CONTENTS

PREFACE

There has probably never been a better time to start up a business of your own. Politicians of all parties now take small business seriously. They realise that the economic future of the country depends upon the wealth creators and that unless new businesses are encouraged to start and prosper, there will be no new industries to provide jobs and create wealth.

The present government has introduced more than 80 measures designed to help new and existing small firms and a mass of new organizations have come into being with the aim of providing advice, practical help and, sometimes, funding, for business start-ups.

Yet, despite all this activity, the failure rate amongst small businesses is very high. In 1983 around 120,000 businesses collapsed, with some 40% of failures occurring within the first few years.

What's the reason for this unhappy state of affairs? Mainly, we're sorry to say, because the potential small business owner hasn't done enough homework before he/she starts up.

The most common mistakes are:

- underestimating the amount of start-up capital required and the amount needed to finance growth (many businesses are forced to close because they run out of money although their order books are full).
- over-optimism about the size of the potential market and the ease of reaching it.
- failure to present a convincing business plan when applying for a loan (there is no shortage of funds but the lenders need to believe in the business competence of those they give money to).
- insufficient grasp of basic business skills such as book-keeping and accounts procedures.

On top of that, running your business is not everyone's cup of tea. Budding entrepreneurs must have courage, imagination and stamina – and many other qualities (we list them in the book). Some people who start up find they don't really have the stomach for it.

Just having good ideas isn't sufficient. Anyone who is seriously contemplating starting up their own business needs advice and information – mountains of it. And that is where this book comes in. It explains in clear, down-to-earth language the qualities you need to run your own business, how to choose the business best suited to your talents, how to set it up, where to find finance and how to run it efficiently. To help the reader the book contains a wealth of actual case histories to illustrate and illuminate the points being made.

The last chapter takes five different business opportunities and analyses them step by step: what qualifications you'll need, the start-up capital required, how to find and fit-out premises, buying stock, how to find the customers plus the special tricks of the trade which make the business prosper.

ACKNOWLEDGEMENTS

The authors would like to thank the following people for their help in preparing this book. Jack Denny and Bob Hale of the University of Stirling for their contributions to chapters 8 and 5 respectively; Jackie Severn and Peter Saunders of Thames Polytechnic for their contribution to chapter 6; Carolyn Patey for typing the manuscript, and Bob Troop for advice and encouragement.

Chapter 1
MAKING THE DECISION

ADVANTAGES OF RUNNING YOUR OWN BUSINESS

Few people get rich working for someone else. Running your own business at least gives you the opportunity to make more money, but whether you become wealthy depends very much on the success you make of it. If the business does well you can determine the amount of money you take out as salary and can claim extra benefits on the firm (e.g. cars, pensions). Big businesses are only small businesses that succeed. If your business makes it to the big time you might consider going public, which will dramatically increase the value of the shares you hold, or you may decide to sell out for a large profit and retire in luxury.

More important than riches to many an entrepreneur, though, is the freedom which comes from being your own boss. You are totally independent and can plan the business and run it on a day-to-day basis the way you want, without any interference from others. It is also an opportunity to work in a field you really enjoy.

There are tax advantages too. Self-employed people have more allowances against income than employees. Directors of their own limited liability companies, though, are not classified as self-employed for tax purposes, but the benefits they can take from the company frequently mitigate their tax bills.

DISADVANTAGES

Running your own business is much more risky than working for someone else. If the business fails you stand to lose far more than just your job. Not only will all your hard work have been to no avail, but you might suffer severe financial hardship if your business owes money since, as a self-employed person, you are *personally* liable to your debtors. This might mean selling your assets, including your home, and, at the worst, may result in bankruptcy. If you form a limited company your personal liability to debtors is limited to the value of the shares you hold – in theory. But, in practice, banks usually require a personal guarantee from the director(s) to secure an overdraft or loan for the business, which to some extent negates the benefits of limited liability status.

You are totally responsible for the success or failure of your business. This can be very exhilarating, but it is, inevitably, very stressful: constant pressure and long hours are par for the course for most entrepreneurs. This can drastically affect your social and family life, also your health.

To give a flavour of what it's like being your own boss, here, in their own words are selected comments from some of the business entrepreneurs we've talked to:

"It gives you a feeling of being totally in control of your own destiny which is very exciting." "You feel totally productive. You use your own time as you wish to spend it. Often this means working all hours of the day, six days a week – permanently. But it isn't a grind if you're doing it for yourself." "I have earned far more in personal reward that I have in financial benefits. It has given me self-confidence which has made me calmer, less neurotic and more prepared to take risks than

1

hitherto." "No longer being involved in office politics has given me an enormous feeling of freedom." "You get pleasure from the simplest things – just the fact that the office copier is working!" "The ability to buy more and better material posse-ssions is irrelevant compared to the sense of achievement you feel." "To begin with it's a very exciting feeling, you've stuck your flag in the sand. Then ... there is a deadly pause while you sit and wait for the business to pour in. The bank manager/your spouse are going berserk and you wonder why you've done it. If you're sensible, you ride out this period by concentrating on planning the business properly and making sure you've got your costings right." "It's food for the soul." "It's good fun."

But ...

"It's very lonely knowing you are totally responsible for the success or failure of the business." "You have to be totally single-minded which can make you appear selfish to family and friends. It bust up my marriage." "You have to be prepared to turn your hand to anything that needs doing. A small firm can't afford all the back-up services – typing help, tea lady, mail boy – you might have become accustomed to as an employee." "Some aspects of the work are unpleasant – e.g. cold canvassing for clients, chasing up slow payers, and doing VAT returns." "You must develop a strong sense of responsibility to your staff. You can't be a cavalier with them, after all, their careers and jobs are in your hands." "You must be prepared to be ruthless however friendly you are with staff or suppliers. If staff are no good you must fire them. If suppliers let you down get rid of them." "It was a great relief going back to being an employee since I no longer had the burden of finding staff salaries every week." "These days everyone is trying to live on credit so the biggest problem is cashflow." "It's very terrifying at the beginning. You sit there waiting for the phone to ring and when it does you hope like hell it's a poten-tial customer rather than someone you owe money to." "The paperwork and form filling is time-consuming and irritating. The Department of Employment returned a form to us because we omitted to indicate the type of business of a client even though the client was called the Bank of America!" "I find the responsibility a constant worry – it brings me out in cold sweats every night."

Despite the carping though, almost all the business owners we talked to said they were very pleased to have gone on their own and would have no hesitation in starting up another business rather than work for someone else.

One woman, however, said that although she gained enormous job satisfaction from her business, she felt it had exhausted her too much to begin again from scratch.

THE QUALITIES YOU NEED TO SUCCEED

To start and run a business successfully, you need to be determined to make a go of it; you need to have, or be prepared to acquire, certain skills and abilities; you must choose a business idea that's right for the market, and get your timing spot-on. To do all this requires a certain sort of personality.

These are the qualities you need to possess to a greater or lesser degree: motiva-tion; initiative; resilience; flair; patience; self-confidence; emotional stability; the ability to get on with people; business acumen; attention to detail; writing and talking ability; and physical and mental energy.

Entrepreneurs come in many shapes and sizes. Business guru Peter Drucker described them thus: "Some are eccentrics, others painfully correct conformists; some are fat and some are lean; some are worriers, some relaxed; some drink quite heavily, others are total abstainers; some are men of great charm and warmth, some have no more personalility than a frozen mackerel."

But, despite visual dissimiliarities, successful business starters do tend to have the following traits in common:

- *they are self-confident all-rounders* Entrepreneurs are usually well-rounded and willing to turn their hands to anything that has to be done to make the venture succeed. They have a universal self-confidence which allows them to move comfortably through unchartered waters.
- *they are able to bounce back* Henry Ford was a two-time loser before he became a winner. His first two businesses folded, and it was not until he was forty that he launched the Ford Motor Company with a borrowed $28,000. Our own Clive Sinclair suffered a disaster with his digital black watch in 1976, but since has become a millionaire several times over. Setbacks are not always of these proportions, but they exist for every business. Entrepreneurs must be resilient if they are to make it past the winning post – it certainly helps if they are healthy too.
- *they are innovative* Almost by definition, business starters are innovators who either tackle the unknown or do old things in new and different ways. It is this inventive streak that allows them to carve out a new market niche, often invisible to others.
- *they are results orientated* They set business goals and their greatest pleasure comes from trying to achieve them. Once a goal is reached, they have to get the next target in view as quickly as possible. The objective could be to reach a certain level of sales, or it could be to buy a Rolls Royce. Whatever it is, the objective acts as the motivator.
- *they are professional risk-takers* One of the most essential characteristics of someone starting a business is a willingness to make decisions and to take risks. This doesn't mean gambling on hunches. It means having the expertise to calculate the odds and deciding which risks to take and when to take them.
- *they are totally committed* Unless you have complete faith in your business idea, you are unlikely to be able to convince anyone else it's a worthwhile venture. You will also need to be single-minded, energetic and hard-working to get things started. Eighteen-hour days are by no means uncommon. The strain this can place on your family relationships means that you have a better chance of succes if they are also involved and committed to the venture.

Do *you* have a suitable personality?

Ask yourself the following questions and count the number of times you answer YES and the number of times you answer NO. If the YES answers easily outstrip the NO answers, you have at least the makings of a successful entrepreneur. However, our capacity for self-deception is enormous, so to do this exercise honestly, ask people close to you to rate you in these areas too.

Are you rarely bored? If something really interests you, can you follow it through? Are you a self-starter – or do you need pushing? Are you the sort of person who frequently has ideas – for your work or for your home? Do these ideas usually get implemented? Do you usually go your own way – rather than follow the crowd? When things go against you do you press on regardless if you believe in what you're doing? Are you fairly stable – i.e. not too many ups and downs? Do you have a supportive family? Do you get invited out a lot? Do you belong to any clubs? Are you on the committees of any clubs or societies? Are your hobbies social hobbies such as dancing, bridge rather than reclusive hobbies such as gardening or fishing? Do you keep promises? List your personal assets and liabilities. Are you going up or down? Do you keep accurate records of your financial affairs? Do you look after your property well? Are you good at organizing? When you buy personal goods do you compare prices? Can you sell? Do you write many letters? Do you find letter-writing very easy? Are you a good listener? Do you often work over the normal hours in your present job?

These are the qualities you, the business owner, need. We now turn to what the business itself needs.

THE ELEVEN DEADLY SINS

That 120,000 businesses go to the wall each year bears witness to the fact that running a business makes large demands, and that many people who start up are ill equipped to do so. The highest risks are in the first few years: nearly 40% of failures come within a mere four years. Some of these budding entrepreneurs lose their life savings, others end up in endless debt. A fortunate few lose only their dignity and rise phoenix-like a few years later, using their experience as a base on which to build a successful venture.

Some academics believe the high failure rate is the price that has to be paid in order to produce a thriving new business sector – the survival of the fittest.

There is no risk-free way to a profitable business but it is as well to know the dangers that lie ahead – and to try and ensure they don't trap *your* business start-up.

New businesses fail for 11 basic reasons:

1. *Lack of expertise* Starting a business from scratch calls for remarkable versatility. The owner-manager types the invoices with one finger in the evenings, does the books at the weekend, sells on Monday, makes the goods from Tuesday and delivers when he can. People with a history in large firms sometimes find it difficult to become a jack of all trades.
2. *No product/marketing strategy* Until you have defined who will buy your product or service, and why, you shouldn't begin to offer it.
3. *Over-optimism about market size* It is a fundamental misconception to believe that people are simply sitting waiting to be sold to. New businesses need to conduct research into the market they are aiming at, see who the competitors are, and make some reasoned estimate of what their anticipated sales will be.
4. *Underestimating the start-up time* There's often a great deal to do before the customers come along – premises to be found and fitted out, equipment and stock to be bought. Estimate how long you think it will all take, double it and add on a bit more.
5. *Lack of working capital* If you haven't calculated 3 and 4 correctly you could easily run out of money. Scarce cash is tied up, and money is flowing in one direction only until customers start buying in reasonable numbers. Assess your capital requirements with a good safety margin at the outset. A well-prepared cash-flow forecast will help you decide how much is needed and when.
6. *Start-up costs too high* New businesses should be lean and mean. Don't spend too much on fixtures, fittings and equipment too soon. People with a background in big business often start with extravagantly high standards. They expect an electronic typewriter and photocopier close to hand, and to sit in an executive-style office from the outset. These overheads have to be spread across the products/service sold and you can lose your competitive edge by being too greedy.
7. *Consequences of early growth* Many people think their problems are over once customers start to roll in – but they may have only just begun. A business changes its shape and size very rapidly in its early days. As sales grow, ever-increasing sums of cash are needed to fuel that growth. And the danger is over-trading: i.e. growing faster than cash resources allow.

8. *Mistaking cash for profit* The cash that flows into the business hasn't had any of the automatic deductions knocked off it as has a pay cheque from an employer. Too often entrepreneurs yield to the temptation to use this cash to maintain their living standards, and when the bills come in – from the suppliers, for National Insurance, for VAT – they can't pay them. The Inland Revenue and Customs & Excise put more businesses into liquidation than anyone else.

9. *Wrong location* Where you conduct your business and how much rent you pay is vital. Don't be tempted to take premises just because the rent is cheap – no customers may pass that way. Equally, don't take on an expensive High Street site if your business turnover is unlikely to cover the costs. Your initial market research should help you identify a suitable location.

10. *Selecting and managing people* Big companies can afford to make the odd mistake when selecting staff. Small businesses can't afford to get it wrong.

11. *No management accounts* New business people often see regular accounting as a bureaucratic nonsense carried out for the benefit of the Inland Revenue alone. For them the end of the first year is often the end of the business.

As you can see, there is no escaping the fact that starting and running a business can be difficult and demanding. But if you have the inclination and think you possess the necessary expertise, don't be daunted. Here's a little success story of someone who at first glance might have seemed an unlikely entrepreneur. The lessons to be learnt from it are that your chances of success are improved if you choose an area where you have specialist knowledge, find a gap in the market, and go about setting up and running the business the right way.

Gill Keenan, a music teacher for 15 years and mother of two young children, felt she needed a "new challenge". She wanted to stay close to the music world and she also knew that colleagues and pupils were unable to obtain adequate supplies of music products locally.

She persuaded her sceptical husband to re-mortgage their home to raise capital so that she could start a music shop in High Wycombe.

She kept on her job while she planned the business, so only weekends were free to scour the area for premises, and every evening was spent trying to work out how much stock, and of what type, she was likely to sell. She estimated her own pupils' expenditure on sheet music, books and instruments, then grossed up the figure for other schools in her catchment area. This gave her an idea of the potential size of her market. From her calculations, she knew that she had to turn over at least £75,000 a year to pay her bills and make a living. This became her first-year target and she planned accordingly.

The plan meant she would have to keep track of over 800 different items of stock – a difficult task if she wished to avoid running out of some items or overstocking others. She solved the problem by liaising with a neighbour who happened to be a computer buff. He loaded details of all opening stock onto his micro and wrote a program which would alert Gill to best-selling lines and slow-moving products. The program also scheduled re-order dates and quantities. The great asset of this program was that Gill was able to tell, early on, which items of stock weren't right for her market – and some weren't – and quickly remedy matters.

Gill called her shop Perfect Pitch and opened it with a cheese and wine party. She organized mail shots to music teachers, plus posters and press releases, to let people know she was in business.

Eighteen months later it is a modest success. Gill beat her sales target by 30%, made a profit and ploughed most of it back into the business to buy new stock. Next year she plans to move into the market for renting musical instruments – a very important, but expensive, sector of the music field. To give herself a chance of success, she has taken on a partner who knows the rental business backwards and is prepared to finance that side of the business. She finds that having a co-worker removes many of the psychological pressures too.

CHAPTER 1 SUMMARY

Running your own business has many advantages; it could make you wealthy and you should enjoy being able to do things the way you want. But it has disadvantages too. You could lose everything you own if things go wrong, and you will certainly have to work much harder than the average employee does.

Successful business starters need a certain sort of personality. They should be self-confident all-rounders who can bounce back when things go wrong – can you?

Whatever sort of business you start things are quite likely to go wrong. If you are skilful and plan properly from the start you can survive. If not, you may join the growing army of business failures. Knowing the eleven reasons why most businesses fail will help you survive.

Chapter 2
CHOOSING THE BUSINESS

The chances are that you already know what sort of business you want to run, which is why you are contemplating a start-up. But even if you do, it's important to evaluate it objectively.

However, perhaps the opportunity to run your own business has only just occurred – through early retirement, redundancy, children leaving home, a legacy from a relative. Or maybe working for yourself is a long-nurtured dream and you're looking for hard facts and encouragement to translate it into reality. Here we offer some advice to those of you who are as yet undecided on the type of business which would suit you best.

WHAT WOULD YOU LIKE TO DO?

There are a myriad different business opportunities to choose from. They range from simple home-based ideas such as extending a hobby like dressmaking, carpentry or flower arranging into, at least, a good source of pin money, through offering standard services like plumbing, car-tuning or typing, selling goods of numerous varieties, running a catering business, a hotel, a nursing home, to the more formidable task of getting your own invention into large-scale production. There are also the more esoteric businesses – oyster farming was one we saw advocated recently. You can start your business from scratch (on your own or with others); you can buy an existing business or you can opt for the increasingly popular franchise route (we cover it in some detail later in this chapter).

There are two publications aimed specifically at people seeking ideas for business start-ups: *The Business Ideas Letter* (published by Stonehart Publications Ltd, 57-61 Mortimer Street, London W1N 7TD) and the *Business Opportunities Digest* (from Business Opportunities Digest Ltd, 11-12 Blomfield Street, London EC2M 7AY). Both are monthly, subscription-only journals which analyse a range of different start-up possibilities in each issue.

If you're determined to start your own business but don't possess any particular skills or qualifications, and don't want to invest, or raise, much money, your best bet is to look around for a service idea you can offer locally. Here are some simple examples:

A reminder service. You maintain an index of dates when clients want their memory jogged (wedding anniversaries, birthdays) and telephone them in advance.
Letter writing. Those with a literary bent can set themselves up as latter-day scribes to help people draft those difficult letters – complaints to the landlord/local authority, job applications, letters of condolence. The task becomes progressively easier as you go along, since you build up a bank of standard letters.
A register of local services. You could consider maintaining a register of people who perform essential services – locksmiths, glaziers, people who will fix a tile back to the roof and the like. Clients then just have one port of call when an emergency strikes.

7

Ice Making. Retailers, pubs, restaurants, hotels, hospitals and private individuals
holding parties need ice-cubes in bulk. You need to buy a large ice-cube making
machine and be prepared to deliver at any hour of the day or night.

Dog-walking is another simple service you could offer. There are many more.

When exploring ideas, look particularly at what you can offer to people in situations where they are prepared to put their hand deeper into their pocket than they
would normally – weddings, barmitzvahs and other celebrations, moving home.
Offering to make a video of peoples' weddings or christenings is one such idea.

A survey conducted in 1981 by the Thames Polytechnic amongst 416 budding
entrepreneurs found that over three-quarters of respondents were interested in starting a business which fell into the categories of distribution or services. The largest
single percentage wanted to start a restaurant, cafe or catering service, but the largest
single group wanted to run unclassified services which included such activities as
steam-cleaning carpets, looking after other people's houses while they were away and
industrial design, plus a whole variety of business consultancy services.

SPOTTING A GAP IN THE MARKET

Many of our most successful entrepreneurs have got where they are today by identifying unexplored areas in fast-growing markets – and plugging the gap. Judy Lever, for
instance, found that no one was catering for pregnant mums in the booming mail
order market. She started her own mail order company Blooming Marvellous and
now has more orders than she can easily cope with.

John Hudson cashed in on the fast-growing take-away food trade by offering a
courier service which not only delivered the food to peoples' doors but provided them
with menus from all the local take-away restaurants and an ordering service.

Peter Fraiman discovered in 1967 that there was a virtually untapped UK market
for *refurbished* electronic equipment. He financed Electronic Brokers from his
savings of £3,000 and a £1,500 bank loan and initially ran it from his home. Now, 17
years later, its sales are over £4½ million.

And here's the story of a Kent housewife who almost single-handedly revolution-
ized beer-drinking habits in Guinness-loyal Ulster.

Two years ago you couldn't get a drop of real ale in Northern Ireland. Beer
drinkers who didn't consider Guinness total perfection were stuck with a choice of
fizzy bitter or lager. Now, real ale drinkers are laughing, thanks to Mrs Skullion.

The Skullions lived in the hoplands of Kent and Mr Skullion is a real ale aficion-
ado. When he was sent to Belfast on a contract, his phone calls home showed less
concern about family affairs than over his desire for something less fizzy and more
full-bodied to imbibe. His wife decided to quench his thirst.

This wasn't just a frivolous attempt to pacify an unhappy husband: born and
brought up in Ulster, Mrs Skullion had witnessed the real ale revolution on the mainland and was convinced there was a profitable gap to fill in her native country.
Neither did she enter into it lightly – she had read too many hard luck stories of small
businesses which had failed through not doing their homework properly.

Her first step was to visit Northern Ireland and talk to the publicans (most pubs
are free houses) and club owners. She found they were excited at the prospect of
something new to increase their bar turnover. She also canvassed drinkers and this
confirmed her suspicions that a real ale would be welcomed.

Mrs Skullion didn't know much about running a business so step two was to enrol
for a course at the Manchester Business School where she learnt the basics of costing
and day-to-day management. They couldn't, of course, instruct her on how to brew
the stuff, so step three was to contact the Heriot Watt University, which runs a brew-
ing course. Through them, she discovered a Northern Irish student who was about to

graduate. "I was terribly fortunate to find someone from the province because it's difficult recruiting people from the mainland. You have to convince them they won't be dodging bullets all day," she says.

With her new-found financial skills and her lucky-find brewer she prepared her budgets. She found she needed £80,000 for the plant and equipment. She raised this from a Belfast bank, who thought the idea exciting and workable, and with a small, but helpful, cash injection from Northern Ireland's Local Enterprise Development Unit, which has a £5m budget to help local small firms. Mrs and Mr Skullion (he gave up his job to become a partner) topped up the shortfall from their own savings, and they bought a converted coach house in a village called Hilden, near Belfast. "Although I could have set up on an industrial estate, I decided that wouldn't give us the right image," Mrs Skullion says. "We called the ale after the village and this was a good move as names mean a lot here and 'Hilden' sounds sufficiently neutral."

Much of the capital was spent on buying the wooden casks needed to provide the special taste peculiar to real ale. A consultant from England was employed to establish the brewery, and once the plant was installed the brewer set it in motion. It has been producing excellent beer ever since.

The brew is priced to keep it within the range of the current cost of a pint, but as an encouragement, publicans are offered a deal which gives them greater profits per pint.

Hilden Brewery employs five people and, now approaching its second year, is about to break even. Mrs Skullion's projected figures turned out to be reasonably accurate – expectations on the top line were not met but all trading figures are well above the bottom line.

Ale drinking is on the increase in Ulster and Hilden Brewery expects to show considerable profits next year. A competitor has come into the market, but Mrs Skullion feels this can only be healthy for trade – she acted as their consultant, a shrewd way of recouping some of her start-up costs!

THE FACTORS WHICH INFLUENCE YOUR CHOICE

1. What are you good at?

It might be that like many people who start up on their own you want to capitalize on the skills you have gained in previous jobs, or you may want to turn your hobby into a financially rewarding proposition. Perhaps you think you are skilled in such things as organizing, selling or dealing with people, and would welcome the opportunity to work in a field where you could put those skills to the test.

If you are considering starting a business in a field you aren't familiar with, some basic training or work experience in the field is a good grounding. And this is one of the distinct advantages of franchise operations – franchisors run intensive training courses for potential franchisees (see below).

2. How much money is required to start it up?

You can, of course, borrow money for start-up capital (Chapter 4 tells you who you can borrow from) but the moneylenders normally require you to raise a near-equal amount yourself. How much can you afford? (Chapter 4 explains how to calculate this). Many people we've talked to who run service businesses – such as consultancy services and secretarial agencies – proudly boast they didn't need any start-up capital since the business was run from home and was self-financing from the start. However, on closer enquiry, they have rarely been able to finance any expansion purely out of profit but have needed, at least, to take on a sizeable overdraft.

3. Is there a market for the product or service?

We can't stress strongly enough the importance of thoroughly researching the market for a proposed new business (Chapter 9 tells you how). Whether there is a big enough market or not depends, of course, to a large extent on where you want to locate your business. If you live in a village, for instance, and wish to work there, you're unlikely to attract enough customers to make a viable business out of running a specialist shop – model trains, tropical fish, even a bookshop or antique shop. If you are in a larger town it could be an uphill struggle to make ends meet if there are several competitive businesses already established there.

4. Will you like the work?

There is no point slogging your guts out for a job you don't enjoy. If you're contemplating a complete change of direction, say, a franchise on a fast food outlet or running a pub when your only experience is in office work, consider this factor carefully and, if possible, talk to those who are already doing the job.

5. How much time are you prepared to put into the business?

Many people who run their own concerns find they work far longer hours than they did in paid employment. And that's not all. They find they are thinking and/or worrying about the business in their spare time, which can have a drastic effect on their family and social life. Are you prepared for that degree of commitment? If not, choose a start-up option which is less demanding.

Which business would be right for you?

Here's an exercise which might help your decision process.

Take a sheet of paper and draw up two columns. In the left-hand column, list all your hobbies, interests and skills. In the right-hand column, translate them into possible business ideas.

For example:

Interests/skills	Business ideas
Motor cars	motor car dealer/repair garage/home tuning service
Cooking	restaurant/home catering service/bakery shop/providing produce for freezer outlets
Gardening	supplier of produce to flower or vegetable shop/running a nursery/running a garden centre/landscape design
Typing	typing author's manuscripts from home/typing back-up service for busy local companies/running a secretarial agency

And so on.

Having done this exercise, you need to balance the possibilities against the criteria which are most important to *you*. These might be: small amount of capital required; good anticipated profit; secure income; work satisfaction; no need to learn new skills; variety of work; the possibility of working hours that suit your lifestyle; opportunity to meet new people; minimal paperwork; opportunity to travel.

You may have other criteria not on this list. Decide the most important criteria and place them in order of importance. Allocate each chosen criteria a *weighting factor* of between 1 and 5. Now list the possible business opportunities you have identified from the first exercise and measure them against the graded criteria.

A simple example: Jane Clark, an ex-secretary with school-age children needed work because her husband had been made redundant and was busy looking for another job. She wasn't in a position to raise much capital, and she wanted her hours to coincide with those of her children. She wanted to run her own show and she wanted to enjoy what she did. The criteria she selected were:

Criteria	Weighting factor
minimal capital required	5
possibility to work hours that suit lifestyle	5
no need to learn new skills	4
minimal paperwork	3
work satisfaction	2
opportunity to meet interesting people	1

Since minimal capital was a very important criteria for Jane she gave it a weighting factor of 5, whereas the opportunity to meet interesting people, being far less important to her, was only weighted one.

Jane then gave each of her three business ideas a rating, in points, against these criteria. A secretarial agency needed capital to start so was given only one point. Back-up typing needed hardly any money and was allocated five points.

Her worked-out chart looks like this:

Criteria	Weighting factor		Secretarial agency		Back up typing		Authors manuscripts	
			points	score	points	score	points	score
Minimal capital	5	×	1 =	5	5	25	4	20
Flexible hours	5	×	1 =	5	3	15	5	25
No new skills	4	×	2 =	8	5	20	5	20
Work satisfaction	3	×	4 =	12	1	3	3	9
Minimal paperwork	2	×	0 =	0	4	8	5	10
Meeting people	1	×	4 =	4	3	3	4	4
Total score				34		74		88

The weighting factor and the rating points multiplied together give a score for each business idea. The highest score indicates the business that best meets Jane's criteria. In this case, typing authors' manuscripts scored over back-up typing since Jane could do it exactly when it suited her.

DIFFERENT BUSINESS OPPORTUNITIES EXAMINED

Below, we look in more detail at what's involved in running some of the more common types of business start-up – retailing, catering, a service business and launching an invention – together with illustrations of how they have, or haven't, worked for other people.

We also tell you about two alternative *techniques* for going into business on your own without starting completely from scratch – a management buy-out and franchising. The other common technique – taking over an existing business – is dealt with in Chapter 3.

Retailing

People tend to think of retailing as opening a small shop, but retailing covers many other things – cash and carry outlets, discount warehouses, market stalls and mobile shops. You can also retail by mail order – perhaps a better option if you don't fancy face-to-face selling – but to sell successfully by mail order you need quite a lot of cash up-front to prepare the literature which will attract your customers.

Shops normally make a living for their owners but rarely make their fortunes. They might, though, if you plan to open a chain of shops or acquire other businesses.

The late Sir Jack Cohen of Tesco fame didn't do badly and he started with just a grocery shop.

The advantages of shops are: they are relatively simple to run; sales are normally for cash, rather than credit; no particular skills are necessary; the prospects should be steady unless inflation bites deep, or the products are likely to go out of fashion; and you can usually sell the shop as a going concern at a later date.

The disadvantages are: hard work; always being there during opening hours (and often outside them because you'll need time to do the books and organize stock when the shop is closed); the difficulty of planning holidays if you have no staff, or only a small staff. Shops are also vulnerable to changes in their immediate environment. Road closures, one-way streets, double yellow lines outside can all affect the shop's accessibility to customers. Competition, too, can drastically affect trade – a new supermarket sited near a grocery store, directly competing shops opening up in a small town.

Some would say another disadvantage is the customers themselves. People can be very awkward sometimes and shopkeepers need considerable patience and tact if they are to ensure the cardinal rule of shopkeeping: "the customer is always right".

We provide a step-by-step analysis of how to set up a health food shop in Chapter 12 (this is relevant for other types of shops too). Here, though, is a story which illustrates the less rosy side of shopkeeping

The toyshop that never took off

Roberta Considine, with her children away at school, decided she wanted to work full-time. Before her marriage Roberta had worked in a specialist London toy shop and had retained her knowledge and interest in toys. Her decision to set up The Toy Box in 1979 was swayed by an offer of low-rent premises in Arundel's Emporium – a warehouse converted into shop spaces designed to cash in on Arundel's booming tourist trade.

She invested £2,000 for advance rent, fixtures and fittings, and purchase of stock. As soon as she began to trade she realized she had severe space problems. The shop was only 196 square feet and there was no extra space to store stock. This meant that a) she couldn't offer as wide a range of toys as she would have liked, and b) she couldn't offer some well-known manufacturers' toys at all since they insisted on sizeable minimum orders.

Business was slow, booming only in the summer months and at Christmas. Takings for the better months averaged around £200 per week but fell to £50 per week for the rest of the year. "The boredom during the lean months was the worst part of it," says Roberta. "You had to be in the shop during opening hours, but some days you hardly saw a customer. Time dragged terribly." She soldiered on for three years before packing it in.

Why didn't The Toy Box do better? Roberta hadn't carried out enough research into local buying habits: "I discovered too late that the resources of the town were really too limited. The locals did the bulk of their shopping in nearby larger towns with toyshops of their own. Also, the tourists who flock into Arundel rarely wander from the High Street. The Emporium was too far off the beaten track. I should have been braver and paid more for premises in the centre of the town." Although the business broke even in the second year, it was hit by the recession in the third year.

Since the premises were only leased on an annual basis and the lease period was up, Roberta had no chance of recouping her losses by selling the shop with stock and goodwill. She sold off as much remaining stock as she could and shut up shop. Three years wiser, but not much richer.

Catering

Doing something in catering is many people's dream of running their own business. It might be a hotel, a restaurant, a cafe or pub, or providing a catering service from home – directors' lunches, office parties, private dinner parties, selling homemade fare to food outlets.

If catering is your thing it can be a highly satisfying way of earning your living, and potentially profitable too. And you don't necessarily need to have any previous experience (it undoubtedly helps, though). But catering has many pitfalls for the uninitiated. Here are some aspects of catering you should be aware of.

For a start, it is an expensive business to get into. Although you can probably get away with a small amount of initial capital if you're catering from home, you can't if you plan to run a hotel, restaurant or cafe. You're unlikely to start a hotel from scratch, more likely to buy an existing one, and a good one will probably cost at least £60,000. If you plan to open a new restaurant or cafe, you have to consider not only the cost of the premises but the cost of fitting out, decorating and furnishing, plus crockery, cutlery and cooking equipment. One restauranteur we know, planning a new restaurant, estimates that his start-up costs will be at least £100,000: £50,000 for the premises (he wants a freehold) and £50,000 to set it up.

Catering concerns are expensive to run too. They consume a lot of heat and power and the amount of space required means rents and rates are high. Andy's Kebab House in London's West End which seats 40 people, has running costs of around £14,000 a year (gas, electricity, rent and rates). On top of that there is stock purchase – food and drink – plus the cost of staff (a good chef in London wants a minimum of £180 clear a week; a waiter £40 a week clear, so allow extra for NHI contributions and PAYE).

Restaurants make most of their money out of liquor sales, usually marked up 100% – which is why waiters are forever replenishing your wine glass! The mark-up on food varies – 50% is normal although many restaurants, French restaurants particularly, level a higher mark-up.

Catering may be a vocation but it requires quite a high degree of business acumen. Apart from all the normal paperwork every business is lumbered with, food catering requires shrewd daily guestimates of numbers of anticipated clientele to gauge the quantities of food to buy. Freezers are a marvellous boon to the catering trade, but not everything can be frozen. Microwave ovens are another indispensable asset – food which used to take 20 minutes to reheat in a conventional oven (which is why restaurants always used to delay the starter) can now be reheated in two minutes.

Hotels require an even higher degree of business flair and strict organization. (We give you the lowdown on setting up a hotel in Chapter 12.)

One caterer described his business to us as "tantalizing but exhausting" And exhausting it certainly is, both mentally and physically. The hours are long but disjointed. Another caterer, who works a 16-hour day, finds the three-hour break between lunch and dinner totally disorientating. You really have to wave goodbye to your social life if you opt for catering, and if you run a hotel you are never actually off duty at all and have little privacy. We read recently that husbands and wives who run pubs have the highest divorce rate in the country, and we're not surprised – the long hours and close working proximity would put a strain on any relationship, particularly if the business has problems.

You have to like the trade and the people you meet and you must be prepared to assume a deferential attitude to customers and not be flawed by the brickbats you'll inevitably receive. Are tact and a thick skin your strong suits? You'll certainly need them!

Before you start a catering concern, you'll need to define your market and the price range in which you want to operate. Assess your seating potential and relate that potential to income. If the business flourishes you'll get immense satisfaction from plates that come back clean, and plenty of money if the place is full most of the time. One caterer's idea of a successful restaurant is that "it should be a party every night".

Below, we relate one man's personal experience of setting up a small restaurant. His story highlights the home truths of catering better than any factual report could.

Running a restaurant – an insider's view

Most one-man business ideas begin with a grand concept. Only shortage of cash cuts the concept down to practical size. My own grand concept was to develop a chain of diners similar to those found in any large Canadian town. Quick, superbly clean, reasonably priced. They were to be open-kitchen style – that is, all food prepared when ordered at gleaming stainless steel cooking counters in full view of the customers.

Menus would be evocative and honest, coffee would taste like coffee and not boiled or scalded tiger nuts, iced water would come with every order. A fast, continuing trade would be vital and this needed to be supplemented by a first-class sendout/takeout sandwich and drinks service. I settled therefore on a busy, commercial area of Holborn, in London, to start operations...

Three months later I moved into my first restaurant – at the end of a side street in a small south coast town filled, in the main, by elderly retired people!

Minimal capital, unco-operative banks and high rents had whittled down my grand design. But all right then, I couldn't afford London – so I would try out my ideas elsewhere.

I got a 40-seater cafe-cum-restaurant with a pleasant self-contained flat of six rooms above. Stock at valuation cost me extra. Most of it turned out to be useless.

Trade figures seemed encouraging but were, I quickly discovered, highly inflated. Equipment was poor and essential things like crockery were in short supply. Most of it was chipped and cracked. All the points I failed to observe before negotiating a price. Enthusiasm can be expensive.

Later, I realized just how anxious the owner was to sell. He would have accepted far less to get out of the place.

I moved in on a sleeting March day. It was the start of the hardest two years' labouring I have ever experienced. Catering, I discovered, included endless washing-up, bricklaying, kitchen renovation, painting and decorating, mouse hunting, cockroach extermination, public relations, humiliation, invention and despair. Yet, oddly enough, there was also a personal sense of achievement in taking a rundown, unprofitable cafe and turning it into a busy and popular eating place.

It was rewarding to see ideas that I had intended for a more sophisticated London trade gain acceptance and flourish in a quiet seaside town. Within three months I knew we were becoming known; poison postcards began arriving – sent, I assumed, by some disgruntled local competitor.

I had learned a lot in the first three months. From complete novice I had learned some essential tricks of the catering trade. Which meat, for instance, to order for minimum wastage. I learned, too, to offer a variety of table d'hôte lunches. I calculated that such a variety would swing a percentage of the customers away from the more expensive (quality) roasts. It worked. Local residents who were by nature conservative eaters quickly accepted new dishes – Chinese food, vegetarian salads, Welsh recipes, all found their way on to our set luncheon list. I even tried making borsch one day from a load of cheap beetroot. It tasted foul and the only customer to try it was the manager of the local repertory company. Next day, we presented him with a pastry Victoria Cross.

Our menu of set lunches became a triumph of editorial invention and cost cutting. The simplest dish was described in glowing adjectives; customers read menus out loud to spot the latest extravaganza. Spinach made the grade one lunch-time with "Fresh, dawn-plucked, hand-cleaned and simmered in dew..." Customers became rivals. One regular, a salad eater, sent a brief note back to the kitchen: "On my 'sparkling crisp, crunchy Sussex lettuce' I have discovered a bright-eyed, exquisitely groomed caterpillar..." That customer received free lunches for the next week. Like his fellow diners, he realized that the food, despite the menu's wild claims, was honest and value for money.

The dishes became an art in cutting costs to compensate for the beef bill. Omelettes contained everything. We even used the previous day's unfinished mock-Chinese dish to add "Canton Omelette: made with thousand-minute old eggs" to our set lunch choice. At that time we were buying crates of eggs (cracked).

The compliments to our "ham" were earned, in fact, by boiled forehocks of bacon; in my opinion, better than ham and half the price. The fatty part joined layers of slightly over-ripe tomatoes and grated ends of cheese to appear on the menu as "Genuine Somerset Harvesters' Pie".

When in doubt we pushed the fish since we could cost out plaice and chips precisely. The kitchen refrigerator was unreliable so I ordered fish daily from a small fishmonger in the next road. If we ran short, I would race round to the supplier for another 30 pieces which would be filleted, collected and fried while the customer was eating his soup. How fresh can fish be!

One Friday we had a local priest in for lunch. I asked the entire restaurant to join him in prayer. It earned me precious extra minutes for yet another sprint round to the fishmonger for fresh supplies.

I needed those prayers. The following lunch time, an elderly woman leaned her elbow on a large fire-extinguisher next to her chair and covered six nearby diners in thick, white foam. We hung their clothes on the oven canopy, the old lady's knickers taking pride of place, and they finished their meal wearing clothes borrowed from my wife's wardrobe.

This, perhaps, was the secret of the quickly growing trade. Customers felt they were playing an essential role in the cafe's development. They were, and we rewarded them handsomely.

Regular customers had dishes named in their honour. Birthdays were discovered and remembered by some small delicacy.

Along the way, I learned that the steamy confines of a restaurant kitchen breed fierce hatreds and squally tempers. One rush hour occasion, I traded a barrage of punches for a split lip with a taciturn chef between taking an order for soup and delivering it to the serving hatch. A matter of seconds. Food inspires ideas, breeds invention. The caterer who allows his cafe or restaurant to become completely predictable – apart from quality – is, in the long term, doomed. A fickle public demands variety; and food lends itself to a sense of the theatrical.

Never over-estimate your capabilities. Seating imposes a rigid limitation; and people won't eat to a time limit. Always ensure your equipment will match demand. If in doubt, buy more. Don't reduce prices to boost bookings; if your prices are fair and the food good, you'll get the bookings anyway.

A service business

There are an immense number and variety of services which can be turned into profitable business ideas, and there's always room for a new, original service idea.

One big advantage of service businesses is that they usually require less capital than other business start-ups since the main equipment needed to do the job is normally you, and your expertise. Home-based services might require no capital at all since you possibly already have the necessary tools, and customers will be found by word-of-mouth. We know one entrepreneur with a busy full-time job in marketing who runs a business with three quarters of a million pound turnover as a "hobby" from his home. His start-up costs were just the price of an ad in the local paper and the cost of forming a company. His "hobby" is buying and selling redundant and liquidated stock, and pretty fail-safe it is too since he never "buys" until he's found someone to sell to. Running costs have rarely been much more than telephone charges so his profits must be staggering. It takes a particular flair, though, to operate as this type of wheeler-dealer.

Many service businesses, of course, do need special equipment and many people prefer, or have, to run the business from premises other than their home. Some high-risk businesses require substantial start-up capital, e.g. tour operating, where on top of the normal costs for premises and office equipment plus the cost of preparing glossy brochures to attract customers, you have to pay sizeable licence fees and security bonds before you can even begin to trade.

To succeed in a service business you need to be good at what you do, to administer well, to project plenty of charm and to be able to sell yourself and your service.

It's impossible to generalize on the disadvantages since services are so varied but, in common with most business start-ups, you'll probably work long hours and worry a lot.

Here's the story of a secretarial agency which just goes to show that all rules are made to be broken! Started by chance with little in the way of business planning, it is now one of the most successful and dynamic agencies in London's West End.

Anne Sanfey and Barbara Lewis met while temping for the same firm. The particular firm, impressed by their obvious administrative abilities, encouraged them to set up on their own. "It wasn't a thought-out decision," says Anne. "More circumstantial, and we never conducted any market research or drew up any corporate strategies since we only envisaged it initially as a short-term proposition."

That was in 1970 and *Action Secretaries* (they chose the name both to reflect the nature of the business and to convey a feeling of immediacy) is now a thriving business in London's Oxford Street with a turnover of over £1m.

They didn't borrow a penny to start up. The business was self financing from the beginning. Clients and temporary staff were contacted by phone and they used an accommodation address to meet the temps and pay their wages. They didn't bother with any paid-for advertising initially since they were able to find enough client and temp contacts by word of mouth.

By 1974 the business had grown to the extent that permanent premises were necessary. They took a short lease on a room in Dryden Chambers, Oxford Street (the very room, they later discovered, where Edward VII conducted his liaison with Lily Langtry). "Our requirements were simply to be near a tube station and as accessible as possible to the Australian and New Zealand girls who make up the majority of our temp force," says Anne. She reckons Antipodean girls are more reliable and work harder than their UK equivalents. "We can't get enough of them."

Business and profits continued to escalate and Anne and Barbara decided to expand by providing permanent as well as temporary staff, also to cater for the temp demand created by the new high-technology word processors. Bigger premises and more staff were required so in 1981, after a fair old hunt around, they found a reasonably priced suite of offices in Oxford Street.

More temps were needed, and were found by advertising in the *Standard* and in magazines for Australians and New Zealanders. Cold canvassing produced additional clients and Action Secretaries now boasts some blue-chip companies amongst its clients, such as Cadbury Schweppes, Trafalgar House and the Bank of America.

The business, started as it was on a shoestring, has never run at a loss from day one. There are few problems, providing clients pay within a month.

What does Anne think are the secrets of Action Secretaries' success? First, a lucky choice of partner. Although she and Barbara barely knew each other before throwing in their lot together, they soon discovered they enjoyed different aspects of the work and this has made for a harmonious work relationship. The fact that Anne and Barbara are themselves highly experienced secretaries means they can quickly gauge which temps suit which jobs, and their success in matching staff with clients has paid dividends in ensuring continuing loyalties.

Launching an invention

This must be the classic way to start up. Many of our major manufacturing companies were started by an individual with a new product idea.

If you get it right, the potential is unlimited. Look at Clive Sinclair. He's a multi-millionaire, knighted and still under 45.

But be warned: most inventors get no further than the invention itself. The problems of getting it into production are enormous. Although we are renowned as a nation of inventors, the moneylenders are actually extremely wary of taking a risk on unknown quantities, so finding finance can be an uphill struggle. Inventors are often their own worst enemies too. Frequently they don't possess the extra skills necessary to present a convincing case to the financiers, or know how to market their product successfully – or even if a viable market exists. Nor are they prepared for all the nitty-gritty paperwork which is part and parcel of running a business.

And even if you *do* succeed in getting the product on the market, it can still go wrong. Here's an example. A husband and wife team invented and started producing a rather interesting triangular mirror. This came to the notice of the *Observer*, who gave it a mention. Orders came flooding in and the husband and wife duly despatched the mirrors. Within a few weeks almost all the mirrors had been returned to them – broken. Sadly, in their rush to fulfil the orders, they had neglected to work out a safe method of packaging.

However, don't be deterred if you think you have an invention which would satisfy a market need. It just might make your fortune. With the help of this book, analyse the market, work out your costings accurately and decide where and how to apply for finance (you might be eligible for the government's Support for Innovation grant – see Chapter 4). If you don't feel confident of your own skills on the financial side, hire an accountant or, if you can't be bothered with the whole business side of the project, consider teaming up with someone you know to be a shrewd business-man. It's sensible, too, to patent your project (we tell you how to do this in Chapter 3 and give some details of information sources for inventors).

The story of David Palmer demonstrates that getting an invention off the ground *is* possible – but can be fraught with difficulties – and offers some guidance to other would-be entrepreneurs.

David was employed as a world-wide troubleshooter for a firm importing a consumer durable product from Japan. The Japanese dominated this particular market with a product which David considered too expensive and too complicated to operate. An engineering graduate and a certified accountant, David decided to go on his own and attempt to design a better, cheaper product which would be more in line with the needs of European markets.

It took him two years of hard work and constant frustration to get it off the ground (from design to first order) during which time his only sources of income were his savings and his wife's earnings.

He needed £100,000 to develop and tool up the product for manufacture. No one was prepared to back a one-man band. The numerous sources he approached included the National Research Development Council, who considered it a "super idea" but said that the only way David would see it produced was by licensing the product to a large manufacturing company.

David contacted all the obvious British manufacturers in his field. He was rebuffed at every turn. They doubted his design and his costing.

David decided to try a different tack – to find a company which would put up money for the initial tooling operation and market and distribute the product. He found a firm that appeared willing to do this and they advanced money to pay for the first instalment of tools.

The basis on which David and the marketing outfit had agreed to do business was by forming a separate company in which the marketing people had a majority stake. Despite interminable meetings, the marketing company dragged its heels and refused to sign the necessary agreements. After a year of this David decided to call it a day and part company from them. At which point the firm turned nasty, claimed title to the tools already made and demanded to be reimbursed for the sum they had advanced – with an additional fee thrown in.

David was now in a real fix: an incomplete set of tools he couldn't get his hands on and not enough money to buy them back.

After a great deal of persistence he eventually negotiated a deal with a finance house whereby they would put up £10,000 for one-third of the equity plus a £50,000 medium term loan with a 17½% fixed (not floating) interest charge plus a charge on assets. The deal was based on David putting up £20,000 himself.

David bought out and finished the tooling but he still had nothing to show – no prototype and no funds for a production run. There appeared to be only one solution: to pick up a substantial order from a retail outlet.

After six months of banging on doors with only drawings to show, a large multiple store ordered 2,000 units. They ordered them, of course, on the basis that stock was available. David had to put his skates on. Sub-contractors and suppliers who were already lined up but who had been strung along and stalled by David while waiting for an order were suddenly asked to spring into top gear, and David himself spent many long nights driving completed machines from the production base to the store to meet delivery dates.

David's machine was composed of 31 different components (compared to several hundred which the competing machines used). However, all these components were made by different suppliers, and finding good parts manufacturers has turned out to be one of the most time-consuming aspects of David's working life. Only one original supplier is still being used. All the other manufacturers have fallen by the wayside.

David had deliberately designed the product so that the final "manufacturing" operation was a simple assembly and packing task. This limits the amount of labour involved and enables the product to be cost effective when manufactured in the UK where labour costs are high.

David had originally planned to organize the assembly and packing himself. However, he discovered he could make substantial savings by sub-contracting it to outside manufacturing firms anxious to make use of spare capacity. They were quoting 80p per unit compared with his own costing of £3.20 per unit. 60% of his selling price is gross profit, 40% the manufacturing cost.

David submitted his design for an innovation award – and won. The benefits of this were both the money prize and the publicity, which gave the product added credibility in the eyes of the banks, suppliers and potential customers.

David took out patents to cover his major markets. He wasn't able to afford a proper patent agent, but he found a moonlighter who did it on the cheap. He patented his design not to prevent copying by the big companies – he wouldn't have had the money to challenge them in the courts anyway – but because financial backers like the security of a product they believe is unique.

David was invited to demonstrate his machine at a series of trade shows around the country. This proved successful and by the autumn of 1981 the product was being sold in stores throughout the country. Not that it was easy to get store buyers to take it. They are notoriously cautious, and David found the best way to ensure repeat orders was to send anonymous friends to buy the machines at his expense. Store buyers watch carefully how sales go in the first few weeks.

David's business is now well under way. His product sells for around £60 which has worried the Japanese, but their nearest competitor still costs twice as much. In the first full 12 months of trading, turnover was £500,000 and net profits £45,000. Export orders are rolling in too – from such diverse places as Iceland, South Africa, the Falklands and the Middle East.

Here are David's tips for would-be inventors:

- Get the design right – the seeds of your own failure can lie in the design of the product. If it is too complicated to manufacture you won't be able to produce enough to satisfy demand or sell it at a price that allows you to offer an attractive enough margin to overseas distributors.
- Get the selling price right – one-man inventors tend to underprice their products. Big firms don't make this mistake due to a combination of expensive overheads and experience of the market. David has been told by department stores that if he had priced his product 50% higher, they would have sold more.
- Be prepared for frustrations – many of the finance houses and agencies you need to approach in the early stages won't have the technical skills to assess the worth of your product.
- Be prepared to exaggerate – people won't take any notice of you if you appear to have little to offer. Tell them now what you anticipate the situation will be in two years time!
- Have the capacity to make mistakes and recover from them – you're bound to make many and you need both emotional resilience and adequate profit margins to ensure you can go forward.
- Be prepared to turn your hand to anything – everyone likes doing the easy things, no one wants the tough jobs. This is probably why many inventors get no further than the "bright idea" – they baulk at rolling up their shirtsleeves and doing the dirty work or putting on a tie and negotiating with financiers.
- Don't neglect even the smallest opportunity – you never know what the spin-offs might be. David's largest export order came through the wife of an overseas businessman watching a product demonstration in a small seaside store.
- Above all, be persistent – no matter how good your product is, the world can exist without it!

MANAGEMENT BUY-OUTS

People who have never thought of running their own business sometimes get the opportunity presented to them on a plate in the form of a management buy-out.

This usually occurs when large companies, rationalizing their activities, decide to sell off subsidiary companies and give the directors a chance to buy them.

The number of management buy-outs has been increasing steadily over recent years. The Industrial and Commercial Finance Corporation, for instance, financed 20 in 1979 (at a value of £3.2m) and 100 in 1982 (£25m).

A management buy-out offers several advantages over other types of business start-up: *less risk* since you are taking over an existing business but, unlike buying someone else's existing business, it is a known quantity. You are familiar with the way it operates and no doubt burning with ideas to improve its performance; comparatively *cheaper* since it will probably be offered to the directors at a lower price than it would fetch on the open market; the combination of the directors' experience and involvement and the fact that the business is a going concern should make it easier to raise the necessary capital.

A report on management buy-outs carried out in 1982 for public relations consultants Nicholas Mendes and Associates suggests that management buy-outs are generally successful. The majority of the buy-out companies interviewed were infinitely better off – in many cases the only alternative was liquidation. Companies which previously operated ineffectively under group control were able to enhance their competitiveness once given their independence, and executives who bought their own companies found no shortage of goodwill in their relationships with customers, employees, suppliers or the general market-place.

The survey indicates that few real problems were encountered by bought-out companies. However, if you are given the opportunity to acquire your company, go into the implications thoroughly: will you have to borrow so much money to finance the change of ownership that the business is put at risk? Do you want to have overall responsibility? Is the market for its products or services viable enough?

TAKING UP A FRANCHISE

Franchising is becoming increasingly popular as a way of setting up in business on your own. It has a much higher success rate than other new ventures. Only about 10% of new franchises fail, compared with around 65% of other business start-ups.

A franchise is a business relationship in which the owner of the name, or method of doing business, allows a local operator to set up a business under that name. The local operator (the *franchisee*) pays the parent organization (the *franchisor*) an initial fee and, usually, royalties for the privilege.

The franchisor lays down a blueprint on how the business should be operated – the content and nature of the goods/services being offered; price and performance standards; type, size and layout of premises; design of stationery. The franchisor also provides the franchisee with training, and other back-up support.

Since the franchise is (usually) for a tried and tested formula and the product or service will be instantly recognizable by customers, the franchisee has a head start over totally new businesses and, theoretically, a better chance of being successful.

The franchising concept stretches back to the start of the tied pub era 100 years ago, but Wimpy, the best-known name in UK franchising, is scarcely twenty years old. There were only a few dozen UK franchisors in the 1970s. Now there are around 300 with some 8,000 franchisees between them, generating sales of over £500 million a year.

The concept goes way beyond the ubiquitous hamburger. It stretches from Phildar Wool shops and Global office cleaning at one end to Computerland and Wordplex word processors at the other. The business fields include professional services such as accounting and veterinary practices as well as more obvious areas such as fast print, health foods and security services.

The field is growing rapidly, and if US experience is anything to go by, we have only just begun. Last year in the USA more new franchisors launched into the field than the whole UK market put together.

The amount of money you need to have, or raise, to take out a franchise varies considerably. It can be as little as £2,500 or more than £300,000 (and all amounts in between). Some franchisors offer financial assistance to franchisees. With others you can raise money through the bank (most of the major clearing banks have now set up specialist sections for franchising – an indication of franchising's growth). But the franchisor will probably only be interested in you as a franchisee if you can find a substantial proportion of the cash from your own resources, since the more you borrow, the more you burden the business in its early stages. The majority of franchises take a royalties fee – usually on turnover or profits. This varies from 5% to 30%. A word of warning: be wary of franchises with a high initial fee and low royalties – they may well take your money and run. However, low royalties may just be a result of a high mark-up on the goods and services controlled by the franchisor. Equally, a low initial fee may mean hidden charges and a high royalty. Some franchisors also demand an advertising levy to go towards the cost of national advertising campaign.

What the franchise package itself consists of varies too. Commonly, it provides the franchisee with all the equipment necessary to operate the business; a training programme; advice on premises and decor; stationery; operating manual; consultancy and other back-up support.

A franchise package must be fair to both parties, the franchisee having ample opportunity to earn a reasonable return on his investment and effort. You need to investigate the franchisor thoroughly before you wade in, and you must be prepared for rigorous scrutiny from him in return. This is essential if a successful partnership is to develop. Ask the following questions to assess the operation and the operator:

- How long has the franchise been going?
- How many outlets are there?
- How successful are they? How does he measure success?
- How many outlets have closed – and why?
- What is the business background and financial involvement of the franchisor and his fellow directors?
- Can you take up any references on him?
- Can you interview his other franchisees? Will he let you choose which ones?
- How does he select his franchisees?
- Is the franchise a member of the British Franchise Association?

As well as making an assessment of the validity of the franchise as an operation, you should also investigate the following:

- How viable is the particular market area? Is it growing, static or declining?
- Does the particular franchise have a good name amongst customers?
- How competitive is it – both in quality and price – with similar businesses (particularly in the area you plan to trade)?

Talk to other people who have taken up the franchise. Ask them:

- Whether the franchisor's projected costs and the revenues were accurate. Were there hidden costs?
- How long did it take to break even?
- Did the franchisor fulfill his obligations on training, help with the launch etc?
- How efficient is the franchisor's supply service?
- Are repairs and problems dealt with promptly?
- Does the franchisor impose many restrictions and checks on franchisees?

You should also take advice from both an accountant and a solicitor to determine whether the franchise is viable financially and that the terms of the contract are fair and reasonable. The accountant will look particularly at the last three years' trading figures for the operation and examine the finances in the contract. The solicitor will explain the terms of the contract to you and look for any major omissions.

Here are some advantages and disadvantages of becoming a franchisee:

Advantages
- Training, provided by the franchisor, overcomes any lack you may have of basic skills or specialized knowledge.

- Risks of setting up a new business are reduced by the fact you are offering a product or service with an established name, and that you can tap the accumulated skills and experience of Head Office.
- Easier to raise finance.
- Layout of premises, management and accounting procedures are already laid down for you.
- Advertising and promotion is often done for you on a national basis.
- The operation is kept up-to-date by a continuous research and development programme.

Disadvantages

- Less freedom than being truly on your own. You can't run the business exactly as you want since you are always accountable to the franchisor.
- You don't keep all the money you take – many franchisors demand a royalty.
- Controls are exercised over the quality of goods and services supplied.
- Policies laid down by the franchisor could adversely affect your profitability.

If you are interested in franchising, investigate the possibilities thoroughly. Two good general books are *Taking Up a Franchise* by G. Golzen, C. Barrow and J. Severn, published by Kogan Page, and *The Guide to Franchising* by M. Mendelsohn, published by Pergamon Press.

The quarterly journal *Franchise World* (37 Nottingham Road, London SW17; 01-767 1371) contains general articles on franchising and details specific opportunities. It also produces a booklet entitled *How to Evaluate a Franchise.*

The British Franchise Association (Franchise Chambers, 75a Bell Street, Henley-on-Thames KG9 2BD; 0491 578049) was founded in 1977 to establish ethical standards in franchising and to provide a public information service. At present the BFA has about 60 members. Admission is only granted once the franchise has been in operation for some time and after a thorough vetting procedure. It's probably a safer bet to go for a franchise with BFA membership but, since franchising is still a relatively new concept, there may well be good, young franchises that don't yet quality for membership.

The BFA, in conjunction with the *Institute of Marketing*, runs seminars for franchisees. Details from the IOM, Moor Hall, Cookham, Maidenhead, Berkshire; (06285) 24922.

At the end of this chapter we provide a directory of franchise opportunities. Contact the franchisors direct for financial and other details.

What's it like to be a franchisee? We talked to John Peters, who's run three franchises.

John was made redundant from his middle-management job in a large company twelve years ago. He'd always wanted to run his own business and taking a franchise seemed a sensible first step since it offered that extra bit of security – a big brother to hold your hand. He used his £1000 redundancy money to buy into a franchised service. It was relatively cheap since there were no fittings or stock to buy.

He built the business up from just himself and a small temporary staff to a permanent team of ten, plus staff in the field, and ran it happily for eight years.

His second venture was less successful. He franchised a business with high overheads which meant higher charges to customers than those of smaller competitors, but the charges weren't high enough to make the business pay.

John stuck it for two years, then bought into an instant print franchise. This wasn't cheap – £50,000 plus buying all your own materials and paying the franchisor a 10% royalty. John has been running it very successfully for a year now (he considers that instant print is a big growth market and there is plenty of room for expansion), but he's thinking of quitting to start a business which will be totally his own. He feels he now possesses the necessary expertise and confidence to do this, and is beginning to resent both paying back hard-earned profits in royalties and the restrictions imposed by a franchise.

However, he strongly recommends franchising as a useful jumping-off point for those who ultimately want to go on their own. Franchised businesses are no longer regarded with the suspicion they were in previous years, but are now considered both acceptable and credible.

But, John warns, a franchise isn't a get-rich-quick operation. Even the most successful franchises take time to get off the ground. John reckons at least 6-12 months to reach break-even point and 2-3 years to get into profit (the same as most businesses).

John's advice: play safe and buy into a proven franchise rather than experiment with an untried idea just on the market. Don't take the word of the franchisor (he's obviously biased) and don't meekly accept all the claims made in the promotional literature – talk to the franchisees. Find out how long they've been in business, what their turnover and profit figures are and what sort of support they receive from the franchisor. Without the right back-up, moral as well as practical, the business may never make it.

Directory of franchises

AIDS, Elscot House, Arcadia Avenue, Finchley Central, London N3 2JE. (01-349-3191).
    Contacts: Mike Salinger or Ivor Davis.
    AIDS has been providing a monthly management accounting service to small businesses for 12 years. AIDS takes the client's normal bookkeeping figures, feeds them onto its mainframe computer, and supplies the client with a complete set of management accounts promptly every month.
    AIDS is managed by accountants who have designed, tested and proven their service, which is complementary to the services normally provided by conventional accounting firms.
    Parent Company: AIDS Computer Services Ltd.
Anicare Group Services (Veterinary) Ltd, 27 Buckingham Road, Shoreham by Sea, W. Sussex BN4 5UA. (079-17-63022).
    Contact: J. Sheridan.
    Promotes the establishment of small animal veterinary services using franchise agreements to establish groups of self-employed veterinary surgeons utilizing the managerial, administrative, financial, promotional and organizational services provided.
Apollo Window Blinds Limited, Johnstone Avenue, North Cardonald Industrial Estate, Glasgow G52 4YH. (041-810-3021).
    Contact: James Watson, Franchise Manager.
    Sell fashion window blinds through their high street retail outlets to homes and businesses. Shops provide total custom made blind service from measuring windows to installation. Company has three factories manufacturing blinds and 60 outlets in the North. Site selection, shopfitting, training and support provided.
Auto-Smart Ltd, Basin Lane, Glascote, Tamworth, Staffs. (0827-54291).
    Contact: Mr. M. E. Fidler, Managing Director.
    Auto-Smart Distributors are self-employed, running their business from either their own homes or a warehouse. Selling specialized products to the Automotive and Transport Industry from a 'Mobile Showroom' – a custom-built vehicle specially designed to carry the products – cases and bulk.

Badgeman Limited, 544 Chiswick High Road, Chiswick, London W4 5RG (01-994-0826).
>Contact: David Mackie, Sales & Marketing Manager.
>A fast service for high quality, personalized name badges on laminated plastic in any quantity. Can be operated from home. Customers range from large companies to local companies and retailers.

Balloon, 26 High Street, Merstham, Surrey RH1 3EA. (07374-4211/3).
>Contact(s): John Gooderham, Hervie Courvoisier (France).
>Paris based franchise, retails up-market maternity wear and accessories, exclusively designed and manufactured in France. Garments include shirts, blouses, cocktail dresses, day dresses, trousers, jeans, swimsuits, underwear and lounge wear. Also sells baby wear and childrens up to two years. Has 42 shops (22 in France) most of which are franchised.
>Parent Co: La Redoute, France.

Baskin-Robbins Ice Cream Europe Ltd, Glacier House, Brook Green, London W6 7BT. (01-603-2040).
>Contact: Susan Brocklehurst, Operations Manager.
>Choice of type of outlet from complete shops, shops within shops or kiosks. Varying range of 31 flavours. Full training and support given.
>Parent Co: Allied Lyons plc.

Bathcare Limited, 106 Main Road, West Huntspill, Highbridge, Somerset. (0278-785950).
>Contact: Mike Scanes, Managing Director.
>Ranges from re-enamelling existing metal baths through to de-limescaling a hotel or RAF camp. Now into fitting bathrooms for the disabled and planning the bathroom installation.

The Big Apple, 10-11 Great Newport Street, London WC2H 7NS. (01-240-1701).
>Contact: Mr. Jim Lewis.
>Health Studios/Gymnasium.

British School of Motoring, 40 North Street, Romford, Essex.
>Contact: Mr. D. Haddon.
>Gives driving instruction. The franchises are existing businesses with accessible trading infomation but new areas may be developed. Training for all kinds of staff is given. The cars are modified and checked for serviceability before issue. Guidance is available on various aspects of the business. Part of the management services levy goes on publicity.
>Parent Co: Taurus Vehicle Leasing.

Bruce & Co., 43 Bridge Street, Leatherhead, Surrey KT28 3BM. (0372-375161).
>Contact: C. B. Jermyn and Mr. I. W. Lynch, Partners.
>Business transfer agents for the sale of businesses, shops, hotels etc.

Budget Rent A Car International Inc, International House, 85 Great North Road, Hatfield, Herts. AL9 5EF. (07072-68266).
>Contact: B. Glover and G. Barkatollah (Directors).
>World's largest franchised vehicle rental system which operates in 90 countries. Package includes support from national sales and marketing activities, modern business systems and training.
>Parent Co: Transamerica Corp.

Burger King Ltd, 20 Kew Road, Richmond, Surrey TW9 2NA. (01-940-6046).
>Contact: R. C. M. Booth.
>Fast food restaurants which the corporation services. There are own brand sandwiches and plans to move into breakfast and other meals. There are 3 types of cooking facility available according to market potential. The site can be corporation or franchisee owned. Full training is given and follow-up advice is available.
>Parent Co: Pillsbury Co.

The City Bag Store, 10 Northfield Industrial Estate, Beresford Avenue, Wembley, Middx (01-903-9448).

Contact: Brian Davies, Franchise Director.

Seeking more franchisees throughout UK to run own successful up-market handbag and leathergoods shop. Can be run by one person with a little part-time assistance. Full training given as is help and assistance in finding suitable shop unit.

Parent Co: The City Bag Store Ltd.

City Link, 13/14 Ascot Road, Clockhouse Lane, Feltham, Middx TW14 8QF. (07842-43721).

Contact: M. D. Farback, Director.

National same day/next morning parcels collection and delivery service, operated in conjunction with the British Rail 'Red Star' and 'Night Star' parcel services.

Parent Co: City Link Transport Holdings Ltd.

Command Performance, High End, Troutstream Way, Loudwater, Herts. WD3 4LQ. (0923-777636).

Contact: Iain Macaulay.

A full service hair salon franchise, new to the UK, but is the largest chain in the USA with 400 outlets.

The Compleat Cookshop, 3 Castle Street, High Wycombe, Bucks. (0494-32631).

Contact: Bryan Wilkes.

Retails pottery, glass and gifts over a wide range. Three types of franchise are available. Much of the stock is bought from clearance lines and need not be from the company. Training is given in preparation for trading.

Condor Clentech, Abbotts Barton House, Worthy Road, Winchester, Hants. SO23 7SJ. (0962-63577).

Contact(s): Derek Ayling and Ray Childs.

Ceiling cleaning specialists.

Parent Co: Conder International plc.

Cookie Coach, Greyhound House, 23-24 George Street, Richmond, Surrey TW9 1HY. (01-940-3323).

Contact: Frank Grindell, or Jack Liquorish.

Vends a range of 'giant cookies' made under licence. Franchisees have a specified area and carry the product in a replica 1901 New York bakery van. The concept is to sell direct on sites of the franchisee's choosing and to top up product supplies at retailers initially serviced by the company. Equipment includes lease of van, starter stock and staff uniform. Training given.

Cookmate Kitchen Shop, Cookshop Supplies Ltd, Unit 5, Southern Road, Aylesbury, Bucks HP19 3AW. (0296-20695).

Contact: Mr. B. Howlett, Franchise Director.

Franchises retailing outlets where items for sale are principally for use in the kitchen. Half the goods are reject, others are imported, bought in bulk or own design products. Full training and an advice service is available and conferences are held for such things as security, displays, advertising and buying.

Cover Right Ltd, Unit 10, Bancombe Industrial Estate, Martock, Somerset. (0935-824866).

Contact: Mr. P. O'Leary.

The company markets and lays a floor– and wall–covering material which is seamless, non-skid, minimizes maintenance and is available in a range of colours and designs. Franchisees have a defined area and are given full training and equipment.

Descamps, 197 Sloane Street, London SW1X 9QX. (01-235-7165).

Contact: G. Gagny.

Selling fine household linen. Colours co-ordinated between bed linen, towelling, table linen and nursery linen. All designs by Primrose Boidier of France.
Parent Co: Descamps Deuneestive (France).

Despatch Post, TNT Despatch Post, 3rd Floor, Blackburn House, Bondgate, Nuneaton, Warks. CV11 4DU. (0203-347932).
Contacts: Mr. R. Crofts and Mr. R. McClellan.
Reception point for parcels which are delivered on any of TNT's express parcel services within the UK, Europe and worldwide.
Parent Co: TNT Roadfreight (UK) Ltd.

Drips Plumbing, 143 Maple Road, Surbiton, Surrey. (01-549-9711).
Contact: Mr. P. M. Slinn.
All year round plumbing service intended to give corporate image to existing plumbing organizations.
Parent Co: Dyno-Rod Ltd.

Dyno-Rod plc, 143 Maple Road, Surbiton, Surrey KT6 4BJ. (01-549-9711).
Contacts: Mr. R. G. Taylor, Mr. R. Stoner.
Offers service on pipe work of various kinds. The services include cleaning, clearance, testing, tracing and emergency work. There is also an Industrial Jetting Division and Off Shore Division. Media coverage varies by area.

Electricure/30, 6/7 Ye Corner, Chalk Hill, Watford, Hertfordshire. (Watford 42678).
Contact: Carole Darley, John Darley, Gordon Rogers.
Seeking qualified electricians. Clients are usually those buying own homes as well as Local Authorities etc. Business can be run from home. Full training given.
Parent Co: J. Darling (Bldrs) Ltd.

Enviraflo, Westone House, 9/11 Horton Street, St. Phillips, Bristol BS2 0LD. (0272-213604).
Contact: Roger Davidge, Franchise Manager.
Structural cleaning service which utilizes a revolutionary wet abrasive surface cleaning system. Used to prepare steel surfaces on offshore oil platforms and to clean exterior of buildings.

Foto Inn Ltd, 12 Oxford Street, London W1N 9FL. (01-580-0434).
Contact: A. Khorshid.
60 minute high quality colour print service using the latest technology. Shops are equipped with easy to operate mini labs which can handle all popular sizes of colour film and some black and white film.

Global Cleaning Contracts, Global House, Lind Road, Sutton, Surrey. (01-642-0054).
Contacts: K. L. P. Wearn, A. N. Hinwood.
The Global franchisee sells cleaning contracts to contractors. The contractor then has to supply the labour, equipment and materials.
Parent Co: Global Cleaning Contracts (Holdings) Ltd.

Holland & Barrett (Franchising) Ltd, Healthways House, Station Approach, West Byfleet, Surrey KT14 6NE. (09232-41133).
Contact: Ken Mullarkey, Chief Executive.
Europe's largest health food retailer which manufactures, markets and distributes a wide range of health foods. Owns a number of brands such as Allinson and Prewetts. Holds headlease while granting an underlease to the franchisee.
Parent Co: Booker McConnell.

Home Tune, Home Tune House, Guildford Road, Effingham, Surrey. KT24 5QS (0372-56656).
Contact: Mr. Duncan Whitefield, Managing Director.
On-site motor vehicle tuning service. Mobile vans, with testing equipment and spares, carry the service to the customer. Full training is given and all vans and equipment are supplied through the company on hire. Central buying is used to

obtain tools and vehicle parts. There is vehicle delivery and a logo. During the first year of trading the franchise is advertised locally.

House of Fraser International, 1 Howick Place, London SW1P 1BH. (01-828-9044).
    Contact: B. A. Evans.
    Provides a total franchising service to create and operate major department stores overseas. Franchises name, retailing expertise and provides senior management, merchandising and promotion, purchasing and delivery and advice on location and design of stores.

Identicar, Identicar House, Wolverhampton Road, Warley, West Midlands B69 4RL. (021-541-1141).
    Contact: J. H. Harris, D. A. Morcom.
    Vehicle security systems, principally the irremovable marking of registration number on to the vehicle windows. Free car rental and reduced insurance premiums are part of the retail package.
    Parent Co: Identicar (Holdings) Ltd.

Intacab, Clock House, Service House, High Road, Laindon, Basildon, Essex. SS15 6NV. (0268-415891).
    Contact: Peter Dance, Franchise Director.
    A taxi service under a company logo. A comprehensive package including advice and instruction is provided. There is also a company marketing campaign using press advertising, mailing shots and leaflets.

Interlink Express Courier Parcels, Portland House, 22/24 Portland Square, Bristol, Avon BS2 8RZ. (0272-40257).
    Contacts: Mrs R. A. Bugden and Mr R. G. Gabriel.
    Guaranteed, nationwide overnight parcel delivery service. Provides a door to door service for industry and commerce.

In-Toto, Wakefield Road, Gildersome, Leeds LS27 0QW. (0532-524131).
    Contacts: Ian Wilkie and Sue Cass.
    Quality fitted kitchen showrooms, furniture by Wellman and electrical fittings by Philips.

Isodan, 12 Mount Ephraim Road, Royal Tunbridge Wells, Kent TN1 1EE. (0892-44822).
    Contact: S. John Holt, Managing Director.
    A system of cavity-wall insulation using dry granules. It involves no on-site hazards or expensive equipment.

Jessop Hall Home Security Ltd, Unit 1, Wharfe Road, Woodston, Peterborough PE2 9PS. (0233-314316).
    Contact: B. Morrell.
    Alarm installation company providing security installations to the home and commercial sector with full maintenance contracts. Comprehensive package provided which includes continuous support.

Kall-Kwik Printing, Victoria Road, South Ruislip, Middx HA4 0JF. (01-841-5151).
    Contact: John. B. Atkinson, Franchising Manager.
    Sole Licensee for US Kwik-Kopy system. Have 100 high street shops in UK. Provide financial start-up package, site selection layout planning, training, pre and post opening support and marketing assistance.

Kenprest, RE Tyre & Rubber Co. Ltd, Mill Lane, Alton, Hants. GU34 2QG. (0420-82122).
    Contact: Mr R. J. Rata.
    Franchise is based on a patented system for retrading truck tyres and also the Kentred sytem for both car and truck tyres.

Kentucky Fried Chicken (GB) Ltd, Wichat House, Camberley, Surrey GU15 3HL. (0276-686151).
    Contact: Mrs Jenny Bassett.

Retails fast food to eat or take away. The company helps in finding and assessing the site and provides drawings for planning permission. Company policy is on shop fittings and equipment, these being proved before use by franchisees. Full training is given and media coverage is provided. Franchisees can be elected to the board responsible for advertising expenditure.

Parent Co: Heublein Inc. (in USA).

Kwik Strip, Units 1/2, The 306 Estate, 242 Broomhill Road, Brislington, Bristol BS4 5RA. (0272-772470).

Contact: Ivor Chivers.

Specializes in serving the growing stripping/restoration market with a process which will strip paint, varnish and polyurathenes from all types of wood and metal. The company offers a comprehensive package which includes a starter-pack and continuous back-up from the Head Office in Bristol.

Lasalign, D.S.B. House, 135 High Street, Bromley, Kent BR1 1JF. (01-466-6021/2/3).

Contact: Graham Ross.

Offers load haulage industry and large fleet operators of articulated vehicles a mobile low assisted trailer axle alignment service. Uses latest laser based equipment.

Leaders Health Food Stores, 105 London Road, Brighton, East Sussex BN1 4JG. (0273-695001).

Contact: Roy Harris.

Health food stores located in the high streets of the south of England. Full training given at existing stores and own training school. £1,000 deposit (returnable) secures town of choice.

Parent Co: Holgran Ltd and Southern Health Foods Ltd.

The Maids, 4-6 Lind Road, Sutton, Surrey. (01-642-0054).

Contacts: K. C. P. Wearn and H. Brogden.

Home cleaning service. Supervised team with special cleaning equipment and materials. Thoroughly clean the home. Additional services include spring cleaning, emergency cleaning and carpet and upholstery cleaning.

Parent Co: Global Cleaning Contracts (Holdings) Ltd.

Med-Ped, Plaza Med-Ped, Palma Nova, Mallorca, Spain. (34-71-68-16-32).

Contact: Dr Daniel C. Denby.

Two-wheeled vehicle hire in Spanish tourist resorts. Expanding soon to France, Italy, Greece, Portugal etc.

Parent Co: Mediterranean Mopeds S.A.

Mixamate Ltd, Station Yard, Bourne Way, Hayes, Kent BR2 7EY. (01-462-8011).

Contact: Peter Bates, Managing Director.

Mixamate supplies concrete for builders and the DIY market. Franchisees should have HGV operating experience as a specialized vehicle, supplied by the company, carries cement, aggregate and water to mix, in amounts as required, on site. A territory is allotted and full training given. There is company policy on appearance of staff and vehicles.

Mobile Tuning Ltd, 7A Nelson Road, London SE10 9JB. (01-853-1520)

Contact: Anton Rowntree.

Car tuning company which specializes in using Crypton electronic engine tuning equipment at customers' homes or places of work. Provides comprehensive training, a fully equipped van, spare parts, diagnostic equipment and tuning data for the different makes of cars. Also receive continuous promotional and technical support.

Mopps & Co., Coniscliffe House, Coniscliffe Road, Darlington DL3 7EX. (0325-84727).

Contact: Sue Rorstad and Christine Sorensen.

Based on a range of high quality domestic and commercial cleaning services. Franchisee has sole rights to territory, use of Mopps & Co. name and logo and associated goodwill. Training is provided and constant help and support is available from Head Office.

Parent Co: Prontaprint Ltd.

Mr. Fish on Wheels Ltd, 26 High Street, Merstham, Surrey RH1 3EA. (07374-4211).
Contact: Michael Way.

Selling fresh sea-food to the housewife and food trade using well equipped, eye-catching sales and delivery vehicles. Fleets range from 10 to 14 vehicles.

Mr. Slade Franchises Ltd, Maritime Chambers, Howard Street, North Shields NE30 1AR. (0632-596421).
Contact: Eunice Hesslegrave.

Dry cleaning units, sited in existing retail outlets. Additionally, agents pass work to the unit. In future the franchisees, who should have business experience, will have independently sited premises. Preparation training is given and the opening phase supported with a launch programme.

Parent Co: Mr. Slade Ltd.

Nature's Way Ltd, 1 Clifford Road, Bexhill, East Sussex TN40 1QA. (0424-222125).
Contact: Barry Howell, Managing Director.

Retail and serve health food. Franchisees should have an interest in the products. A defined area is allotted and company assistance is available on choice of sites. Company policy covers layout and fittings and stock must be bought from an approved list. Promotion is funded from a turnover levy.

Olivers Hot Bread & Coffee Shops, Leeds House, 64 George Street, Luton, Beds LU1 2BD. (0582-417408).
Contact: Gordon Paterson.

Combination of units comprising a bakery, take-away and coffee shops with seating between 70-150. Shops have a range of in-store equipment and are supplied with special bakery mixes and other ingredients.

The Pancake Place, 30 New Road, Milnathort, Kinross KY13 7XT. (0577-63969).
Contacts: Mr. A. Miller and Mr. R. Kay.

"Olde-worlde" style restaurants aimed at popular end of market. Menu consists of pancake based snacks and three course meals.

Pass & Co., Passco House, 635 High Road, Leytonstone, London E11 4RD. (01-539-1105).
Contact: J. Frankling, Franchise Director.

Specializes in the remedial treatment of woodworm, dry rot and rising damp giving a guarantee each time.

PDC Copyprint, Head Office, 103 Oxford Street, London W1H 9DL. (01-439-8937).
Contacts: Mr. D. Campbell Nisbet, Mr. H. Stokes and Mr. W. Slade.

Experienced quickprint company with unique features. Reducing royalty – buying out licence, full training, holiday relief, private insurance, site finding, shop fitting, machinery installation and supply.

Parent Co: PDC Holdings.

Phildar UK Ltd, 4 Gambrel Road, Westgate Ind. Estate, Northampton NN5 5NF. (0604-583111).
Contact: G. C. Houston or T. Moreav.

Makes and retails own brand knitting wools, rug making and tapestry work supplies together with related hobbies accessories. Interest in handicrafts would be an advantage. Premises have a company logo and colours, with layout and interior design plans drawn up by the company. Training is given and support is provided on promotion, legal and financial guidance.

Pip Instant Printing, 166 West End Lane, London NW6. (01-435-8027).
Contact: Ivor Freedman.

Shops provide a full instant-print service from copiers and offset presses; with over 700 locations worldwide it is the largest instant printers.

Pizza Express Ltd, 29 Wardour Street, London W1. (01-437-7215).

Contact: Ian S. Neill.

These restaurants offer a choice of 14 pizzas, a selection of desserts and Italian wines and beer. Comprehensive training and advice on running a Pizza Express.

Prodata, Churchfield Road, Frodsham, Cheshire. (0928-35110).

Contact: C. I. Piff.

Specialized, professional bookkeeping service for small to medium sized firms. They visit their clients regularly taking a compact microcomputer with them which is used to record current financial information.

Prontaprint, Coniscliffe House, Coniscliffe Road, Darlington DL3 7EX. (0325-55391).

Contact: Peter Brennan and John Atkinson.

High-speed printing and instant copying shops. Printing experience is not required, as full training is offered and all equipment is tested for suitability.

Pronuptia de Paris Bridalwear, 70/78 York Way, London N1 9AG. (01-278-7722).

Contact: Edward Young, Chairman.

Has international outlets retailing bridal wear exclusive to the company. There is a commercial association with Young's menswear. Training is given in various aspects of the business. Company advice is available on suitable locations and shopfitting. National advertising in women's magazines, with fashion shows, point of sale aids and local publicity.

Parent Co: Young's Dress Hire Ltd.

Safeclean, Pound House, Stream Road, Upton, Didcot, Oxon. (0235-850387).

Contact: Desmond Cook, Managing Director.

Offers an on-site service to clean upholstery and carpets. Materials can be treated for anti-static and flame retarding. Hand cleaning methods are used and the equipment is patented. Franchisees must be fit and could start business on a part-time basis. Training is given both before and after start-up.

Parent Co: D. G. Cook Ltd.

Seekers, Thornganby Ltd, Suite 10, Priory House, Kingsgate Place, London NW6. (01-328-7251).

Contact: M. Nyman and M. Davis.

A fast-growing chain of shops introducing home buyers to home sellers offering a low-cost alternative to the established estate agents.

Servicemaster Ltd, 50 Commercial Square, Freemans Common, Leicester LE2 7SR. (0533-548620).

Contact: Mr. J. R. Major.

A carpet and upholstery cleaning organization specializing in on-site cleaning of carpets and upholstery in domestic, commercial and disaster situations.

Parent Co: Service Master Industries Inc.

Silver Shield Windscreen, 38-42 Holbrook Lane, Coventry CV6 4AB, West Midlands. (0203-661311).

Contact: John Oliver.

Offers on-site motor vehicle windscreen replacement. The service is day and night throughout the year and contact can be made by freefone. A complete training, promotional and advice package is given. Company equipment and materials are provided.

Singer, 255 High Street, Guildford, Surrey GU1 3DH. (0483-5771144).

Contact: Angela Auger.

Retail outlet for sale, and after-sale servicing, of the Singer company sewing machines and related products. The franchise can be added to an existing business or started independently. Full training is given and a pre and post trading advice package is available.

Parent Co: The Singer Company (USA).

Snap-on-Tools Ltd, Dunham House, 85/99 Cross Street, Sale, Cheshire M33 1FU. (061-969-0126).

Contact: Jonathan Ward.

Retail tools for the motor vehicle garage trade, the role of the franchisee being to sell a range of company supplied products to appropriate outlets. Full training is given but someone with previous sales experience is envisaged as a franchisee.

Sovereign Services (SE), 39 Osborne Road, Eastbourne, East Sussex BN20 8JJ. (0323-20814).

Contact: B. R. Southon.

Offers a private ambulance service with fully qualified medical attendance. Vehicles and staff move patients, including out-patients, to and from hospitals and nursing homes over any distance. Repatriation abroad can be provided.

Parent Co: Sovereign Medical Services Ltd.

Sperrings Convenience Store, Sperring House, 1 Spring Crescent, Portswood, Southampton SO2 1FZ. (0703-552550).

Contact: Mike Trusler and Debi Bunker.

Large chain of convenience stores, more than 45 outlets. It is a full business format franchise.

Spud-u-Like, 34-38 Standard Road, London NW10 6EU. (01-965-0181).

Contacts: G. Heath and R. Patmore.

Restaurants specializing in a large variety of filled baked potatoes.

Parent Co: British School of Motoring.

Stop A Thief, Knightsford House, Church Road, Wombourne, Wolverhampton, West Midlands WV5 9EX (0902-893870).

Contact: Phil Aston.

Security marking of vehicles and property. System is easily operated by one person who operates from a fully equipped, signwritten vehicle. Full training and on-going assistance are provided.

Strikes Restaurant, 289 Oxford Street, London W1R 2AD. (01-629-4680).

Contacts: Mr. John Connell and Miss R. Eliades.

Licensed table service restaurants, with take-away facilities. Possible outlets are considered for viability and suitable premises are prepared with company advice. Although training is given franchisees are expected to select their own staff. At time of opening publicity is given but later franchisees must pay for advertising.

Tandy Corps (Branch UK), Tameway Tower, Bridge Street, Walsall, West Midlands. (0922-648181).

Contact: Bob Cleaver, National Manager.

A retailer of consumer electronics, whose range inlcudes hi-fi, radios, micro-computers, electronic components and general electronic durables.

Parent Co: Radio Shack in the USA.

J. W. Thornton, Derwent Street, Belper, Derbyshire DE5 1WP. (077382-4181).

Contact: Mr. R. E. Smith, Commercial Sales Manager.

Retails own brand sugar and chocolate confectionery. The franchise can be run independently or in an existing business retailing compatible products. Shops are stocked and fitted exactly as company-owned outlets. Training is given. This is a fractional franchise, and only of interest to people looking for add-on products.

Tie Rack Limited, 2 Montpelier Street, London SW7 1EZ. (01-584-8129).

Contacts: Mr. T. D. Jennnings and Mr. J. S. W. Tonks.

Retailing of quality ties through rented premises with stock supplied from franchisor.

Parent Co: Associated Investments Ltd.

Torlink, C. & J. Clark Ltd, Street, Somerset BA16 0YA. (0458-43131).
Contact: J. E. Dixon, Torlink Manager.
Effects the assisted Venture Scheme of the Clarks footwear organization, to install franchisees as retailers of company footwear products. Training is given. Company policy covers selection and fitting of retail outlets, which are sub-let to franchisee. There is a comprehensive franchise package. Products are nationally advertised.
Parent Co: C. J. Clark Ltd.

Trace Heat Pumps Ltd, Trade House, Eastways Ind. Park, Witham, Essex CM8 3YU. (0376-515511).
Contacts: G. A. Sills, N. R. Smart, T. J. Cook.
Sells, installs and services their own heat pumps. Have largest range of pumps in UK, over 350. Will provide training and ongoing support.
Parent Co: Trace Cleveland Ltd.

Uticolor, Sheraton House, 35-37 North Street, York TO1 1JD. (0904-37798).
Contact: Eric S. Bottomley, Director.
An invisible repairing service for vinyl– or leather–covered furniture. The bonding technique is taught. Customers include schools, pubs, hotels and offices.

Vinyl Master (UK) Ltd, Avonbridge, King Johns Island, Tewkesbury, Glos. GL20 6EB. (0684-295511).
Contact: Mr. N. Scanlan.
Offers an on-site repair and re-covering service for vinyl covered upholstery. Market includes homes and businesses of various kinds.

Watertite Ltd, Unit 4, Wall End Close, Leamore, Walsall, West Midlands WS2 7PH. (0922-409178).
Contacts: J. Oliver and C. Evans.
Installation of new and replacement guttering, by aluminium guttering formed on site in 'bespoke' lengths.

Wimpy, 214 Chiswick High Road, London W4 1PD. (01-994-6454).
Contact: Ian Petrie, Managing Director.
A world-wide network of hamburger restaurants. Wimpy offers franchise in its new counter-service style.
Parent Co: United Biscuits.

Woodcure-Dampcure/30, 6/7 Ye Corner, Chalk Hill, Watford, Herts. (Watford 23842/41514/42678).
Contacts: Carole Darley, John Darley, Gordon Rogers.
Established business which treats timber infestation and rising damp. Provides training, equipment, the guarantee for each job and full marketing support.
Parent Co: J. Darling (Bldrs) Ltd.

Youngs Formal Wear for Men, 70/78 York Way, London N1 9AG. (01-278-7722).
Contact: Edward Young, Chairman.
They retail and hire out men's formal morning and evening wear. Menswear can also be ordered in Pronuptia bridal wear shops. Training is provided as is promotion and various forms of guidance and advice.

Yves Rocher Beauty Centres, Chapel Court, 169B Borough High Street, London SE1. (01-403-4944).
Contact: Mr. S. Partridge, Managing Director.
Attractively designed and equipped small shops offering a complete range of cosmetic products and treatments. Over 600 outlets world-wide.
Parent Co: Yves Rocher.

Ziebart Appearance & Protection Services, Zeegard Car Care Ltd, Crescent House, Crescent Road, Worthing, Sussex. (0903-203170).
Contact: L. F. Smith, Managing Director.

Specialists in the treatment of rust protection of new and used vehicles. Backed by Ziebart International Corporation, Ziebart UK is able to offer total protection for vehicles, inside and out.

Parent Co: Ziebart International Corporation.

CHAPTER 2 SUMMARY

- Various factors will influence your choice when deciding what sort of business to run. Not least, what you would *like* to do and where there is a gap in the market.
- There are a great number of possible business ideas – service businesses of many types, retailing, catering and getting your own invention into production. There are also two increasingly popular techniques for getting into business – management buy-outs and taking a franchise on an existing business.

Chapter 3

FORMING THE BUSINESS

The decision to start your own business can be an immensely difficult one to make, and, once made, planning and structuring your business can cause an awful lot of headaches. However, the actual mechanics of *forming* the business can be surprisingly simple. In this chapter we tell you the legal and other requirements of the different forms of business, their advantages and disadvantages. We also give some advice on business names; points to watch when buying an existing business. We list the types of businesses which need licences and registration, tell you which professional advisers can help, and show you the ways you can protect a business idea.

WHICH BUSINESS STRUCTURE?

Legally, all businesses fall into one of the following categories: *Sole Trader*, *Partnership*, *Company* (limited or unlimited, public or private, limited by guarantee) or *Co-Operative* (or common ownership enterprise). Franchises are not included here since they are not a business structure as such – see Chapter 2.

You need to decide which structure is most suitable for your type of business. It's an important decision since the form you choose will affect most aspects of your business life – your legal liability to customers and suppliers; your tax position and your methods of financing and accounting. It's sensible to seek advice from a solicitor and/or accountant as to which structure you should adopt. You can change the structure at a later date but not without some expense. Many people who start up on their own in a small way without any formalities (classified as sole traders although they might not realize it!) find that as their business grows, they need the tax advantages and protection against putting their personal assets at risk which a private limited liability company offers.

The factors which affect your decision are the number of people involved, the scale of the operation, the amount of capital required – and the means by which you need to raise it, plus your own temperament.

Making a choice

Penny Chalmers, who found that her friends were willing to pay for the dolls she made for her own amusement, but was unsure whether doll-making could make a living for her (or whether she wanted it to) elected to become a sole trader. Accountants Roger Howells and Tony Bingham set up their accountancy practice as a partnership since their professional association doesn't allow accountants to form limited companies. Roger Curry had no hesitation about opting for limited company status for manufacturing and selling the knitting machine he had invented because of the high-risk capital involved.

SOLE TRADER

Being a sole trader is just a method for one person to start their own outfit. It doesn't have to be a trade and you can employ as many people as you like.

35

Setting up as a sole trader is the most simple business structure to adopt. You are not required by law to do anything in the way of registering the business (although you should register for VAT if your anticipated turnover is £18,700 or more). You can start up without any formalities. However, it is probably the most risky way to trade since you are totally responsible for the business. Its success or failure depends entirely on you, and if it fails, you have to pay your creditors – which could mean selling your house and other personal possesions if the debts are large.

Although there is nothing you are required to do legally as a sole trader, it is sensible to do the following:

- Open a separate bank account for the business.
- Tell your local tax inspector (or get an accountant to do so). The inspector will give you some indication of allowable business expenses.
- Take out full insurance cover against possible loss or damage to any equipment – if you have invested in any.
- Take out a personal injury/illness insurance since your National Health Insurance won't cover you if you are injured or ill while operating your own business.

The advantages and disadvantages of being a sole trader are as follows:

Advantages

- Easy to set up – you can start the business in a small way, from your home if you want (but see Chapter 5: Working from home).
- You are the boss. You can run the business at your own pace and in your own way.
- You keep the profits.
- You can offset some business expenses against earnings for tax purposes.
- No public disclosure of your affairs.
- Profit or loss in one trade can be set off against profit or loss in any other business you run – or past PAYE.

Disadvantages

- You are totally responsible for any debts your business incurs. If you go bankrupt, your creditors are entitled to seize and sell your possesions – personal as well as business.
- Can be lonely.
- Low status.

PARTNERSHIP

If two or more people want to club together to start a business without actually registering it as a company, they can form a partnership. Like sole traders, partnerships are informal business arrangements. They can be created without any legal formalities – although it is advisable to have a written document drawn up by a solicitor which set outs the terms of partnership (see below for details).

Partnerships can consist of up to 20 partners. Certain categories of professionals, such as solicitors and accountants, can have more than 20 partners. These professions are prohibited by their professional associations (the Law Society and the Institute of Chartered Accountants) from trading as limited companies since these bodies decree that their members must be publicly accountable to their clients and therefore can't hide behind the protection of limited liability (however, this is likely to change). Many professional partnerships continue for many years. As older partners retire, they are replaced by younger ones who join at a cost they can afford and the retired partners continue to draw an income from the partnership.

Why You Might Consider a Partnership

- As a means of starting up with increased capital (presuming both you and your partners put money in).
- You might not feel confident to start a business entirely on your own and would prefer to share the responsibilities with someone else.
- You have complementary skills – one of you may have specialist skills and the other management flair, or one the money, the other the ideas.

Choosing a Partner

If the business is going to have any chance of success, it is essential that the partners trust each other and can work together harmoniously. Also, since you and your partner(s) have unlimited financial liability for the firm, if things go wrong – regardless of whose fault it is – creditors can claim the personal possesions of each and every partner. A partnership is therefore almost as close a relationship as a marriage. So the choice of partner must be made with as much care as selecting a wife or husband.

If you are considering a partnership, ask yourself first if you have the right temperament to be a partner. Some people are too individual to be able to cope with pooling their ideas and resources on an equal footing.

The intolerant entrepreneur. Eric O'Keefe opted out of the highly successful Spanish bar he had painstakingly set up and nurtured for seven years within a year of taking a partner. He took the partner because he needed finance to expand but Eric couldn't tolerate what he saw as the partner's "interference" with the way the bar was run. He now admits – with hindsight – that the partner was perfectly entitled to express his views on what had, after all, become a joint project. Eric agrees that his personality was the problem. "I'm better on my own," he admits and, perhaps equally significantly, "alcohol always causes personality clashes but it's the only business I would contemplate working in."

There are no hard and fast rules about selecting a partner, but the most successful partnerships do seem to be those where the partners have known each other for some time – either as friends or business associates – and where they have *complementary* skills and personalities. If one partner, for instance, is a technical person who looks after the manufacturing side of the operation while the other is good at dealing with people and looks after sales, or the combination of an "ideas" person with a down-to-earth practical man or woman who can implement the ideas.

If you want to go into partnership but don't have a particular partner in mind, publications such as *Daltons Weekly* have classified advertising sections of people seeking partners. Examples of the ads they run are shown below:

Partnerships

Partnership Agreements

Partnerships are covered by the Partnership Act 1890. Its main provisions are:

1. Partners are entitled to share equally in the capital and profits of the business and must also contribute equally to all losses of the business. (They can also put in different amounts and share proportionately.)
2. Every partner may take part in the management of the business, but is not entitled to a salary for his services, only a share in the profits.
3. New partners cannot be introduced without the consent of existing partners.
4. Every partner must have access to the partnership books, which should be kept at the place of business.

The provisions of the Partnership Act apply if there is no other agreement between the partners but it is sensible, if not essential, to get a solicitor to draw up a Deed of Partnership between you and your partners. You may want to vary the rules laid down in the Partnership Act and to cover points not mentioned. This document also regulates exactly how the business is run. It should cover the following:

Profit sharing: how profits and losses are to be divided. If, for example, one partner has sunk more capital into the business than the other, profits won't be shared in equal proportions; or you might decide to distribute profits according to the number of contracts completed, the number of hours worked, or by some other method.

Withdrawing money: it is important to limit the amount of money each partner can take out of the business each month otherwise you may find you have insufficient working capital.

Time off: the length and frequency of holidays should be laid down, as well as what rules apply if a partner is incapacitated through illness. He will be entitled to his share of the profits, so you may consider it important to stipulate a time limit after which the partnership can be dissolved.

Voting rights: unless the agreement states otherwise, all partners have equal voting rights. You might wish to vary this.

Duration of partnership: how long do you want your partnership to last – one, three, five or ten years? Or you might prefer it to be for an indefinite period, terminating after, say, three months notice.

Admitting or expelling a partner: the consent of every partner is necessary before a new partner can be admitted. If you want the right to have a relative, e.g. your son, admitted as a partner later, this should be stated in the agreement. Unless the agreement states otherwise, you must get a court order if you want to expel a partner, so the partnership deed should set out in detail the circumstances in which a partner can be expelled.

Dissolving or rescinding the partnership: dissolution will occur automatically on the death or bankruptcy of a partner – unless the partnership agreement provides otherwise. If you discover your partner has given you false information you may apply to the court to rescind the partnership agreement.

Getting capital out: when dissolution occurs, a partner is entitled to have the partnership property sold and all assets distributed. After the assets have been realized and outstanding debts paid, any surplus must be distributed among the partners in equal shares – unless you make a different arrangement in the partnership deed.

The proceeds from the sale of assets must be applied in the following order, although, again, the partnership deed can vary this:

(1) Payment to creditors who are not partners.
(2) Repaying loans made by partners.
(3) Paying back partners their capital contribution.
(4) Surplus divided amongst partners.

If there aren't enough assets partners must make up the deficiency in the proportions in which they shared profits.

Notice of withdrawal from a partnership: the agreement should state how much notice should be given to each of the other partners if one partner wants to withdraw. Remember, if you are withdrawing, that you are still responsible for all obligations which your firm incurred while you were a partner. Give notice to all customers and suppliers that you are withdrawing and make sure your name is removed from all stationery. Advertise the fact in the *London Gazette.*

Conflicting interests: partners are free to engage in other business activities unless the partnership agreement prohibits this. However, no partner may engage in any activity which *competes* with the partnership business. It might be sensible to provide in the partnership agreement for the contingency of a partner leaving and setting up in competition.

Limited Partnership

A partner who is prepared to put capital (or property of a stated amount) into the business but who wants no part in running it can protect him or herself against liability for the debts or obligations of the partnership beyond the amount he or she has contributed by registering a "Limited Partnership" with the Registrar of Companies (see below for address). Such a person is usually referred to as a "sleeping partner" and is prohibited by law from taking part in the management of the business, from making contracts or drawing cheques on the firm's account.

The advantages and disadvantages of trading as a partnership are as follows:

Advantages
- No formalities involved in setting up (although it's sensible to have a Partnership Deed drawn up between you)
- Less lonely than starting up totally on your own (in theory anyway!)
- Secrecy – no obligation to submit copies of your accounts for public scrutiny
- A chance to start off with increased capital
- No limitations on capital, assets or scope of business as with a limited company.

Disadvantages
- Each partner is liable for the debts of the company – regardless of which partner is at fault
- Risk of personality clashes between partners
- The death or bankruptcy of any partner automatically disolves a partnership unless there is an agreement otherwise.

LIMITED COMPANY

There is one very good reason for setting up in business as a limited company: should the business fail, or run into debt, your liability is "limited" to the amount you have paid for your shares. Quite often this is no more than £1. It is a way of forming a business without putting your personal assets at risk. (But see *disadvantages* below: directors of new businesses are now often required to give personal guarantees for money borrowed or owed.)

Like a person, a limited company is a separate entity in law. It can enter into contracts, sue and be sued, independently of its shareholders. Unlike its shareholders, it has an everlasting life unless deliberately put to to death.

Limited companies must be conducted according to the rules laid down in the Companies Acts. Although there have been a number of acts, the basic design of a limited company hasn't changed for over a century. It is easier and cheaper to form a limited company in the UK than probably anywhere else in the world.

One word of caution, though. Be very careful who you start your company with. The first flush of enthusiasm might lead you to invite any members of your family or close friends to become shareholders, regardless of the contribution they can make. Sometimes this can be disastrous.

The unco-operative brother Starting their own business was a tradition in the Francis family. Grandfather had done it, so had father, and brother John had been running his own market research firm for several years when younger brother Steven decided to take the plunge with a computer consultancy firm. Inviting John to contribute his experience as a director and shareholder seemed a logical step, and all went swimmingly – until Steven's business became more successful than John's. John's jealousy manifested itself as a total withdrawal of co-operation and this negative approach made it exceedingly difficult to implement decisions at board level, so that the company was unable to push forward. After a protracted struggle, Steven managed to buy John out, but not without damage to the company and a complete souring of family relationships.

Here are some of the advantages and disadvantages of running a limited company:

Advantages
- Members' (the directors and shareholders) financial liability is limited to the amount of money they have paid for shares
- The management structure is clearly defined which makes it easy to appoint, retire or remove directors
- If extra capital is needed it can be raised by selling more shares privately
- It is simple to admit more members
- The death, bankruptcy or withdrawal of capital by one member does not affect the company's ability to trade
- The disposal of the whole or part of the business is easily arranged
- High status

Disadvantages
- Requirement to register the company with the Registrar of Companies and provide annual returns and accounts – which must be audited. All details of the company are available for public inspection so there can be no secrecy. There are penalties for failing to make returns.
- Can be more expensive to set up
- May need professional help to form
- As a director you are treated as an employee and must pay tax through PAYE and class 1 National Insurance contributions both as an *employee* and as an *employer*.
- The advantages of limited liability status are increasingly being undermined by banks, finance houses, landlords and suppliers who require personal guarantees from the directors before they will do business.

Other types of company

The information in this chapter applies only to *private limited companies* since this is the most appropriate company form for a business start-up. There are, however, other types of company:

Public companies offer their shares to the public through the Stock Market, the Unlisted Securities Market or the Over the Counter Market, and style themselves PLC (public limited company). They require a minimum share capital of £50,000, at least seven shareholders, and a special trading certificate from the

Registrar of Companies. To "go public" the company has to be launched on the relevant share market by a firm of stockbrokers, who need to be convinced of the firm's commercial viability before they will undertake the launch. The cost of flotation is very high. Many private companies do eventually transfer to public company status but only after a period of successful trading.

Unlimited companies are governed by the same rules as limited companies but are not required to send accounts and annual returns to the Companies Registration Office. Although registering an unlimited company protects your affairs from public scrutiny, the loss of limited liability means that the directors are personally liable for all the company's debts.

Companies limited by guarantee don't issue shares but get assurances from their members that they will contribute a fixed sum (usually a nominal £1) in the event of the company's liquidation. This is a convenient company form for clubs, societies and associations, but not for businesses where the pursuit of profit is the main objective.

HOW TO START A COMPANY

You have two options: to buy a *ready-made company* or have one *tailor-made*.

Ready-made

Organizations known as Company Registration Agents are in the business to form "ready-made" or "off-the-peg" companies to sell on to people wanting to trade as limited companies. The companies the agents form are named and registered with the Companies Registration Office, but these companies don't trade.

It is extremely quick and cheap to buy a ready-made company. All you do is contact a Companies Registration Agent (they are listed as such in the Yellow Pages), tell him the type of business you intend to start and he will look through his files for a company with a suitable Memorandum (i.e. the statement of the company's objectives – see below for details). Since the company already has a registered office and directors, it is necessary for you to fill in two forms – *9b Change of Directors and Secretary* and *4a Change of Registered Office* – to transfer the company to your ownership (two signatures are needed). Apart from paying the Agent £133.25 (the company registration fee, the agent's fee and VAT) and organizing the transfer of the shares, that is all you have to do. The Agent then supplies you with the Memorandum and Articles of Association, the Certificate of Incorporation, a book which contains the Register of Members, minutes etc. and a company seal. And, hey presto, you are a fully fledged company director with a company ready to trade – although if you anticipate that your turnover will be more than £18,700 you need to register for VAT (get form VAT 1 from your local VAT office).

You may dislike the name of the company you have bought – or want to change it for other reasons. To do this you and your fellow directors pass a "special resolution" to change the name and send a typed document laying out the special resolution to the Companies Registration Office together with a fee of £40. Within three to four weeks they will send you a Certificate of Incorporation on Change of Name unless for any reason they don't approve the name you have selected (see below for details on names).

Tailor-made companies

Setting up a company from scratch gives you the advantage of selecting the name you want and getting the exact specifications for your company laid down at the beginning. But unless you are experienced in company law and procedure you will need professional help, and it will take a good deal longer – probably around two months minimum. A draft copy of the Memorandum and Articles of Association have to be prepared and submitted to the Companies Registration Office for approval. Prior to the registration procedure itself, you will have to arrange – and pay for – the Memorandum and Articles to be printed, as well as having a company seal made and purchasing a book to contain minutes, the register of members etc. (All the above are provided with a ready-made company.)

The approximate costs of starting up a tailor-made company will be around £400/£500. This figure is made up of the standard £50 registration fee, printing costs and accountant's fee.

Companies Registration Agents will also arrange a tailor-made company for you by doing a patch-up job on one of their ready-made companies. This takes longer than buying a company off-the-shelf and is more expensive.

However, unless your requirements are out of the ordinary we can see no sense in forming a tailor-made company. Ready-made companies are available with a wide variety of Memoranda, and if the Memorandum and Articles aren't quite right for your enterprise it is easy to change them by passing a special resolution at a board meeting. Also, it is simple enough to change the name as outlined above. Ready-mades can be formed in as little as two days and are generally much cheaper.

Companies Registration Offices:

All enquiries relating to the registration of companies in England and Wales should be addressed to The Registration of Companies, Companies House, Crown Way, Maindy, Cardiff CF4 3V2 (tel: 0222 388588).

Companies records in microfiche form can be inspected at the above address and at the London Search Room, Companies House, 55-71 City Road, London EC1Y 1BB (tel: 01-253 9393). They can also be purchased for £1 a company.

Enquiries relating to companies having a registered office in Scotland should be addressed to The Registration of Companies, 102 George Street, Edinburgh EH2 3DJ (tel: 031 225 5774).

Documents which need to be delivered by hand can go to either the Cardiff or London address for companies with a registered office in England or Wales and to the Edinburgh address for Scottish companies.

Northern Ireland operates entirely independent Companies Acts and all enquiries about companies with a registered office there should be addressed to The Registration of Companies, Department of Commerce, 43-47 Chichester Street, Belfast BT1 4RJ (tel: 0232 34121/4).

Requirements for a Private Limited Company

(1) *A registered business name* followed by the word "Limited" or Ltd. (Cyfngedig may be used instead if the company has a registered office in Wales.) The Companies Registration Office exercises some control over the choice of name – it can't be identical (or very similar to) the name of an existing company. It won't be considered if it is offensive or illegal and the use of certain words in a company (e.g. "Institute", "International") can only be used in certain circumstances (see below for details). The company name must be displayed in a conspicuous place at every office, or other premises where the company carries out business.

(2) *A registered office* This need not necessarily be the same address as the business is conducted from. Quite frequently the address used for the registered office is that of the firm's solicitor or accountant. This is the address, though, where all official correspondence will go. EEC regulations now require the name of the company to be prominently displayed at the Registered Office address.

(3) *Shareholders* There must be a minimum of two shareholders (also described as "members" or "subscribers"). There must be at least one director and a separate individual as company secretary. In small companies these are usually the two shareholders (often husband and wife) but the directors and secretary do not necessarily have to be shareholders. A private company can have up to 50 shareholders.

(4) *Share Capital* The company must be formed with a stated, nominal share capital divided into shares of fixed amounts. Small companies are frequently formed with nominal share capital of £100.

(5) *Memorandum of Association* The Memorandum is the company's charter. It states the company's name; the situation in Great Britain of its registered office i.e. England, Scotland, Wales (but not the town); its share capital; the fact that liability is limited and, most importantly, the objects for which the company has been formed. In theory, the company can only operate in the areas mentioned in the *objects clause* but in practice the clause is drawn to cover as wide an area as possible and anyway a 75% majority of the members of the company can change the objects whenever they like. Nevertheless, it is worth bearing in mind that directors of the company will incur *personal* liability if the company engages in a type of business which is not authorized by the objects clause. The memorandum must be signed by at least two shareholders.

(6) *Articles of Association* This document contains the internal regulations of the company – the relationship of the company to its shareholders and the relationship between the individual shareholders. Many companies don't bother to draw up their own Articles but adopt (sometimes with some modification) Articles set out in Table A of the 1948 Companies Act, which are quite satisfactory for the majority of private companies. The Articles must be signed by the initial shareholders.

(7) *Certificate of Incorporation* This is the document (see illustration overleaf) which the Registrar of Companies issues to you once he has approved your choice of name and your Memorandum. When you receive this document your company legally exists and is ready to trade.

(8) *Auditors* Every company must appoint a qualified auditor. His duty is to report to the treasurer whether or not the books of the company have been properly kept, and that the balance sheet and profit and loss account presents (or doesn't present) a true and fair view of the company's affairs and complies with the Companies Acts. Auditors are appointed or re-appointed at general meetings at which annual accounts are presented, and they hold office from the conclusion of that meeting until the next general meeting.

(9) *Accounts* The Companies Acts lay down strict rules on accounting. Every company must maintain a set of records which show the financial position at any one time with reasonable accuracy. The accounts comprise a profit and loss account and balance sheet with auditors' and directors' reports appended. A new company's accounting reference period begins on its incorporation and runs until the following March 31st – unless the company notifies the Registrar of Companies otherwise.

Within ten months of the end of an accounting reference period, an audited set of accounts must be laid before the shareholders at a general meeting and a set delivered to the Registrar of Companies.

(10) *Registers etc.* In addition to the accounts books, companies are required to have: a register of members and a share ledger; a register of directors and secretaries; a register of share transfers; a register of directors' interests in shares or debentures etc.; a register of charges; a register of debenture holders; a book of share certificates and a minutes book. One book can be purchased to hold all the above. This will be provided automatically if you buy a ready-made company. Jordan

CERTIFICATE OF INCORPORATION

OF A PRIVATE LIMITED COMPANY

No. 1662727

I hereby certify that

RUSTICROSE LIMITED

is this day incorporated under the Companies Acts 1948 to 1981 as a private company and that the Company is limited.

Given under my hand at Cardiff the 8TH SEPTEMBER 1982

Assistant Registrar of Companies

C.173

& Sons Ltd, 15 Pembroke Road, Bristol BS99 7DX offer a Company Kit which assists in the maintenance of essential records and in the preparation of necessary returns.

(11) *Company Seal* All companies must also have an engraved seal. This must be impressed on share certificates and must be used whenever the company has to execute a deed. Again, this is included in the ready-made company package.

Useful Reading

Notes for Guidance on Incorporation of New Companies (Companies Registration Office);

How to Form a Private Company, edited by Alec Just (Jordans).

CO-OPERATIVES

An alternative business structure for a group of people who wish to (and are prepared to) work together on a democratic basis – i.e. to share all the control and all the profits – is to form a co-operative (sometimes called a common ownership enterprise or a workers co-op).

The term "co-operative" usually brings to mind the Co-op shop in the high street, which is a "consumer co-operative" – ultimately controlled by its customers who elect the management committee which in turn appoints the managers.

However, industrial and service co-operatives, which are defined as enterprises owned and controlled by the people working in them, have been around for over a century and, thanks to support from all the major political parties who hope co-ops will focus local energies and create new employment, have increased in popularity as a way of trading over the last ten years or so.

There are now over 700 worker co-operatives in Britain and they're on the increase at the rate of 20% a year. Their total turnover is at least £175 million a year and they provide jobs for some 5,500 people. Despite the well-publicized débâcles of Meriden Motor Cycle and the Scottish Daily News, the survival rate of co-operatives compares very favourably with conventional small businesses.

Co-operatives are controlled by entirely different legislation from companies. They are governed by the Industrial and Provident Societies Act 1965 which is administered by the Chief Registrar of Friendly Societies, 17 North Audley Street, London, W1Y 2AP. Tel: 01-629 7001.

Instead of the Memorandum and Articles of Association, a co-operative has a book of "rules" which must be approved by the Registrar of Friendly Societies and registered with him. The rules cover such things as *the way the business is conducted* – the members must benefit primarily from their participation in the business; *control* – each member has equal control through the principle of "one person, one vote". To become a member anyone may first have to satisfy certain qualifications such as minimum age and length of time in the company; *interest repayments* – co-operative cannot pay an unlimited return on loan or share capital even when times are good. Interest payments will be limited in some specified way; *surplus* – this may be wholly retained in the business or distributed in part to members in proportion to their involvement, e.g. according to hours worked or gross wages; *membership* must be open, i.e. anybody satisfying the stipulated qualifications for membership who wishes to become a member must be accepted.

The conditions can be varied but it is almost twice as expensive to register a co-operative with an original set of rules than it is to register one which adopts the "model rules" already accepted by the Registrar of Friendly Societies.

A number of organizations, notably the Industrial Common Ownership Movement (see below), have developed sets of model rules which they will supply to you. It costs £50 to register a co-operative with model rules. Registration requires at least seven members, but not all of them have to start as full-time workers.

Like a limited company, a registered co-operative has limited liability for its members and must file an annual return (but there is no charge for this). Not all co-operatives bother to register (it isn't mandatory) in which case they are treated in law as a partnership with unlimited personal liability.

Advantages and problems

As well as the advantages of a co-operative as a business structure outlined above, co-ops supposedly offer the prospect of improved industrial relations, greater commitment and motivation throughout the workforce to achieve the company's agreed goals, better decisions as a result of the pooling of ideas and experience between shop-floor and management, and the fact that the firm can possibly get by with lower levels of profitability and growth than conventional companies – with investors demanding a given capital return to justify their continued backing. However, human nature being what it is, it doesn't always work like that, and it certainly doesn't happen automatically. Among co-operatives only a few years old, relationships have been found to be the major problem – particularly where there is an imbalance between the input made by different members and when new members join.

This is in no way supposed to warn you off starting as a co-operative – many co-operatives run very successfully – but to advise you to think very carefully about your own personal philosophy, business aims and objectives before you decide on co-operative status. You and your colleagues should ask yourself such questions as:

- What do you understand by democracy and how much do you want?
- How much do you value congenial working life against, for example, making large profits?
- How much equality do you want? What does this mean in terms of: how much we are paid, how we share out the work, how we make the decisions?

Only go ahead if you can agree on these points and there is real commitment to the idea of running a democratic business.

As well as the conventional sources of advice and finance mentioned elsewhere in this book, there are additional sources of information for co-operatives. The main ones are:

Industrial Common Ownership Movement (ICOM), 7 Corn Exchange, Leeds LS1 7BP. Tel: 0532 461737

Co-operative Development Agency, Broadmead House, 21 Panton Street, London SW1Y 4DR. Tel: 01-839 2988

The Co-operative Union Ltd, Stanford Hall, East Leake, Loughborough, Leicestershire LE12 5QR. Tel: 050982 2333

Beechwood College, Elmete Lane, Roundhay, Leeds LS8 2LQ. Tel: 0532 72025 (Runs courses on how to start co-operatives.)

Industrial Common Ownership Finance, 4 St Giles Street, Northampton NN1 1AA. Tel: 0604 37563

The Co-operative Bank PLC, Head Office, 1 Balloon Street, Manchester M60 4EP. Tel: 061 832 3456.

There are also thirty or more local co-operative development agencies around the country designed to promote co-operatives. One of the bodies listed above should be able to tell you whether there is one in your area.

Some co-operatives are conversions from ordinary companies, others have been established by workers whose factories have closed down, but most are new businesses started from scratch. One such is Paper Back. Here's their story:

Tropical forests are being decimated and natural woodlands sacrificed to conifer plantations. A forest the size of Sweden is cut down every year to meet the world's insatiable appetite for paper – around 170 million tonnes. In Britain we use up 7 million tonnes a year, only 2 million tonnes of which is reclaimed. According to a recent Department of Industry report this figure could easily be doubled, bringing environmental and economic benefits.

Information and statistics like these prompted a group of environmental activists to set up Paper Back, a co-operative selling a range of recycled papers and paper products.

Paper Back was started in February 1984 by a group of eight friends including an ex-teacher, ex-planner and ex-carpenter. What they have in common is a concern for the environment and a strong belief in working together and sharing decision-making.

They registered Paper Back under the Industrial and Provident Societies Acts 1965-78 with ICOM, the Industrial Common Ownership Movement. Control is in the hands of two full-time working members, Frank Broughton and Jan Kuiper, who pay themselves £110 a week gross. The other co-op members offer valuable advice and feedback, but are not on the payroll.

The original idea was to open a shop selling ecological products, but extensive research over a 20-month period revealed the gap in the market – no one was selling recycled paper on a commercial scale and making it pay. National and local feasibility studies were carried out and enquiries to sample firms, local authorities, voluntary organizations and environmental groups like Friends of the Earth brought an encouraging response.

The next step for the Paper Back team was to acquire the necessary knowledge and business skills to give their enterprise an even chance of succeeding. Frank Broughton took a job in a paper company, learning the complexities of running a business and finding out about the product – there are, for instance, over 40 different grades of waste paper. Another member of the group enrolled on the London Co-operative Enterprise Programme, a business management course specifically aimed at start-up co-ops. The free, 16-week course (a pilot scheme organized jointly by the Manpower Services Commission, the GLC and the Polytechnic of Central London) was run in conjunction with the network of London Co-operative Development Agencies. It offered a range of advice on subjects like fund-raising, marketing techniques and accounting skills. Course members spent two weeks on secondment to existing co-ops and then a considerable time was devoted to working up detailed business plans for the would-be co-operators. Following its success a similar programme is being planned for the end of 1984.

The business plan, which includes budgets, two years of projected cashflow and three years' balance sheets proved invaluable to Paper Back when they went in search of finance. They raised £3,000 among their members and turned to ICOF (Industrial Common Ownership Finance) for a loan. Unfortunately at the time of application ICOF's annual quota was fully taken up. Undeterred, Paper Back looked around for alternative sources of finance and applied to the Greater London Enterprise Board, who granted them a loan of £12,000. The conditions of loan were free use of the money for one year and repayment over five at a fixed 5% interest. They also secured a £1,000 start-up grant from their local authority, the London Borough of Hackney. Initial capital was used to purchase stock, valued at £9,000, equipment and a van for deliveries (£2,000).

Finding suitable premises proved to be Paper Back's biggest problem. They wanted a location on the edge of Central London, accessible for suppliers, central for distribution and close to home (Islington); premises large enough for storage, in reasonable condition (clean, dry and secure) and at a reasonable rent. After searching for over nine months they tracked down a second-floor unit of 1800 square feet in a refurbished warehouse in Hoxton at a rent of £2 per square foot. The space consists of two offices and a large storage area, and although it is on the second floor a hoist eases access problems. Under the Inner Urban Areas Act, Hackney provided them with a rent grant of £3,500 p.a. for the first two years of trading.

Recycled paper has a variety of uses from toilet paper to writing paper. The quality isn't perfect but it's certainly more than adequate for a great many purposes. Paper Back deal in a range for printing, photocopying, sugar paper for artwork and ticket board as well as memo pads, jotters, envelopes and greetings cards. Stocks of paper are bought direct from the mills and cut to size on a magnificent 1904 guillotine found abandoned in a basement.

Paper Back's prices are competitive, particularly for bulk buying, and their marketing strategy is aimed not only at individual cranks and eccentrics who want to "save trees" but at commercial customers – cost-conscious local authorities, schools, trade unions, charities, churches, voluntary groups and firms in the private sector. They offer a mail order service and have a retail outlet via a stall in Camden Lock market.

Nearly 1000 catalogues mailed to potential customers and distributed at the London Co-operative Trade Fair resulted in a steady flow of enquiries and orders, and Paper Back intend to gear up and extend their promotion and advertising.

For the future Paper Back hope to extend their market and expand their product range and services (they recently acquired an old Minerva printing press). And by the end of their first year's trading they expect to have created three full-time jobs – a realizable aspiration since they are already over target for their first year's projected turnover of £65,000.

CHOOSING A BUSINESS NAME

A rose by any other name may smell as sweet but this isn't necessarily true in business. A clever choice of name will enhance the image of your business in the eyes of your customers which can lead to more sales more quickly.

Unless you have decided to trade under your own name, which many people prefer to do, it's worth giving a fair amount of consideration to what you should call your firm. Apart from giving your business its public identity, it affects the design of everything the name appears on.

Ideally, the name should be easy to remember, easy to say, easy to write, and look good on stationery, in advertisements and painted on the side of vehicles.

The best names are those which are catchy and easily identify the type of business. Examples of clever business names: Flymo, Mothercare, Dial-a-Van, Ansafone, Kwik-Fit Exhausts.

Name Formalities – Sole Traders and Partnerships

Sole traders and partnerships have always been allowed to start up under their own name (or names) without any registration or legal requirements attached. Prior to 1982, people who wanted to trade under a different name, or make some addition to their own name (e.g. Jones & Company rather than plain Albert Jones) had to register the name with the Registry of Business Names. The Registry of Business Names was abolished under the Companies Act 1981 which laid down the following new requirements for businesses trading under other than the owner's name:

(1) The name of the owner(s) of the business must be stated on all business letters, written orders for goods and services, invoices and receipts, and on written demands for payment of business debts.

(2) For each person named, an address must be given at which any document relating to the business will be accepted.

(3) A notice must be displayed in a prominent place containing the names and addresses of the owners in all premises where the business is carried on.

There are penalties for not complying with these requirements, and failure to give the proper information may make any contracts you enter into legally unenforceable.

The abolition of the Registry of Business Names was an unpopular move – searching the Registry made it easy for new businesses to discover whether the name they wished to use was available. It also made it possible for customers and creditors to trace responsible owners when a business ceased trading.

There is, however, an organization which will still search the Registry of Business Names for you plus a substitute list of business names (also, alas, now defunct). If the name you want to use is not listed there is a good chance that it's safe to use it. Contact Business Registry Searches, Greyhound Chambers, Chepstow, Gwent NP6 5DB. Tel: 02912 70138. Searches cost from £5 per name.

Name Formalities – Limited Companies

If you are setting up as a limited company you have to submit your choice of name to the Registrar of Companies along with other documents required for registration. It will be accepted unless (a) there is a company with that name already on the Register (b) the Registrar considers the name to be obscene, offensive or illegal. (There are also certain words you can't use in a company name – see below.)

Prior to the implementation of the Companies Act 1981, names were submitted to the Registrar of Companies for *provisional* approval which meant you could be reasonably sure you could use that name as soon as you received your Certificate of Incorporation. Cut-backs in the Civil Service mean that provisional approval has been dispensed with, and the Department of Trade is now allowed twelve months after the company's incorporation to direct a company to change its name if it falls into one of the unacceptable categories mentioned above. This could be expensive if you have printed a load of stationery.

Names you can't use – or only with care

Although you are entitled to trade under your own name, if another sole trader is already using the same name you must not take unfair advantage of the similarity. If you do, the other trader can protect his business by getting a court order to stop you.

You might be tempted to cash in on existing publicity by calling your firm after a famous name or personality – but you could run into trouble. In the Kojak Lollipop case (1975) a sweets manufacturer had paid a considerable sum of money for a franchise to call his lollipops after that famous lollipop-licker. An injunction was slapped on him by another lollipop manufacturer who was already selling Kojak lollipops – but without permission. The judge held that the firm which first started selling Kojak lollipops was entitled to protect its sales. Although the latecomer had paid for a franchise, no permission was needed.

Another firm started business as "Womble Skips". The real Wombles brought a court action to stop them. The judge said they had no complaint in law since they weren't involved in hiring out skips or any other sort of building business so Womble Skips wasn't interfering with their trade. However, it would have been a very different story if the business had been called "Womble Toys".

You cannot use a name that is "misleading" – i.e. you cannot call yourself a building society unless you really are one and not just a small-time money lender, or anything else that suggests you are trading on a large scale over a wide field. Similarly words like "British" will not be allowed unless your business is pre-eminent or nationally representative in its field. You cannot use a name which suggests a connection with the Crown or members of the Royal Family.

The Department of Trade has compiled a list of "sensitive and prohibited names" which require specific consent before they can be incorporated into a business name. We reproduce it here. These restrictions apply to all types of business structure – sole traders and partnerships as well as companies.

Department of Trade List of Sensitive and Prohibited Names

The following words and expressions will require the consent of the Secretary of State for Trade before their use will be allowed in a company name. The words fall into the following categories:

a) Words which imply national or international pre-eminence

International	British	Wales
National	England	Welsh
European	English	Ireland
United Kingom	Scotland	Irish
Great Britain	Scottish	

b) Words which imply governmental patronage or sponsorship

Authority	Board	Council

c) Words which imply business pre-eminence or respresentative status

Association	Society	Institution
Federation	Institute	

d) Words which imply specific objects or functions

			Friendly Society
Assurance	Patent	Group	Industrial &
Insurance	Patentee	Holdings	Provident Society
Reinsurance	Chamber of Commerce	Post Office	Building Society
Ressurance	Chamber of Trade	Giro	Trade Union
Insurer	Chamber of Industry	Trust	Foundation
Assurer	Co-operative	Stock Exchange	Fund
Re-assurer	Chemist	Register	Charter
Reinsurer	Chemistry	Registered	Chartered
			Sheffield
			Benevolent

The following words and expressions also require the Secretary of State's consent and normally a company would be registered by a name containing any of the following words or expressions only if the applicant had obtained a letter of non-objection from the relevant Department or Body. Any correspondence should be submitted with the appropriate registration documents.

Words	Department/body
Royal, Royale, Royalty, King, Queen, Prince, Princess, Windsor, Duke, His/Her Majesty	Home Office (or Scottish Home & Health Department)
Police	Police Department, Home Office (or Police Division, Scotland)
Special School	Department of Education and Science
Contact Lens	General Optical Council
Dental, Dentistry	General Dental Council
Nurse, Nursing	General Nursing Council for England and Wales (or General Nursing Council for Scotland)
Midwife, Midwifery	Central Midwives Board (or Central Midwives Board for Scotland)
Health Visitor	Council for Education and Training for Health Visitors

Words	Department/body
District Nurse	Panel of Assessors in District Nurse Training
Health Centre	
Health Service	
Nursing Home	Department of Health and Social Security
Pregnancy	
Termination	
Abortion	
Breed, Breeder, Breeding	Ministry of Agriculture Fisheries and Food
Charity, Charitable	Charity Commission
Apothecary	The Worshipful Society of London Apothecaries (or the Pharmaceutical Society of Great Britain)
University, Polytechnic	Department of Education and Science

The use of certain words in company names is covered by other legislation and their use may consitute a criminal offence (see Section 22(1)(d) of the Companies Act 1981). Some of these words are listed below, but the list is not exhaustive. Applicants wishing to use any of these words may therefore be asked to seek confirmation from the relevant body that the use of the word does not contravene the relevant legislation. The Department of Trade also reserves the right to seek the advice in each case direct with the relevant body if necessary.

Words	Department/body
Architect, Architectural	Architects Registration Council of the United Kingdom
Credit Union	The Registrar of Friendly Societies
Veterinary Surgeon	Royal College of Veterinary Surgeons
Dentist, Dental Surgeon, Dental Practitioner	General Dental Council
Drug	
Druggist	
Pharmaceutical	
Pharmaceutist	Pharmaceutical Society of Great Britain
Pharmacist	
Pharmacy	
Ophthalmic Optician	
Dispensing Optician	General Optical Council
Registered Optician	
Bank, Banker, Banking	
Deposit	Bank of England
Red Cross	
Anzac	Seek advice of Companies Registration Office
Insurance Broker	
Assurance Broker	
Re-Insurance Broker	Insurance Brokers Registration Council
Re-Assurance Broker	

For more detailed information see *Companies and Business Names Regulations 1981*, SI 1685.

TAKING OVER AN EXISTING BUSINESS

Many people prefer to begin in business on their own by buying a going concern rather than starting from scratch.
   The advantages of doing this are:

- less risky, provided the business is sound
- you get the benefit of someone else's experience and hard work
- it should provide you with an immediate income, so you don't have to suffer a period of low profits or losses while getting established

- you can dispense with many of the hassles of getting a new business off the ground – assessing the viability of the market, finding premises, forming a company
- if the previous owner wasn't exploiting the business opportunity fully, you have a chance to expand the operation and make money.

But it would be naive to regard an existing business as a totally trouble-free way to start up. You won't know its good points and its bad points until you take over, and customers and staff (if you keep them on) might resent a change of ownership. It can be a more expensive way to start up too – good businesses don't come cheap.

How to find a business

To get an idea of what's available, buy *Daltons Weekly* and *Exchange and Mart*. Both contain dozens of pages of classified advertisements listing businesses for sale – newsagents/tobacconists, village stores, guest houses, gift shops, launderettes, pubs and many more (see below for some examples).

BUSINESSES FOR SALE
— EXAMPLES FROM DALTONS WEEKLY

Cotswolds

HISTORIC TOWN RESTAURANT. First class proposition, serving morning coffee, lunches, tea. Prime high street position, overlooking market square. Easy hours, no evenings, licence unexploited. Living accommodation, attractive lounge, 3 bedrooms, bathroom, full gas central heating, garden, excellent order throughout. Turnover £50,000 plus. Profitable easily run business with sound all year trade. Ever popular tourist area. £115,000 freehold. Box No. 3359, Daltons Weekly, Apex Tower, New Malden KT3 4EE.
[0566—11SA

GARAGE BUSINESS, sit. in a picturesque village on the Essex/Suffolk borders comprising car display rms. & usual offices. Large basement workshop. Sale inclds. all machinery & gge. equipment. Forecourt facilities with petrol agency & Fiat service agency. A.A. & R.A.C. reg. Frhd. Price £85,000.

ATTRACTIVE hairdressing salon in select Oxon. village. Averages £250 wkly. S.-c. two bedrm. flat. Gdn., gge. Lshd. £12,950 s.a.v. Box No. 3350, Daltons Weekly, Apex Tower, New Malden KT3 4EE. [5202—11SA

Essex

HOME SALES BUSINESS. Property shop in busy town for sale, due to sudden family commitments. Full training given. Really first or second business as easy to run. Box No. 3407, Daltons Weekly, Apex Tower, New Malden KT3 4EE. [5318—12SA

Superior

GIFTWARE, COOKWARE, fashionwear business. Spacious period listed property, lovely situation, Norfolk coast. Sales over £90,000 at 42% gross. Established thirty years. Retirement sale £89,500, freehold. Box No. 3401, Daltons Weekly, Apex Tower, New Malden KT3 4EE.
[5293—12SA

Health Foods

HERBS, VITAMINS, HOMEBREW. (West Midlands). Owner retiring after 12 years successful trading. Takings £700 p.w. Large three bedroom flat available. Clean, easy to run (no staff). £10,000. S.a.v. Box No. 3319, Daltons Weekly, Apex Tower, New Malden KT3 4EE. [5122—10SA

DEVON

NEWS./CONF./TOB. GEN. Delivery round. Plus well maintained family accom. 4 bedrms., 2 recs. Gge. etc. Thriving all yr. round tde. in busy North Dartmoor town. £79,000 frhd.

LEATHER/FANCY GOODS. Prime mod. shop unit in recently developed pedestrian precinct in town centre. Scope for wider tde. in associated lines. Allocated parking. Rent £1,625 p.a. Lse. about 17 yrs. unexpired. £10,000.

CARAVAN PARK. ½ mile Dartmoor National Park. Approx. 5.5 acres gently sloping land, perm. permission & lic. for 45 units, toilet blocks, showers, stabling etc. A.A. & C.C. listed. £70,000 frhd.

HOTEL — NORTH DARTMOOR TOWN. 11 bedrm. det. Hotel within easy walking distance of the Moor and about ½ mile from 18 hole Golf course. Car parking for 12 cars. Gdns. & grounds. £85,000 frhd.

Norwich Outskirts

RESIDENTIAL CARE HOME. registered 19. Attractive Victorian detached property in tranquil village setting of 1½ acres. Fully approved fire precautions. Excellent reputation. Ample scope for expansion. Well established with £75-80,000 turnover. Offers around £178,000 considered for freehold, goodwill, working contents. Box No. 3358, Daltons Weekly, Apex Tower, New Malden KT3 4EE. [5210—11SG

Many of these businesses include living accommodation. Are you willing to move from your present home?

The national and local press also advertise businesses for sale and, for people only interested in a specific field, the relevant trade journals are a good source (you will find trade journals listed in *Benn's Press Directory*, a copy of which should be in your local library). There are also firms called *Business Transfer Agents* (listed as such in the Yellow Pages) who operate like estate agents putting vendors and sellers together and charging the vendor a percentage of the sales figure.

Questions to Consider

Once you have decided on the type of business, consider which area of the country you want (or are prepared) to trade in; the target net income you want your business to provide; how much cash you have available, and your borrowing capacity. Do you want freehold, leasehold, or rented premises? This will probably depend on the type of business and on the availability of living accommodation. Have you got your own staff or are you prepared to take over existing staff? Do you want the existing owner to stay on for a handover period? Do you have any preference for a sole tradership, partnership or company? Remember that if you buy a company, you take over all obligations of that company (debts, tax arrears etc.) unless you make an agreement to the contrary.

What to look for

Buying a business is like buying a house, but far more complicated. There are many points to consider. It is therefore essential to have the help of professional advisers – a solicitor, an accountant and a surveyor. However, you don't need to involve them until you are thinking of making an offer. So the first step is to go and inspect some likely businesses.

Have a good look round the outside as well as the inside. Does the area appear prosperous or run down? Is it convenient for public transport? How easy is it to park? Do the premises look well maintained or neglected? What are the first impressions when you enter? How are you greeted? Make as thorough an inspection as you can, including storerooms and outbuildings. Does any of the stock look as if it has been there a long time? What do you think of the staff? Does the place look as if it is run efficiently?

If you are still interested try to collect as much information as you can from the vendor. Most important, why does he want to sell? It could be he is retiring, wanting to start up a different business somewhere else, can't raise the cash to develop the business, or that the business simply isn't paying its way. If it is either of the latter reasons, ask yourself honestly whether you could do any better. Perhaps you could. Ask the vendor to show you the figures for the last three years turnover, gross profit, net profit, overheads, outstanding debtors and creditors (see Chapter 7). If the asking price for the business is broken down into (1) premises (2) fixtures and fittings (3) stock (4) goodwill (see below for explanation), enquire what the basis is for each of these four figures and ask whether the vendor will accept an independent valuation for the stock and goodwill.

Try to establish whether he is open to offers and find out how and when he wants to be paid.

Make notes of all these points while they are fresh in your mind and go away to mull it over. When you are ready to make an offer call in the professionals. The surveyor will survey the premises and tell you whether, given their condition and the price of similar property in the area, the asking price is reasonable. The accountant will give you his opinion as to the viability of the business from an examination of the books, and guide you on the right price for fixtures and fittings, stock and goodwill. The solicitor will examine terms of the contract and ensure that necessary clauses are included – e.g. if you are purchasing the goodwill, a clause preventing the present owner from opening a similar business just down the road and taking his goodwill with him.

Making the decision

You now need to delve deeper into the business, with the help of the professionals, to see whether you can afford it and what offer you are going to make. Bear in mind that even if your thorough investigation proves the business is sound and the price fair and reasonable, there will be other initial expenses on top of the asking price. Work out your budget to include these.

Turnover/profits Does the business make enough profit to meet your target income? In other words will you be able to live off the proceeds? Have profits been increasing – at the very least along with the rate of inflation?

Location How does the price compare with similar properties in the area? Are the premises in reasonable state of repair? (See Chapter 5.) Are they suitable as they stand or would you need to modify them?

Costs involved: all the expenses you will incur in buying the premises and making them suitable for your purposes e.g. legal fees, survey fees, modification repairs, and redecoration.

Fixtures and fittings (also plant and machinery if applicable): there are two widely differing methods for assessing the value of fixtures and fittings: (1) what it would cost to replace them with new or secondhand materials (2) what the existing equipment would fetch if sold secondhand or for scrap. The asking price will no doubt fall somewhere in between but it should take into account the condition and suitability for purpose. Do you find the fixtures and fittings satisfactory or will you want to replace them?

Costs involved: buying the existing fixtures and fittings, installing any new ones required and/or refurbishing existing ones.

Stock You will see from advertisements that many businesses contain the letters "SAV" which means "stock at valuation". This is a common method of estimating a price for stock. An independent stocktaker (they are listed under Stocktaking Services in the Yellow Pages) is employed to value the stock and advise on a fair price. Bear in mind that stock which is out of fashion, damaged, shop-soiled or unsaleable for any reason isn't worth anything.

Costs involved: the amount of the stock valuation plus the cost of additional purchases needed to bring stocks up to levels required.

Goodwill Most businesses either itemize separately, or build in a price for goodwill. Goodwill is the value of the name, reputation or intangible assets of the business (it is very difficult to value). A method commonly used is to say that goodwill equals so many years profits – but you need your accountant's advice on this. Try to assess whether the present reputation of the business is a liability or an asset. How much does it depend on the personality of the owner? Is the business heavily dependent on a few large customers?

Costs involved: buying the goodwill plus building up your own by writing to existing customers, advertising etc.

Negotiating the sale

You can handle all the negotiations yourself or you can appoint one of your advisers to do the deal for you. It is a matter of personal preference.

Decide on the target price at which you would like to buy the business and the highest price you are prepared to pay. The tactics followed will depend upon the difference between these and the asking price. If the gap is small you may seek to negotiate on the total price, concentrating on the weak points revealed by your evaluation. If the gap is large, it may be more effective to break up the total price into the constituent parts – premises, fixtures and fittings, stock and goodwill – and try to negotiate a price for each which gives you a total price nearer to what you are prepared to pay. If the gap is still too wide you could suggest making part of the payment dependent on profits or sales achieved over the first year.

Terms of payment are also important. If only part of the payment need be made immediately, with the balance by instalments at no extra charge, this is equal to an interest-free loan, the value of which you can calculate. Here's what *not* to do when buying an existing business:

Philip Harley needed work and somewhere to live. He spotted a grocery shop for sale with a flat above it. It looked cheap at £16,000 (£8,350 for a 15 year lease, £6,650 for goodwill and £1,000 for fixtures). The business wasn't showing much of a profit but the vendor confided to Philip that he was pocketing most of the takings to keep them out of sight of the taxman. Philip took him at his word and bought the place on a mortgage.

Trade was going badly so Philip decided to turn the shop into a delicatessen. An accountant warned him against it because he didn't have the money to pay for the necessary refitting. Philip ignored the advice and got a bank loan.

Within nine months he was in deep trouble. He owed money to 22 different creditors including the local authority and the electricity board. His debts totalled £13,850 but the business, even if he could sell it, was valued at only £11,000.

Philip is now bankrupt as well as having no job and no home.

Moral? Don't believe all the vendor tells you, take advice at the outset – and don't ignore what the professionals say.

LICENCES AND REGISTRATION

Certain types of business are not allowed to operate without first obtaining a licence, or registering themselves. The chart below lists these businesses together with details of who licences or registers them, the cost and the renewal period.

Although not listed here, there are other types of business which you can't or would be unwise, to set up without official approval. You are not able to set up, for instance, as an accountant, doctor, lawyer or other professional unless you hold a practising certificate from the relevant professional body. Neither can you function effectively in many businesses, e.g. the travel trade, unless you belong to the relevant trade association. Many associations now operate strict codes of practice to which members are expected to conform, and they warn enquirers not to deal with firms who don't comply with the standards. To discover whether there is a trade association in your intended area of business look at the *Directory of British Associations* (most reference libraries will have a copy).

Getting a licence

If your business needs a licence or registration, contact the relevant authority early on in the planning stage of your business. They will want to know quite a lot about you and your past record to satisfy themselves that you are a suitable person to operate in the particular field. Some people have found getting a licence is quite a lengthy process. We know two girls who run an employment agency who had to wait three months for their application to be granted because ten years earlier one of the girls had worked for a company that went broke. The licensing people insisted that she produce the cheque to confirm that the company concerned had paid her.

Businesses which require Licences or Registration

Business	Who licences it	Renewal	Cost
Accommodation agencies	Police	Annual	Nominal charge
Alcohol production (for sale)	Customs & Excise	Annual	£5.25 wine £15.75 spirits
Alcohol sales (pubs, restaurants, clubs, off licences)	Licensing Justices	Annual	£12.50
Amusement machine operators	Licensing Justices	Every 3 years	£8.50

Business	Who licences it	Renewal	Cost
Animals:			
breeding cats & dogs	Local authority	Annual	£43
performing animals	Local authority	Annual	£11
pet shops	Local authority	Annual	£45
boarding kennels	Local authority	Annual	£37
riding schools	Local authority	Annual	£79
keeping wild, dangerous animals	Local authority	Annual	£86
Betting shops	The Betting Licensing Board Committee of the Licensing Justices	Annual	£100/£6
Billiard and Snooker Halls	Licensing Justices	Annual	£8.50
Bingo Halls	Gaming Board of Great Britain (for certificate), Licensing Justices (for licence)	Annual	£1,450/£510
Boarding Kennels (see Animals)			
Cafes (late night)	Local authority	Annual	£63
Caravan sites	Local authority	Once only registration	Varies
Casinos	Gaming Board of Great Britain (for permit), Licensing Justices (for licence)	Annual	£18,000/£3,000
Child Care (crèches, day nurseries, child minders, playgroups)	Local authority	At present only need to register once (but might become annual)	No fee at present
Chiropodists	Local authority (but not many authorities currently require registration)	Annual	Varies
Cinemas	Local authority	Annual	£82
Credit facilities – any retailer who sells on credit, or anyone who offers a credit reference service, a credit advisory service or arranges loans, mortgage or insurance, needs a licence NB sole traders and partnerships arranging transactions for £30 or less are currently exempt	Office of Fair Trading	Every 10 years	From £80, but depends on type of business and facilities offered
Dance hall/discotheque	Local authority	Annual or occasional	Varies
Debt collecting/counselling (see Credit)			
Ear piercing	Local authority	Annual	£72
Employment agencies	Department of Employment (local regional office)	Annual	£114
Escort Agencies	Department of Employment (local regional office)	Annual	£114

Business	Who licences it	Renewal	Cost
Executive search agencies	Department of Employment (local regional office)	Annual	£114
Explosives – use of in demolition, mining work	Local authority	Annual	£80 (under review)
Finance houses *see* Credit			
Firearms dealers	Police	Annual	Initially £58 renewal £36 (Also need a firearms certificate – £25)
Firework sales	Local authority	Annual	£5
Football pools operators	Local authority for permit & registration	Annual	£300
Food hawking	Local authority	Once only	Varies
Foods – preserved (sale or manufacture)	Local authority	Once only	Varies
Food storage premises	Local authority	Once only	Varies
Game food dealers	Local authority	Annual	Varies
Gambling/gaming	Gaming Board of Great Britain and licensing Justices	Annual	Depends on activity *see* separate entries
Heavy goods vehicles haulage	Department of Transport (local office)	Every three years	£5
Hiring – cars, domestic equipment, office equipment etc.	Office of Fair Trading	Every 10 years	From £80 Depends on type of business & number of categories
Kennels *see* Animals			
Liquor *see* Alcohol			
Lotteries/raffles	Gaming Board of Great Britain & Licensing Justices	Annual	£20
Massage parlour	Local authority	Annual	Varies
Mail order firms *see* Credit			
Milk & dairy products distribution	Local authority	Registration once only	Free
Mobile shops	Local authority	Registration once only	No set fee
Moneylenders *see* Credit			
Music – as paid for entertainment	Local authority	Annual	Varies
Nursing agency – auxiliary nurses	Department of Employment (regional office)	Annual	£114
Nursing home: (1) providing 24hr qualified nursing care	District health authority	Once only	£100 (for 50 beds or less, more for additional beds)
(2) residential home	Local authority	Annual	£1
Off licences *see* Alcohol			
Offensive trades (e.g. fat rendering)	Local authority	Registration once only	Free
Pawnbrokers	Office of Fair Trading	Every 10 years	£80 £150 (Ltd. Co.)
Pet shops *see* Animals			
Pharmacies & others who sell poisonous drugs	Local authority	3 certificates needed	Varies

Business	Who licences it	Renewal	Cost
Rag/flock upholsterers	Local authority	Annual	Varies
Refreshment stalls (late-night)	Local authority	Annual	£33
Riding schools *see* Animals			
Scrap metal dealers	Local authority	Every 3 years	Free
Sex shops	Local authority	Annual	Varies
Street traders	Local authority	Annual	Varies
Snooker halls *see* Billiards			
Taxi services	Police	Every 3 years	No fixed fee – depends on type of taxi and what it's licensed to do.
Tattooing	Local authority	Annual	£72
Theatrical agencies	Department of Employment (regional office)	Annual	£114
Theatres	Local authority	Annual or occasional	Varies

Notes to the chart

1. The fees quoted are intended only as a guide. They were correct as at March 1984, but there is no *national* scale of fees for businesses licensed by local authorities and they do differ from authority to authority; the charges quoted here are those recommended by the London Boroughs Association (General Purposes Committee) Taberner House, Park Lane, Croydon. Tel: 01-686 4433.
2. The department within the local authority which has the responsibility for issuing licences varies from authority to authority. It is usually – but not always – the Trading Standards Department or the Environmental Health Department. In the case of child care facilities and nursing homes it is more likely to be the Social Services Department.
3. Bear in mind that the licence fee may only be the tip of the iceberg. For instance, a lot of expensive legal work may be required to prepare a case to present to the Licensing Justices. Similarly, meeting all the rules and regulations which apply to nursing homes may cost a great deal.
4. All licences are obtained locally apart from those issued by the Gaming Board for Great Britain and the Office of Fair Trading (although your local trading standards department should be able to supply you with an application form).

Here are their addresses:

The Gaming Board for Great Britain Berkshire House, 168-173 High Holborn, London WC1. Tel: 01-240 0821.

The Office of Fair Trading Government Building, Bromyard Avenue, London W3 7BB. Tel: 01-242 2858.

PROTECTING YOUR IDEA

The man who invented "cats' eyes" lived off the proceeds of this simple idea for the rest of his life, which suggests that anyone with a humdinger of an idea should take steps to protect it from exploitation by others. However, the legal means by which you can protect an idea are costly and time-consuming so you need to be fairly sure that the resulting commercial benefits will be worthwhile before you go ahead.

The four categories of protection are: *patenting*, which protects technological and other inventions; *design registration*, which protects the shape or appearance of a commercial product; *copyright*, which protects literary, artistic and musical works; and *trade mark registration*, which protects symbols, logos and pictures.

Some products may be covered by two or more categories – e.g. the mechanism of a clock may be patented while its appearance may be design-registered.

Each category requires a different set of procedures, offers a different level of protection and extends for a different period of time. They all have one thing in common, though. In the event of an infringement your only redress is through the courts, and going to law can be wasteful of time and money, whether you win or lose.

Patents

A patent can be regarded as a contract between an inventor and the state. The state agrees with the inventor that if he is prepared to publish details of his invention in a set form and if it appears that he has made a real advance, the state will then grant him a "monopoly" on his invention for 20 years – "protection in return for disclosure". The inventor uses the monopoly period to manufacture and sell his innovation; competitors can read the published specifications and glean ideas for their own research, or they can approach the inventor and offer to help develop his idea under licence. However, the granting of a patent doesn't mean the proprietor is *automatically* free to make, use or sell the invention himself, since to do so might involve infringing an earlier patent which has not yet expired.

A patent really only allows the inventor to stop another person using the particular device which forms the subject of his patent. The state does not guarantee validity of a patent either, so it is not uncommon for patents to be challenged through the courts.

Which inventions can you patent? The basic rules are that an invention must be *new*, must involve an *inventive step* and must be capable of *industrial exploitation*.

You can't patent scientific/mathematical theories or mental processes, computer programs or ideas which might encourage offensive, immoral or anti-social behaviour. New medicines are patentable but not medical methods of treatment. Neither can you have just rediscovered a long forgotten idea (knowingly or unknowingly).

If you want to apply for a patent, it is essential not to disclose your idea in nonconfidential circumstances. If you do, your invention is already "published" in the eyes of the law, and this could well invalidate your application.

There are two distinct stages in the patenting process: (1) from filing an application up to publication of the patent; (2) from publication to grant of the patent. Two fees are payable for the first part of the process and a further fee for the second part. The whole process takes some two and a half years. Relevant forms and details of how to patent are available free of charge from the Patent Office. Briefly, the procedure is as follows.

(a) On forms provided by the Patent Office you file a patent application (current fee £10) with a specification of the invention. (If the invention isn't yet fully developed, the specification at this stage need only be a summary but it should contain sufficient detail to ensure that any claim can be upheld should a dispute arise.) You now have 12 months in which to pursue development, or exploitation, of your invention before proceeding further with the patent application – or deciding to let it lapse. During this period you need to consider whether you want protection in the UK only or in other countries as well. Foreign patenting is not as complicated as it might appear initially. It is already possible to file one single patent application to cover you for 12 European Countries (you pay, currently, £76 for each country together with total costs of approximately £1,600). And, for other countries, there is now the patent Cooperation Treaty which covers many countries throughout the world (the USA, Japan, and USSR included). A single application can cover the countries you choose to designate. Your application is sent to an International Searching Authority, and after about 18 months, it is published. Copies are sent to you and to the designated National Offices. To proceed further you have to file specifications with the countries you have designated and pay the appropriate fees.

(b) If you want to pursue your application, you pay a fee (currently £76) and file a
     claim, plus a more substantial specification of the invention.

The Patent Office then conducts a search to see if any earlier published description of the invention exists, and, decides whether the idea is "inventive" enough. The
Patent Office sends a report to the inventor. If everything is in order, the application
is then published (this is usually 18 months from the original filing date).

With publication, the inventor's secrecy is ended. Third parties, such as other
inventors, can write to the Patent Office making observations on the patentability of
the invention.

That's stage 1. To embark on the second stage you request (within six months of
publication) a "substantive examination" (this currently costs £90) which is much
more thorough than the previous search. The idea is now closely scrutinized to see
whether it complies with all the requirements of the Patent Act. Does the invention
work? Is the description sufficiently clear to enable a skilled person to put the invention into effect? Is the invention novel and truly *inventive*? The Examiner then sub-
mits a report to the applicant. If the application is defective, amendments can be
made.

Once all objections have been dealt with, the patent will be granted and published
in a finally agreed form. The grant is for 20 years from the date of filing, subject to
payments of annual renewal fees from the fifth year onwards.

It is possible – and cheaper – to make your own patent application but this is not
really recommended. Drafting a specification to give you as wide a monopoly as you
think you can get away with is the essence of patenting and this is the skill of professional patent agents. They also know the tricks of the trade for each stage of the
patenting procedure. A list of patent agents is available from the Chartered Institute
of Patent Agents (see List of Addresses below).

What can you do with your idea? If you have dreamt up an inspired invention but
don't have the resources, skill, time or inclination to produce it yourself, you can take
one of three courses once the idea is patented:

Outright sale You can sell the rights and title of your patent to an individual or com-
     pany. The payment you ask should be based on a sound evaluation of the market.
Sale and royalty You can enter into an agreement whereby you assign the title and
     rights to produce the product to another party for cash but under which you get a
     royalty on each unit sold.
Licensing You keep the rights and title but sell a licence for manufacturing and
     marketing the product to someone else. The contract between you and the licensee
     should contain a performance clause requiring the licencee to sell a minimum
     number of units each year or the licence will be revoked.

Whichever option you select, you'll need a good patent agent/lawyer on your side.

Trade Marks

A trade mark is the symbol by which the goods of a particular manufacturer or trader
can be identified. Trade marks can be: a word, a signature, a monogram, a picture, a
logo or a combination of these.

To qualify for registration the trade mark must be distinctive, must not be decep-
tive and must not be capable of confusion with marks already registered. Excluded
are: misleading marks, national flags, royal crests, insignia of the armed forces. A
trade mark can only apply to tangible goods, not services (although pressure is
mounting for this to be changed).

The Trade Marks Act of 1938 offers protection of great commercial value since,
unlike other forms of protection, your sole rights to use the trade mark continue
indefinitely.

To register a trade mark, you, or your agent, first conduct preliminary searches at the Trade Marks branch of the Patent Office to check there are no conflicting marks already in existence. You then apply for registration on the official trade mark form and pay a fee (currently £42).

Your application is then advertised in the weekly *Trade Marks Journal* to allow any objections to be raised. If there are none, your trade mark will be officially registered and you pay a further fee (currently £53).

Registration is initially for seven years. After this, it can be renewed for periods of 14 years at a time, with no upper time limit.

You can protect the trade mark internationally but this is fairly complex and you would need an agent to help you.

If you want to employ an agent to deal with trade mark registration anyway, and, again, it is advisable since there are often quibbles to sort out over various aspects of the trade mark, contact the Institute of Trade Mark Agents (see List of Addresses below).

It isn't mandatory to register a trade mark. If an unregistered trade mark has been used for some time and could be construed as closely associated with the product by customers, it will have required a "reputation" which will give it some protection legally, but registration makes it much simpler for the owner to have recourse against any person who infringes the mark.

Design registration

You can register the shape, design or decorative features of a commercial product if it is new, original, never published before or – if already known – never before applied to the product you have in mind. Protection is intended to apply to industrial articles to be produced in quantities of more than 50. Design registration only applies to features which appeal to the eye – not to the way the article functions.

To register a design, you apply to the Design Registry (unless it is a textile design when you apply to a separate office in Manchester – see end of section for address) and send a specimen or photograph of the design plus a registration fee (currently £42). This is examined to see whether it is new or original and complies with other requirements of the Registered Designs Act 1949. If it does, a certificate of registration is issued which gives you, the proprietor, the sole right to manufacture, sell or use in business, articles of that design.

Protection lasts for five years but can be renewed for two further five-year periods. You can handle the design registration yourself but, again, it might be preferable to let a specialist do it for you. There is no register of design agents but most patent agents are well versed in design law.

Copyright

Copyright is a complex field and since it is unlikely to be relevant to most business start-ups we only touch on it lightly here.

Basically, the Copyright Act 1956 gives protection against the unlicensed copying of original artistic and creative works – articles, books, paintings, films, plays, songs, music, engineering drawings. To claim copyright the item in question should carry this symbol: © (author's name) (date).

You can take the further step of recording the date on which the work was completed (plus a £15 fee) with the Registrar at Stationers Hall (address at end of section). This, though, is an unusual precaution to take and probably only necessary if you anticipate an infringement.

Copyright protection lasts for 50 years after the death of the author (or whoever holds the copyright).

Copyright is infringed only if more than a "substantial" part of your work is reproduced (i.e. issued for sale to the public) without your permission, but since there is no formal registration of copyright the question of whether or not your work is protected usually has to be decided in a court of law.

Sources of further information

Patent Office, 25 Southampton Buildings, London WC2A 1AY. 01-405 8721 (open to public Mon-Fri 10-4pm). Publishes the following pamphlets: *Applying for a patent, Introducing patents – a guide for inventors, How to prepare a UK patent application.*

Design Registry, 11th Floor, State House, High Holborn, London WC1 4TP 01-405 8721 (Mon-Fri 10am-4pm) and at Baskerville House, Brown Cross, New Bailey Street, Salford M3 5PU. for textile designs. Publishes free of charge: *Protection of Individual Designs* and other guides for filing an application.

Trade Marks Registry, 25 Southampton Buildings, London WC2 1AY (Mon-Fri 10am-4pm). Textiles at Manchester branch, 7 Trade Marks Registry, Baskerville House, Brown Cross, New Bailey Street, Salford M3 5FU. Publishes free of charge *Applying for a trade mark*; *Trade Marks Journal* (every Wednesday).

Stationers Hall, Ludgate Hill, London EC4M 7DD. 01-248 9279 (Mon-Fri 10-4) for registration of copyright. Provides details and forms for registration.

The Chartered Institute of Patent Agents, Staple Inn Buildings, High Holborn, London WC1V 7PZ. 01-405 9450. No advisory service but will put you in contact with a patent agent in your area. Publishes a Register of Patent Agents which lists names and business addresses of all patent agents qualified to practice before the Patent Office.

Institute of Patentees & Inventors, Staple Inn Buildings South, 335 High Holborn, London WC1 7PZ. 01-242 7812. A membership organization (membership costs £20 pa). Looks after the interests of patent holders and inventors. Can provide useful advice and guidance on almost every aspect of intellectual property from idea conception to innovation and development. Publishes quarterly journal and *New Patents Bulletin*. The latter acts as liaison with industry bringing members' inventions to the notice of specialized manufacturing firms.

Institute of Trade Mark Agents, Suite 3, Panther House, 38 Mount Pleasant WC1X 0AP. 01-833 0875. Can put you in contact with a trade mark agent in your area and give general advice. Shortly to produce a register of trade marks.

The organizations listed below can help you with the commercial exploitation of your invention:

British Technology Group, 101 Newington Causeway, London SE1 6BU. 01-403 6666. The government-funded BTG is one of the main channels for exploiting technology from universities and research councils, but is always keen to hear from innovative entrepreneurs (more details in Chapter 4).

QMC Industrial Research Ltd., 229 Mile End Road, London E1 4AA. 01-790 0066. Wholly owned company of Queen Mary College, University of London. Makes available the invention expertise and equipment of the college. Offers help with all aspects of research and development. (Many universities now offer similar help.)

Ventures Division of Investors in Industry, 91 Waterloo Road, London SE1. 01-928 7822. Co-owned by leading clearing banks and Bank of England. Funds available usually as equity capital in amounts of £250,000 to £2 million. Apart from financial help, offers specialized support systems. Currently looking for propositions in biotechnology, industrial automation and electronics fields.

PA Technology, Melburn, Royston, Herts SG8 6DP. 0763 61222. Offers a comprehensive technology service. This can take client's ideas to either the licensing stage or full commercial exploitation. They have a highly qualified specialist staff with international experience.

Prutec, 17 Buckingham Gate, London SW1E 6LN. 01-828 2082. Wholly owned subsidiary of Prudential Assurance which seeks out investment opportunities in the UK. Its investment strategies include: basic research; developing technological applications; commercial developments. They do have specific areas in which they are actively seeking clients.

Your local enterprise agency may also be a useful starting-off point. Many throughout the country now have a free innovations service.

PROFESSIONAL ADVISERS

We know from experience that many people who are thinking of starting up on their own never seek advice from the professionals. We also know, sadly, that a lot of them come unstuck as a result – frequently they can't raise the cash because they haven't been able to present their case convincingly enough, or the business founders in the early stages because it wasn't properly costed from the outset. Understandably, you may fight shy of calling in an accountant or solicitor because of the expense, but the investment can often mean the difference between success and failure.

The three professional advisers who can help you most are: your *bank manager*, your *accountant* and your *solicitor*. You may also need to use the services of other professionals from time to time (see below).

Bank Manager

Bank managers vary in their understanding and backing of small businesses. Some are fantastically supportive, others less so. If you already have a bank account, the manager there is your obvious first port of call. If you don't like him, consider switching your account to another branch of the same bank. If there isn't one close enough, or the manager there is no better, you are stuck unless you change banks – but this can raise problems over negotiating a sizeable overdraft until the new manager has had the chance to see something of your track record. If you don't have a bank account, take soundings from friends and acquaintances as to which local managers are sympathetic to small businesses and get the contact to arrange a personal introduction.

Make an appointment to see the bank manager at an early stage in the planning of your business. Explain what you intend to do and ask him if he is happy to open a business account for you. If he is interested, he should offer you some sound advice on the factors to consider before going ahead and, should you require a loan, tell you how you should present your "business plan" (see Chapter 4). He may also be able to recommend an accountant who specializes in helping a small firm start up and/or put you in touch with other business people in your field.

Charges As a rule, the bank will not charge you for the time spent discussing your affairs, but there might be a fee if the manager obtains advice for you from the bank's experts. There will, of course, be bank charges – and these vary from bank to bank. If the bank draws up a loan or overdraft agreement for you, there is likely to be an extra charge for this.

Accountant

How do you find one? The best way is still by recommendation from other people operating a business or, perhaps, from the bank manager. Most professional bodies cling to the pretence that all their members are whiter-than-white and specialize in all aspects of their field. This works against the interests of potential clients. Professionals are only human and obviously some either enjoy or are more experienced in certain aspects of their trade than in others. Until 1982, accountants weren't allowed to advertise which meant there was no easy way to find one who had the particular type of expertise you required – it was a matter of sticking a pin in the relevant section of the Yellow Pages. The advertising restrictions have been relaxed somewhat and accountants are now allowed to advertise with certain provisos.

So, if you can't get a personal recommendation, look for the more informative listings in the Yellow Pages – e.g. "ACCOUNTANTS FOR THE SELF EMPLOYED ... FOR ALL TYPES OF BUSINESSES INCLUDING LIMITED COMPANIES" or for similar ads in the local press or the accountancy journals (consult *Benn's Press Directory* in the local library for a list of these).

Interestingly, many large accountancy firms – for instance, Price Waterhouse – have recently started up special sections to service small businesses. Some of them also produce a series of free informative booklets on various aspects of business practice ("Incentives for Industry" and "Employment Legislation" are two titles in the Price Waterhouse Business Information Series). Look for an accountant who is qualified either as a member of The Institute of Chartered Accountants or the Association of Certified and Corporate Accountants.

What he can do Once you've found him, give him an outline of the kind of business or service you intend to set up; tell him how much money you have available and what you think your financial needs are going to be over the first year of operation; how many people are going to be involved, either as partners or shareholders; and what your plans for the future are.

The accountant will then give you an opinion on the apparent financial viability of the project; will advise you on the right business structure to adopt; will organize the formation of a limited liability company – if that is the most suitable structure; explain the tax situation to you and help you prepare budgets and "business plans" to present to the bank (if you need to raise funds).

Few small businesses can afford to employ an accountant full-time. It is cheaper to do your own bookkeeping (or employ someone to do it) and your own monthly monitoring to establish how you stand financially. You could, though, ask the accountant's advice on the best system of bookkeeping to adopt.

You will need him again when the time comes to make up your accounts and have them audited and when you are preparing your annual returns for income tax (any accountant who doesn't tell you how to organize your tax affairs in such a way that you can minimize tax liability isn't worth his salt).

Your accountant should be thought of as a doctor. He cannot compel you to look after the health of your business properly, he can only diagnose and treat any sickness. But he *can't* treat any illness that has become incurable.

Charges Limited companies are required by law to have their accounts audited. Sole traders and partnerships aren't, but tax-wise it is of great assistance to have a loose audit carried out by an accountant who issues a "qualified certificate" confirming that the accounts correspond to the books. For this reason, most firms employ an accountant on a yearly retainer (£300-£400 p.a. seems to be the average fee paid by a small firm but, of course, it depends very much on the amount of work he is required to carry out). Many accountants won't charge for initial consultancy on the basis that they will be employed on a retainer. If you don't wish to have your books audited but occasionally require accountancy advice, reckon on paying around £20-£25 per hour.

Solicitors

How to find one It's best to find a solicitor through a recommendation. Otherwise, you can look in the Yellow Pages listings, or the *Solicitors Diary* (a copy of which should be in the local library).

There is, however, a new and potentially much more useful *Solicitors Regional Directory* currently being produced by the Law Society (due to be published in 1984) which lists those solicitors who wished to be included with details of the fields they specialize in. It was produced in response to requests from Citizens Advice Bureaux and other advice agencies who are frequently asked to recommend solicitors in a particular field. It should be available in your local library or CAB.

What they do You are not likely to require the services of a solicitor very often. You will need him initially if you are buying, leasing or renting property. Apart from carrying out the conveyancing, he can sort out for you any necessary planning permission. He can also advise you on the type of business structure to adopt (but so can the accountant) and will draw up a partnership deed for you – if that is the business structure you plan to adopt.

When the business is running, you will probably need his help in drawing up any contracts you want to enter into, or in scrutinizing other people's contracts, and if you are threatened with, or contemplating, legal action.

Charges You can employ him on a yearly retainer or pay him per consultation. He will charge a scale fee, though, for any conveyancing work he does.

An accountant and solicitor are useful allies for any small business, but view them as a guide – not a crutch. Resist the temptation to lean on them too heavily or your bills will be astronomical. Before you automatically reach for the phone think carefully whether you couldn't figure out the problem on your own.

Other professional advisers you might need from time to time:

Insurance broker In addition to property, fire and theft, car insurance, life and accident insurance, you may also need cover against employer's liability, product liability and, perhaps, professional indemnity. You may also require advice on pension schemes. Few insurance companies have a complete range of policies which are ideal for every purpose. Unless your needs are simple, it is better to go through a reputable broker who can select the best policies from different insurers. (See Chapter 6.)

You don't pay the broker – he gets commission from the insurance companies.

Surveyor If you are acquiring property you should have an independent survey carried out. Use a surveyor who is a member of the Royal Institute of Chartered Surveyors otherwise the bank or mortgage company might not accept his report. A surveyor can also help if you want to check your rating assessment. He is the best person to argue the case with the local authority if you decide to challenge it. (See Chapter 5 also.)

Other professional advisers you may need at one time or another particularly as you grow are *architects*, *advertising agents*, *management* or *business consultants*.

CHAPTER 3 SUMMARY

- The structure you choose for your business has important legal and tax implications and you need to carefully consider the alternatives – sole trader, partnership, limited company or co-operative.
- You also need to select a name for your venture which will help to market its products or services and which complies with the law.
- Taking over an existing business offers some advantages over starting out from scratch but there are many points to consider when looking at businesses for sale.
- With some types of business you are required to register or licence with the local authority (or another body) before you can start to trade.

- If your business idea or product is innovative, creative or unique you may be able to protect it from exploitation by others through patenting, copyright, trade mark or design registration.
- Any business start-up needs advice from the professionals – your bank manager, accountant and solicitor are your most likely three wise men.

Chapter 4
RAISING THE MONEY

HOW MUCH DO YOU NEED?

Underestimating the amount of money required to start up in business is one of the most common mistakes made by potential new businesses – with disastrous results. Don't let it happen to you.

An amount of fixed capital is required to establish the businesss on a sound financial basis. This capital will be required to buy the initial fixed assets and stock, and to provide adequate working capital. Fixed assets are items such as property, plant, fittings, vehicles and equipment which last for many years. The working capital is the amount required to pay for the continuing outgoings until cash is received from customers.

Inevitably, the total amount of capital necessary varies substantially from one type of business start-up to another. A service business, for example, could get going with maybe just a few hundred pounds, whereas a large manufacturing operation would need hundreds of thousands.

Whatever type of business you plan, you should prepare detailed estimates of the amount of money needed. Here are some guidelines.

Fixed assets

Property Unless you plan to run your business from home you need to rent or buy premises. Calculate how much floorspace you need for equipment, storage and working purposes. If you intend to buy, find out how much suitable premises would cost and assess how much mortgage you will need. If you've decided to rent, find out the going rents per square foot in the area you wish to trade (rent payments count as working capital but you are likely to be charged a "premium" as well).

You will need extra money to fit and equip the premises the way you wish to use them, so allow for this in your calculations. (See Chapter 5 for more details on premises.)

Equipment If you are a manufacturer this could mean plant, machinery and tools. If a retailer, shop fittings, cash registers, freezer units etc. Service and other businesses may need equipment such as typewriters, photocopiers, office furniture, filing equipment, answering machines, telephones (remember that British Telecom levy a charge for installing a phone), computers, word processors and vehicles. Bear in mind, though, that office equipment and vehicles can be acquired on a lease or hire purchase basis. This often makes more sense than purchasing them outright (see p. 87 for an explanation of the pros and cons) and it frees your capital for other uses.

Tangible assets, such as property, vehicles, machinery are something on which to value the business if it goes bust, or you want to sell it at any time. This explains why it is often easier to raise money to start up a sizeable business requiring substantial fixed assets than a smaller business which requires little in the way of assets. Assets can also be used as security against which to raise a loan since they have a continuing value.

Working capital

This means the amount of money which will be required to cover the operating expenses until such time as your "cash flow" generates enough to cover all outgoing payments. And *this* is where so many new business proprietors go wrong. They frequently don't realize, for instance, that the payments they will receive for goods and services won't normally come in for at least a month (often much longer). You must either budget for this or ask for extended credit from your suppliers – who may charge extra for it.

When you assess your working capital requirements you need to budget for the following:

Stock – initial stocks of raw materials, or goods for sale. Stock is also regarded as an asset since it can be converted into cash.

Staff – the wages of any employee you want to take on, plus NHI contributions, overtime payments, pension contributions (if you decide to offer a pension scheme). See Chapter 8.

Running costs of your premises – rent, rates, electricity, gas and telephone bills. See Chapter 6.

Advertising & promotions – cost of initial publicity to get the business underway and ongoing advertising/promotional expenses. See Chapter 9.

Insurance – there is a variety of different insurance cover you can have – some is mandatory, some is strongly advised. See Chapter 6.

Sundries – this includes a wide number of things. Some examples: running costs of vehicles, postage, stationery, purchase of essential directories/reference books/ magazines, paying professional advisers and delivery costs.

Paying yourself – assess how much you, your partners, or fellow directors, will need to live off for your first year of operation – at least. (Many businesses don't begin to show profits until year three.)

Here is an example of a "Capital requirements schedule".

Capital Requirements Schedule for a retail store

Fixed assets		
Goodwill of existing business	£10,000	
delivery van	7,500	
shop fittings, replacement equipment, including cold storage,	2,000	
tills, trolleys and blinds	2,500	
shop sign and flooring	2,000	
Total Fixed Assets		£24,000
Opening stock		6,000
Other working capital needs (e.g. wages, living expenses, bad debts and contingency for other items)		£4,000
Total start-up capital needed		£34,000

IS THE BUSINESS VIABLE?

To determine whether your business idea will work financially and make you money, you now need to prepare a cash forecast which shows the estimated proceeds from the business and the estimated payments out.

Preparing a cash forecast is not an easy task for a start-up. It's rather a chicken-and-egg situation. How do you know what your sales will be before you've even begun? But you can't decide on the viability of your idea until you've made a stab at guessing them. And this is why it's so essential to carry out some initial market research into who and where your customers are, how much they are likely to buy of the products you sell, or use the service you're offering, and what you should charge (see Chapter 9). You need to assess your potential *turnover* (i.e. how much money you will receive from sales and other revenue); your potential *outgoings* (i.e. costs) and what your *profit margin* will be (i.e. what is left when you subtract the outgoings from the turnover).

When preparing your cash forecast bear in mind the limiting factors which will influence sales – e.g. the capacity of a restaurant will be determined by the number of tables available and the average time it takes to consume a meal; a transport operation is limited by the number of passenger miles or ton miles that can be carried out in a given period of time; a service business by the amount of time you can spend performing the service as distinct from the time you'll need to spend touting for business, travelling and doing paperwork; and a shop by the number of customers you can deal with in, say, a week during opening hours. Obviously, the capacity of the business needs discounting for slack periods, particularly in its early development stages.

We provide more information on constructing a cash forecast in Chapter 7, but bear in mind too that since sales and costs will undoubtedly vary from month to month, the forecast should be prepared on a monthly, or at least quarterly, basis and because the first year is likely to be one of development as well as the year in which you have the highest capital expenditure, it is sensible to extend your cash forecast, along broad lines, into the second and third years.

Once you have worked out how much you need, you will have to decide where to get the money from.

WHAT ARE YOU WORTH?

How much money do you have available to put into the business? You may, like many people who start their own businesses, be able to finance it entirely from your own resources – savings, redundancy payments, money from friends and relatives, a second mortgage on your home. The advantage of using your own money is that you avoid interest payments – which can be as high as 15% a year or more – on money borrowed from a bank or other financial organization. Whether it's sensible, though, to risk your own money depends very much on the type of business you intend to run and the amount of capital you require.

To discover your own true worth, list the value of your assets (remember to deduct outstanding HP or credit payments). Here are some guidelines on what to include. There could well be others.

Cash in hand, bank current and deposit accounts, building society accounts, savings certificates, premium bonds, unit trusts, stocks and shares, life insurance policies, your house (less outstanding mortgage), cars, antiques, furniture and furnishings, domestic equipment, clothes, sports and hobby equipment, jewellery, stamp/coin collections etc.

If you are married, is your spouse prepared to put his or her share of the resources into the business? If not, make up two lists, one for your own resources and one for your share of joint resources.

Having found out what you are worth, decide (a) how much you *want* to commit to the enterprise, (b) an extra sum you might be prepared to use, (c) how much you need to keep back (for somewhere to live, education fees etc) in the event of the business collapsing. This latter amount should, ideally, be put in a form where creditors can't get at it if you run into debt – in the name of your spouse (unless he/she is involved in the business), or in a trust fund. The money that you are prepared to put up should be easily accessible – bank or building society accounts.

You may be able to raise money on some of your assets. For instance:

1. *Your home* If you have a small mortgage could you increase it? Or you could, perhaps, take out a second mortgage.
2. *Your life insurance or endowment policy* If your policy has been in force for several years there are various ways it can provide you with cash. (a) The policy can be deposited as security with a bank or building society. This may enable you to get a bigger loan than you would otherwise. (b) You can borrow from the insurance company itself, often on more attractive terms than from other lenders. The policy remains in force, you continue the premium payments and, on maturity, you receive the final payment less any loan still outstanding. (c) You can surrender the policy. However, since surrender terms are not usually very attractive, it is better to borrow than surrender.
3. *Your car* You could organize a sale and lease-back arrangement with a leasing company. The lessor buys the car and leases it back to you (we explain how leasing works later on in the chapter).
4. *Your friends and relatives* People who start their own business often discover that their friends and relatives find it exciting to be involved with a new venture and are prepared to lend money at little or no interest. The Business Expansion Scheme (see p. 77) has made it more tax-efficient for wealthy friends to invest in your company, too. Remember, however, that borrowing money from people close to you can cause dreadful problems if things don't work out.

Can you finance the business entirely from your own resources or will you need to borrow? Even if you have sufficient funds to provide capital for the business it is sometimes more economic to borrow. It depends on the rate of interest you would have to pay (although interest is tax deductible) especially if your own funds are tied up in investments which give you a good tax-free bonus. In any event, it's questionable whether it's really wise to commit too much of your capital to the business with the inevitable risks involved. It's always sensible to have funds to meet the crises that befall most people at some time in their life.

However, if you do need to borrow, remember that lenders like to see evidence of serious commitment to the enterprise and are usually more forthcoming if the borrower is prepared to put in a substantial amount of his own capital. Often, they will simply match the amount he puts in. Sometimes, though, they will lend a higher proportion.

RATIONALIZING YOUR REQUIREMENTS

If you don't think you can find the funds for the business on the forecasts you have prepared, go through your financial calculations again and see if you can't trim off some fat. These are some suggested ways to scale down capital requirements:

1. *Premises* Renting rather than buying outright releases capital for other uses. Can you sublet part of the premises? Would you be better off to start in a communal workspace where various services and equipment are included, so saving you some initial overhead costs? (see Chapter 5 for more details). If you already own your own business premises you could consider a sale and lease-back arrangement (see p. 88).
2. *Plant, machinery and equipment* Can you lease, rather than buy outright, the plant, machinery and/or equipment you need? If you only use equipment occasionally, can you hire it when you need it? Can you contract out some aspects of your business to save buying equipment? If you need to buy equipment, is it available secondhand?
3. *Stock* Have you done enough research to discover which supplier will give you the best credit terms? Can you get supplies "on consignment", which means you don't pay for them until you sell them? Can you carry less stock but organize a rapid delivery service if you run short?

4. *Selling policy* Can you narrow the range of goods you offer to reduce stocks? Can you concentrate on cash sales or cash with order, instead of credit sales?
5. *Scale of business* Assess what turnover would correspond to the capital you can raise. Re-do your profit and cash flow calculations. Is it still feasible?

Before we explain the different ways of raising money to start a business, it's worth mentioning a Government scheme which is designed to fund *you* while you are trying to get your business established.

The Enterprise Allowance Scheme run by the Manpower Services Commission went national on 1 August 1983 and at the time of writing was due to run until at least March 1985.

This scheme is for *unemployed* people who want to start their own business but don't want to lose their unemployment or supplementary benefit.

Under the scheme, the Manpower Services Commission pays previously unemployed people an allowance of £40 per week for a year to supplement receipts from the business. There's a catch, though, buried away in the small print – you must have at least £1,000 of your own to invest in the business over the first twelve months.

The business you propose to run must be *new* – if you plan to take over an existing business this won't be acceptable under the scheme. *Independent* i.e. it can't be a subsidiary of, or financially supported by, another company. *Small* – applications won't be accepted from people who intend to employ more than 20 workers during the first twelve months.

And the scheme is not available to support businesses which involve the establishment of nightclubs and licensed clubs, including gambling establishments, or which involve the promotion of particular political or religious views.

To be eligible for the Enterprise Allowance you have to meet *all* the following conditions:

- you must be receiving unemployment benefit or supplementary benefit at the time of application.
- you must have been out of work (or under notice of redundancy) for at least 13 weeks before your application.
- your proposed business must be approved by the Manpower Services Commission as suitable for public support. But there will be no test of the business's likely success.
- you must be able to show that you have at least £1,000 available to invest in the business.
- you must be over 18 and under pensionable age.
- you must have no other employment while you are receiving the Enterprise Allowance and you must work full-time (at least 36 hrs per week) in the business.

If you think you might be eligible, ask at your Jobcentre to be included in an Enterprise Allowance Scheme information session. This gives you more details on how the scheme operates, also advice on starting up a business from a counsellor of the Government's Small Firms Service.

Once you have attended the session you will be given an application form for entry into the scheme (application forms are *only* available to people who attend an information session).

After completing the form you will be interviewed at the Enterprise Allowance Scheme jobcentre. The interviewer will want evidence that you have at least £1,000 to invest in the business (a bank statement will be enough but the money must be in a separate bank account from your personal account and in the name of the proposed business).

If both you and the jobcentre are satisfied, you sign an agreement and this marks your entry into the scheme.

At the time of writing, around 27,000 people are using Enterprise Allowance Scheme funds to help start their business. Here's the story of one of them.

Roy Kempson, at the age of 55 with two years redundancy behind him, was feeling incredibly gloomy since the chances of finding work in his home town of Bacup, Lancashire were remote.

Roy and his wife Eileen had for many years nurtured a dream of owning a restaurant, but redundancy had made him abandon hope.

Then Eileen saw an advertisement on a bus about the Rossendale Enterprise Trust, which was set up to advise and help small businesses. They went to see the director who told them they were entitled to both the government regional development grant (Bacup is in an assisted area) and help under the Enterprise Allowance Scheme. The Enterprise Trust steered their ideas favourably through the banks and they were accepted on the Enterprise Allowance Scheme.

They opened the Heritage Wine Bar and Restaurant in November 1982 serving lunches in their 30-place dining room. Now they have extended the business to cater for 120 people and the next string to their bow will be bed and breakfast in flats they have rented next door. It is not uncommon to see a "Restaurant Full" sign outside the door.

Roy says, "It is like a dream come true. Everyone has benefited. We received good financial advice from the Enterprise Trust and a steady income from the Enterprise Allowance Scheme. The government has also received a good return for its investment since now I'm an employer, I'm keeping another five people off the dole."

RAISING MONEY FROM OUTSIDE SOURCES

This can be in the form of *grants* (which you don't have to pay back); *loans* (which you do, with interest – often hefty) and *equity finance* (where the lender takes a share stake in your business and therefore a percentage of the profits).

Potential lenders include: individuals, clearing banks, merchant banks, finance houses, insurance companies, pension funds, local authorities, central government, the EEC. There are also additional financial sources for certain types of operations (e.g. co-operatives).

Bank loans (which include the Government Loan Guarantee Scheme) are the most usual method of raising start-up money and, in theory, available to any type of start-up idea. Equity finance is only available to limited companies but it is often the *only* source of cash for new business ideas which require a large capital injection, such as getting an invention into production.

Grants are a much scarcer commodity. Whether you are eligible for a grant will depend largely on *where in the country you plan to locate your business* and *what type of business you intend to run*. We explain the grants available and who can apply below.

Whether you can get financial help from your local authority varies from authority to authority (many don't offer any assistance whatsoever).

Since government schemes and local authority initiatives are constantly changing, use what we tell you only as a guide. We believe this information was correct as at April 1984 but double-check with the relevant body before you go ahead.

Some points to remember when raising money:

● it is never cheap to borrow since lending money for new business start-ups is a risky business for the financier. In general, the greater the risk, the higher the charge. If you are able to reduce the risk by providing security for the loan (in the

form of personal guarantees, insurance policies, property deeds) the rate of interest should be lower.
- shop around. Different lenders charge different rates of interest, it can vary by as much as 5%.
- don't give up if the first lender you try turns you down. Find out why your request has been refused, and either amend your original proposition accordingly, and/or approach another source of finance.

And two rules of borrowing:

- *Gearing:* the ratio of money borrowed to the money put in by you (see also Chapter 7). Some lenders are reluctant to let you borrow sums which represent too high a proportion of the total resources of the business since the interest payments could become too high for the business to bear, and the risks too great if the business doesn't do well. In the past the gearing ratio was 1:1 but lenders have become more flexible in recent years.
- *Matching:* choosing the right type of finance for the purpose. The principle is to keep the life of the assets and their relevant financing to roughly the same length of time. For example, office equipment such as photocopiers, computers, vending machines is normally reckoned to have a five-year lifespan so it wouldn't be appropriate to finance it with a ten-year loan since you would still be paying for it long after it had packed up, a five-year lease arrangement would be sensible.
The chart below provides some guidelines on matching finance to purpose.

Which Finance for What Purpose

Term of finance	What for	Method of financing
Short-term (up to 3 years)	stock; debtors; other working capital needs; seasonal finance fluctuations; financing export orders	overdrafts, short-term loans, factoring, invoice discounting, bill finance, creditors
Medium-term (3-7 years)	financing fixed assets – premises, plant, machinery, vehicles and other equipment; long-term working capital needs – hard-core stock, debtors; technological innovations; developing a new product	Medium-term loans, leasing, hire purchase, public sector finance
Long-term (7-20 years)	permanent working capital; major fixed assets; buying another business; broadening borrowing base	long-term loans, equity finance, mortgage loan, sale and lease-back, venture capital

Overdrafts

You and the bank agree an overdraft limit. When your account is in credit the credit balance usually attracts an allowance to reduce bank commission charges. When in overdraft, interest is charged.

Interest rates are normally 2% to 4½% above bank base rate – which makes overdrafts one of the cheapest ways of borrowing.

The bank may, additionally, charge you a small fee for arranging the overdraft.

Overdrafts are suitable to cover fluctuating day-to-day working capital requirements but not for the purchase of assets. Because overdrafts are cheap and convenient there is a temptation to use them for the wrong purposes. Resist it, since overdrafts have the disadvantage of fluctuating interest rates and the fact that the bank in theory (and sometimes during a credit squeeze in practice) can ask you to reduce or even repay the sum overdrawn.

Term Loans

These are a more formal borrowing arrangement than overdrafts and the interest charges are normally higher.

The lender agrees to advance you a sum of money for a set period which you repay with interest. Term loans are either *short-term* (0-3yrs), *medium-term* (3-7 years) or *long-term* (7-20 plus years). It's important to negotiate the right term for the purpose. It wouldn't be sensible, for instance, to acquire factory premises on a short-term loan of, say, a year since it's unlikely that the business would be able to generate enough profit to repay it in that period. The chart above provides some guidelines on which type of loan is right for what purpose.

Interest rates on loans can either be fixed for the term of the loan or can vary according to the bank base rate (some loans, though, are related to other variable rates such as the London inter-bank base rate, LIBOR).

A fixed-rate loan makes forward planning easier since you know exactly how much money you will be required to pay each month. It also works out cheaper if interest rates rise sharply during the loan period, but dearer if interest rates fall.

When negotiating a loan you can arrange to build in a capital repayment "holiday". This means you initially only pay back the interest on the loan and start to repay the capital later. If you're a tax paying company the interest can be set off against income for Corporation Tax purposes and it allows the plant, equipment and building you're investing in to come fully into profit by the time the capital repayment programme starts. It is usually a good idea to negotiate the longest capital repayment "holiday" you can.

As well as the interest, you might be charged a setting-up fee for arranging the loan.

Lenders normally require security against the loan (but see Government Loan Guarantee Scheme below). This can be in the form of personal guarantees from the owners/directors; insurance policies; your home (this is called a mortgage loan) and/or a charge on the assets of the business.

Who gives loans?

The *clearing banks* are the main source for term loans. For businesses only requiring a small injection of cash, banks such as the Co-op and Trustee Savings Bank may be better bets than the Big Four. They are aggressively marketing their loan facilities to small firms as a way of competing with their larger brethren. In addition to offering straight term loans, the major clearing banks have set up various special schemes aimed primarily at the small independent business.

Foreign banks will sometimes lend to small businesses but you have a better chance of borrowing from them if your business has a connection with the country.

Finance houses will consider loans to new businesses but they almost always require an equity stake so we'll come to them in a minute. There is, however, one finance house which is a prime lender to small businesses which *doesn't* always require a share stake. This is the *Industrial & Commercial Finance Corporation* (ICFC) which is owned by the four major clearing banks and the Bank of England. It is interested in any sound business proposition requiring funds of between £5,000 and £2m. The corporation treats every application on its own merit so interest rates may vary depending on the type of company and the repayment term – loans of up to 20 years can be negotiated.

Interest rates are usually fixed but ICFC has now introduced a "drop-lock" provision. The borrower starts off paying a floating rate but at any time during the term of the loan he can elect to fix the rate and "lock-in". ICFC's interest charges, though, don't look cheap against the competition. ICFC has 17 regional offices. Contact

ICFC head office at 91 Waterloo Road, London SE1 8XP, 01-928 7822 to get the address of the office nearest to you.

Local authorities Some offer specific start-up loans or "topping-up" finance for new businesses. Usually, though, only in the more depressed areas of the country.

Finance is often only available when it hasn't been possible to raise it from other sources. Local authority loan schemes vary substantially from area to area so check what's available from your authority with your local Industrial Liaison Officer/ Planning Department/local enterprise agency.

Government Loan Guarantee Scheme Of all the government initiatives for small business, this is probably the most helpful. It is designed to provide capital to small firms who haven't sufficient security to qualify for a normal bank loan, or whose directors are unwilling to provide personal guarantees.

The scheme is administered on behalf of the Department of Industry by many of the clearing banks and several of the financial institutions including ICFC (mentioned above).

Currently, under the scheme, the government guarantees 70% of the loan, up to a maximum of £75,000. This means that if the customer runs into trouble the bank picks up only 30% of the tab and applies to the DOI for the rest. The scheme is intended to encourage lenders to look more favourably on business propositions they might normally have turned down.

Loans can run for any period between two and seven years. As well as the bank's own interest charge (currently 1½%-3% above base rate) the government levies a 5% premium on the amount lent, and there is an arrangement fee. The GLGS, therefore, isn't exactly the cheapest way to raise money, but for businesses which can't put up collateral it is often the only way. Initial demand for the scheme was so strong that the money allocated for the first three years was eaten up in the first 12 months. Of course a lot of it went to wily companies who saw it as a heaven-sent opportunity to get unsecured borrowing and thus free up other lines of credit – some even spun off associate companies with completely separate directors. Also, many of the companies who tapped into the scheme have since gone bust (about one in three at the last estimate). Although the government has now put in more money, these two factors may mean the government calls a halt to the scheme sooner rather than later.

The British Technology Group (an amalgamation of the National Enterprise Board and the National Research and Development Corporation) aims to stimulate innovation and investment in British Industry. It has two schemes which offer money:

The Small Company Innovation Fund, which requires a minority equity stake (so we deal with it under *equity finance* below) and *Oakwood Loan Finance Ltd*, which offers standardized five-year loans of up to £50,000 to companies in England who need finance for growth but are unable to provide the security normally required. The interest is fixed at 2% above base rate throughout the life of the loan. You also have to pay an arrangement fee. Oakwood *likes* to take an option to buy shares in your company but you are given the right to prevent its doing so.

CoSIRA (the Council of Small Industries in Rural Areas) will, in certain instances, lend funds for building/plant/equipment (up to 50% of the project cost). The CoSIRA fund is limited, though, and only offered to firms in rural areas that have been unable to raise money from normal commercial sources.

Development agencies The Welsh, Scottish and Ulster Development Agencies make loans to businesses in their areas. They might require an equity stake if adequate security isn't available.

BSC (Industry) Ltd offers loans (typically for a two or three year period) to both start-up and existing businesses in the eighteen areas it supports (see chapter 11 for a list). BSC loans have the advantages that security is not normally required and interest charges are slightly lower than commercial rates, but BSC will usually only lend where a funding gap exists after all other possible sources have been explored.

Money from EEC. Businesses setting up in coal and steel closure areas may be eligible for loans from the European Coal and Steel Community. The business can be of any type but must offer employment prospects suitable for redundant coal and steel workers.

The European Investment Bank also lends to certain types of small firms who set up in Assisted Areas. EIB loans carry no absolute requirement that new jobs will be created.

Since EEC loans usually carry a lower interest rate than comparable funds in the UK, they're nice if you can get them!

ICFC and some of the clearing banks act as agents for EEC loans, as do the various regional development agencies.

Equity Finance

Raising money by equity finance means the financier takes shares in your business. You relinquish overall control and quite often have to accept an outside director on the board. Nobody likes parting with a share stake in return for a cash injection. After all, if the shares go up in value mainly because of your hard work, why should somebody else reap part of the benefit? However, you might not be able to get your proposed business off the ground without a financier risking some money in it and it's better to have a slice of the cake than no cake at all.

Equity finance for new businesses usually goes under the name of "venture capital". The number of organizations offering venture capital is on the increase and the government has provided an incentive to private individuals to invest in small businesses with the "Business Expansion Scheme" (see below). But evaluating the commercial prospects of a new business is a difficult, expensive and time-consuming process and providing money as venture capital is risky, so financiers are very choosy about who they offer it to.

For a start you have to be – or about to become – a limited company. Financiers are looking for companies with evidence of a strong management team with good ideas which can be translated into a commercially viable business that will grow quickly. The project is only usually likely to appeal to a venture capitalist if it is *innovative*, *creating a new market* or *filling a gap* in an old one.

Commercial lenders want a stake in a growing company's equity for a very good reason. When they provide medium and long term finance, as a loan, even at what looks (to you) to be a high rate of interest, they still reckon the return on their investment is quite low, particularly when inflation reduces the real value of the money they've advanced.

However, if they can get 15%, 20%, 30% or 40% of the borrower's equity (ordinary shares or variations thereof) at a knockdown price when the company is new, that equity stake can be worth a very great deal when the company makes it to the big time, and either sells out or widens the market in its shares on the Unlisted Securities Market, the Over-the Counter-Market or via a full Stock Exchange quotation.

Venture capitalists vary enormously in who they lend to, how much they lend and what they want in return. On average, though, they look to lend a minimum of £50,000 (although some, notably the banks, lend less). The amount of equity stake in your business they require varies between 10-50%.

Some venture capital organizations simply invest direct into ordinary shares but others increasingly are doing their best to minimize their risk by going for what is called "the low-risk option technique". It works like this: finance is injected by means of a five, seven, 10 or even 15 year loan which is secured on the assets of the business, plus personal guarantees from the owners and, if necessary, second mortgages on their houses. When the loan is made, an option is written into the deal allowing the financier to convert part of the loan, or subscribe new money for, a percentage of the borrower's share capital at a price fixed at the time the loan is made. ("Converting" means the amount of the outstanding loan is reduced by whatever the financier pays for the shares; "subscribing new money" means he pays for the shares over and above the amount of the outstanding loan.)

The option technique allows the lender to have his bread buttered on both sides. If the borrower prospers, the lender exercises his option. If the borrower doesn't prosper, the option is allowed to lapse.

Sources of venture capital

Private individuals You might have friends or relatives willing to participate in funding your business in return for a share stake. Or you could find a complete stranger now that the government is actively encouraging private investment in small business through the *Business Expansion Scheme*. Basically, the BES provides tax relief for those in high tax brackets if they invest in new or existing unquoted companies. A 60% tax payer can claim tax relief at his marginal tax rate if he invests up to £40,000 a year. This means the actual cost of his investment is only £16,000. Most businesses are eligible for BES investment (but not financial services, dealers in commodities, shares, securities, futures and land; legal, insurance and accountancy business; leasing companies; farming concerns).

All well and good. But how do you find such an investor? One company that keeps a register of them is Electra Risk Capital (Electra House, Temple Place, Victoria Embankment, London WC2. 01-836 7766). Some Enterprise Agencies run "marriage bureaux" designed to put investors and people seeking investment together. The London Enterprise Agency's Business Introduction Service can be used by anyone regardless of where they are located.

There are also business expansion *funds* which have sprung up to cope with the problem of matching people and needs. Potential investors under the Business Expansion Scheme put their money into a special fund – most are administered by the merchant banks – which pools the resources and lends to companies they consider eligible. This is a more expensive method of finding a private investor, though, since the funds take their cut in the form of arrangement and annual management fees. Arrangement fees can vary from nil to 9% and the option the funds exercise over your company's equity can be anything from 10%-30%. So you need to shop carefully amongst the funds. The terms of the BES mean they have to invest in ordinary shares in order to get the tax clawback – so they have the advantage of no low-option technique. For a directory of business expansion funds see *The Small Business Guide* published by the BBC.

Banks The clearing banks have moved into the venture capital business, often establishing subsidiaries for the purpose.

Public Sector Sources The British Technology Group, an amalgamation of the National Enterprise Board and the National Research Development Corporation aims to stimulate innovation and investment in British Industry. BTG's Small Companies Division offers two schemes for companies in the high technology sector. Oakwood Loan Finance Ltd offers standardized five-year loans up to £50,000 to companies that can't provide the normal security. Capital repayments start at the beginning of the fourth year of the loan, interest payable at a fixed annual rate of 2% above base rate throughout the life of the loan. Oakwood normally seeks to subscribe to up to 20% of the equity at a fixed future date but you, the borrower, have the right to buy out this entitlement at the end of the loan period according to a predetermined formula which reflects profit growth. The second BTG scheme is the Small Company Innovation Fund, which specializes in providing individually designed investment packages for small companies where the business as a whole is innovative. They take a minority equity stake.

Private Sector Sources The big boys in the venture capital field are the merchant banks, finance houses, insurance companies, pension funds and institutions such as ICFC. Some US venture capital organizations have moved into the UK, and investors from Europe have become interested in the British scene and are channelling money into it. Large industrial firms in the UK are also starting to back new and young firms with growth potential.

If you think, in the light of this section, of venture capital as the right method to finance your proposed business – or as part of a financial package – prepare your business plan carefully and shop around. Resist grabbing the first offer that comes your way and worrying about the terms later. Remember, the job of a venture capitalist is to pay the lowest price for the equity, yours is to ensure you get the highest. Never forget that once an offer is made, you can take it around the market place to see if you can improve on the terms.

The directory which follows lists organizations providing long-term finance, both as loans or equity. The guide to their services will give you a clue to their lending policy. The £25,000 threshold was selected because a vast majority of new businesses are not looking for a greater level of external long-term finance.

Directory of Institutions giving long-term finance

(This table is abridged from the *The Small Business Guide*, BBC Publications, 1984.)

Key

(I)   Invest less than £25,000
(S)   Start-up loans provided
(E)   Equity stake not required
(M)   May not put a director on your board
(N)   No special restrictions
(H)   Help with Business Plan

Abingworth (various City Institutions, including Barclays Bank), 26 St. James's Street, London SW1A 1HA. (01-839-6745).
   Contact: P. Dicks (S)

Alan Patricof Associates Ltd, 24 Upper Brook Street, London W1Y 1PD. (01-493-3633). (S)

Allied Combined Trust Ltd (Allied Irish Bank Group), Pinners Hall, 8/9 Austin Friars, London EC2N 2AE. (01-920 9155).
   Contact: Nicholas Condon. (I)(S)(M)(H)

Anglo-American Venture Fund Ltd, 8th Floor, Bank House, Charlotte Street, Manchester M1 4ET. (061-236-7302). (I)(S)(E)(M)

A P Bank (Norwich Union), 21 Great Winchester Street, London EC2N 2HH. (01-638-4711).

Barclays Development Capital (Barclays Bank), 3rd Floor, Chatsworth House, 66/70 St. Mary Axe, London EC3A 8BD. (01-623-4321).
   Contact: M. R. Cumming. (S)(H)

British Railways Pension Funds, 50 Liverpool Street, London EC2P 2BQ. (01-247-7600 ext 2784).
   Contact: Peter Croft. (M)(N)(H)

British Steel Corporation (Industry) Ltd, (BSC), NLA Tower, 12 Addiscombe Road, Croydon, CR9 3JH. (01-686-0366). (I)(S)(E)(M)(H)

British Technology Group (government financed organization), 101 Newington Causeway, London SE1 6BU. (01-403-6666).
Contact: D. M. James. Ⓘ Ⓢ Ⓔ Ⓜ

Brown Shipley Developments, Founders Court, Lothbury, London EC2R YHE. (01-606-9833).
Contact: Mrs. C. Howlett. Ⓔ Ⓜ Ⓝ

Business Mortgages & Investment Trust PLC, Manager, 1 Marlborough Road, Sherwell, Plymouth PL4 8LP. (0752-669286).
Contact: R. V. A. Peachey. Ⓘ Ⓢ Ⓔ Ⓜ

Candover Investments, 4/7 Red Lion Court, London EC4A 3EB. (01-583-5090).
Contact: P. Symonds. Ⓝ Ⓗ

Capital Partners International Ltd (private European investors), 40 Edgerton Crescent, London SW3 2EB. (01-351-4899).
Contact: C. von Luttitz and P. Cammerman. Ⓘ Ⓢ

Castle Finance (Norwich Union), Norwich Union Insurance Group, Surrey Street, Norwich NR1 3TE. (0603-22200). Ⓢ Ⓜ

Cayzer, Ltd, Cayzer House, 2-4 St Mary Axe, London EC3A 8BP. (01-623-1212).
Contact: Jonathan Hawksley. Ⓢ Ⓔ Ⓜ Ⓝ Ⓗ

Charterhouse Development Capital (Charterhouse Group), 65 Holborn Viaduct, London EC1A 2DR. (01-248-4000).
Contact: Richard Duncan. Ⓢ

CIN Industrial Investments (National Coal Board Pensions Funds), 33 Cavendish Square, London W1M 0AL. (01-629-6000). Ⓢ Ⓜ Ⓝ

Citicorp Development Development Capital Ltd, Melbourne House, 33 Melbourne Place, Aldwych, London WC2B 4ND. (01-438-1277).
Contact: Jon Moulton. Ⓝ Ⓗ

Clydesdale Bank Industrial Finance Ltd (a member of the Midland Bank Group), 30 St. Vincent Place, Glasgow G1 2HL. (041-248-7070).
Contact: S. B. Keir. Ⓢ Ⓜ

Commercial Bank of the Near East (private shareholders, mainly Greek), 107/112 Leadenhall Street, London EC3A 4AE. (01-283-4041).
Contact: R. F. Coyle. Ⓘ Ⓢ Ⓔ Ⓜ Ⓝ

CoSira. Council for Small Industries in Rural Areas, 141 Castle Street, Salisbury, Wilts SP1 3TP. (0722-336255).
Contact: Info. Officer. Ⓘ Ⓢ Ⓔ Ⓜ Ⓗ

County Bank, County Bank Ltd, 11 Old Broad Street, London EC2N 1BB. (01-638-6000).
Contact: C. A. Bloomfield. Ⓢ Ⓔ Ⓜ Ⓝ

Creative Capital Fund (British Linen Bank), c/o The British Linen Bank Ltd, 4 Melville Street, Edinburgh EH3 7NZ. (031-226-4071). Ⓢ Ⓜ Ⓝ

Dawnay, Day & Co. Ltd, Managing Director, Corporate Finance, Garrard House, 31 Gresham Street, London EC2V 7DT. (01-726-4080).
Contact: B. Pincus. Ⓢ Ⓔ Ⓜ Ⓝ Ⓗ

Development Capital Group Ltd, 88 Baker Street, London W1M 1DL. (01-486-5021).
Contact: M. Burrell. Also
Baker Street Investment Co. plc (BASIC) Same address. Also
Lazard Development Capital Ltd, 21 Moorfields, London EC2P 2HT. (01-588-2721).
Contact: N. Falkner. Ⓢ

East Anglian Securities Trust Ltd, 3 Colegate, Norwich. (0603-660931).
Contact: John Cox, Group Secretary. (I)(S)(M)(N)

East of Scotland Onshore plc (ESO plc), 42 Charlotte Square, Edinburgh EH2 4NQ. (031-226-4471).
Contact: D. M. Munro. (S)(M)

Electra Risk Capital (Electra Investments), Electra House, Temple Place, Victoria Embankment, London WC2R 3HP. (01-836-7766).
Contact: O. J. H. Huntsman. (S)(N)

English & Caledonian Investment PLC, Cayzer House, 2-4 St Mary Axe, London EC3A 8BP. (01-623-1212).
Contact: John Parkin. (S)

Equity Capital for Industry (City Institutes), Leith House, 47/57 Gresham Street, London EC2V 7EH. (01-606-8513).
Contact: Tony Lorenz. (S)(N)(H)

European Investment Bank (EEC's long term bank), 23 Queen Anne's Gate, London SW1H 9BU. (01-222-2933).
Contact: Guy Baird. (I)(S)(E)(M)

Exeter Trust Ltd (ET Ltd), Sanderson House, Blackboy Road, Exeter, Devon EX4 6SE. (0392-50635). (I)(S)(E)(M)(N)

F & C Management Ltd, Secretary, 1 Laurence Pountney Hill, London EC4R 0BA. (01-623-4680).
Contact: J. Nelson. (S)(M)(N)

Fountain Development Capital Fund, Hill Samuel & Co. Ltd, 100 Wood Street, London EC2P 2AJ. (01-628-8011).
Contact: D. Osborne. (N)(H)

Greater London Enterprise Board, 63-67 Newington Causeway, London SE1. (01-403-0300).
Contact: Mrs. J. Pegg. (I)(E)

Gresham Trust (Gresham), Barrington House, Gresham Street, London EC2Z 7HE. (01-606-6474).
Contact: T. A. Jones. (S)(N)

Grainger & Co. Ltd, 18 Woodside Terrace, Glasgow G3 7NY. (041-332-8751).
Contact: Adam I. Armstrong. (I)(S)(E)(M)(N)(H)

Growth Options Ltd, (Member of National Westminster Bank Group) Business Development Division, 6th Floor, 4 Eastcheap, London EC3M 1JH. (01-726-1919).
Contact: Colin Peacock. (I)(S)(M)(N)(H)

Guidehouse Ltd, 1 Love Lane, London EC2 7JJ. (01-606-6321). (S)(E)(N)(H)

Hafren Investment Finance Ltd, (Welsh Development Agency), Peal House, Greyfriars Road, Cardiff CF1 3XX. (0222-32955). (I)(S)(N)(H)

Hambros Advanced Technology Trust, 41 Bishopsgate, London EC2P 2AA. (01-588-2851).
Contact: G. J. Chalk, A. Ryden. (S)(N)(H)

Highlands & Islands Development Board (HM Government & Scottish Office), Bridge House, 27 Bank Street, Inverness IV1 1QR. (0463-234171).
(I)(S)(E)(M)(N)(H)

Industrial and Commercial Finance Corporation (ICFC) (Bank of England & Clearing Banks), 91 Waterloo Road, London SE1 8XP. (01-928-7822).
Contact: Miss S. L. Palmer. (I)(S)(E)(M)(N)(H)

Regional Offices: Aberdeen, 38 Carden Place, Aberdeen AB1 1UP. (0224-638666).
Contact: Keith Mair. Ⓘ Ⓢ Ⓔ Ⓜ Ⓝ Ⓗ

Birmingham, 112 Colmore Row, Birmingham B3 3SA. (021-236-9531).
Contact: Peter Williams, Malcolm Gloak. Ⓘ Ⓢ Ⓔ Ⓜ Ⓝ Ⓗ

Brighton, 47 Middle Street, Brighton BN1 1AL. (0273-23164).
Contact: Paul Waller. Ⓘ Ⓢ Ⓔ Ⓜ Ⓝ Ⓗ

Bristol, Pearl Assurance House, Queen Square, Bristol BS1 4LE. (0272-277412).
Contact: John Kingston. Ⓘ Ⓢ Ⓔ Ⓜ Ⓝ Ⓗ

Cambridge, Jupiter House, Station Road, Cambridge CB1 2HX. (0223-316568).
Contact: Richard Summers. Ⓘ Ⓢ Ⓔ Ⓜ Ⓝ Ⓗ

Cardiff, Alliance House, 18/19 High Street, Cardiff CF1 3TS. (0222-34021).
Contact: Ray Braddick. Ⓘ Ⓢ Ⓔ Ⓜ Ⓝ Ⓗ

Edinburgh, 8 Charlotte Square, Edinburgh EH2 4DR. (031-226-7902).
Contact: Jim Martin. Ⓘ Ⓢ Ⓔ Ⓜ Ⓝ Ⓗ

Glasgow, 9th Floor, Pegasus House, 375 West George Street, Glasgow G2 4AR.
(041-248-4456).
Contact: Sandy Walker. Ⓘ Ⓢ Ⓔ Ⓜ Ⓝ Ⓗ

Leeds, Headrow House, The Headrow, Leeds LS1 8ES. (0533-25223).
Contact: David Thorp, Barry Anysz. Ⓘ Ⓢ Ⓔ Ⓜ Ⓝ Ⓗ

Leicester, Abacus House, 32 Friar Lane, Leicester LE1 5QU. (0533-25223).
Contact: David Wilson. Ⓘ Ⓢ Ⓔ Ⓜ Ⓝ Ⓗ

Liverpool, Silkhouse Court, Tithebarn Street, Liverpool L2 2LZ. (051-236-2944).
Contact: Jeremy Dawson. Ⓘ Ⓢ Ⓔ Ⓜ Ⓝ Ⓗ

London, 91 Waterloo Road, London SE1 8XP. (01-928-7822).
Contacts: Andrew Holmes, Brian Larcombe, Roger Lawson, Philip Marsden,
Donald Workman. Ⓘ Ⓢ Ⓔ Ⓜ Ⓝ Ⓗ

Manchester, Virginia House, 5 Cheapside, Manchester M2 4WG.
(061-833-9511).
Contact: Peter Folkman. Ⓘ Ⓢ Ⓔ Ⓜ Ⓝ Ⓗ

Newcastle, Scottish Life House, Archbold Terrace, Jesmond, Newcastle-upon-
Tyne NE2 1DB. (0632-815221).
Contact: Colin Chadburn. Ⓘ Ⓢ Ⓔ Ⓜ Ⓝ Ⓗ

Nottingham, 38 The Ropewalk, Nottingham NG1 5DW. (0602-412766).
Contact: Graham Spooner. Ⓘ Ⓢ Ⓔ Ⓜ Ⓝ Ⓗ

Reading, 43/47 Crown Street, Reading RG1 2SN. (0734-861943).
Contact: Roger Cottrell. Ⓘ Ⓢ Ⓔ Ⓜ Ⓝ Ⓗ

Sheffield, 11 Westbourne Road, Sheffield S10 2QQ. (0742-680571).
Contact: Paul Gilmartin. Ⓘ Ⓢ Ⓔ Ⓜ Ⓝ Ⓗ

Southampton, Capital House, 11 Houndwell Place, Southampton SO1 1HU.
(0703-32044).
Contact: Richard Scrase. Ⓘ Ⓢ Ⓔ Ⓜ Ⓝ Ⓗ

Industrial Common Ownership Finance Ltd, 4 St. Giles Street, Northampton NN1
1AA. (0604-37563). Ⓘ Ⓢ Ⓔ Ⓜ Ⓝ

INTEX Executive (UK) Ltd & E. P. Woods Investments Ltd, Chancery House, 53/64
Chancery Lane, London WC2A 1QU. (01-831-6925 or 01-242-2263).
Contact: D. Bruce Lloyd. Ⓘ Ⓢ Ⓔ Ⓜ Ⓝ Ⓗ

Investors in Industry Group plc. *See* 3i Ventures.

James Finlay Corporation (James Finlay Group), 10/14 West Nile Street, Glasgow
G1 2PP. (041-204-1321). (H)

Larpent Newton & Co. Ltd, 7th Floor, 18 Breams Buildings, London EC4A 1HN.
(01-831-9991).
Contact: Simon Ashton. (S)(N)(H)

Leisure Development Ltd, Mountbatten House, Victoria Street, Windsor, Berkshire
SL4 1HE. (07535-57181).
Contact: J. A. Knight. (H)

Leopold Joseph & Sons Ltd, 31-45 Gresham Street, London EC2. (01-588-2323).
Contact: Paul Thrussell. (I)(S)(E)(M)(N)(H)

Local Enterprise Development Unit, (Department of Commerce Northern Ireland),
Lamont House, Purdys Lane, New Town Breda, Belfast BT8 4TB.
(0232-691031).
Contact: George Mackey. (I)(S)(E)(M)(H)

London Wall Industrial Consultants Ltd (Smithdown Investments Ltd), 15 South
Molton Street, London W1Y 1DE. (01-408-1502).
Contact: G. L. Taylor. (I)(S)(E)(M)(H)

Lovat Enterprise Fund (National Coal Board Pension Fund & Others), 27/28 Lovat
Lane, London EC3R 8EB. (01-621-1212).
Contact: Tom Sooke, Guy Eastman, A. Hawksley. (H)

Mathercourt Securities Ltd, 1 Lincoln's Inn Fields, London WC2A 3AA.
(01-831-9001).
Contact: Ian Taylor. (S)(M)(N)(H)

Melville Street Investments (Edinburgh) Ltd, (British Linen Bank) 4 Melville Street,
Edinburgh EH3 7NZ. (031-226-4071). (S)

Meritor Investments Ltd, (Midland Bank & Rolls Royce Pension Fund), 22 Watling
Street, London EC4M 9BR. (01-638-8861). (N)

Midland Bank Industrial Finance (Midland Bank), 22 Watling Street, London EC4M
9BR. (01-638-8861).
Contact: J. R. Beevor. (S)(N)

Midland Bank Venture Capital Ltd, 22 Watling Street, London, EC4M 9BR.
(01-638-8861).
Contact: B. L. J. Warnes. (I)(S)(M)(N)(H)

Minster Trust (Minster Assets), Minster House, Arthur Street, London EC4R 9BH.
(01-623-1050). (S)

Moracrest Investments Ltd (Midland Bank, Prudential and British Gas Pension
Fund), 22 Watling Street, London EC4M 9BR. (01-638-8861).
Contact: D. G. Hutchings. (S)(N)

National Coal Board Pension Fund (NCB), Hobart House, Grosvenor Place, London
SW1. (01-629-6000). (S)(E)(M)(N)

National & Commercial Development Capital (National & Commercial Banking
Group), 88 Baker Street, London W1M 1DL. (01-486-5021).
Contact: Mr. Robinson.

National Commercial & Glyns Limited, (Royal Bank of Scotland Group), 26 St.
Andrew Square, Edinburgh EH2 1AF. (031-556-8555).
Contact: James S. Lindsay ext 2621. (E)(M)(N)(H)

National Westminster Bank, under the terms of Capital Loan Scheme. Approach
through local branch but if guidance is needed to identify a suitable branch tel:
01-726-1891.

Newmarket Co. (1981) Ltd. (UK Subsidiary Newmarket (Venture Capital) Ltd), 57 London Wall, London EC2. (01-638-4551).
Contact: Tim Earl.

Noble Grossart Investments (Scottish Investment Institute), 48 Queen Street, Edinburgh EH2 3NR. (031-226-7011). Ⓢ

Northern Venture Capital Syndicate, Hodgson Martin Ventures Ltd, 4A St Andrew Square, Edinburgh EH2 2BD. (031-557-3560). ⓈⓃⒽ

Norwich General Trust (Norwich Union Insurance), 12 Surrey Street, Norwich NR1 3NJ. (0603-22200). Sister organization: Castle Finance: (01-493-8030). ⒾⓈⒺ

Oakwood Loan Finance Ltd (British Technology Group), 101 Newington Causeway, London SE1 6BU. (01-403-6666). ⒾⓈⒺⓂⓃⒽ

P. A. Developments Ltd (P.A. Ltd), Bowater House East, 68 Knightsbridge, London SW1X 7LJ. (01-589-7050).
Contact: P. T. Grundy, D. E. Hemming. ⓃⒽ

Pegasus Holdings Ltd (a member of the Lloyds Bank Group), General Manager, 11-15 Monument Street, London EC3R 8JU. (01-626-1500 ext 2231). Ⓝ

Rainford Venture Capital, (Pilkington Brothers, Prudential Assurances, Community of St Helen's Trust & others), Prescott Road, St. Helen's, Merseyside WA10 3TT. (0744-682336). ⒾⓈⒽ

Royal Bank Development Ltd (Royal Bank of Scotland), Edinburgh House, 3-11 North St. Andrews Street, Edinburgh EH2 1AF. (031-556-8555).
Contact: James S. Lindsay. ⒺⓂⓃⒽ

Safeguard Industrial Investments (Major Insurance & Pension Funds), 2a Pond Place, London SW3 6QJ. (01-581-4455).
Contact: H. E. King. ⒺⓃⒽ

Scottish Allied Investors, James Finlay plc, 10/14 West Nile Street, Glasgow G2 2PT. (041-204-1321). Ⓗ

Scottish Development Agency (UK Government), 120 Bothwell Street, Glasgow G2 7JP. (041-248-2700).
Contact: Mr. J. Fisher. ⒾⓈⒺⓂⓃⒽ
Also
Small Business Division, Roseberry House, Haymarket Terrace, Edinburgh EH12 5EZ. (031-337-9595).
Contact: Mr. B. Rutherford. ⒾⓈⒺⓂⓃⒽ

Scottish Offshore Investors (James Finlay & Others), 10/14 West Nile Street, Glasgow G2 1PP. (041-204-1321). Ⓗ

Shandwick Consultants Ltd, Wamford Court, 29 Throgmorton Street, London EC2N 2AT. (01-588-4278).

Sharp Unquoted Midland Investment (Legal & General Royal Insurance, Sun Life Assurance & Others), Edmund House, 12 Newall Street, Birmingham B3 3ER. (021-236-5801). Ⓝ

Small Company Innovation Fund (SCIF) (British Technology Group), 101 Newington Causeway, London SE1 6BU. (01-403-6666).

Smithdown Investments (private individuals), 141 North Hyde Road, Hayes, Middlesex (01-573-3783). Also at: 15 South Moulton Street, London W1Y 1DE. (01-408-1502).
Contact: G. L. Taylor. ⒾⓈⒺⓂⒽ

Stewart Fund Managers Ltd, 45 Charlotte Square, Edinburgh EH2 4HW. (031-226-3271).
Contact: J. H. Murray. Ⓢ Ⓜ Ⓝ Ⓗ

Thamesdale Investment & Finance Co. Ltd, Manager, Hamblin House, 1-2 Langham Place, London W1N 8HS. (01-636-2557). Ⓢ

Thomson, Clive & Partners Ltd (TCP Ltd), 24 Old Bond Street, London W1X 3DA. (01-491-4809).
Contact: Mr. Fitzherbert. Ⓘ Ⓢ Ⓜ

3i Ventures, 91 Waterloo Road, London SE1 8XP. (01-928-7822).
Contact: Vicki Bowman or Geoff Taylor. Ⓢ Ⓔ Ⓗ

Trust of Property Shares Ltd, Managing Director, 6 Welbeck Street, London W1M 8BS. (01-486-4684). Ⓢ

UKP-EA Growth Fund Ltd, 7th Fl., 18 Breams Blds, London EC4A 1HN. (01-831-9991).
Contact: Mr. C. Breese. Ⓢ Ⓝ

Venture Founders Ltd (British Investment Trust), 39 The Green, South Bar Street, Banbury, Oxon OX16 9AE. (0295-65881). Ⓢ

Welsh Development Agency (UK Government) Treforest Industrial Estate, Pontypridd, Wales. (044-385-2666). Ⓘ Ⓢ Ⓔ Ⓜ Ⓗ

West Midlands Enterprise Board Ltd, Lloyds Bank Chambers, 75 Edmund Street, Birmingham B3 3HD. (021-236-8855).
Contact: Mr. N. R. Holmes.

Woodside Securities Ltd. (See under Grainger & Co. Ltd).

GRANTS

Starting your business with free money from the public purse sounds great. But don't be too hopeful. Although there are numerous different grants available most of them are only for very specific purposes or are rather obscure, e.g. Inland Waterways Freight Facilities Grant, Forestry Grant Scheme, Fibre Optics and Opto-Electronics Scheme, or only for firms in certain areas of the country. However, don't skip the grants section completely as there are some grants around – not so much for setting up as for financing aspects of the business – which could save you money.

We can't list all the grants available here. We concentrate on those we consider most relevant. For more information contact your regional office of the Department of Trade and Industry. Or get a copy of *British Business, Guide to Industrial Support* (January 1984) from Department of Trade and Industry, Eleventh floor, Millbank Tower, Millbank, London SW1 4QV. (01-211 6088).

Regional Development Grants

The Government, anxious to boost wealth and employment in depressed areas of the country, has designated certain areas *Assisted Areas* and some types of business locating in an assisted area are entitled to financial assistance in the form of a Regional Development Grant.

At the time of writing, RDG's were only available to manufacturing firms for capital expenditure on buildings and for acquiring certain items of plant and machinery.

However, the whole subject of regional aid was being reviewed whilst we were preparing this book and the government was also planning to revise its map of the

Assisted Areas. Details of the new legislation and the new designated areas will be available in late 1984.

It is proposed to restructure the grants so that they relate to *approved projects* as opposed to *qualifying premises* and to target grants more closely to job creation. The present bias towards manufacturing firms will be removed, the business activities which qualify being more widely defined and extended to include service industries considered appropriate.

For details of Regional Development Grants contact the Regional Policy and Development Grant Division, Department of Trade and Industry, Room 431, Kingsgate House, 66-74 Victoria Street, London SW1E 6SJ (01-212 6712).

Grants outside Assisted Areas

Some grants are available for businesses outside the Assisted Areas. They:
1. *Depend on location* – for start-ups in the Highlands and Islands of Scotland (from the Highlands and Islands Development Board), for urban areas in Scotland (under the LEG UP scheme of the Scottish Development Agency), for areas in Wales which have lost their Assisted Areas Status (contact the Welsh Development Agency) and for the conversion of redundant farm buildings in rural parts of England (from the Council for Small Industries in Rural Areas).

   Northern Ireland offers various grant schemes which resemble the RDG (contact LEDU or the Department of Economic Development for more details). See Chapter 11 for addresses.

   Some local authorities offer *grants*, as opposed to loans, for premises, plant and working capital. Several offer relocation grants for firms moving into the area. A few offer small start-up grants and/or New Enterprise Grants. (Check what your authority does and what the terms are.)
2. *Depend on business sector.* Hotels and tourist projects throughout Great Britain can be eligible for grants from the English, Scottish and Welsh Tourist Boards. The grants are discretionary and, generally speaking, priority is given to projects that: aid the development of tourism in the off-season; encourage visitors to less popular tourist areas; and create employment directly or indirectly (more details from the individual Tourist Boards). Micro-electronic projects can attract grants of up to 33% under the Micro-electronics Industry Support Programme – more details from the Electronics Applications Division, Department of Industry – and the Software Products Scheme (contact the Software Products Scheme Administrator at the National Computing Centre Ltd, Oxford Road, Manchester M1 7ED. 061-228 6333). Telecommunications equipment manufacturers may be eligible for grants under the Telecoms Product Scheme (contact IT Division – Department of Industry).

   There are also various grants for businesses involved in agriculture, horticulture and fisheries (details from the Ministry of Agriculture, Fisheries and Food); for shipping (Department of Industry); for transport (Department of Transport); for forestry projects (Forestry Commission) and for mineral exploration (Department of Industry).
3. *Depend on activity* As well as the grants mentioned above, which are designed to help businesses finance capital expenditure, there are various grants for different aspects of activities. Here are some of them:

The Microelectronics Application Programme. Financed by the Department of Industry, MAP's aim is to encourage the use of microcomputers in industry. MAP will pay towards the costs of employing a consultant to conduct a "feasibility study" (which determines whether or not your business will benefit from computerizing, and if so how). In certain cases MAP will also fund the development of the systems themselves, especially in the fields of automation and production control. All companies with a manufacturing base are eligible for MAP grants, some other types of company too, depending on individual circumstances. (Contact MAP Information Centre, Department of Industry.)

Support for innovation. The aim of this grant, which helps finance the costs of research and development projects, is to improve the technological base of UK industry and help companies get new, or significantly improved products and processes, onto the market more quickly and more effectively. Companies in, or closely associated with, the manufacturing sector are eligible. (Contact Research and Technology Policy, Department of Industry.)

Flexible Manufacturing Systems Scheme. This aims to accelerate the investment by the UK engineering industry in systems, combining microelectronics and mechanical engineering, which bring economies of scale to batch production. Grants are available for professional consultancy fees and towards development and capital costs. (Contact Mechanical and Electrical Division, Department of Industry.)

Industrial Robots Scheme. Grants are available for employing a consultant to determine the commercial applications of installing robots and for the capital development costs associated with developing a new application for industrial robots and grants for installing them. (Contact Mechanical and Electrical Division, Department of Industry.)

The government initiatives designed to alleviate unemployment means there are grants available for employing certain categories of staff:

The Young Workers Scheme whereby employers can claim £15 a week if they take on young people (under 18) at wage rates which reflect their lack of training and relative inexperience (they must be in their first year of employment); *The Youth Training Scheme* whereby the employer gets £1,850 per annum for employing a school-leaver (out of which he has to pay the trainee £25 per week and pay off-the-job training education fees). The YTS might sound like a good source of cheap labour but it doesn't suit all small firms. The *Job Splitting Grant.* A £750 grant is available to employers for splitting a full-time job into two part-time jobs, one or both of which must be given to somebody unemployed, or threatened with redundancy. *Job Introduction Scheme for Disabled People* offers employers a weekly grant of £45 per head towards the cost of employing certain registered disabled people. There are also grants to adapt premises and equipment (up to £6,000 per person) if you need to make essential adaptations to premises or equipment in order to recruit a disabled person. More details on all these schemes from your regional office of the Department of Employment.

To discover whether you might be eligible for any type of government assistance, you might like to take advantage of a useful free service provided by the Bank of Scotland. You put forward the details of your project and the bank runs it through their GAINS (Government Assistance Information Service) computer program. This produces a print-out listing the government assistance you may be eligible for. Contact: GAINS, Bank of Scotland, Uberior House, 61 Grassmarket, Edinburgh EH1 2JF. (031 229 2555).

OTHER METHODS OF FINANCING A BUSINESS

You can raise money by methods other than loans, grants or equity finance. We outline them briefly below. Some of them will only apply when your business is already under way but you need to know about them so that you can take them into account when planning your business.

Leasing

A third of all equipment used in British industry today is now leased, rather than bought outright, bought on hire purchase or rented, and a vast industry has grown up offering leasing facilities – it includes banks, merchant banks, specialist leasing companies and leasing brokers.

Almost anything can be leased: cars, computers, plant, machinery, aircraft, even North Sea oil rigs.

Under a lease agreement you select the equipment you want to acquire and arrange for a leasing company to buy it and then lease it to you for an agreed rent for a set period. At the end of the period you may be able to continue using it on payment of a "peppercorn" rent or you may be offered the chance to sell it to a third party as the leasing company's "agent" for which you will receive a substantial "commission" – normally 95-99% of the second-hand price.

The advantages of leasing are:

● *releases capital for other uses* – by allowing you to have the use of the equipment by payments out of your business income.
● *aids cash-flow forecasting and forward planning* – since you know exactly what the payments are going to be over a period that is, if you opt for a *fixed* rather than a *floating* rate lease. The first makes sense when interest rates are low and expected to rise; the second is best when the reverse situation applies.
The disadvantages are:
● *expensive to cancel* – if the goods you lease become obsolete, or your business runs into trouble, you either have to keep up payments for the full term of the lease or pay a cancellation charge – which can be swingeing. If you lease items such as photocopiers or computers where improved models are constantly being introduced you're stuck with the model you lease – unless you have an arrangement which allows you to trade up.
● *loss of allowances* – companies which are liable for Corporation Tax (see Chapter 6) can't normally claim the 75% first-year capital allowances on equipment which they lease, rather than buy outright (capital allowances, though, are due to be abolished completely after March 1986).
Leasing is now a highly competitive business and lease-rental rates vary from leasing company to leasing company – so shop around. For more details on leasing contact the Equipment Leasing Association (address in Chapter 11).

Hire purchase

Buying equipment on HP (which works like domestic HP) releases capital for other areas of the business. HP differs from leasing in that you *own* the equipment from the start. Interest is usually fixed at the outset and usually works out more expensive than a bank loan. As always, it pays to shop around since interest rates vary.

Factoring

Factoring allows you to receive up to 80% of the cash due from your customers more quickly than they are likely to pay.

Factoring means you hand over the book debts of your business to a specialist factoring company which deals with all aspects of your debt collection.

This saves you running your own sales accounting department.

You do, of course, have to pay for the factoring service. Fees vary and can be anything between ½% and 5% of turnover.

The factor advances you 80% of the value of your invoices – you get the remainder when your customer settles – which you can use as working capital. Since service fees are not cheap and often outweigh the savings, factoring only suits certain types of business – those with a turnover of £50,000+ who sell a large number of low-priced items.

You can get a list of factoring companies from the Association of British Factors, 12th Floor, Moor House, London Wall, London EC2Y 5HE; 01-638 4090.

Invoice discounting

This is a variation on factoring whereby only selected invoices are sold to the factor. You still control your own cash-collection system so customers never discover you are using a factor.

The factor pays you up to 75% of the value of the invoices. You pay him a fee of between ½% and ¾%.

Invoice discounting can be useful if you have a few relatively large orders to collect from reputable customers.

Most factoring companies offer an invoice discounting service but there is also a separate association: the Association of Invoice Factors, PO Box 37, Kimberley House, Vaughan Way, Leicester LE1 9AT.

Mortgage loans

These operate in a similar way to ordinary mortgages: the money borrowed is used to buy the freehold on business premises. This then acts as the main security for the loan with regular repayments made up of interest charges and principal, paid to the lender.

Building Societies do not provide mortgages for industrial purposes but they are available from insurance companies and pension funds.

Sale and leaseback

You can sell your freehold premises or items of capital equipment to a financial institution – normally a pension fund or insurance company – which then leases them back to you on a long-term lease for which you pay a rental charge. As a method of raising permanent capital for a company it has the advantage of say, not parting with an equity stake to an outsider. But it has drawbacks: it reduces the company's ability to borrow at a later stage since the asset you now lease can no longer be used as collateral against a loan. The tax aspects of sale and leaseback are complex, too, and work more in favour of some types of business than others so you need to take professional advice before entering into a sale and leaseback agreement.

On a smaller scale, sale and leaseback can be used when raising money for starting up. You can, for instance, sell and lease-back your car.

Bills of Exchange

This is a source of short-term finance, mostly used in exporting and importing, but which can be used for domestic business as well.

A bill of exchange is, in effect, a form of post-dated cheque which can be sold to a third party for cash – usually a bank or discount house. You have to pay for this service, usually in the form of a discount on the face value of the bill, often directly related to the credit-worthiness of the particular customer.

A bill of exchange has several advantages as a form of short-term finance: it is competitive with bank overdrafts; you can calculate the cost of financing a transaction accurately because the discount rate is fixed and not subject to interest rate fluctuations; you can free up capital for other purposes. This may seem like a longshot but we know of one entrepreneur who exhausted every other source for start-up capital and only managed to get going with a £75,000 Bill of Exchange.

Trade Credit

Once you've established yourself as credit worthy you may be able to take advantage of the trade credit extended by your suppliers as a means of short-term finance. Credit terms can be anything from seven days to three months from receiving the goods before having to pay for them.

But, weigh up carefully the benefit of taking the credit against the cost of losing any cash discount on offer.

PRESENTING YOUR CASE

Government support for new business ventures has meant that, in theory anyhow, there is plenty of money around to finance would-be entrepreneurs. Yet far more people are turned down by banks or finance houses than are accepted. Why? Quite often simply because the moneylender's experience tells him that the project isn't commercially viable but sometimes, regrettably, because the moneylender doesn't have the commercial savvy to assess the potential of the proposed product or service.

According to the financial institutions themselves, though, the main reason why applications for loans fail is because the would-be borrower hasn't done enough homework to come up with a *convincing proposal*.

If your business idea falls, as most do, into the grey area between an obvious winner and a complete dead duck, then the way you present your case can make all the difference between getting off the launching pad or going back to the drawing board.

The first thing to remember is that the moneylender sees himself as making an investment in your business which has to be profitable to him. So when you present your case you are, in effect, doing a selling job – perhaps the most important one you'll ever do. And since the finance institution, after you, may own the largest stake in your business, your sales pitch deserve to be prepared with at least the same effort and skill you would use for your most important customer. Proper preparation is the key to a successful presentation. Inadequate preparation is the most common reason for getting a refusal.

Many would-be business owners think it's enough to go and chat to the lender with all the essential points of their plan scribbled on the back of an envelope. But paper is the lifeblood of financial organizations and to stand a real chance of success you should be prepared to send the potential lender a *written report* in advance of your visit to give him the opportunity of studying your proposal and assessing its potential. The written report is important too, in that the man you see may not be empowered to authorize the amount of money you require so, however convincing an impression you make in his office, your proposal may well have to be sent higher up the organization.

The report should be concise, to the point and well presented – typed double-spaced with wide margins on each side of the page with pages numbered, section headings and a contents page.

This is what it should contain:

1. *Basic information* The business name and names and addresses of the directors/ partners.

2. *What you're asking for* How much money you want; why you want it; how you intend to use it and when and how you intend to repay it, e.g. £X in year one, £Y in year two; how much money you (and your partners/fellow directors) are able to raise.
3. *Your business* The nature of the proposed business and a description of it's products/services; production processes used; information on the potential market – how large it is, where it is, how you intend to sell to it; preliminary customers and details of orders (if any); a description of the present state of the project (e.g. have premises been found).
4. *Yourself* A short biography of yourself your partners or fellow directors. Lenders like solidity and respectability so mention facts such as age, marital status, children, whether or not you own your own house, any positions of trust or responsibilities held – e.g. local councillor, church warden, social club committees etc. Give details of your professional qualifications, previous employment and experience.
5. *Financial information* Forecasts of expected profit and loss accounts for at least the first one to two years. Explain the assumptions behind the figures. Allow for contingencies.

A 10% margin (at least) for emergencies – whether shown in the accounts or hidden – is quite acceptable. It is better to include it in the figures and then state in a note that a 10% allowance has been included.

Always tell the truth in your financial calculations and if challenged on the facts, be prepared to substantiate them. In your forward projections, be realistic. Cautious optimism is allowed, flights of fancy are not.

If you find the idea of preparing this report on your own too daunting, rope in an experienced adviser to help you. You may find one through the DOI Small Firms Service or your local Enterprise Agency (see Chapter 11) or use an accountant experienced in dealing with new business ventures.

It's useful, too, to ask your adviser or a business colleague to review the proposal before you send it to the bank (or financial organization) and then to cross-examine you in a simulated interview.

The next stage is to contact the bank manager or other lender, send in your written proposal and fix up an appointment. If your business has already started, it's a good move to invite him to come and see the business in action. Don't be surprised if he turns up unexpectedly – too many lenders have been caught out by prepared "busy company" visits. The classic example was a domestic appliance entrepreneur whose business subsequently collapsed. The bank manager was invariably steered to the end of the conveyer belt where finished appliances were being loaded onto vans for delivery. It later transpired that the vans only drove the appliances around to the other side of the factory where they were placed on the start of the conveyor belt!

The interview

Whether your potential business becomes a reality or is totally scuppered could hinge on the brief time you have to convince the lender, although if you have submitted a thorough report the task should be a great deal easier.

He wants to be convinced that he won't lose his money, and will actually see some return on it. He needs to be satisfied on the following points:

- *Character* – are you honest and reliable? Can you be relied on to uphold your side of an agreement?
- *Capability* – you might be honest and reliable but are you competent to run a business and manage money? Can you adapt to change? Can you get things done? Can you manage people?

- *Capacity* of the business – is the idea good enough and the market large enough for the business to generate the necessary profits *and* cash flow to repay the bank within the stated period with a sufficient margin of error if things go wrong? A proposal that relies upon everything going to plan will *not* be acceptable to the lender. He needs to be convinced that you will be using the money correctly and that you are asking for the right amount – neither too much nor, even worse, too little. Since start-up businesses are usually unable to provide much in the way of security, the financier will probably want to see you have enough money of your own at stake – this, too, is a way of testing your commitment. How much do you stand to lose if the project fails?

When you get to see the financier try to project an air of confidence, self assurance and decisiveness. Everybody is nervous in an interview situation and the financier knows this – but try not to let it show. Lenders are usually busy people so don't waste their time with unnecessary waffle – if you do he might suspect you'll waste his money as well! Let him dominate the interview and answer all his questions frankly. If you don't know the answer, say you'll find out and come back to him as soon as possible.

Don't dress outrageously. We heard of a swanky kitchen furniture manufacturer with a potentially profitable business who went to see the bank manager clad in a shirt open to his navel, bell-bottomed trousers and loaded with gold jewellery. The manager was not impressed and the meeting was deteriorating badly until the entrepreneur's minority partner, a sober-sided accountant, found an opportunity to tell the man to push off. The accountant was able to regain the bank's support, albeit on tight terms, and the couple sold out some years later for several million pounds. A briefcase, apparently, inspires confidence – even if it's empty. But don't do what we once saw an interviewee do, open it and allow a fusillade of pills to drop to the floor!

If and when it comes to talking terms, don't let yourself be pushed around too much. Talking terms implies that you will get the loan – the question is at what price.

Preparing your case and presenting it properly can be a long-drawn out and difficult process but it is well worth the slog.

PERSONAL GUARANTEES

As we've already mentioned, financiers feel it's a risky business to lend money to a company – especially a new one with no track record behind it. So, unfortunately, personal guarantees, which mean you undertake to pay back the money if the business fails, are now the rule, rather than the exception, for new businesses who need to borrow (apart, that is, from businesses which borrow under the Government Loan Guarantee Scheme). Guarantees make lenders feel more secure since they tie the business owner more closely to the fate of his business. From the point of view of the business owner, though, guarantees negate most of the benefits of incorporating as a limited liability company.

You may not be able to avoid signing a personal guarantee so here is some advice. First of all, a cautionary tale to show what you could be letting yourself in for.

In June 1970 a Mr Harry Goodman and his co-directors signed a guarantee for the borrowings of a company. In September, three months later, Mr Goodman and the company parted. He ceased to be a director or shareholder and severed all contacts with the company. Years passed and even the company's bankers who had received the guarantee were taken over.

In September 1979 Mr Goodman received a letter. It was a demand from the company's new bankers for £338,165 under his guarantee *plus* accrued interest. Mr Goodman was, to put it mildly, shocked.

His guarantee was made many years previously. He had since lost all contact with the company. Why should he be responsible? He hadn't been a director or shareholder for years. Anyway, the bank claiming the money wasn't even the bank to whom he had given his guarantee. It seemed unreasonable. He fought the case all the way to the Court of Appeal. And lost. The Court judged that he should pay £338,165 under his guarantee, and interest of £129,368. He probably also had to pay the legal costs of both parties.

The Court decided he was liable since he had not taken any "steps to terminate his liability under the guarantee".

The moral of this story is to make sure you cancel guarantees no longer needed.

We think it's sensible to note down the details of any guarantee you sign in a safe place where you will be periodically reminded of it – e.g. against 31 December in your 1985 diary. You can then decide each year whether to leave the guarantee effective or cancel it.

If possible, sign a guarantee for a fixed period, say five years. The bank will not always accept this – it depends upon the relative strength of the parties involved and who needs whom more. This way there is eventual automatic cancellation. You can always sign another one at the end of the five years.

CHAPTER 4 SUMMARY

- You need to calculate carefully how much money is needed to start and run your business. And, once calculated, whether the business is likely to be a commercial proposition.
- Are you able to finance it entirely from your own resources? Should you anyhow?
- The banks are not the only source of money for small business funding. Private investors, public and local bodies, merchant banks and venture capital providers will also lend on viable propositions.
- Money is available in the form of overdrafts, term loans, equity finance (where the lender takes a share stake in your business) and, in certain cases, as a straight grant.
- Other methods of financing a business are leasing, hire purchase, factoring, invoice discounting, sale and leaseback, bills of exchange and trade credit.
- The Business Plan is a crucial document when presenting your case to a lender. It should be prepared with great care. Remember, though, that the lender is not only weighing up your business idea, but assessing you (and your partners) to see if you have what it takes to succeed.
- If you opt for limited company status you might find you are required to give a personal guarantee for a loan. Examine carefully what you are letting yourself in for.

Chapter 5
PREMISES

The type of premises you need are inevitably dictated by the business you plan to run. It could be an office, a shop, a factory, a warehouse, or any combination of these. Alternatively, you may be planning to run your business from home. In this chapter we give you some guidelines on the main points to consider when selecting and fitting out premises, and what you'll need to know if you run the business from home.

Finding suitable premises is rarely easy but there are many organizations that offer free or economical help. The Department of Industry has staff around the country to help businesses find small industrial and offices premises. They, like county councils and chambers of commerce, often maintain a register of available premises.

CoSIRA (see Chapter 11) assists firms wishing to locate in rural areas of England by telling them of redundant buildings, and can sometimes help with the design and financing of the necessary conversion work. The relevant Development Agencies can provide advice and information to people in Scotland and Wales (see Chapter 11).

British Steel (Industry) Ltd (NLA Tower, 12 Addiscombe Road, Croydon CR9 3JH. 01-686 0366) runs a number of workshop complexes for small businesses in eight of the areas it supports. Premises are available on an "easy-in, easy-out" licence arrangement and each workshop is managed by an experienced businessman who can also provide general business advice (we list the BSC Industry workshops later in this chapter). There are also a growing number of initiatives at local level to provide small office and workshop facilities at modest prices; for example, LENTA Properties Ltd (69 Cannon Street, London EC4 5AB; 01-248 4444 ext. 226) was formed in 1981 to act as a catalyst in the supply of premises in and around London. It also buys and develops property itself. Whether any of these initiatives are relevant to your business start-up will depend on where you decide to locate. Otherwise you will need to find your premises by the conventional methods – business transfer agents, estate agents, local papers etc. (We'll come back to them later.)

LOCATION

Where should you run your business? You may intend to start up in your home town where you have contacts and where travelling to and from work is easy. But you would be foolhardy to set up shop locally without establishing, at least, that in the catchment area there is sufficient demand for your products or services to make the business viable, and that the economic characteristics of the trading area are unlikely to decline for any reason you know of, or are able to discover.

If you are totally flexible it's worth bearing in mind that financial assistance is available to firms who relocate to the designated Assisted Areas (see Chapter 4). It can be in the form of grants, reduced rents and/or rate-free periods. Whether these areas offer a rich enough market to make your business commercially viable, though, is something you should consider carefully. (The whole subject of regional aid was under review when this book went to press so please check the position when you come to start *your* business.)

Here are the factors you need to weigh up when deciding where to locate:

1. Is there a market for the particular type of business you plan? If you're selling a product or service aimed at a particular age or socio-economic group, analyse the demographic characteristics of the area. Are there sufficient numbers of people in the relevant age and income groups? Are the numbers declining or increasing?
2. If you need skilled or specialist labour, is it readily available?
3. Are the necessary back-up services available?
4. How readily available are raw materials, components and other supplies?
5. How does the cost of premises, rates and utilities compare with other areas?
6. How accessible is the site by road, rail, air?
7. Are there any changes in the pipeline which might adversely affect trade – e.g. a new motorway bypassing the town, changes in transport services, closure of a large factory?
8. Are there competing businesses in the immediate neighbourhood? Will these have a beneficial or detrimental effect?
9. Is the location conducive to the creation of a favourable market image? For instance, a high fashion designer may lack credibility trading from an area famous for its heavy industry but infamous for its dirt and pollution.
10. Is the area generally regarded as low or high growth? Is the area pro-business?

DECIDING ON PREMISES

Once you've selected the location, you have to consider the sort of premises you need, the size and how to acquire them. If you're interested in buying an existing business you can circumvent these decisions to some extent (we give advice on buying a business in Chapter 3). But choice is critical to your potential success.

What are the options? You can purchase the lease or freehold of an existing property, purpose-build your own premises, rent space in premises offering limited security of tenure (where many services are provided) or you can work from home. Here are some pros and cons.

Existing premises

Taking over an existing shop, office or any other form of accommodation has the advantage that the building is designed and designated for business use and can usually be adapted to your requirements without too much work. The disadvantage is that if you need substantial alterations, it might take some time arranging for the work to be carried out, and this will not only delay the start of the business but put severe strains on cash resources if it takes longer than originally anticipated. If planning permission is needed (see below) the wheels tend to grind slowly, and you can waste many weeks of non-productive time.

Lease or buy?

Purchasing premises outright frequently makes sense for an existing and viable business as a means of increasing its asset base. But for a start-up, interest and repayments on the borrowing will usually be more than rental payments – in the settling-in period most firms want to keep cash outgoings to a minimum.

Building new premises

If you have specific requirements which can't be fulfilled by available vacant premises you may have no option but to build from scratch. There are distinct advantages in starting off in a tailor-made building: given good design, the premises are exactly right for your operation and should allow enough flexibility to accomodate future growth so that there will be no need to relocate when you extend; it also may be cheaper to build new premises than to bring an old existing building up to the standards required by law. Again, you may qualify for government assistance which could make the proposition even more financially attractive.

The disadvantages are, obviously, the amount of time it takes to a complete a new building project – anything from six to eighteen months plus – and the costs and the amount of work and supervision involved in planning and seeing it through.

Purpose-built premises are not the route recommended for most start-ups. As well as requiring a hefty cash injection, the time delays could mean you'll miss the boat with your product or service.

Workspace premises

Finding premises small enough for a new business has always been a problem, and this is an area where initiatives have been taken in recent years. The government has made a number of important tax provisions with the aim of encouraging developers and others to build or renovate small industrial premises. Consequently, there are an increasing number of small workshops available in shared premises for light industrial businesses, craftsmen, new high-tech industries, small service businesses and others. Many of these are run by private companies who charge commercial rates but some local authority-built "nursery units" offer subsidized rents as a way of promoting employment in the area. They may even offer rent-free periods. If you opt for a workspace or a subtenancy in a building where the landlord has surplus space you may be able to enjoy communal facilities such as a receptionist; a telephone switchboard; a mailing room; telex, photocopying, word- and data-processing facilities; secretarial help; cleaning; conference rooms; and tea and coffee round the clock.

Workspaces provide an interesting alternative to conventional offices for one-man bands and young enterprises who don't want to tie up cash in office equipment or permanent staff. Apart from the cost savings of shared facilities, the proximity of other business people can lessen the sense of isolation suffered by start-up entrepreneurs. Communual contact can boost your business since tenants feed each other with ideas, goods and services, and sometimes sub-contract work to fulfil a rush order. We know one tenant of a London workspace who pays her rent entirely from in-house jobs! The flexible design of the building makes it easy to expand without moving – or, conversely, to contract gracefully. However, expanding in a workspace doesn't always make economic sense. Because service charges are worked out on a square footage basis, expanding without giving thought to increased turnover and profit means you pay for services you are not using.

Most workspaces are offered on short-term (generally monthly) licences, so there are fewer legal formalities than with ordinary premises. There are no complex lease agreements to sign, with the added problems of collateral and personal guarantees. And, should things not work out, there is no lease to dispose of.

However, there are drawbacks: since workspaces are often arranged on an open plan basis the working environment can be noisy, with little privacy or security. Neither do workspaces necessarily work out cheaper than conventional commercial property. But as charges are generally inclusive of rates, heating, insurance, fire protection and cleaning your admin costs are minimal.

Here are two examples of people who opted for workspace accommodation and why:

When inventor David Palmer finally got his product into production, (see pages 17-19), he needed basic office accommodation from which to co-ordinate the manufacturing/assembling operation and from which to co-ordinate the marketing and sales side of the business. Although many people are involved in making David's business succeed – factory workers, packers, salespeople – his office contingent numbered only two, himself and his wife. David had enough on his plate without the added worry of organizing and maintaining an office, so renting space in a redundant warehouse converted into small units proved the ideal solution.

When Sue Lovell-Greene decided to run a conference and seminar-organizing consultancy she considered working from home but rejected this for a variety of reasons, not least because she felt she needed the stimulus of a work environment. So a workspace with shared overheads and facilities suited her well.

To find out whether there are any workspaces planned or operating in your area contact the Industrial Development Officer or Planning Department of your local authority, or your local enterprise agency (see Chapter 11).

We give below a list of these we know about.

England
BIRMINGHAM,
   Birmingham New Enterprise Workshop, 99 Clifton Road, Balsall Heath, Birmingham (021 449 8125)
   Contact: Mr Isherwood
BRISTOL,
   Avondale Workshops, Woodland Way, Kingswood, Bristol BS15 1Q (0272 603871)
   Contact: Michael Winwood
CORBY,
   BSC (Industry) Ltd, Central Works Site, Northants NN17 1YB (05363 64215)
   Contact: G. Bent
COUNTY DURHAM,
   BSC (Industry) Ltd, Berry Edge Road, Consett, Co Durham (0207 509124)
   Contact: E. Hutchinson
CUMBRIA,
   Moss Bay Enterprise Trust, Mobet Trading Estate, Workington, Cumbria (0900 2197)
   Contact: Max de Redder
HARTLEPOOL,
   BSC (Industry) Ltd, Hartlepool Workshops, Usworth Road, Hartlepool, Cleveland TS25 1PD (0429 65128)
   Contact: B. Elsdon
LONDON,
   Aladdin Workspace, London Borough of Ealing, Industrial Information Unit, 24 Uxbridge Road, London W5 2BP
   Barley Mow Workspace Ltd, 10 Barley Mow Passage, Chiswick, London W4 4PH (01-994 6477)
   Contact: P. G. Shearmur
   Clerkenwell Workshops, 31 Clerkenwell Close, London EC1 (01-271 4821)
   Contact: T. Haines
   Great Eastern Workspace Ltd, Coldharbour Works, 245a Coldharbour Lane, London SW9 8RR (01-274 7700)
   Contact: Bob Gunning
   Kirkaldy's, 99 Southwark Street, London SE1 0JF (01-928 9515)
   Contact: Vivian Church
   Old Loom House, Black Church Lane, London E1 1LU (01-488 0144)
   The Old Nichol, 19 Old Nichol Street, Shoreditch E2 7HR (01-729 4243)
   Omnibus Workspace, 41 North Road, London N7 (01-607 7021)
   Contact: Gillian Harwood

Panther House, 38 Mount Pleasant, London WC1X 0AP (01-278 8011)
Contact: A. S. Perloff
The Portobello Green Centre, North Kensington Amenity Trust, 1 Thorpe Close, London W10 5XL (01-969 7511)
Rotherhithe Workshop, Hope Sufferance Wharf, 61 St Mary Church Street, London SE16 4GE (01-237 5299)
Contact: Ron Perfield
LIVERPOOL,
New Enterprise Workshops, South West Brunswick Dock, Liverpool L3 4AR (051 708 0952)
NEWCASTLE UPON TYNE,
Newcastle upon Tyne New Enterprise Workshop, Albion Row, Byker, Newcastle upon Tyne NE6 1LQ (0632 764244)
Contact: R. Dolman
NOTTINGHAM,
Hyson Green Workshops, Lindsay Street, Hyson Green, Nottingham NG7 6AP (0602 708779)
Contact: Brian Sweet
Sharespace, 13/15 Bridlesmith Gate, Nottingham NG1 2GR (0602 583851)
Contact: Virginia Stunt, Andrew James
SCUNTHORPE,
BSC (Industry) Ltd, Normanby Park Workshops, Normanby Road, Scunthorpe, South Humberside DN15 8QZ (0724 843411)
Contact: Alan Henderson
SHIPLEY,
Saltaire Workshops, Ashley Lane, Shipley (0274 596746)
Contact: Frank Khune
TYNE AND WEAR,
Tyne and Wear Innovation and Development Co. Ltd, Green Lane Industrial Estate, Pelaw, Tyne and Wear NE10 0UW (0632 382468)
Contact: Dr J. A. Hedley
WEST MIDLANDS,
Waterfall Lane, c/o A & J Mucklow, Halesowen Road, Cradley Heath, Warley, B64 7JB (021 550 1841)
WEST YORKSHIRE,
Pennine Heritage Ltd, The Birchplace Centre, Hebden Bridge, West Yorkshire HX7 8GD (042 284 3626)
Contact: Jennifer Holt

Scotland
DENNY,
The Denny Bonnybridge Project, 42 Stirling Street, Denny, FK6 6DJ (0324 825574)
DUNDEE,
Dundee Enterprise Workshop, Logie Avenue, Dundee DD2 2ER (0382 67951)
Contact: Mr Finan
GLASGOW,
BSC (Industry) Ltd, Clyde Workshops, Fullerton Road, Tollcross, Glasgow G32 8YL (041 641 4972)
Contact: S. Morrison
Govan Workspace, 6 Harmony Row, Glasgow G51 3BA (041 445 2340)
Contact: Pat Cassidy

HAMILTON,
   Hamilton New Enterprise Workshops, Dept of Strathclyde Regional Council,
   Portland Place (behind Brown's Car Wash), Hamilton (0698 283082)
   Contact: Tom Clark
PAISLEY,
   Paisley New Enterprise Workshop, Storey Street, Paisley (041 889 0688)
   Contact: R. Wright
FORT WILLIAM,
   Enterprise Workshops, Locgaber, Annat Point, Corpach, Fort William,
   Inverness-shire (0397 7391)

Wales
BRYNMAWR,
   BSC (Industry) Ltd, Blaenau Gwent Workshops, Unit 6, Pond Road, Brynmawr,
   Gwent NP3 4BL (0495 311625)
   Contact: Ray Davies
CARDIFF,
   BSC (Industry) Ltd, Cardiff Workshops, Unit A, Lewis Road, East Moors, Cardiff
   CF1 5EG (0222 486661)
   Contact: Graham Blackburn
PORT TALBOT,
   BSC (Industry) Ltd, Port Talbot Workshops, Addison Road, Port Talbot, West
   Glamorgan SA12 6HZ (0639 887171)
   Contact: Ivor Vincent
SWANSEA,
   The Swansea Business Centre, Alexandra House, Alexandra Rd, Swansea SA1
   1ED (0792 476076)

WORKING FROM HOME

Obviously, for a new business which doesn't require much in the way of equipment,
using your own home as your work premises has tremendous advantages: you save on
rent, rates, telephone rental, cleaning and, perhaps, additional staff.

Using a home for business purposes has always been something of a grey area.
Strictly speaking you need planning permission to do so. Many local authority planning bodies turn a blind eye to small businesses which occupy one room inconspi-
cuously and plenty of small business people get away with it. But if your work is
noisy, disruptive, or inconveniences neighbours, local planners may take enforcement action to stop you operating until you obtain their consent. If you prefer to be
above-board, or if your house needs to be altered in any way for the purpose (such as
building an extension), you should apply to the local authority for "change of use",
submitting the appropriate fee.

If your application is successful, you may have to pay higher rates for commercial
occupation. Again, permission may only be given with some qualifying conditions –
restrictions on hours of work, callers to the house, a set time before permission is
reviewed.

If permission is refused you have the right to appeal, but if the appeal fails you will
have to find other premises.

Some house deeds also prohibit use for business purposes, so check carefully for
restrictive covenants – the Building Society might well enforce them if they get to
know about it. You must also decide what to do about your house insurance. Using
your house for business, particularly if you store goods which are combustible, may
invalidate your buildings and contents insurance.

Also, you may be liable for capital gains tax if part or whole of the accommodation is designated for commercial use.

SELECTING A SITE

If you plan to operate a shop, restaurant or any business that relies on passing trade, choosing the right site to operate it from will be crucial to its potential success. Service firms and other businesses which conduct operations mainly by phone or post can put more store on cost and convenience.

Whatever your needs, it's worth spending some time just walking around the area where you plan to locate to get the feel of the business environment. Such an exercise can highlight problem sites, potential customer behaviour, when and why business activity is brisk or depressed.

It is useful, too, to chat to other business people in the area. They can tell you the pros and cons and provide information about available services. Reactions to the arrival of a new business can vary from outright hostility to friendly co-operation and it's good to know where you're likely to stand.

Also, as an application for planning permission gives adjoining businesses the opportunity to object, it is prudent to anticipate such battles by putting your potential neighbours fully in the picture. Courtesy does pay handsome dividends.

Some points to consider when selecting a site:

- *Financial constraints* You must strike a balance between the costs of operating the site and the likely income it will generate. For example, a site on the edge of town might have a rent of £200 p.a. but only attract 200 customers per week. A high street site with a rent of £20,000 p.a. could have the potential to attract 20,000 a week. However, it would be nonsensical to pay the higher rent if most of the 20,000 weren't likely to be interested in your product or service.
- *Marketability* Is the appearance of the premises attractive enough for customers to want to shop there? Are adjoining businesses healthy? Are there other commercial or retail businesses nearby which enhance your prospects or compete with you? Is there a steady flow of people passing by? Is the site accessible by public transport? What about parking? Can people park in front of the premises? Will a narrow pavement inconvenience customers? What are the noise and pollution problems?
- *Ease of operation* How easy is it for delivery vehicles to get to the site – and to park and unload once there? Check that there will be no difficulties with the mains services, that there will be enough electric power, water, gas, adequate drainage, and no problems installing a phone. Are there any restrictive clauses in the lease which would prevent you operating the way you want to? Is there any restriction on the time or days you can gain access to the premises?
- *Converting the premises* Will it be simple and not too expensive to alter the premisese to suit your needs, and create the right image? Is there any convenant preventing you making changes?
- *Personal constraints* Can you, the owner, get to the premises easily? If you drive, can you park without paying a fortune in car park charges? Although personal reasons are less important considerations, you might regret ignoring them if the police are constantly getting you out of bed to de-activate the burglar alarm.

CALCULATING SPACE REQUIREMENTS

It's always difficult to calculate just how much space you'll require, since your initial preoccupation is probably just surviving. Generally you won't want to use valuable cash to acquire unnecessarily large premises. However, if you make it past the starting post you are inevitably going to grow, and if you haven't room to expand you'll have to begin looking for premises all over again. This can be expensive, not to say disruptive. One possible solution is to take larger premises than you initially require and sublet the surplus accommodation on a short-term lease (provided the landlord agrees). If this isn't possible, it's more prudent to think small and gauge your requirements by where your business plan suggests you'll be in two or three years time.

To calculate your space requirements, prepare a layout which indicates the ideal position for the equipment you're going to need, allowing adequate circulation space. Shops require counters, display stands, refrigeration units etc. Offices need space for desks, copying equipment, filing cabinets, telephones etc. In a factory, plant, machinery may not only need careful positioning but you may have to consider in great detail the safe positioning of electricity cables, waste pipes, air extractors etc.

Always make cut-out scale models of the various items and lay these on scaled drawings of different size premises – 400sq ft., 100sq ft. etc.

By a process of trial and error you should arrive at an arrangement which is flexible, easy to operate, pleasant to look at, accessible for maintenance, and comfortable for both staff and customers.

The next stage is to adapt your ideal layout to the premises on the market. When you receive details of premises, a layout will normally be included. Make sure you determine precisely what *usable* space the premises have and what access you will have to services: a "cheap" office could become very expensive if the provision of additional telephone lines requires structural alterations and repairs to the fabric of the building.

The rental may relate to gross space rather than usable space. Older premises often include disused basements or attics which may contribute substantially to the rateable value, and to standing charges for electricity and gas.

Make sure there is enough storage space. Many business managements are frustrated when they can't take advantage of discounts on bulk purchases due to inadequate storage room.

Premises have to conform to a variety of regulations (see below) so the layout will have to be approved by the five appropriate planning, health and safety authorities.

SEARCHING FOR PREMISES

High street estate agents usually handle commercial as well as residential property. There are also specialist commercial property agents. Use them the same way you would when searching for a home. Tell them your requirements and ask to be placed on their mailing list. Look for their sign boards and press ads. As with house purchase, agents don't make any charge to buyers/tenants, only to vendors. Business transfer agents, who specialize in selling existing businesses, are also a valuable source.

Local newspapers contain advertisements of vacant commercial property, as do publications such as *Dalton's Weekly* and *Exchange and Mart*. Particular types of premises are regularly advertised in the appropriate trade magazines. The *Estates Gazette* contains details of property auctions and other commercial and industrial property.

However, since there are now various initiatives to help new businesses find suitable premises, we think it would be a sensible first step to contact the local authority (Industrial Development Office or Planning Department) to see whether they maintain a register of available property, and can help. Also your local enterprise agency (see Chapter 11) and the other organizations we mentioned at the beginning of this chapter may be worth contacting.

There is also the government-sponsored organization English Estates (St George's House, Kingsway, Team Valley, Gateshead, Tyne and Wear NE11 0NA; 0632 878941), which develops advance factories and offices nationwide, but especially where job creation is at a premium.

If you don't want to spend time and effort searching for premises, you can pay a property agent or surveyor to act on your behalf. Terms for finding property may be expressed in several ways – e.g. 10% of the premium or 1%-3% of the first year's rent. Fees are negotiable, but be careful of what you are committing yourself to.

SURVEYS

You will need to employ a surveyor to report on the condition and repair of the building. This is a wise move even if you are only taking out a short lease. The surveyor should determine the precise repairing liabilities from the lease. He can also advise on likely costs of repairs and alterations. You'll be charged on the basis of the time involved.

You should use a surveyor who is a member of the Royal Institution of Chartered Surveyors (they use the initials RICS after their name) or the Incorporated Society of Valuers and Auctioneers.

Surveyors are listed in the Yellow Pages or, you can contact the Royal Institution of Chartered Surveyors (12 Great George Street, London SW1 01-222 7000) or the Incorporated Society of Valuers and Auctioneers (3 Cadogan Gate, London SW1X 0AS 01-235 2282).

AGREEMENT

Whether you are taking out a lease, a licence, a tenancy agreement, or purchasing the freehold, the documentation must be examined very thoroughly to ascertain terms and conditions, and evaluate the restrictions hidden away in the small print. With a lease, there are some particular points to watch. Does the lease limit the use of the property? Can the premises only be used for certain types of business – this might clobber you should you want to diversify into a different activity. Are you forbidden to sub-let? What are your repairing liabilities? You may be just responsible for internal repairs and perhaps, external painting, or the lease might insist on responsibility for repairs and dilapidations – which means the tenant is responsible for all repairs and decoration, including the repair and maintenance of the structure, usually at specified intervals. What insurance payments are required? When are rent reviews due? What are the service charge implications? In a multi-tenanted building you could well find yourself liable for major repairs to lifts and central heating – or expensive security services.

You must employ a solicitor to check the conditions in the lease and generally assist with the conveyancing (see Chapter 3 for details of how to find one).

RENT

Assess whether the asking rent is reasonable given the property's current value on the open market. How does it compare with similar properties in the area? No two offices or shops are identical, of course, but finding comparable rentals for neighbouring properties should assist you in your negotiations. Also, check that you are being charged the right sum for the right amount of space. Commercial rents are normally quoted on a square footage basis and a slip of the tape measure could result in you paying for more than you're getting.

Commercial property leases almost invariably contain built-in provisions for regular rent reviews. And, unless the lease states otherwise, the landlord has carte blanche to demand any figure he likes. This can sometimes be double or more. So look at what the lease says about rent reviews, and what provisions it makes about challenging a rise. Does it, for instance, contain a clause agreeing to settlement by arbitration in the event of a dispute? If not, and you are unable to negotiate a settlement when the rent comes up for review, you may have to get a court order to take it to arbitration.

PREMIUM

If you are being assigned an unexpired lease you may be charged a "premium" by the outgoing lessee. The amount of premium can be substantial, especially for shops in prime locations.

The premium payment should be balanced against the length of the lease remaining. Premiums don't always reflect the value of the fixtures, fittings and goodwill of the previous tenant. Premium payments are not allowed to be offset against tax.

RATES

Eighty three per cent of small firms interviewed by the Economist Advisory Group in its "Small Firms Survivors" survey identified rates as having the single most negative impact on their business and it's undoubtedly true that rate bills are the biggest tax burden for many companies.

Non-domestic ratepayers provide more than half the rate revenue and many firms, understandably, don't feel they get value for money especially since they don't make use of such services as education, social services etc.

One way to avoid rates is to locate in an Enterprise Zone. During the lifetime of an Enterprise Zone (usually ten years), industrial, commercial and retail businesses are exempt from local authority rates and are only liable for water rates. The Department of the Environment will supply full information.

Since rates will inevitably account for a sizeable proportion of your outgoings it's as well to find out your liability early. Although estate agents particulars might give a figure for rates, any alterations to the premises or a change of use can affect the rates bill quite considerably. If you can't get quick information from the rates office (which often moves at a snail's pace), find out what comparable businesses are charged.

It's important to notify the rating authority if you're carrying out building work before you move in since rates are not charged on empty industrial premises. Some local authorities also exempt empty commercial premises.

If you consider your rating assessment too high, you can challenge it by appealing to the local authority Valuation Office. The tests to apply are: (1) Can I reasonably expect to let the property on the open market at a rent not less than the amount of the rating assessment? (2) How does my rating assessment compare with that of other similar properties in the area? If it appears to be higher then you may have a valid case for appeal.

You could have grounds for appeal if drastic changes take place in your trading area – one-way road systems, new parking restrictions, road closures, opening of new shopping centres – but the onus is on you to prove that trade has decreased for these specific reasons, rather than through seasonal factors or ineffective management.

You can appeal yourself or employ an expert rating surveyor, who will usually charge a fee based on the rateable value appealed against. Names are available from the Royal Institution of Chartered Surveyors (12 Great George Street, London SW1 01-222 7000) and from the Rating and Valuation Association (115 Ebury Street,

London SW1 01-739 7258) and the Rating Surveyors Association (c/o J. R. Clark, Montague Evans & Son, Awdrey House, 11 Kingsway, London WC2).

INSURANCE

The different insurance policies you'll need are dealt with in Chapter 6 but, briefly, your premises need to be insured against damage and destruction and your stock and machinery against damage and loss. If your premises are freehold you should insure the whole building. If you are a tenant you may only need to insure the fixtures and fittings because the landlord insures the building (the lease should tell you).

When employing outside contractors – builders, decorators etc – to refurbish the property it is a sensible precaution to find out what liabilities they are insured for and what the business is indemnified against. Painters have been known to set light to a building when removing peeling paintwork with a blow torch!

PLANNING PERMISSION

It is important to ensure that the premises you want can be used for your intended business *before* you enter into the legal transactions necessary to acquire them. The main categories of "use" are: *retail*, *office*, *light industrial*, *general industrial* (there are other special cases too).

If your business falls into a different category than that of a previous occupant you may have to apply to the local authority for a "change of use".

Planning permission is also required for all building operations, including new shopfronts, erecting illuminated (and some non-illuminated) signs. In conservation areas, for example, any change to a facade may be totally prohibited.

Applying for planning permission can be a lengthy operation for which you pay a fee. Information must be submitted on:

- the existing and proposed use
- details of external appearance and parking space
- details of floor space
- number of employees and their working hours
- the movement of vehicles to and from the site
- waste disposal methods
- details of hazardous materials stored

The application must be accompanied by a site plan and drawings.

Your surveyor or architect will help you with your planning application. He will prepare the specification and drawings, apply for permission and arrange planning consent. He may charge you a fixed fee or a variable fee of between two and ten per cent of the cost of the work, depending on how much he has to do. There are also separate planning consultants who make planning applications for clients and act for them in appeals against refusals. For details of a planning consultant in your area contact the Royal Town Planning Institute (26 Portland Place, London W1 01-636 9170). Sometimes a building contractor or even the landlord may be prepared to handle the planning permission details for you and at minimal cost.

CONVERSION WORK

The chances are that your planned alterations will be simple enough to be implemented with the help of the surveyor and a competent builder. If, however, they are more complex and you need to employ an architect or structural engineer you will need to give him a detailed brief on the work you want. He will then prepare a design for your approval, consult with the planning authority on whether the scheme is likely to be acceptable and obtain the necessary consents.

While it's usual for all the work to be done under the architect's directions and supervision, there are forms of building contracts where a specified person will represent your interests. When placing a contract ensure that your solicitor thoroughly checks and substantiates who is responsible for what. Depending on the size and complexity of the contract, architects' fees are likely to range between 6% and 12% of the cost of the job, excluding consultant's fees. If possible try to negotiate a fixed fee contract. Architects are listed in the Yellow Pages, and the Royal Institute of British Architects (66 Great Portland Place, London W1 01-580 5533) can tell you whom to contact in your area. However, it's always preferable to find an architect by recommendation – someone who has brought a job in on time and within the estimate without loss of design flair.

Regardless of whether you need an architect, you will almost certainly need a builder. Again, try and find one by recommendation. Be very precise as to what work you want carried out and get several builders to quote. Provide the builder you choose with a written schedule of the work together with a sketch plan. (Remember that once the schedule and price are agreed, variations can be very costly.)

Get the builder to acknowledge instructions in writing to avoid any hassles when it comes to finalizing accounts. Never authorize changes to a contract without first getting a fixed estimate of the cost.

OTHER LEGAL REQUIREMENTS

Fire, Health and Safety Regulations All offices, shops or factories employing more than 20 people are required to have a fire certificate, as are premises where more than 10 people are employed elsewhere than on the ground floor, or if explosives or highly inflammable substances are stored there. The fire certificate is granted by the local Fire Prevention Officer and it pays to consult him before you clinch the deal on premises since you may not be able to afford the work needed to bring the premises up to the required standard – and the Fire Officer can close you down without notice if you don't comply.

If you are moving into premises which have been previously occupied you need to check whether there is a current fire certificate and, if so, whether it will cover your business. Structural alterations or change of use may mean you need a new certificate.

You are also obliged to comply with legal requirements of the Environmental Health Department and the Health and Safety Executive (the former are generally responsible for commercial premises, the latter for industrial buildings).

The Health and Safety at Work Act (1974) is complementary to the Factories Act (1961) and the Offices, Shops and Railway Premises Act (1963). The HSAW applies fully in England and Wales and, with few exceptions, throughout Scotland. It does not apply in Northern Ireland, which has its own legislation.

Almost all workers are affected by this Act, including the self-employed and members of the general public.

The Health and Safety Executive is the operating and enforcement arm of the Health and Safety Commission which administers the Act. The main duty of the H & S Executive is to see that the health and safety laws and regulations are enforced. It does this through the appointment of inspectors who have the task of investigating accidents and dangerous situations.

Full information can be obtained from the Health and Safety Commission (Regina House, 259 Marylebone Road, London NW1 5RR 01-723 1262) or the Health and Safety Executive (25 Chapel Street, London NW1 5DT 01-262 3277).

Local authorities under the guidance of the Health and Safety Commission continue to have many responsibilities, mainly in relation to non-industrial processes and premises including offices, most shops, and coin-operated launderettes.

Inspectors appointed by the local authorities have the same status and powers as those appointed by the Health and Safety Executive.

Inspectors are empowered to take action through informal approaches to the owners of premises. If the breach is not too serious they will ask you to put it right without resorting to legal powers. However, they may serve an Improvement Notice if they are of the opinion that you are contravening any of the regulations. The notice will be withdrawn as soon as you comply with it. In more serious breaches, the inspector will issue a Prohibition Notice which means that you must stop trading altogether. Appeals against Improvement and Prohibition Notices must be made within 21 days. You can continue to operate under an Improvement Notice until the appeal is heard, but not so with the Prohibition Notice.

The areas where inspectors will be most diligent are:
1. Unsafe floors, passages and stairs
2. Inadequate and inefficient sanitary conveniences
3. Room temperatures too low
4. General uncleanliness
5. Poor ventilation
6. Too little light

Under the Fire Precautions Act (1971) you will need a Fire Certificate if you share a building with other tenants and the total number of people working in the building exceeds 20. The *owner* of the building must obtain the fire certificate.

You have the right to appeal to a Magistrates Court within 21 days if you are refused a certificate or you think the conditions are too onerous.

Even if you are too small to be legally obliged to obtain a certificate you still have to meet certain basic legal requirements such as:

- All doors which are entrances to, or exits from, the premises must open outwards
- Every form of fire escape must be distinctly and conspicuously exhibited
- Doors must not be locked during working hours in such a way as to prevent easy opening
- Contents and layout in a room must be arranged to allow free passage in case of fire
- You must provide and maintain appropriate fire fighting equipment
- Every liftway used in a factory must be completely enclosed by a construction with a fire resistance of 30 minutes

The fire authority can grant exemptions if they feel it is inappropriate for you to meet all these conditions.

Useful advice can be obtained from the Association of Consulting Engineers (Alliance House, 12 Caxton Street, London SW18 0Q1 01-222 6557) or the British Property Federation (35 Catherine Place, London SW1E 6DY 01-828 0111).

If your lease prevents you from making substantial alterations and these are nevertheless needed to conform with the health and safety laws you can make an application to the county court, which has power to order variations in the lease.

Remember that inspectors check that everything is in order and thereafter carry out spot checks. Penalties for non-compliance can be severe – closing the business until improvements have been made.

The Offices Shops and Railways Premises Act lays down minimum standards covering density of occupation, natural light, ventilation and heating. The Act also specifies standards for staff welfare in terms of number of toilets, provision of washing facilities, first-aid provision among others.

The Building Control and Environmental Health Department will advise you on relevant provisions.

In factories there must be at least 400 cubic feet of space for every worker. With offices and shops every worker in a room other than one to which the public is admitted must have at least 40 square feet of floor space *and* at least 400 cubic feet of room space. And, remember, you must take into account the space occupied by furniture and equipment.

There are also discretionary powers which can be used against you if you do not provide adequate facilities for ensuring the health of employees.

New shops have to fill in a registration form and you have to notify a shops inspector (an Environmental Health Officer).

FITTING OUT AND EQUIPPING THE PREMISES

New businesses, anxious to get going, often allow too little time for decorating, fitting out and equipping their premises, often only a couple of weeks. This can be a false economy. Not only can the mechanics of actually organizing the premises and acquiring the necessary equipment take much longer than anticipated but, since your internal layout is the face you present to the public, buying the first items that come to hand, rather than the best for the job, may burden you with a poor public image – and of course, if you've made wrong decisions on equipment, your business is not likely to function efficiently.

It goes without saying that for a shop, restaurant or any other business that relies on visual appeal to attract customers, the internal design is all important. If you're not confident that you can create the effect you want by yourself, it may be worth calling in professional help. It could be an architect (but this may be unecessarily expensive) an interior designer or a professional shopfitter (they are listed in the Yellow Pages).

Interior image-creating is perhaps a little less important for factories or offices – but a good designer ensures that space will be utilized effectively and that staff will be happy with the environment. Office planners and designers aren't always listed in Yellow Pages but you can be put in touch with them through the Royal Institute of British Architects or the Royal Institution of Chartered Surveyors.

Here are a few tips on layout. Ironically, the two wings of accommodation design – industrial and commercial – are drawing closer. With technology moving so quickly the key word in accommodation is *flexibility*. In other words, your office, shop or factory should be seen as a shell into which all the functional ingredients can be placed. Thus any building should preferably be symmetrical in shape. Dog-legged shapes are uneconomic and difficult to fit out.

There should be general floor to ceiling heights so that either floor or ceiling voids can be created to accommodate the cables and tracking required to service the ever-growing amount of high-technology equipment needed in any efficient small business.

Even starter businesses may require word processors, desk top computers, copying machines etc.

Flexibility also means that your business – industrial, retail or office-orientated – can expand or contract with minimum disruption. Modern office furniture contains all the trunking, switching etc to accommodate cables which a decade ago would have been permanent fixtures of the building proper.

Modern partitioning is not only soundproof but it can be adapted to accommodate shelving, doors and display units.

Of course, the cost of so much flexibility doesn't always come cheap, but before you decide irrevocably on permanent walls, corridors etc, it would be wise to consider the advantages of such flexiblity.

Deciding what fitments, furniture and equipment would be right for your business should be part of your overall planning operation. Spend time looking at what other businesses use and noting details of make and model. Go to exhibitions where relevant items are displayed. Get catalogues from a variety of manufacturers and suppliers and compare prices and suitability. Here are some publications you might like to consult (the reference sections of good public libraries should stock them):

Exhibition Bulletin – monthly publication which lists forthcoming exhibitions at home and abroad.

Business Equipment Guide – lists manufacturers and models for various types of equipment.

Shop Equipment & Shopfitting News – lists racking and display systems and up to date news on shopfitting techniques and trends.

Unfortunately, there is no *Which?* magazine for business, but there are many journals which cover business equipment. They not only tell you about new products coming on the market but run feature articles which can help your buying decisions. There are too many to mention here but you'll find them listed under subject categories in *Benns Press Directory*.

If cash is tight there is a large market in secondhand furniture and equipment. Local papers and *Industrial Exchange & Mart* carry ads, as do the appropriate trade magazines. And, with so many businesses going into liquidation, you can often pick up bargains when the assets of a bankrupt business are being auctioned off (look in the trade mags and the local paper for details of forthcoming auctions).

You can, of course, improvise if things are really bad. We know an electronics start-up business that economized on showroom fittings by buying a cheap load of ordinary scaffolding, painting it in bright colours and assembling it with planking. Very nice it looked too! The business incidently now has sales of over £3m a year.

HEAT, LIGHT AND POWER

Fuel bills will account for a fair proportion of your business costs but it's difficult to estimate their effect on your cash flow until your business has been going for a time (unless you move into a workspace where fuel is inclusive of service charges).

Utility services impose a standing charge and this can be high for commercial and industrial premises. Like rates, charges are levied on the size of the premises regardless of whether they contain areas you can't use, such as basements.

Here are some tips to help you economize on fuel:

- Make sure you are on the right electricity tariff. There are many different ones on offer.
- Don't waste energy. Leaving the heating on all night in winter uses up about four times as much energy as starting from scratch every morning. Turning down your thermostat by three degrees could knock up to 15% off your heating bill (but you are obliged by law to maintain a temperature of not less than 61°F).
- Similarly, lowering the washroom hot water temperature from, say, 150°F to 120°F could net you a 30% saving. Lighting uses only a fraction of the power that heating requires, but it can become significant if you get too neglectful about switching off. Likewise typewriters, drinks machines, photocopiers, fans and other office paraphernalia.
- Draughtproofing doors, windows, letterboxes, keyholes, skylights and floorboards pays for itself in fuel savings within six months, according to the Department of Energy.
- Carpets are the warmest way of covering a floor. Double glazing is expensive to install and probably won't reduce your heating bills sufficiently to pay for itself (but it might be well worthwhile to keep out traffic noise).

- If you are installing a central heating system remember that natural gas and solid fuel systems are the cheapest to run. If you don't have central heating, gas and paraffin fires have lower running costs. The Department of Energy estimates that it would cost £153 a year to heat a 4 × 3m room for 12 hours a day to a temperature of 68°F with an electric bar fire. That compares with £25 using a paraffin fire, £89-96 using an electric storage heater and £52-£84 with a gas heater.

CHAPTER 5 SUMMARY

- You should think carefully about where you start your business. There's little point setting up in an area which won't produce enough customers to make the operation viable.
- When deciding on premises your options are: to work from home, buy the freehold on, or lease part of, an existing property, purpose-build your own premises or start off in one of the new, but increasingly popular, workspace developments where tenants have the benefit of shared back-up facilities.
- Finding the right premises can be difficult, especially if you plan to start the type of business that relies on passing trade where the site is crucial to its success. You have to strike the balance between accessibility and affordability. As well as estate agents and the other conventional methods, several organizations now maintain registers of vacant premises and generally assist new businesses in their search.
- You need to calculate your space requirements accurately and once you've found suitable premises, organize a survey, scrutinize the small print in the agreement and assess whether the rent, rates and premium asked are fair.
- You may also have to apply for planning permission and you must take note of the legal requirements business premises have to comply with.
- Make sure you allow sufficient time to organize and equip your premises before you start to trade and learn how to keep your fuel bills down so that your running costs aren't exorbitant.

Chapter 6
RUNNING THE BUSINESS

KEEPING ACCOUNTS

The way a business records and stores financial facts is by keeping books. The owner/manager may keep these himself at the start, if the business is small and the trading methods simple. Later on you may feel your time could be spent more usefully helping the business to expand, and you might employ someone to do the books for you, perhaps initially on a part-time basis. Or you could use an outside bookkeeping service, sending them information periodically. Many small retailers now have cash tills that are programmed to analyse sales, to produce information about product gross margin, stock levels, and even to signal when and how much new stock is needed. Finally, if the work and profits warrant it, you might decide to employ a bookkeeper (or even an accountant) full-time.

In any event, the owner/manager will need to appreciate the basics of bookkeeping and choose the best system for his purpose.

THE RECORDS TO BE KEPT

It is essential to remember that having lots of cash, either in the till or in the bank, does not necessarily mean you are making a profit. Conversely, pursuing a profitable business can often lead to cash flow problems (see Chapter 7). The records must keep track of all items that affect both cash and profits.

Day books, sometimes called journals, or books of original entry, are where every transaction is initially recorded in the order of occurrence. Each day book is used to cater for one kind of transaction, so if there are enough transactions of a particular kind, you open a day book for it. For example, there are always enough cash transactions to warrant a *cash* day book. If your firm sells on credit, then you will need a *sales* day book.

Many small businesses trade in both notes/coins and cheques. For bookkeeping purposes these are both called cash, although initially a separate record is kept of each. The *petty cash book* is used to record transactions in notes and coins. Money in is noted on the left-hand page and money out on the right. Money out can include items like stamps, office coffee. Try to keep receipts since you may need to verify these records. Once a week, or daily if the sums involved justify it, total the money in and out to get a cash balance. Check that it agrees with actual cash from the till or cash box.

Receipts and payments made by cheque are recorded in the *cash book*. Again, money in on the left-hand page, money out on the right. Add up both pages every week to arrive at a cash at bank balance. Check this against your monthly bank statement and make sure that the basic information you are working with is correct.

Sales and purchase ledgers are where you enter details of suppliers and customers if you give, or take, credit. Ideally, there should be a separate page in the ledgers for everyone you deal with.

On the right-hand side of the purchase ledger you list the date, description, amount and cost of each item bought on credit. On the left-hand side you record details of payments made to suppliers.

The sales ledger deals with customers in much the same way. One important difference, though, is that credit sales are shown on the left-hand side and payments on the right. This is merely an accounting convention to deal with credits and debits. It is useful to keep records of the address, telephone number and person to contact with each ledger entry, to save time when chasing up payments, or dealing with queries.

Limited companies have to keep a *capital register* which records their capital assets – such things as land, buildings, equipment, vehicles – together with how much they cost to acquire. It also records disposals of capital items and the cumulative depreciation.

All the information from the "primary" ledgers (your basic records) are brought together in a *nominal ledger*. Expenses from the cash books and purchase ledger are "posted" on the left-hand side; income is posted on the right.

Each month every page in the nominal ledger is totalled, and used to prepare a *trial balance*. The sum of the left-hand totals should equal the sum of the right-hand totals, i.e. debts equal credits. This is the basis of double-entry bookkeeping and is what gives you confidence that the figures are correctly recorded. From the trial balance an accountant can produce a set of accounts, comprising Trading, Profit and Loss Account and Balance Sheet.

It is vitally important to keep records of everything relating to your business, and to maintain them religiously. Large stationers stock ready-ruled and prepared accounts books. There are several more sophisticated variations on the standard books, such as the *one-write* system where your double entry only has to be made once with the aid of sensitized paper. Get your accountant to advise you on which bookkeeping system would best suit your business.

The books don't have to be kept manually, though. There are special accounting machines which speed things up and reduce the likelihood of errors. However, these are fast being superseded by computers which are quicker, quieter and have the ability to produce and provide additional information.

There are now many microcomputers with readymade software able to perform the bookkeeping and accountancy functions. Whether it makes sense to acquire one for your financial records will probably depend on how the computer could help other aspects of your business.

The most common uses for computers beside accounts are for *stock control, payroll, sales and purchasing analysis*. Many small businesses also use them for *order entry, client records, mailing lists* and *word processing*.

Since the costs of microcomputers and the programs to run on them are tumbling fast, acquiring a computer is no longer the major capital investment it once was. Computers suitable for small business use can cost as little as £2,500 (you can, of course, lease them too). You need to add to that figure the cost of the programs you require, storage disks and a printer, which will bump it up somewhat.

Buying a computer isn't a decision to be taken lightly. Although the time saved and the number of potential methods of analysis possible could be valuable to your business, computers are unlikely to make economic sense unless you have, or anticipate having, a moderately large amount of data to process. And deciding which system to go for can be a major headache: of the thousands of systems on the market, no single one is ideal for all small firms since needs differ; the market is intensely competitive which often causes salesmen to behave unscrupulously and, to make matters worse, computer technology is muffled in jargon.

If you want a computer, spend some time mugging up on the technology and terminology so the salesmen can't blind you with science. There are any number of basic books on computers and masses of trade magazines which will enable you to get an idea of the different systems available. Computers are displayed in their droves at business exhibitions which gives you an opportunity to compare them. There are also twelve Microsystems Centres throughout the country, run by the government-backed National Computing Centre (Oxford Road, Manchester M1 7ED 061-228 6333). These centres offer impartial advice and "hands-on" experience of the systems they keep on permanent display. The service isn't free but could well justify the cost. Contact the NCC for more details and the address of your nearest Microsystems Centre.

If you don't justify the investment in a computer but would prefer not to do your accounts manually, you could make use of a computer bureau.

AUDITING THE BOOKS

If you are operating as a limited company you must have your annual accounts audited. After all, your creditors have no claim on your personal assets so the accounts filed at Companies House each year are their only way of knowing that your company is in a position to pay them. Therefore, an independent check on the accuracy of your accounts is required by law; and the only people authorized to do this are qualified Chartered and Certified Accountants. You can choose which firm you hire to audit your accounts but you must have one. Chartered Accountants have the letters ACA or FCA (according to how many years they have been qualified); Certified Accountants ACCA or FCCA.

It is important to remember that an auditor's duties are laid down in the Companies Acts, and neither you nor he has any power to change them. His job is to attach an auditor's report to your accounts which should read something like this:

> In our opinion, the attached accounts show a true and fair view of the state of the company's affairs as at ...... 198X and of the profit/loss for the year ended on that date, and are in accordance with the Companies Acts 1948-1981.

In other words he is saying that in his professional opinion your accounts are "true and fair", and to enable him to reach this judgement he has the legal right to inspect whichever of your books and records *he* sees fit, whenever he sees fit. Obviously, it is to the advantage of both parties to co-operate, but you should remember that you cannot legally refuse him access to information. If he feels you have not been truthful he will "qualify" his report, i.e. express his doubts about the accuracy of your accounts, which will inevitably damage your reputation with your creditors and the Inland Revenue.

Normally, for a small firm, the auditors (these will usually be a qualified accountant together with a trainee to do the number-crunching and boring leg-work) will come in a couple of months after the end of your accounting year and stay for a few days checking the books before finalizing the accounts back at their office. For a larger firm they may use one of the slack periods to come in part way through your year and break the back of the work (an "interim audit") thereby shortening the year-end work period.

Accountants base their charges on a combination of what they think you are likely to be willing to pay (if they don't think you are likely to pay a realistic fee they will not accept you as a client – after all, they're in business too!) and on an hourly rate. So if you present them with a disorganized heap of scraps of paper you will end up paying much more than if you had kept up a good bookkeeping system.

TAXATION REQUIREMENTS

There are two areas where taxation affects the small business – VAT (although this is not strictly speaking a tax, in that it is run by the Customs and Excise, not the Inland

Revenue) and either Income Tax (if you are a sole trader or partnership) or Corporation Tax (if your business is being run as a limited company).

VAT

VAT is a horrendously complicated tax. Essentially, you must register if your taxable *turnover*, i.e. sales (NOT profit), exceeds £18,700 in any twelve-month period. The general rule is that all supplies of goods and services are taxable at the standard rate (15%) unless they are specifically stated by the law to be zero-rated or exempt. In deciding whether your turnover exceeds £18,700 you have to include the zero-rated sales (things like most foods, books and children's clothing) as they are technically taxable, it's just that the rate of tax is 0%. You leave out exempt items. There are three free booklets issued by the Customs and Excise: a simple introductory booklet called "Should you be registered for VAT?" and two more detailed booklets, "General Guide" and "Scope and Coverage". If in doubt (and the language is not easy to understand) ask your accountant or the local branch of the Customs and Excise; after all, they would rather help you get it right in the first place than have to sort it out later when you have made a mess of it.

Each quarter, you will have to complete a return which shows your purchases and the VAT you paid on them, and your sales and the VAT you collected on them. The VAT paid and collected are offset against each other and the balance sent to the Customs and Excise. If you have paid more VAT in any quarter than you have collected you will get a refund. For this reason it sometimes pays to register even if you don't have to – if you are selling mostly zero-rated items for example; also being registered for VAT may make your business look more workmanlike and less amateurish to your potential customers.

Here's a simple example: You buy goods with a selling price of £100. On this you have to pay VAT at 15% so you actually write a cheque for £115. You then sell these goods at a basic price of £150, on which you have to charge VAT, so you will actually receive £150 + £17.50 = £167.50. You have paid VAT of £15.00; you have collected VAT of £17.50 so you send £2.50 to the Customs and Excise. You should note that this has absolutely no effect on your profit margins. If VAT did not exist your profit would have been £150-£100 = £50. Allowing for VAT you have paid out £115 + £2.50 = £117.50 but you have received £167.50, so the difference is still £50. In other words, VAT has no effect on a registered trader except to involve him in more detailed and tedious record-keeping than he might otherwise require. In fact, if you sell for cash, thereby collecting your VAT immediately, but buy on credit, you may derive a cash flow advantage through not having to pay over till the end of the quarter.

WARNING! The Customs and Excise started out as a body of men recruited to stop smuggling and other such criminal activities. To enable them to carry out their duties they have powers of search, entry etc which are sometimes said to be the envy of the fraud squad, so you would be well advised not to upset, deceive or otherwise get on the wrong side of them. Remember, ignorance of the law is no excuse. You may also need proof of your inputs and outputs; you should keep invoices etc for at least three years.

Income Tax

If you are operating as a sole trader or a partnership there is no legal distinction between you and the business. The business profits, therefore, are just part of your total income, and the amount of tax you pay will depend on what other income you and your spouse (if you have one) have in total.

The first point you should note is that *the onus of disclosure is on the taxpayer* – in other words, it's your responsibility to tell the tax inspector about your profits, it's not his responsibility to ask (though he will). So, as soon as you start trading, or getting any sort of regular income from a hobby, you should write to the local Inspector of Taxes and tell him that you have got income from trading, or which might develop into a trade, and that you will send in accounts in due course. You cannot then be accused of trying to conceal a source of income. Eventually, after some months or even years depending on how busy your Inspector is, he will get tired of waiting for these accounts and onto your doormat will drop an "Estimated Assessment" – a form which says your profits from dealing in second-hand Wurlitzer organs or whatever are £4,000; tax due at 30% £1200. This is not generally a serious assessment; it is really the Inland Revenue's way of forcing you to produce accounts. The reason is that unless you appeal against this assessment within 30 days (and the Revenue are quite strict about this) you will have to pay the tax even if you didn't make any profits.

Bearing in mind that you can forget anything you ever thought about being innocent until proved guilty – in tax *you* have to prove your case – your main means of defence is a well-kept set of books and a plausible set of accounts, preferably prepared by a qualified accountant. You will then negotiate with the Inspector about any doubtful items (for example, did you really use your car 80% for business or was it more like 40%?) and you will eventually come to an agreement and you will get a revised estimate. If you cannot come to an agreement there is an appeals procedure, but before embarking on this you should carefully weigh up the tax saving if you win against the time, effort, worry and professional fees it will involve.

Business profits (or Schedule D Case I as they are sometimes known) are taxed on a preceding year basis; that is, a year in arrears. So, if your accounting year ends on 31 December each year, your profits for 31 December 1984 would not be taxed in 84/85 when they actually happened, but in 85/86 – the next fiscal year. In a time of inflation this is a particular advantage, because you will be paying the tax out of the current year's (hopefully) higher turnover.

Choice of accounting date has a considerable impact on your cash flow, because Schedule D Income Tax is payable in two equal instalments on the 1st of January in the fiscal year in which the profits are assessed and the following 1st July. The effect of different accounting dates can best be shown by an illustration.

Suppose you draw up your accounts to 31 March 1984. This is in the fiscal year 83/84 (just – as the fiscal year ends on April 5th) and so will be taxed in 84/85. The tax will be payable on 1st January 1985 (9 months after the year end) and 1st July 1985 (15 months after). You are therefore getting interest-free credit averaging 12 months.

On the other hand, suppose you postpone drawing up your accounts for a month, to 30 April 1984. You have gone over the end of the fiscal year, the 30 April 1984 is in 84/85 and will therefore be taxed in 85/86. The tax will then be payable on 1 January 1986 (20 months later) and 1 July 86 (26 months) giving an average credit period of 23 months as opposed to 12. So for most businesses an April, May or June year end is better from a cash flow point of view than January, February or March. If, however, your trade is seasonal, you may want a year end half-way through it, so the profits of a good year may even out the profits of a poor one.

It is completely up to you to choose your year end, or to change it. You do not have to make up your first set of accounts for twelve months – they can be three, nine, fifteen – whatever is most beneficial.

There are special and rather complicated rules for working out the tax in the first few years, but the general rule is that the profits for the first year to eighteen months or so will determine the amount of tax to be paid for three years. It is therefore vital that these early *taxable* profits should be as low as legally possible, or preferably a tax loss; whereupon no tax would be payable for the three years.

There is nothing wrong or unethical about having an accounting profit but a tax loss; it's just that the rules and conventions are different in some areas and give different results. This is *not* an area for DIY attempts; get professional advice before 5 April each year, and a couple of months before your year end prepare draft accounts so your accountant can see what needs to be done to minimize your liability.

NOTE None of the above relating to fiscal years, payment dates or opening years relates to limited companies.

One point that frequently causes confusion is that the taxable profits do not depend in any way on the amounts actually taken out of the business by the owner. Suppose the profit and loss account looks like this:

		£
Gross Margin		15,000
Expenses:		
Rent, rates, light & heat	3,000	
Wages	4,000	
Management Salary	6,000	
	———	13,000
Net Profit		2,000

The owner has withdrawn £6,000 from the business to cover his living expenses. This is not regarded as an expense of running the business and is added back to the profits for tax purposes; so the taxable profits would be £8,000.

Corporation Tax

Because a limited company is a separate legal entity it has its own tax liability. The computation of the taxable profit is much the same as for Income Tax, but there are a few important differences. The major difference is that the amounts taken out of the business by the owners will be in the form of either directors' emoluments or dividends. In Income Tax any amounts taken from the business by the proprietor are regarded as drawings. The directors of a company are legally employees of the company and therefore the company has to pay Class 1 NHI contributions on their behalf, and the directors themselves have to pay Class 1 employees contributions. This may work out very much more expensive than the Class 2 and 4 contributions paid by the self-employed, particularly at the lower profit levels. Moreover, as employees, the directors have to pay tax on their emoluments under PAYE.

As far as payment dates are concerned, new companies pay their tax nine months after the accounting year end. There are no special rules for the opening years of the business.

The 1984 Finance Act reduced the main rate of Corporation Tax to 45% for the Financial Year commencing 1 April 1984, dropping to 40% in 1985 and 35% in 1986. This, however, only applies to companies with profits of over £500,000, so most new companies will pay the special "Small Companies" rate of 30%.

Losses and Capital Allowances

As mentioned earlier, it is perfectly possible to have an accounting profit but a tax loss. This is usually because the business has invested in plant and machinery on which Capital Allowances (sometimes called Tax Depreciation) were given. These are now being reduced; until the last Finance Act a First Year Allowance of 100% was given, so if you decided you wanted to reduce your taxable profits, by, say, £10,000, all you had to do was to go out and buy a useful piece of plant – a lorry, or a mini-computer perhaps – before you reached your accounting year end (hence the need for forward planning!). Now, until March 1985 the allowance is 75%, from April 1985 to March 1986 50%, and thereafter nil. Writing down allowances of 25% on the reducing balance will continue as at present. There is therefore an advantage in investing in capital equipment before 31 March 1986. There are very few restrictions on the type of equipment – it can be new or second-hand, purchased for cash or on hire-purchase; but there are no First Year Allowances on motor vehicles suitable for private use i.e. cars and estate cars. Vans are allowable.

Whether the loss is one created by Capital Allowances, or a genuine commercial loss, the form of the business is important. If it is a limited company then the losses belong to the company and can only be offset against company profits. There is no way that the directors can get the losses out of the company and into their own affairs. If the business is unincorporated, the business profits or losses form part of the individual's total tax liability, so business losses can cancel out other income of the proprietor and his or her spouse. There is particularly generous loss relief in the opening years, where if the business makes a loss in any of the first four years this can be offset against any income of the taxpayer or spouse in the previous three years; so if you have given up a job to start your business you may be able to reclaim some of the PAYE deducted from your salary. (See also Chapter 8 for PAYE.)

It can be seen from the above that there are definite tax advantages to operating as a sole trader in the early years when profits are likely to be low, or there are losses; whether this outweighs the protection and peace of mind offered by limited liability is a decision each entrepreneur must make for himself.

INSURANCE

It is essential to obtain insurance cover for your business. Just as the householder insures the home against events such as fire, flood, "acts of God" and the theft of treasured household contents, your business requires a similar guarantee against loss.

You have to decide on the level of insurance cover necessary by assessing the extent to which the assets of the business are exposed to risk, and the consequences the business would suffer in the event, say, of a break-in. Therefore, by its nature, the decision as to how much cover to carry is a commercial one and many find that the temptation to make that cover as meagre as possible is considerable.

Employment law requires that you carry some insurance cover, and you may very likely find that you are obliged to cover certain risks through contractual commitments on a mortgage, for example.

Business Premises, Plant and Equipment

These items all require insurance cover, but there are a variety of ways you can do this.

'Reinstatement' cover provides for full replacement cost, whilst 'indemnity' will only meet the current market value of your assets, which will involve deducting the depreciation first.

There are other factors which also require consideration. Removal of debris, architect's fees, employees' effects and, what can prove to be most expensive of all, the possible insistence of local authorities that the standards required for replacement buildings exceed those previously required for the buildings they replace.

Commercial Vehicle Policy

If you use your present vehicle for commercial purposes, it is unlikely that the private use cover you already have also insures the vehicle for commercial use. As such, the vehicle(s) in question should also be covered by a commercial use policy.

Consequential Loss

Insurance for consequential loss is designed to restore the finance of your business to the position it would have been in had not a disaster befallen it. Even if the replacement costs of plant, buildings, equipment and stocks are met by insurance, it will not compensate you for loss of business and profit incurred as a direct result of, say, a fire. You may still have to meet your overheads, and pay employees' wages etc, even though you may not actually be trading.

Employer's Liability

You must carry at least £2m cover to meet your legal liabilities for death or bodily injury incurred by any employee during the course of business.

Generally such insurance cover is unlimited, and the premiums would be directly related to the size of your business.

Fidelity Guarantee and Other Thefts

A Fidelity Guarantee will cover you from threats within and outside your business. Such a policy can protect you from fraud or dishonesty by your employees. A normal theft cover policy can be taken to protect your business premises and contents from the "outside" threats to your livelihood.

Goods in Transit

It may be prudent to protect yourself from loss or damage to goods in transit to customers. Until those goods reach the customer, and the customer accepts them, the said goods are still at your risk. This type of cover may prove especially useful if you trade in fine arts, antiques or fragile goods.

Personal Accident

Only those accidents in which the employer is held to be legally responsible are covered by employers' liability insurance. Further cover may be extended, on your behalf, to insure any individual(s) in your employ who fulfills a particularly hazardous function, for example, manipulation of dangerous machinery or heavy loads.

As a further safeguard, you could cover your own financial security, particularly if the business depends on your sustained good health and fitness.

Professional Liability

Anyone involved in giving professional advice would be wise to consider their possible liability arising from wrongful advice and negligence to their client.

Such insurance cover is particularly relevant to accountants, solicitors, management consultants and the like.

Public Liability

This protects employers against legal liability for death or injury to a third party on their property caused by defects in premises, negligent acts by you or your employees or from liabilities arising from certain products that you market (although you may need separate product liability cover for this).

Stock

In the event of a fire or another such disaster, your stock, from raw materials through to finished goods, would be at risk. It makes sense to insure these items against such risks.

Some other cover you might consider worth having is *credit insurance*. This covers you against defaulting customers and might be particularly important if you sell a large proportion of your output to one customer and are therefore at his financial mercy. *Legal expenses insurance* would pay the legal bills of any dispute in which you become embroiled.

Many insurance companies now offer "package" policies for different types of small business in an attempt to save shopping around the different insurers to find the best deal for each type of cover. Package schemes lump together the major risks in one policy and you decide how *much* cover you require (within set limits).

The established insurance companies offer schemes for shopkeepers, hoteliers, garages, farmers, to cover offices and many more besides. Each company differs in which schemes it offers and in the cover it provides, though.

We think package policies are worth considering if you plan a small business with fairly conventional insurance needs, and with contents to cover worth less than £100,000. They will certainly save you time – less literature to wade through (and what there is couched in plain English rather than insurance jargon) and fewer decisions to make as to the type and amount of cover required. They are far easier to administer, too, since you have only one policy and one premium to remember to renew each year.

Package policies may not work out any cheaper than policies bought individually – it depends very much on the complexity of the cover you require.

In any event, a sensible first step when thinking about insurance is to consult an insurance broker. He can offer help in sorting out your priorities, assessing the amount and type of insurance needed as well as discovering the best policies for your purpose.

Brokers are required to be registered with the Insurance Brokers' Registration Council (15 St Helen's Place, London EC3A 6DS 01-588 4387).

CREDIT CONTROL

Because of the high interest charges on borrowed money, it is tempting to have as little money tied up in working capital as you can get away with. However, you need to calculate carefully – if you have insufficient stocks you may lose valuable sales. If you don't have enough cash to pay your bills, creditors might become tired of waiting and cut off supplies. What you do want to avoid, though, is having too much of that working capital owed to you by debtors if you sell on credit.

Look at it this way: an unpaid debt is a loan being financed by your company. If you were carrying debts of £100,000 and paying 12% in overdraft charges, you would be losing £12,000 a year.

When deciding whether or not to offer credit terms, you need to calculate whether the profits contributed by the additional sales outweigh the cost of the funds tied up in the amount owed to you and the (hopefully few, but inevitable) bad debts where you'll never recover any money for the particular sale.

If you sell on credit, it's essential to get your debts paid as fast as possible. To do this you need to establish a *credit control procedure*. This means simply setting up a system for coping with cash collection. In other words deciding when invoices, statements and follow-up letters should be sent out and what to do if there is no response.

Here are some guidelines:
1. Send invoices as soon as possible. Don't wait until the end of the month, or even later, as many small firms do. Ideally, send your invoices at time of despatch.
2. Send statements to your debtors every month, as soon as possible after the month end. A low-cost device which might speed things up is to affix an "overdue" label to the statement (self-adhesive overdue labels can be bought from most commercial stationers).
3. Devise standard letters to be sent out at defined intervals after the due date. These should be carefully worded – friendly but firm. Too blunt and you'll arouse the mule in your customer; too polite and he'll ignore it. Set a deadline for payment, say 10-14 days after the first reminder which, if ignored, will trigger the next stage.
4. After two written reminders, switch to personal contact. Telephone the person whose job it is to schedule debts for payment and go back to him or her within seven days if there's been no result. Be prepared to be flexible – some money is better than none, and you build up strong customer loyalty if you help them over a temporary bad patch.
5. If the customer still doesn't pay, consider calling in a debt collection agency to chase the debt for you. Reputable agencies don't operate by sending in the heavies to make the debtor an "offer he can't refuse". They have evolved collection techniques based on their skill and knowledge which shouldn't harm your trading relationship with the customer. Most agencies charge a commission based on the percentage of the amount the agency actually collects, usually between 2½% and 10% depending on age, value and number of debts passed to them. Although debt collectors are listed as such in the Yellow Pages, there are rogues in this, as in any other business, so it's better to have a debt collector recommended to you. Failing that, you could contact the Collection Agencies Association (c/o The Grange, 1 Hoole Road, Chester CH2 3NQ). The CAA was created specifically for the smaller independent debt agency and members are required to comply with a code of practice.
6. Take your debtor to court. Many firms are reluctant to go this far, either out of fear of offending the customer (but who wants him if he doesn't pay?) or because of the legal fees involved. But you don't *have* to use a solicitor. The Small Claims procedure in the County Court is designed for people who want to sue and defend actions without a solicitor (more details from your local county court).

To identify where you should concentrate your effort and to alert you to customers' paying patterns, it's sensible to prepare an "aged debtor analysis" at the end of every month. For example:

Customer	Total due	Under 30 days	30-60 days	60-90 days	Over 90 days
Joe Blow & Co	£1,400	900		500	
Arthur Mind Co	£1,000	1,000			
Little Earner Co	£700				700
D. Grafter	£25		25		

You may also be able to speed up payment by using the "carrot and stick" approach, i.e. rewarding those who pay debts quickly by offering a discount for prompt payment (say, within 14 days) and charging interest on debts that aren't paid within your stated credit term period. The discount is supposed to be both an inducement to customers and a compensation for the additional interest on their overdraft incurred by paying you early.

If you intend to levy interest on overdue debts, you must ensure that this is written in your "terms of business" (see below) otherwise you probably won't be able to enforce it legally.

Regrettably, the carrot and stick approach isn't always effective since some customers take advantage of the discount, and still don't pay; others may pay a late bill but omit the interest payments, and it's debatable whether it's worth your while taking them to court on what, after all, will only be a relatively small sum.

Bad debts

If you religiously implement a credit control procedure along the lines suggested above, this will certainly reduce the risk of debts turning "bad". But, undoubtedly, there will be some debts which are impossible to collect despite your own energies, the intervention of a debt collector, solicitor or a county court judgement.

The only precautionary measures you can take are to carry out checks on potential customers before you offer them credit.

Ask the customer to supply you with a banker's reference and at least a couple of trade references. Do take up these references if for no other reason than to ascertain that the customer really exists (it's not unknown for unscrupulous people to print bogus letterheads to get credit). Even if the customer turns out to be legitimate, don't place too great a store on the trade references; after all, he's highly unlikely to have given you the name of a firm with whom he has had a bad trading record.

You can also check out a customer's credit-worthiness through a firm offering credit investigation services (they're listed as such in the Yellow Pages; the best-known firm is Dun and Bradstreet).

If the references prove inadequate, the credit check unsatisfactory or you simply don't have confidence in the customer's ability to pay, then it isn't sensible to offer him credit. Instead, if you want the custom at all, invoice him on a "pro-forma" basis. Pro-forma means cash before delivery – the required goods or services are forwarded only after the customer's cheque has been received and, hopefully, cleared by the bank. If this arrangement works satisfactorily for a period you can then reconsider your decision to offer credit.

If you think certain customers might go "over the top", you can set credit limits and, once the customer reaches his limit, stop supplies until some of the debt has been paid. You will have to rely on your personal judgement to determine the particular credit limit you set – assess how sound a risk you think he is. Ideally, keep the decision out of the hands of any sales staff you may employ – they are often biased.

Scrutinizing your customers' payment patterns can sometimes alert you to potential bad debts. Customers who occasionally send you a cheque for a round sum – £100, £1,000 – may be experiencing cash-flow problems and are merely trying to keep you sweet with a minimum figure while they try to resolve their difficulties, and sometimes they fail.

CREDIT CARDS

A retailer cannot accept credit cards willy-nilly. He must first register (or become "accredited") with the firms that offer them. Barclaycard and Access are the two most common credit cards in this country, although American Express and Diners Club are becoming more widely accepted.

Once accredited, the credit card company provides you with pre-printed sales vouchers and a machine on which to record details of the card on the voucher. There are three copies of the completed sales voucher: one for the customer, one for the trader, and one for the bank.

The credit card company will set a limit on the amount of sales the firm can make to any one person without referring to the credit card company. If sales exceed the stated amount the trader must ring the company for authorization. This is not as bad as it sounds as set procedures keep the calls very brief.

In an age of ever-increasing plastic money, credit cards undoubtedly increase sales, and businesses not accepting them are bound to lose out. People tend to spend more too when using cards.

Another advantage is that the credit card company takes the risk of non-payment, freeing the seller from bad debt worries. It is, in short, the simplest form of credit trading.

You do, of course, have to pay for it. The credit card company takes around 5% of each transaction. You may be able to negotiate a better rate than this, depending on the nature of your business. Another disadvantage is that sales staff are tied up longer with a credit sale than with a cash sale.

Holders of credit cards are supposed to notify the issuing organization if their card is lost or stolen. If you accept a stolen card in good faith, though, the credit card firm will pay you. Credit card companies, however, do send details of stolen cards to card-taking organizations with instructions not to accept them.

With cheques, you should insist on a cheque card and note down the number on the back of the cheque. This guarantees payment from the bank *provided* the cheque is for less than (currently) £50 even if the cheque book and card turn out to have been stolen.

LEGAL REQUIREMENTS

A great many laws govern the way you run your business. We look briefly at those concerning your premises and your staff in Chapters 5 and 8 respectively. Here, we tell you something about the laws designed to protect the consumer from the unscrupulous trader (needless to say, there are far fewer laws to protect the trader against the dishonest customer!).

The laws are both criminal, i.e. enforced by the police or the local authority (usually through its Trading Standards Department) or civil, i.e. you are taken to court by the customer.

The penalties for not complying with the main criminal laws may be a fine, closure of unhygienic premises, or even imprisonment.

A conviction under the criminal law may also enable the consumer to bring a separate civil action against you for damages. Consumers are often able to take legal action, though, without a previous criminal conviction. Their redress is a monetary figure to compensate them for damages caused by your breach of contract or negligence. This figure can be high. If, for instance, you sold your customers a faulty washing machine which ruined their clothes, they may be able to claim both the purchase price of the machine *and* the cost of the damaged clothes.

The fact that the trader doesn't know about defects in the products he sells doesn't absolve him from responsibility. Similarly, he is also guilty if he has done all he can to comply with the law and is unaware that a criminal offence has been committed.

The criminal laws which most concern traders are: the Trade Descriptions Act, the Weights and Measures Acts and the Food and Drugs Act. They cover many things but basically make it an offence to sell, or offer for sale, goods which are falsely described; to give short weight (or measure) and to sell food unfit for human consumption.

The Trade Descriptions Act covers the supply of both goods *and* services. It means you must take great care not to misrepresent whatever it is you are selling in any description you make. The description can be written (brochures, circulars, catalogues, advertisements), verbal, or even an illustration. For instance, you can't advertise a hotel as having "hot and cold water in every room" if it hasn't, or state that a product is "made in England" if it isn't.

With prices, you must not make false comparisons with manufacturers' recommended prices, or your own previous prices. If you want to make a "reduced price" offer, you must have offered the goods at the higher price continuously for 28 days during the last six months (although you can get away with it if you state that this condition hasn't been met).

Pure "sales talk" is unlikely to constitute an offence under the TDA. Describing a second-hand car as "a lovely little runner" shouldn't land you in trouble; stating that the car had just had a reconditioned engine fitted (if it hadn't) certainly would.

The most important piece of civil legislation is the Sale of Goods Act, which sets out the conditions which govern the contract between buyer and seller. Basically, it states that goods must be of "merchantable quality", "as described" and "fit for the purpose" for which they are required (we explain this more fully below).

"Merchantable quality" is a somewhat relative term and the interpretation will obviously vary with, for example, price – somebody paying £4,000 for a car is entitled to expect more of it than if he paid £400.

If the trader points out any defects at the time of sale, then the customer cannot complain later; nor can he bring an action if the defect is something a reasonable examination would have revealed.

As stated above, traders are liable to prosecution under the Trade Descriptions Act if they misrepresent their wares. Customers can also bring a civil action under the Sale of Goods Act if the goods aren't as described (the Sale of Goods Act doesn't apply to services). This can either be a verbal description or something stated on the packaging or on the product itself (a pair of shoes described as leather shouldn't turn out to be plastic).

Traders must be careful of customers who tell them the specific purpose for which they require the goods. If the customer buys on the trader's recommendation and the goods turn out to be unsuitable, the customer has redress even though the goods may be of perfect quality. For instance, if a customer told you he wanted a glue to mend broken china, then the glue must be capable of doing this. If it isn't then he's entitled to compensation.

If you have delivered goods to a customer and not been paid, you can't normally take them back. They belong to the customer even though he hasn't paid for them. Your remedy is to sue for the price. You can claim interest on overdue accounts *provided* you have drawn up written terms of business which give you the right to do so.

People who supply services are expected to carry out their functions with reasonable skill and diligence, and to charge a fair price. The Supply of Goods and Services Act codifies these principles and sets out the conditions which are implied when you provide a service.

Other criminal and civil legislation which may affect your business is the Consumer Credit Act (which imposes conditions on credit and hire-purchase agreements); the Consumer Safety Act (which makes it an offence to manufacture or sell an item which is in breach of the various safety regulations); and the Competition Act (which is designed to prevent anti-competitive practices against the public interest. Examples of such practices are price discrimination or exclusive dealing arrangements. This act is of more concern to big business but it does apply to small firms and individuals too).

Another piece of legislation, the Unfair Contract Terms Act, forbids you to contract out of your legal responsibilities by inserting clauses to that effect in your small print (this used to happen). Other trading clauses are subject to a test of "reasonableness".

There has been no room here to do more than give you a thumbnail sketch of the legislation which will affect your business. Inevitably, it's a complex subject, but it is important to familiarize yourself with trading laws – court cases are time-consuming and expensive, as well as giving your business the sort of publicity it could well do without.

Free pamphlets on various legal matters are available at your local Citizens Advice Bureau, or from your Trading Standards Department. There are also many legal books written in lay language. One such is *Your Business and the Law* by John Harries, published by Oyez Longman. A preliminary briefing from your solicitor is always sensible too.

DEALING WITH CUSTOMERS

Remember, when you sell goods and services, you enter into a legally binding contract. As we've seen, your customers have certain legal rights, and you can't take these away from them. You cannot insist that a customer accepts a credit note if whatever you've sold turns out to be defective, not as described, or unfit for the specific purpose the customer told you they wanted it for. The customer is entitled to a refund or, if they prefer, a replacement or repair. However, there is nothing to stop you offering a credit note if the customer has simply changed their mind. It is now an offence for shops to display notices like: "No cash refunds", "Refunds only within 14 days".

Some manufacturers give guarantees with their products. This, though, doesn't absolve retailers from their legal liability to customers. It's a bonus for the customer, and gives him/her a choice of who to complain to if things go wrong.

It's worth giving some thought as to how you are going to handle complaints. You're bound to get them – some legitimate, others not. Try always to take a complaining customer somewhere where they won't be overheard by other customers – it's not good for your image. Keep calm, be reasonable, and try not to argue. If the customer appears to have a good case it's best to act promptly to rectify matters. Even if the grounds for complaint appear slim, being generous, or even over-generous, might be a good, cheap form of promotion since the complainant is bound to tell friends how well you dealt with them.

The law doesn't cover all aspects of business, though, and most firms (except, perhaps, those who only sell cash-on-the-nail) need to draw up their own "terms of business" to cover such things as when payment is due, interest charges on overdue accounts and what guarantees are given about delivery. It's sensible to have your terms drawn up by a solicitor, since if the terms are inadequate you may not be able to rely on them in the event of a dispute, and the deal you've made won't become a legally binding contract.

Your terms won't be any use either unless customers know about them, and accept them, at the time the deal is made. So play safe, print them on the back of your order form, and get the buyer to sign that he has read your terms and agrees with them.

CHAPTER 6 SUMMARY

- Running your business will call for a regular flow of financial information.
- At the outset you must understand how the books are to be kept and choose a bookkeeping system that is appropriate to your size and type of business. Computers can drastically speed up and aid your bookkeeping and accountancy functions, and it may make economic sense to buy a computer for your business at the outset if it can also help other aspects of your operation.
- If you are going to trade as a limited company you will need to have your annual accounts audited.
- Whichever form of business you choose you will have to deal with the Inland Revenue on income or corporation tax matters and when your turnover exceeds (currently) £18,700 in any twelve month period, you must register with H.M. Customs and Excise for VAT.

- It is essential to obtain insurance cover for your business but you will have to weigh up the costs, and choose what type and how much cover you need.
- If you are selling on credit you should check the credit worthiness of your customers, and evolve an effective system of credit control to ensure they pay quickly, and know what to do if they don't pay.
- You also need to be aware of your legal responsibilities to customers and how to deal with complaints.

Chapter 7

CONTROLLING THE BUSINESS

The records described in the previous chapter are used to provide the owner manager with the means of controlling the business. From time to time these books are "balanced" and some financial statements prepared. The frequency of these statements will be an important factor in deciding a business's chances of survival.

WHY YOU NEED ACCOUNTING FIGURES

Liquidators say almost all the businesses they are called in to wind up have no reliable management accounts. "If only I'd known the financial situation earlier" is the failed entrepreneur's stock exclamation. New businessmen often see accounting as a bureaucratic nuisance carried out for the Inland Revenue's benefit alone. Those same people would never drive a car without a fuel gauge, speedometer or oil pressure indicator. Yet they set off at break-neck speed running their business with only a "gut feel", or perhaps the annual accounts to guide them – and break their necks. For them the end of the first year is the end of the business.

These words of Luca Pacioli, the Italian monk who wrote the first comprehensive book on accounting in 1494, are as true today as on the day they were written: "Frequent accounting makes for long friendships."

This case study will show you just how quickly and disastrously things can go wrong, without accounting data to guide you.

Fiona left a nationally known high-street fashion fabrics shop after fifteen years. She started at the bottom when the business was comparatively small and rose with it to finish up as the manager of a group of shops. She was offered voluntary redundancy terms in 1982 that left her with £8,000 cash and a company car worth £4,000. This seemed a golden opportunity to start up on her own and, together with a new boyfriend, she formed Fiona's Interiors Ltd, interior designers, contractors, decorators and contract furnishers. They used Fiona's redundancy money, together with an overdraft of £20,000 secured on her London flat, to finance the venture.

Neither of them knew anything about accounting, but good fortune brought them nearly 200 customers in the first ten months. This brought in the best bit of £75,000 with which they paid their workers, ran two cars and lived very well. The only people they did not pay were the creditors, who were surprisingly sloppy in calling for their cash. By January 1984 the company had run out of cash and overdraft facility. Fiona's personal credit card was at its limit and she began to borrow from friends to keep the business going.

The first time Fiona put any financial information together was when she had to prepare her accounts for the Inland Revenue, but by then it was too late.

The business was wound up in the spring of 1984 and the liabilities, shown overleaf, totalled £71,750.

Of this sum Fiona and her long-gone partner are personally responsible for £41,700. In less than fifteen months she had managed to lose her redundancy money, her home, her friends and saddled herself with debts that would take the rest of her life to pay. As if this were not enough some impatient building trade creditors took to making threatening phone calls late at night.

Fiona's Interiors Ltd

Creditors	Amount
Trade Creditors	30,000
Wages owed	2,500
Bank overdraft	21,500
Personal overdraft	5,300
Loans from friends	9,800
Credit cards	1,700
Arrears of rates, mortgage	950
	£71,750
Assets	NIL

Before you can really have control of a business, you need to prepare three financial statements. The Profit and Loss Account, the Balance Sheet and the Cash Flow Forecast. Using these as your guide, you can usefully analyse and even anticipate the performance of your business. Let's look at these in turn.

THE PROFIT AND LOSS ACCOUNT

From the information in your books your accountant can compile the profit and loss account. This account assembles in a logical order all the income – that is, money that has come in from sales, and the expenditure – that is, money that has been paid out to get those sales. It is prepared for a specific interval of time, as the example opposite shows.

But with some additional knowledge, a new business venture does not have to wait until the first year has elapsed before preparing a profit and loss account. It can be prepared in advance from anticipated events and assumptions and used as a guide to action.

The Medsoft case study will illustrate how this, and the other essential financial statements, can be prepared for a new business.

Medsoft is a new and very small high-tech venture situated in a town half way along the much-publicized Silicon Valley, off the M4 motorway. The company is in the business of selling dedicated micro-computer systems to hospital consultants. Their products allow the clinician to diagnose symptoms and monitor treatment results in a way that would not be possible without immediate access to a very powerful computer and a tailor-made program.

The business concept grew out of a chance meeting at a computer exhibition between Richard Kensall, then a successful programmer, later to be Medsoft's founder, and an up-and-coming young doctor. The doctor's problem was that he had too large a volume of patient data to classify and analyse.

Kensall solved the problem by writing a program that could be run on a micro that was being used as a word processor in another part of the hospital. In the process he had a stream of enquiries from other consultants, and eventually Kensall began to realize that he had stumbled across a significant market opportunity. He was confident that he could develop a range of software that could meet clinician's needs, and as most did not have access to a micro computer he could sell them one at the same time.

But Kensall made another important discovery when he was developing his contacts in the health service. Although hospitals were by and large "blue chip" customers, once you had them, getting an order for capital equipment out of them was a long slow haul. The path to an order started with convincing a consultant that you had the solution to his problems. This could involve several meetings, a demonstration of the system in action and perhaps even a period of clinical trials. Once the consultant is "sold" he in turn has to convince his fellow specialists, for example pediatricians, that the system is both worthwhile and would work.

At this stage the proposal then goes forward to a meeting of the medical executive, a group made up of consultants from various specializations such as general surgery, cardiology, pediatricians etc. They have to agree between themselves, on strictly medical grounds, which new projects should be put forward for approval to the Hospital Management Board. This Board in turn evaluates all requests for money, including those from the medical departments. Those they approve are passed on to the Regional Health Authority (RHA) for them to review.

In March or April of each year, just after the Chancellor's Budget, the RHA would be advised by the DHSS how much money it would be getting for the year. This news would eventually percolate down to individual consultants during May. If he did not get his cash then, there were two other opportunities, one in September after the half year budget review by the hospital board, and the other at the year end in February if any money was left over.

So all in all it could take four or five months to get a firm order and a further six to eight weeks to get the cash in from the hospital.

Medsoft's problems were further compounded by two other factors. Firstly, another computer company had begun to investigate the market. Secondly, the fragmented nature of hospital buying, meant that the decision-making power resided in over a dozen regional health authorities up and down the country. This called for a national sales effort if any volume of orders was to be achieved, and the competitors be kept at bay.

Profit projections

Despite these problems the profit prospects looked good. With the help of an adviser Kensall prepared a profit and loss account for the first three years. It was based on getting fifteen customers in the first year, all from consultants he could readily identify. It built up to 35 orders a year by the third year, a total of 75 over the three-year period. This represented a fairly modest 8% market penetration.

Medsoft's Profit and Loss Accounts for the Years Ended 31.12

	£000's	1984 £000's	£000's	1985 £000's	1986 £000's
SALES			225	375	525
Purchases in period	122				
Opening Stock	0				
	122				
Less Closing Stock	36				
= Cost of Goods Sold	——	86			
Gross Profit					
EXPENSES					
Salaries/Wages (Admin)	60				
Rent & Rates	55				
Advertising	16				
Salesforce	57	188	274	300	350
Net Profit (or Loss)			(49)	75	175

The first year's expenses were expected to be high as both the products and the markets had to be developed quickly. It looked as though Kensall would need most of his £50,000 savings just to stay afloat for the first year. But after that costs were projected to rise at a slower rate than sales, profits coming through in the second half of the second year's trading.

Now let us look in a little more detail at the elements of the profit and loss account.

The date is an essential ingredient in every account. For the profit and loss account it is usually stated "the year/month/week ended". This tells you the interval of time covered by the record.

The layout of the first year's figures include three columns of £000s simply to make the arithmetic easier to calculate and understand.

"Sales" is the name given to the income from customers for your goods and services. A particular prudent sales manager once said that a sale was not a sale until the customer's cheque had cleared, he had consumed the product, had not died as a result, and finally, he had shown every indication of wanting to buy again.

Most of us know quite different salesmen who can anticipate the most unlikely volume of sales. For profit and loss purposes sales income is usually recognized as having been earned when the goods (or services) are despatched and the invoice sent out. This has nothing whatever to do with when an order is received, or how firm an order is, or how likely a customer is to pay up promptly – if at all!

It is also possible that some of the products despatched may be returned at some later date – perhaps for quality reasons. This all means that sales, and consequently profit, can be brought into the business in one period only to have to be removed in another. (Obviously, if these returns can be accurately estimated, then an adjustment can be made at the time.)

Cost of goods sold. You may consider that everything you have spent in the business has gone into "making" the product, but to calculate the cost of goods sold, only costs strictly concerned with making are considered. These will include the cost of all materials and the cost of manufacturing labour. It is calculated in this example by adding the opening stock to the purchases and deducting the closing stock.

All the basic principles and practices of the manufacturing business apply to a service or professional business. For example, a travel agent would calculate his gross profit as follows:

Sunburn Travel

	£
Sales	200,000
Payment to carriers	130,000
Net commission income (or Gross Profit)	70,000

The money that is left after Sunburn Travel has paid the companies that carry their customers is the Gross Profit.

Gross profit is arrived at by deducting the cost of sales from the sales. This figure gives an indication of how efficient a business is at putting its product or service together. It also shows the maximum sum of money available to market and to administer the business, if you hope to make a profit.

Expenses is the general name given to the costs incurred in selling, marketing, administering, distributing and advertising your products or services. Some of these expenses may be for items that you have not yet paid for. The profit and loss account sets out to "match" income and expenditure to the time period they were incurred. So if you were preparing a monthly profit and loss account, for a month in which you did not receive a quarterly telephone account you would not enter a nil expense. You would properly estimate what you think you spent. Accountants call this "accruing".

Depreciation is an item we have not shown in Medsoft's accounts. Depreciation is how we show a Fixed Asset being "consumed" over its working life. It is simply a bookkeeping record to allow us to allocate some of the cost of an asset, such as a car or a photocopier, to the appropriate time period. So a car costing £4,000 with an expected life of four years could be depreciated at the rate of £1,000 per annum.

From a cash point of view you may pay out the full sum on Day One. But as far as an entry in the profit and loss account is concerned an expense called depreciation of £1,000 is incurred.

Net profit is what is left after all the expenses have been deducted from the gross profit. More properly called operating profit, net profit is what is left after interest charges on money borrowed have been deducted. If the business makes a profit then it may be liable for tax and a further heading would appear – net profit after tax.

The accounting requirements of the Companies Acts generally does not concern small businesses. A very sizeable majority of these are either sole traders or partnerships. There is no obligation for them to prepare accounts in any particular way, but obviously they would be prudent to follow the guidelines in this chapter. Limited companies do have to prepare accounts and file them with the Registrar of Companies. The Companies Act 1981 lays down a standard profit and loss account and balance sheet. These are similar to the ones described in this chapter but are by no means as clear to the layman as they are really designed for the company's auditors to use.

Fortunately, small companies are exempt from following the Companies Act guidelines – but all limited companies have to have their accounts audited by a suitable qualified accountant.

THE BALANCE SHEET

The balance sheet is the second essential financial statement and this shows the picture of a business at a particular moment in time. It shows where a business has got its money from and what it has done with that money once it has got it. Like a photograph, it is only true at the moment it is taken. A picture taken of you in a few years' time will be an accurate likeness of you, but it won't necesarily look much like the old you! We'll return to Medsoft to see how this balance sheet is constructed.

Kensall, Medsoft's managing director, realized that the techical issues surrounding his products were almost of secondary importance to the short-term financial problems. If he was going to survive long enough to reap the forecasted profits that were coming in the second and third years of his business plan, he needed more capital. He needed capital to pay for typewriters, cars and some packaging equipment. But, more important, he needed working capital, to finance amongst other things the build-up of stocks and a large debtor balance caused by the long delay between getting an order and getting paid; to pay for advertising and to keep his sales force on the roads; and, being a new business, Medsoft could not expect to be able to take much credit from suppliers.

With the help of his financial adviser he calculated that his financial picture at the end of the first year would look like the table shown overleaf.

Of the £124,250 that would be needed to finance the business at the year end, £103,250 would be needed for *working capital* (that is, the difference between current assets and current liabilities). His injection of £50,000 would be consumed by the first year's losses, but Kensall had excellent connections that could help with raising the Loan Capital, so he was not too concerned by this revelation.

Now let us look in more detail at the structure of this account.

The date. This is an essential record of when the financial picture was taken.

The lay-out. The balance sheet comprises two main sections. The "what have we done with the money" section is headed *Fixed Assets.* The "where did we get the money from" section is headed *Financed by.* And surprise, surprise, they have to balance, as the things a business has done with its money must equal the sum of money invested in it.

Medsoft Balance Sheet at 31.12.84.

		£
Fixed Assets		21,000
Current Assets		
Stock	36,000	
Debtors	75,000	
Bank	250	
	———	
	111,250	
Less Current Liabilities		
Creditors	8,000	
	———	
Net Current Assets		103,250
NET ASSETS		124,250
		———
Financed by:		
Share Capital		50,000
Profit or Loss from 1st year		(49,000)
LOAN CAPITAL REQUIRED		123,250
		———
		124,250
		———

Assets are the valuable resources owned by a business, which were acquired at a measurable money cost. There are really only three types of asset a business can hold.

Fixed assets include such items as premises, machinery and motor cars. These are assets that the business intends to keep over the longer term. They will be used to help make "products" and eventually profits too, but they will not physically vanish in the short term (unless sold and replaced, like motor cars, for example).

Working capital is the money tied up in "things" immediately involved in the business's products (or services), that will vanish in the short term. Stocks get sold and are replaced; debtors pay up, and creditors are paid; and cash circulates. The working capital is calculated by subtracting the current liabilities from the current assets. (Current is a term used to describe something that has a financial "life" of up to a year – although you will always have debtors, hopefully they will be different.) This is the net sum of money that a business has to find to finance the working capital. In the balance sheet this is called the net current assets, but on most other occasions the term working capital is used.

Investments. Finally, a business can put money aside over the longer term, perhaps in local government bonds or as an investment in someone else's business venture. In the latter case this could be a prelude to a take-over or merger; in the former it could be a reserve for future capital investments. It is not shown in this example as it is a fairly rare phenomenon in a new or small business, and these are usually cash-hungry rather than rich.

The *Financed by* section shows where the business got its money from. Once again there are really only three sources of funds.

Share capital, sometimes called equity; if the business is not a limited company it will be called 'owners capital introduced'. This is the money invested by the owner(s) or shareholders in the business. It can be put in at the start and increased at a later date. Shareholders are entitled to all the profits the business makes, after everyone else has been paid. They can reinvest that profit rather than take it out as dividends.

The Profit (or Loss) from previous years, ploughed back into the business is a second possible source of funds. In the second year of trading it will be possible for

Medsoft to reinvest the £75,000 profit it has made, into the business. Other terms frequently used to describe this source are Retained Earnings and Reserves.

This latter term conjures up pictures of sums of cash stored away for a rainy day. It is important to remember that this is not necessarily so. The only cash in the business is that shown under that heading in the current assets. The reserves, like all other funds, are used to finance a business and are tied up in the fixed assets and working capital.

Loan Capital is the final source of money open to a business. These long-term loans are from outside parties and could be in the form of a mortgage, hire purchase agreements or long-term loans from a bank. (An overdraft would be treated as a *current* liability and dealt with in the working capital equation.) The common feature of all such loans is that businesses have to pay interest on the money, and eventually have to repay the capital whether or not the business is successful. Conversely, if the business is a spectacular success the lenders, unlike the shareholders, will not share in those profits.

THE CASH FLOW FORECAST

One of the characteristics of most new or small businesses is a tendency to change their size and shape quickly. In the early months and years, customers are few and each new customer (or a particularly big order) can mean a large percentage increase in sales. A large increase in sales in turn means an increase in raw materials, and perhaps more wages and other expenses. Generally, these expenses have to be met before your customer pays up, not, however, before his order appears on your Profit and Loss Account as additional income, and perhaps profit. Remember that income is realized in the P and L Account when the "goods" are despatched and the invoice raised. But until the money comes in, the business has to find cash to meet its bills. If it cannot find the cash to meet these day-to-day bills then it becomes "illiquid" and very often goes bust.

Bankers have a name for it. They call it overtrading. Put simply it means taking on more business than you have the cash to finance.

The way in which a business attempts to predict the movement of cash is by preparing a cash flow forecast. Lets return to Medsoft to see how they prepared such a statement.

While the balance sheet gave some idea of the funds that the business would need to finance the first year's trading, it did not reveal Medsoft's cash requirements. Kensall knew that for the first six months, cash would only flow one way – out. Only after six months' sales effort would any cash start to come in, and then only a trickle at first.

Making some educated guesses together with his financial adviser he put together the cash flow forecast shown overleaf.

Salaries would be high in the first quarter, while programs were being developed and tested, and the stock build-up would have to start from Day One.

All in all it looked as though the business would need to find £178,000 cash if it was to survive the third quarter trough. This was much more than the £124,000 or so Kensall had predicted at the start of his calculations.

He needed to find a further £54,000 to survive his cash flow trough: £178,000 cash needed less the £124,000 loan he had already planned to raise.

Kensall and his financial adviser put together a report packaging Medsoft's projected financial statements, together with a market appreciation, a resumé of Kensall's achievements in the software field, and the background details of the others involved with the business.

They asked the bank for an overdraft facility of £70,000 but explained that they expected only to need about £54,000, and only for about three months of the year at that.

Now let us look in some more detail at the cash flow forecast.

Cash Flow Forecast (£'000s) for Medsoft Ltd to Year Ending 31.12.84

	Quarter 1	Quarter 2	Quarter 3	Quarter 4
IN				
Cash introduced	50	–	–	–
Sales receipts	0	0	20	130
	50	0	20	130
OUT				
Purchases	29	25	30	30
Salaries/wages	30	10	10	10
Rent/rates	14	14	14	14
Advertising	2	4	5	5
Salesforce	8	15	17	17
Fixed assets	21	–	–	–
	104	68	76	76
CASH BALANCES				
Monthly	(54)	(68)	(56)	54
B'fwd	0	(54)	(122)	(178)
Net Cash Flow	(54)	(122)	(178)	(124)

The top of the cash flow forecast shows the cash coming into the business, in this case each quarter. (It would be more usual for a new business to prepare a month by month cash flow but this is quite satisfactory as an illustration of the procedure.) Medsoft's owner put in his own £50,000 at the start of the year, and no further cash came in until the third quarter when customers' cash started to arrive.

The middle of the cash flow forecast shows the cash payments out of the business. Purchases of computer equipment, salaries/wages, and rent and rates make up the largest element of this.

The bottom of the cash flow forecast shows the cash balances. The quarterly cash balance shows the surplus (or deficit in brackets) for each quarter; the balance brought forward (B'Fwd) shows the amount brought forward from the preceding quarter; and the balance to carry forward shows the cumulative cash position, or net cash flow as it is usually called.

As a general rule if a business is alternating between periods of cash surplus and cash deficits, an overdraft is the answer. If there are no periods (or projected periods) of cash surplus then the business is undercapitalized.

In other words the owner must put in more cash, or if the prospects warrant it, more outside money can be borrowed, long term.

If you are asking other people to invest in your business proposition, the cash flow forecast will be even more interesting than the projected profit. This forecast will reveal your chances of surviving long enough to collect your "profits".

BUSINESS RATIOS

An understanding of financial reports is essential to anyone who wants to control a business, but simply knowing how these reports are constructed is not enough. To be effective, the businessman must be able to analyse and interpret that financial information.

It is highly likely that a business will want to borrow money either to get started or to expand. Bankers and other sources of finance will use specialized techniques to help them decide whether or not to invest. These techniques are the same as those used by the prudent businessman. Understanding them will help you to speak the same language as the bankers.

The starting point for any useful analysis is some appreciation of what should be happening in a given situation. If, for example, you fill your car up with petrol until it flows out, you expect the fuel gauge to read full. If it does not you would think the gauge suspect. (If you had left someone else to fill up the car you might have other doubts as well.) This would also be true for any other car you may come across.

Ratios, the tools of analysis

All analysis of financial information requires comparisons and there are three yard-sticks against which business performance can be measured.

First, you can see how well you are meeting a personal goal. For example, you may want to double sales or add 25 per cent to profits. In a more formalized business this activity would be called budgeting, then comparisons would be made between actual results and the budget.

Second, you might want to see how well you are doing this year compared with last, comparing performances against a historical standard. This is the way in which growth in sales or profits is often measured.

Third, you may want to see how well you are doing compared with someone else's business, perhaps a competitor, or someone in a similar line of business elsewhere. This may provide useful pointers to where improvements can be made, or to new and more profitable business opportunities. For this type of analysis you need external information. Fortunately the UK has an unrivalled wealth of readily available financial data on companies and industries. The chief sources of this information are explained later in this chapter.

The main way in which all these business yardsticks are established is through the use of ratios. A ratio is simply something expressed as a proportion of something else, and it is intended to give an appreciation of what has happened. For example, a percentage is a particular type of ratio, where events are always compared with a base of 100.

What results are you looking for?

Every business is looking for financial results in two areas that are vital to its survival. The first result looked for is a satisfactory level of profit. If you had some cash that you wanted to invest you would shop around and look for an organization that paid a good "interest rate" for the risk you were prepared to take. Once you had decided on, say, building societies, you would research for the best interest rate for the term you were prepared to tie your money up for.

A business is in exactly the same position. It has to give a satisfactory return to shareholders – or the owner(s) – bearing in mind the risk they are taking. If your proposed venture is highly speculative and the profits are less than building society rates, your shareholders (yourself included) will not be happy.

Also you must make enough profit to allow the company to grow. If a business wants to expand sales it will need more working capital, and eventually more space or equipment. The safest and surest source of money for this is internally generated profits – reserves.

The second result looked for is for survival, and to survive the business must be financially sound. Clearly, all businesses are exposed to market risks: competitors, new products and price changes are all part of a healthy commercial environment.

The sort of risks that investors and lenders are particularly concerned about are high financial risks. These risks include the danger of running out of cash, as Medsoft

FACTORS THAT AFFECT RESULTS

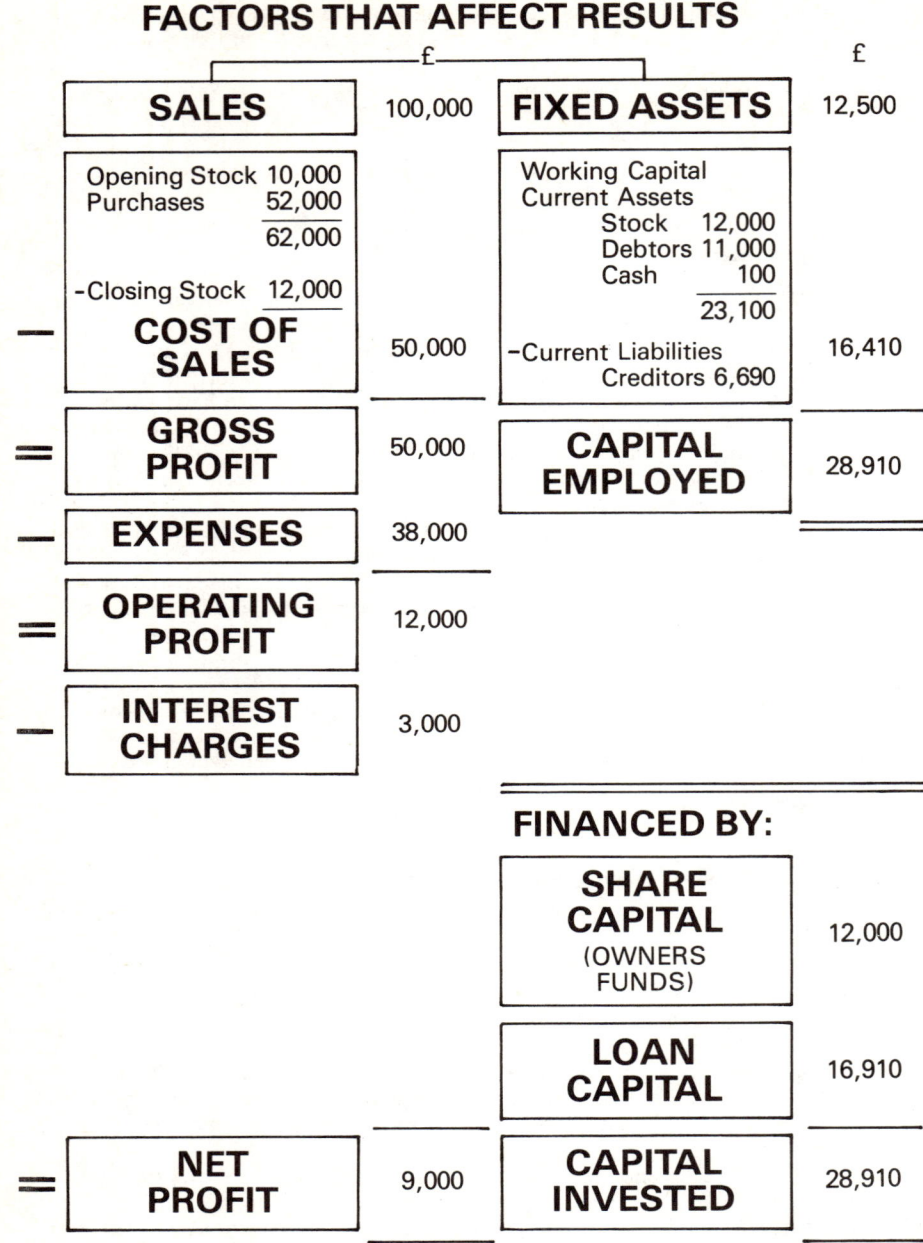

	£		£
SALES	100,000	**FIXED ASSETS**	12,500

Opening Stock 10,000
Purchases 52,000
62,000

−Closing Stock 12,000

— **COST OF SALES**   50,000

Working Capital
Current Assets
    Stock   12,000
    Debtors 11,000
    Cash   100
                  23,100
−Current Liabilities   16,410
    Creditors 6,690

= **GROSS PROFIT**   50,000

CAPITAL EMPLOYED   28,910

— **EXPENSES**   38,000

= **OPERATING PROFIT**   12,000

— **INTEREST CHARGES**   3,000

FINANCED BY:

SHARE CAPITAL
(OWNERS FUNDS)   12,000

LOAN CAPITAL   16,910

= **NET PROFIT**   9,000

CAPITAL INVESTED   28,910

nearly did. Or borrowing so much money that the interest charges weigh the business down.

Factors that affect results

Look at the table opposite and you will see how the results of the business, as measured in the profit and loss account and the balance sheet, affect business performance.

The *profitability* of a business can be measured in two ways. Both are important and to a large extent interdependent. *Return on Investment (ROI)* relates the profit to the capital invested in the business. In the example here this ratio is calculated in this way.

$$\text{ROI} = \frac{\text{net profit}}{\text{capital invested}} = \frac{9,000}{28,910} = 31\%$$

This is the fundamental performance ratio of any and every business and can be used to compare and contrast results. You could say of this result, for example, that it is more than three times greater than a building society's rate.

Profit margins relate various levels of profit to the level of sales activity. The first of these is the *gross profit* which is calculated by deducting the cost of sales from the sales and expressing the result as a percentage. In this example this is £100,000 (sales) – £50,000 (cost of sales) = £50,000 (gross profit); then £50,000 (gross profit) ÷ £100,000 (sales) = 50%. This ratio gives an indication of how efficient a business is at "producing".

Operating profit is calculated by deducting the expenses from the gross profit. This figure is then divided by the sales and expressed as a percentage. For this example this ratio is 12% (12,000 ÷ 100,000).

This tells you how well (or badly) the business is performing if you ignore all the factors outside your direct control. Those factors include interest rates and levels of corporation tax. Clearly changes in these will affect your overall results, but the changes themselves are decided by people outside the business's control or influence.

Net profit is calculated by deducting the interest charges (and tax, if any) from the operating profit, and expressing it as a percentage of sales. For this example the ratio is 9% (9,000 ÷ 100,000).

These ratios are useful when comparing one period's performance with another, or when comparing similar businesses. They are not universal, however, so comparing a butcher's profit margins with a paint manufacturer's would be meaningless.

A SOUND FINANCIAL POSITION

Maintaining a sound financial position for most small or new businesses seems to be focused on keeping away from overgearing or overtrading, the two rocks on which many founder.

Overgearing

A business has access to two fundamentally different sorts of money. Equity, or owner's capital, including retained earnings (reserves), is money that is not a risk to the business. If no profits are made then the owner and other shareholders simply do not get a dividend. They may not be pleased, but in the short run there is little they can do about it. Loan capital, or debt capital as it is sometimes called, is money borrowed by the business from outside sources; it puts the business at financial risk and is also risky for the lenders. In return for taking that risk they expect an interest payment every year, irrespective of the performance of the business.

High gearing is the name given when a business has a high proportion of outside money to inside money. For a new business with no substantial historical profits to invest in future growth, borrowing money represents perhaps the only option.

Gearing

Capital Structure	No Gearing	Average Gearing 1:1	High Gearing 4:1
	£	£	£
Share Capital	100,000	50,000	20,000
Loan Capital		50,000	80,000
Total Capital	100,000	100,000	100,000
Interest on loan at 12%	0	6,000	9,600
Profit before interest	9,000	9,000	9,000
Times interest earned	–	1.5X	0.94X

Look at this example. Our hypothetical business needs capital of £100,000 to make profits of £9,000 (before interest charges). If all the money is provided by the owner (or shareholders) there is no gearing, as this relationship between share capital and loan capital is called. If the owner decided to borrow £50,000, the gearing ratio would be 1:1. If he decided to go for £80,000 of borrowed money his gearing ratio would rocket to 4:1. This may seem to him at the time to be his only option. But if he pursues this course he will become overgeared. His £9,000 profits are not enough to cover the interest charges on the borrowing. Recent evidence from research into reasons for the failure of companies given loans under the Government Loan Guarantee scheme, show that a start-up gearing greater than 4:1 is nearly always fatal.

As well as looking at gearing, lenders will study the business's capacity to pay interest (that is, once you have been trading for a few years). They do this by using a ratio called "times interest earned". This is calculated by dividing the profit before interest by the loan interest. There are no hard and fast rules on what this ratio should be, but much less than three times interest earned is unlikely to give lenders confidence.

Overtrading

Overtrading is the term used to describe a business which is expanding beyond its capacity to get additional working capital resources. Sales growth in the early months and years of a business is as natural as physical growth is to a baby. As sales expand, the money tied up in stocks and customers' credit grows rapidly. Pressure also comes from suppliers who want payment for the ever-increasing supply of raw materials. The natural escape valve for pressures on working capital is an overdraft (or a substantial increase in the current one). Unfortunately, many small or expanding businesses do not have the financial controls to alert them to the dangers in time.

Here are the most important control ratios to monitor working capital.

The Current Ratio (a measure of liquidity)

A business's ability to meet its immediate liabilities can be estimated by relating its current assets to current liabilities. If for any reason current liabilities cannot be met, then the business is being exposed to an unnecessary level of financial risk. Suppliers may stop supplying or could even petition for bankruptcy if they are kept waiting too long for payments. In our example this ratio is:

$$\text{Current Ratio} = \frac{\text{Current Assets}}{\text{Current Liabilities}} = \frac{23,100}{6,690} = 3.4$$

This shows current liabilities covered 3.4 times, and the ratio is usually expressed in the form 3.4:1. There is really only one rule about how high (or low) the current ratio should be. It should be as close to 1:1 as the safe conduct of the business will allow. This will not be the same for every type of business.

A shop buying in finished goods on credit and selling them for cash could run safely at 1.3:1 (Marks and Spencer's current ratio is usually 1.1:1). A manufacturer with high raw material stocks to store and customers' credit to finance may need over 2:1. This is because the period between paying cash out for raw materials and receiving cash in from customers is usually longer in a manufacturing business than in retailing.

It is a bit like the oil dip-stick on a car. There is a band within which the oil level should be. Levels above or below that band pose different problems. So for most businesses, less than 1.2:1 would probably be cutting things a bit fine. Over 1.8:1 would mean too much cash was being tied up in such items as stocks and debtors.

An unnecessarily high amount of working capital will lower the rate of return on investment because it makes the bottom half of the sum bigger – ROI = Profit ÷ (FIXED ASSETS + WORKING CAPITAL).

Credit Control

Any small business selling on credit knows just how quickly customers can eat into their cash. This is particularly true if the customers are big companies. A key ratio in this area is:

$$\text{Average Collection period} = \frac{\text{Debtors}}{\text{Sales}} \times 365 \text{ (or days in period)}$$

$$\text{For our example this sum is } \frac{11,000}{100,000} \times 365 = 40 \text{ days.}$$

This shows that on average customers are taking 40 days to pay up. This area has been comprehensively covered in the preceding chapter. If you want to know something of a particular company's credit record then Credit Ratings Ltd (51 City Road, London EC1Y 1AY; 01-251 6675) can help.

Stock Control

Manufacturing, subcontracting or assembling businesses will have to buy in raw materials and work on them to produce finished goods. They may have to keep track of three sorts of stock: raw materials, work in progress and finished goods. A retailing business will probably only be concerned with finished goods, and a service business may have no stock at all. A key ratio in this area is:

$$\text{Day's Stock Held} = \frac{\text{stock}}{\text{cost of sales*}} \times 365 \text{ (or days in period)}$$

*Cost of sales is used because it accurately reflects the amount of stock. The sales figure includes other items such as a profit margin.

For our example the sum is $\dfrac{12,000}{50,000} \times 365 = 88$ days.

This shows that the business has enough stock in hand to last for 88 days. It is impossible to make any general rules about stock levels. Obviously a business has to carry enough stock to meet customers' demands or production requirements.

Credit taken from suppliers and others

Of course the credit world is not all one-sided. Once a small business has established itself, it too will be taking credit. You can usually rely on your suppliers to keep you informed on your indebtedness – but only on an individual basis. It would be prudent to calculate how many days' credit, on average, are being taken from suppliers: a very similar sum to average collection period. The ratio is as follows:

$$\text{Average credit period} = \frac{\text{creditors}}{\text{purchases in period}} \times 365 \text{ (days in period)}$$

Which for our example is $\dfrac{6,690}{52,000} \times 365 = 47$ days

As a rough rule of thumb you should be looking for at least as much credit from your suppliers as you are giving to your customers. (In our example we are giving 40 days and taking 47.)

Remember also it is useful to have more than one source of supply for important materials, and you should gather some facts and figures on suppliers' credit policy before dealing with them. The directories described in Chapter 9 will tell you how to go about finding sources of supply.

Cash Control

The residual element in the control of working capital is cash or, if there is no cash left, the size of overdraft needed in a particular period.

Usually, the amount of cash available to a small business is finite and specific, as is the size of overdraft it can take. Stock levels, creditor and debtor policies and other working capital elements have to be decided with these limits in mind. This information is assembled in the cash flow forecast, which was explained above.

SOURCES OF FINANCIAL INFORMATION

To help you prepare your start-up financial plans it will be very useful to know ratios for another company or even an industry as a whole. A number of organizations have been set up to help you find this information.

Some of the most useful sources in this field are listed below, together with an outline of their services. At least one of these, the Centre for Interfirm Comparisons, carries out its work both inside an individual business and in the industry sector in general. Many of these organizations' services extend to cover international markets. Much of their published information is freely available in the reference section of major public libraries. Examples of one of these services is given at the end of this chapter.

The Centre for Interfirm Comparison Ltd, 8 West Stockwell Street, Colchester, Essex CO1 1HN; 0206 62274, and 25 Bloomsbury Square, London WC1A 2PJ; 01-637 8406. This is a non-profit making organization, established in 1959 by the British Institute of Management and the British Productivity Council to meet the need for a neutral, expert body to conduct interfirm comparisons on a confidential basis, and to help managers to improve business performance. Participating firms feed a range of information into the centre, who in turn provide yardsticks against which they can compare systematically the performance of every important aspect of their business with other, similar firms. Together with the yardstick ratios come written reports on the findings and ideas for action, but only, of course, to the participating firms, and even then only on a 'comparative' basis so that no one company's data can ever by identified.

The uniqueness of this method rests in part on the data itself which goes far beyond anything supplied in companies' annual returns to Companies House or production monitor figures. Thousands of companies, large and small, have participated, and comparisons are made in over 100 industries, trades, services and professions both in the UK and abroad.

The centre publishes a number of free booklets that explain their activities, the ratios they use and why, and, more importantly, how you can use them to improve performance.

Credit Ratings Ltd, 51 City Road, London EC1Y 1AY; 01-251 6675. This company provides an ad hoc subscription service credit report. The cost varies from £15 to £12 for each report, which can normally be provided within 24 hours. Each credit report provides a company profile, financial performance figures for the past two years, and eight credit ratios (including an estimate of how long they normally take to pay their bills). These ratios are then compared with the average for that industry, and are followed by a short commentary bringing important factors to the reader's attention.

The Companies Registration Office keeps records of all limited companies.

The records kept include financial statements, accounts, directors' names and addresses, shareholders, and changes of name and structure. The information is available on microfiche at £1 per company, and can be photocopied at 10p per sheet. This service is available to personal callers only. There are a number of commercial organizations who will obtain this information for you. Two such organizations are: The Company Search Centre, 1-3 Leonard Street, London EC2A 4AQ; 01-251 2566; and Extel, 37-45 Paul Street, London EC2A 4PB; 01-253 3400, telex 262687. The charges for this service are about £3 to £3.50 for a microfiche of each company, or for a photocopy of the report and accounts, around £8.

Extel Quoted Service cards are published each year by the Exchange Telegraph Co Ltd. Cards for each of the 3,000 UK companies quoted on the Stock Exchange contain the following information: name and business of the company together with details of subsidiaries and associates; the date on which the company was registered (formed), along with any change of name or status (e.g. private to public); directors – their positions (chairman, managing director etc) and their shareholdings, as well as the names of the company secretary, bankers, auditors and solicitors. Ten years' profit and loss accounts and at least three years' balance sheets are given, together with sources and applications of funds statements. The highest and lowest share prices over the ten-year period are also given, as well as the chairman's latest statement on the company position.

A news card is published three or four times a year, giving details of dividends declared, board changes, acquisitions, liquidations, loans raised and other elements of operating information. A selection of these cards is held in many reference libraries. Individual cards can be bought for £1.95 from Extel Statistical Services Ltd at the above address or from the Manchester Office; 061-236 5802.

Extel Unquoted Service provides a similar service for some 2,000 ordinary companies. These cards cost £5.85 each, as considerably more work has to be done to get at this information, and the call for it is less.

The Financial Times Index, introduced in 1981, provides a monthly and yearly index to the references to some 35,000 companies. Instead of thumbing through back issues, you can locate the abstract of each story by using the corporate index, the general index covering products and industries, or the personality section covering key people. It costs £240 per annum, and is available from Financial Times Information Ltd, Minster House, Arthur Street, London EC4R 9AX. The index is also available on microfiche, floppy disk and magnetic tape.

ICC Business Ratios produce 150 business sector reports analysing the performance of some 12,000 leading UK companies over a three-year period. For each sector (for example, window manufacturers, retail chemists, the toy industry or computer equipment) key performance ratios are shown for each company in the sector and an average for the sector as a whole. You can therefore use this information to compare your performance, actual or projected, against an industry standard. There are 19 key ratios, and they cover profitability, liquidity, asset utilization, gearing, productivity and exports. Growth rates are monitored, including sales, total assets, capital employed, average wages and exports. It is thus possible to see quickly which company is growing the fastest in your sector, and to compare your growth against the best, the worst or the average. Reports are priced at about £100 each, and further details are available from The Business Ratio Manager, ICC Business Ratios, 23 City Road, London EC1Y 1AA; 01-638 2946.

Jordan's Business Information Service, Jordan House, 47 Brunswick Place, London N1 6EE; 01-253 3030. They also have offices in Bristol, Cardiff, Edinburgh and the Isle of Man. The Company Search Department can get you information on any UK company in Companies House, and their rapid reply service can guarantee a despatch within a few hours. Alternatively, if you really are in a hurry, they have a telex and telephone service. They also produce a range of annual business surveys covering some 80 industries, priced between £8 and £85.

Jordan's new companies service could be particularly useful for a small company looking for sales leads. Over 5,000 new companies are incorporated each month, and Jordans report on about half. They eliminate the companies with convenience directors and registered offices (each of which offers no contact point), leaving several thousand 'genuine' new potential customers each month. Naturally, these companies could be anywhere in the UK, so in order to make the service more useful to small businesses, they produce a county-by-county service, with London split into eight. These selected services cost from £60 to £600 per annum. The whole UK service could cost around £4,000, and London alone around £2,000. At just over 13p a 'lead', this could prove a cost-effective way to expand sales.

CHAPTER 7 SUMMARY

- A large proportion of businesses fail because they don't keep reliable management accounts.
- As well as recording financial events as they occur, the "books" mentioned in the last chapter have to be balanced each month and the following financial statements prepared: *a profit and loss account* which matches income to expenditure; a *balance sheet* which shows your assets and liabilities at the end of the period; a *cash flow forecast* which assesses the likely pattern of cash in and out of the business in the future.
- These accounts need to be interpreted to produce ratios which monitor the performance of your business. Done properly, this exercise should enable you to avoid two of the common pitfalls for new businesses: overtrading and overgearing.
- There are many sources of financial information to help you find suppliers and important customers, and to help you discover how your competitors are performing.

Chapter 8
EMPLOYING STAFF

You may not yet have considered it necessary to think about employing staff. However, demands on your time, limitations in expertise or just good business sense may point to the need to take on an extra pair of hands.

This chapter focuses on the key factors relating to employment in small business. We hope it will help you avoid some of the common pitfalls, and make the best of your investment in human resources.

Finding good employees can be a costly and time-consuming business, but not half as difficult as getting rid of the wrong people. Start by deciding why you need to employ someone, and for what tasks. Avoid the natural temptation to think in standard job-title terms. The chances are that it isn't just a typist you need, but a multi-skilled, multi-experienced person who can handle everything from reception and correspondence to stock control and bookkeeping.

DEFINING YOUR NEEDS

Before writing an advertisement or approaching an employment agency you need to prepare a specification and description for the job. Don't worry about the jargon; these are simply checklists which indicate:
- the qualifications, knowledge, experience, personal qualities etc that the job demands.
- the main responsibilities, functions, tasks that you expect the person appointed to take on.

Following this process will ensure that you have a clear awareness of your needs, and will provide you with a valuable, time-saving aid to selection when the applications start flooding in.

Job title This may be more difficult in the small firm where a job involves a range of activities, but hopefully you can come up with something that reflects the nature of the job.

Description of the job A brief statement of the main purposes, responsibilities and tasks. Think in terms of: What has to be done? How will it be done? What equipment will be used? Will it involve working with others?

Performance standards What do you expect the job-holder to achieve? How will they know what you expect from them by way of results?

Working conditions Where will they work? What are the hours? What about overtime? Holidays? What will they be paid? Will they be entitled to sick pay? If they have to travel as part of the job, will they get the use of a car or van? What about travelling and meals allowances?

Special features Will the job involve driving on the public highway? Driving Heavy Goods Vehicles? Are there any other aspects of the job that are likely to require specific knowledge or ability?

At first sight this may seem like an unnecessary and laborious task. Certainly it is one that very many small business owners ignore – often to their cost! Failure to think through these questions may save you an hour or two today, but could lead to stressful time-consuming situations later on, especially if the employee wants to argue the toss over what his or her job involves in the event of a dispute.

Here is an example of a job description:

JOB DESCRIPTION

Job title: SALES REPRESENTATIVE

Responsible to: SALES MANAGER

Job summary: To promote the company's products and achieve agreed targets for sales turnover and new customer development.

Key tasks:
1. Achieve budgeted monthly sales volume.
2. Analyse potential market and increase number of customers by x% per month.
3. Maintain cost of sales within agreed budget.
4. Maintain sales records including company calls report, quotations, credit rating, customer complaints.
5. Liaise with production manager on current order status.
6. Ensure that all existing customers are visited, at least quarterly.
7. Provide an effective customer service and respond to customer queries without delay.
8. Report on current situations at monthly sales meetings.
9. Assist in the planning and organization of sales promotion activities.
10. Complete and submit travel and subsistence expenses monthly within agreed guidelines.

Once you know what the job involves, you will be able to prepare a profile of the ideal person for the job. At this point it is important to appreciate that the ideal candidate probably doesn't exist. If they do, the chances are that they live too far away, or are looking for a much higher salary than the one you are offering. But don't despair; if you tackle the selection process systematically you have a good chance of finding someone with most of the qualities you desire. Using your job description, list the skills, knowledge, experience and personal attributes that are needed to do the job. A well-tried method for doing this is the Seven Point Plan:

1. *Physical make-up* What does the job demand in the way of general health, strength, appearance, manner, voice?
2. *Attainments* What standard of education is needed? What specialized training or previous experience is required?

3. *General intelligence* What level is required to do the job satisfactorily?
4. *Special aptitudes* Does the job require manual dexterity, verbal skills, numeracy etc?
5. *Interests* How far does the job require a special interest in, say, outdoor life? working with other people? Are hobbies or spare time activities relevant?
6. *Disposition* Does the job demand qualities of self-reliance? leadership? acceptability to others? reliability?
7. *Circumstances* How will the pay, working conditions, location, status of the job affect the job holder's private life?

Having worked through these seven points you should have a person specification which will enable you to match each candidate's intellectual, physical and personal circumstances to your specific requirements. You are now in a position to communicate your needs to the employment market.

FINDING EMPLOYEES

What you do next will be determined by the nature of the job you wish to fill, the local employment situation, and personal choice. Regrettably – but not for you – high unemployment means that you can reach many well-qualified and experienced people through the Job Centre. We mention briefly the various government subsidised schemes to encourage employment in Chapter 4. If you are looking for someone out of the ordinary however, you will need to look at more specialized sources.

Some potential sources are more obvious than others: Job Centres, Careers Offices, schools, colleges (particularly those running courses relevant to the job), local firms closing down or reducing staff, professional institutes, trade unions. The "local grapevine" is also a ready source, as are friends and relatives – but beware: they are inevitably, if unconsciously, prejudiced; if it doesn't work out you could lose more than just an employee!

Employment agencies can save you time, but they vary in their levels of professional ability and they can be expensive. Unless you are looking for someone with particularly specialized or scarce expertise you would be better advised to try other sources first. If you feel that you have to use an agency, be selective. Like choosing an accountant, seek the advice of those who have used them before. Apart from the well-established national and international names, the field is strewn with poorly trained wheeler-dealers whose sole concern is their bottom line.

Whatever means you decide to use, make sure you give them specific instructions on your requirements. If you don't do this you will be inundated with a mass of keen but unsuitable candidates – 50 is not unusual today, and many recruiters have been faced with over 500 applications for one job. So be firm and precise in stating your requirements; it will save you time and a lot of job-seekers disappointment.

If you choose to advertise bear the following points in mind:

- the less precise your wording the more applications you will receive. This means more time sifting through a high proportion of totally unsuitable candidates.
- using box numbers can turn people off – including potentially suitable, eminently qualified candidates.
- exclusion of wage or salary indicators will put off some people, but can also have the same effect as imprecise wording and lead to the "ideal" candidate rejecting your offer at the crucial stage.
- select the right medium for the job. The local paper is an ideal source for general office, secretarial, technical, trade and industrial personnel particularly for part-time or flexi-time jobs. Professional, technological and management people are

best reached through the "quality" dailies or appropriate trade or professional journals. Remember that the glossier it is, the higher the cost.

● agencies will advertise for you – but think about your budget first.

If you are not used to writing advertising copy you can do four things: get a particularly literate friend to do it for nothing; scan the ads, decide what you like about the good ones and dislike about the bad, and use this as a guideline; pay an agency to do it for you; or just write it anyway and accept the consequences.

"Apply in writing" might be ideal if you want to recruit a trainee journalist. Editors are experienced speed-readers, but the chances are that you aren't and don't need to be. Application letters come in all shapes and sizes with varying amounts of irrelevant information which you will have to plough through to get to the essential facts from which you will decide whether to interview or not. Without basic guidelines, many job applicants labour under the misapprehension that the way to impress potential employers is to present a full life history!

Application forms can save you time at the initial screening stage, but their value depends upon how well they are designed. They are open to abuse both by employers who may make unwarranted assumptions from limited information, and candidates who may distort the facts or omit crucial points. In designing your form decide what information you need; why you need it; and how you propose to use it. Remember also that you won't want to design a different form for every type of job in the future, so make it as widely applicable as possible.

An example of a fairly simple standard application form is shown opposite.

Of course, there is no such thing as an "ideal" format, and a form can't do the selection for you. But well designed and sensibly used, it can act as an early screening process by relating the profile of the applicant to your specification for the job. One of an application form's main benefits for the small business is that it limits the information provided to the things that matter.

THE SELECTION PROCESS

The selection process is akin to an investment decision. In simple terms, an employee costing you £5,000 per annum who stays with you for five years represents an investment of £25,000. With employment-related costs and inflation it could represent a much higher figure. Compare this with a decision to invest a similar amount in new machinery or computer equipment. Are you likely to reach a decision on the basis of a few general questions, a liking for the appearance of the equipment, and a half-hour interview with the salesman? No? Surprising though it may seem, that's precisely what many employers do when selecting employees for key jobs.

If you have worked through the process described above you may well find yourself with more applications than you can reasonably handle. But you have your job/person specification: use it to identify those candidates who have what you are looking for. This should thin the pile quite a bit, but don't discard the others at this stage, you may well have overlooked a potential superman or wonderwoman. (It's sensible to send a standard "holding" letter to those you might like to interview if the initial ones disappoint.)

The Job Interview

The interview is an essential part of the selection process – but not the only part, as you will see later. Despite criticisms of the interview as an effective means of selection there is, as yet, no satisfactory alternative to enable you to make a decision on the likely suitability of a candidate for the job.

GENERAL APPLICATION FORM

Position applied for	

Surname (block letters)	First names
Address	Telephone number

Age now	Date of birth	Place of birth	State of health (mention any disability)

Marital Status	Number, age and sex of children

EDUCATION AND TRAINING

Schools (after 11 yrs.)	Dates	Examinations passed and qualifications
Universities/Colleges		
Professional/craft/ other training		

EXPERIENCE
(start with most recent employer and work backwards. Include military service)

Name of employer and nature of business	Dates From To	Position held and reason for leaving

Any other information you would like to give about yourself or your experience

May we contact any of your previous employers? YES/NO (no approach will be made to present employers at this stage)

If yes, please give below the names of any of your previous managers with whom we may speak about you

If selected when could you start?

To be completed by interviewer

Interviewing is a skill that takes years of practice. A few fundamental guidelines will help you to sidestep some of the more serious traps in this particular minefield:

- Remember the 80/20 rule: you speak 20% of the time and listen for 80%. The more time you spend talking to the candidates, the less you will know about them at the end of the interview.

- If the candidate is panic-stricken he or she won't communicate much. Put them at ease, show an interest and, please, don't make them paranoid with unveiled reactions to their apparent shortcomings.
- Ask open-ended questions – those that can't be answered with a simple "yes" or "no". Try starting with "how", "what" or "when", and avoid "Do you", "Can you", "Will you".
- Be aware of your own prejudices and the dangers of stereotyping. Someone who looks like you and has a similar cultural background may not be the best person for the job in question.
- Don't rely on first impressions. If you do, the interview will tell you little more than appears in the application form.
- Take notes of the facts as they come out – but leave the assessment until later.
- Don't be reluctant to explore any aspect of the candidate's career. If they consistently avoid certain issues, gently draw the interview to a close and seriously consider exclusion from your final list.
- For your own peace of mind – and theirs – avoid embarrassing personal questions, and don't offer unsolicited personal advice or comment.
- Comparative questions are a useful way to test the candidate's ability. Set a scenario and ask which of several courses of action the candidate would take, and why. The candidate's thinking-out-loud can be illuminating. Have two or three questions that you can put to all candidates in exactly the same way. You can then directly compare the answers.
- Don't rush the candidate. Allow him or her time to think before answering a question. Silence can be a strong weapon in interviewing. The interviewee will be even more conscious of a silence than you are and it will often spark off a spontaneous remark which may tell you more about the candidate than any of your questions.
- Allow five minutes at the end of the interview for the candidate to ask questions, amplify any points made or to raise any other factor in support of the application.
- Explain what the candidate can expect to happen after the interview – when you think you'll make the decision, when they will hear from you, when the job will begin, and conditions of service for the successful applicant.

Avoid making snap judgements on the people you've interviewed. Allow time afterwards to reflect on them, and if you're interviewing with others, discuss them.

One of the problems of seeing several people over a short period is that you forget which was which: "Mr So and So? Wasn't he the chap with the red tie?" This is where it pays to devise an *assessment form* which you fill in after each interview. Candidates, anyway, should be assessed against a set of criteria which relate to the job specification. The criteria used should be those which make sense to you, but opposite for guidance is an example of a fairly standard interview assessment form.

Other Aids to Selection

You don't need to rely on the interview as the sole process of selection, particularly where key skills are concerned. Just because someone obtained RSA I and II with distinction doesn't mean that he/she is necessarily a highly proficient shorthand typist, or an expert in using the word processor. How do you know that Joe Bloggs, Class 'A' welder of 1978, is capable today of working to the standards your product demands? You certainly won't find out from encouraging answers to interview questions.

Although it takes more time, remember the investment factor. Why not get them to demonstrate their skills to you? It needn't be a major operation – just enough to

Vacancy		Candidate						
Factor	*Comments*			*Rating* A B C D E				
Qualifications and training								
Experience								
Knowledge and skills								
Personality characteristics								
Overall impression								
Recommendation								

A = Very much above average; B = Above average; C = Average; D = Below average;
E = Very much below average.

Interview Assessment Form

demonstrate their familiarity with the equipment and their ability to use it effectively. Make allowances for the fact that your particular model or application may be unfamiliar to them however; this, together with natural nervousness, will affect their performance. All you are looking for is a realistic level of competence and potential to get it together in a relatively short time after starting the job.

There are numerous selection techniques that we have not mentioned such as psychological tests, personality profiles, graphology and group selection processes, to name but a few. The small businessperson has neither the time nor the expertise to become involved in such esoteric and possibly unrewarding activities.

The process, as we have already stressed, is concerned with relating your requirements – as specified in the job specification – with the candidate's profile, built up from the application form, interview and practical tests. Your task will be that much easier, and hopefully the results more satisfactory, if you think in terms of "matching" rather than "selection". It's a bit like a marriage bureau; you are looking for that mix of desirable factors which most closely meets your needs, whilst minimizing the risks!

TERMS AND CONDITIONS OF EMPLOYMENT

This chapter began with selection, but before you start to inverview candidates you will need to consider certain essential factors such as wages, hours of work, arrangements for holidays and sickness. No matter how small your organization, you will need to think about employee grievances and how you propose to deal with them. What action do you take if your new secretary takes every second Wednesday off for reasons unknown? If your scrap rate increases by 25% because the well-qualified sheetmetal worker you employed doesn't really know his job, what do you do? Ideally, these are things that you will think about, and devise policies and procedures for in advance – before you are faced with conflict or an industrial tribunal. This section seeks to provide you with general information which will assist you in devising such strategies.

Salaries and Wages

In determining wage and salary levels you will need to take a number of factors into account:

- Wages and salaries paid by other employers in the area for similar jobs. Will you match them or pay over the odds to attract and keep the right person?
- Will payment be a straight wage or salary cheque or will you offer an incentive scheme, commission, bonus system?
- Differentials between jobs. If you don't sort your grading out at the start it could cause you headaches later on.
- Increases. Employees will expect compensation for rises in the cost of living; if you fail to recognize their increased contribution to the business, and their increased experience, they may become less co-operative or leave.
- The cost of wages and salaries can be high, make sure that you have made adequate provision for them in your financial plan.
- Directly or indirectly you will be obliged to recognize the minimum levels of pay set by Wages Councils or rates negotiated locally, whether or not you recognize a trade union. Both the Fair Wages Resolutions and the Employment Protection Act demand that wages, hours and conditions of employment are no less favourable than those established by negotiation and standard practice.

You must also be aware of the rights of your employees regarding payment in cash (unless otherwise agreed); deductions from wages; itemized pay statements, and equal pay for equal work. Leaflets on the range of employment legislation which affect you are available from the Department of Employment or HMSO.

Remember also that the working hours of women and young persons are regulated by law.

Contracts of Employment

The Employment Protection (Consolidation) Act 1978 requires you to issue every employee who works more than 16 hours a week with a written statement of the main terms and conditions of their employment within 13 weeks of commencing employment. This must include:

- the names of the parties
- the date employment commenced
- the job title
- payment terms – how much? when? how calculated?
- hours of work and what are normal working hours?
- holidays, sickness, pension – sufficient for the employee to calculate his entitlement, know arrangements for payment during sickness, and the details of any pension scheme
- period of notice – remembering that there are minimum periods set by law depending upon length of service
- disciplinary and grievance procedures

At this point it may also be worth noting that every employee who has been with his employer for 12 months – or 2 years if you have 20 employees or less – has the right not to be unfairly dismissed. In general, dismissal is potentially fair when it relates to lack of capability or qualifications, misconduct, redundancy or a statutory bar, such as loss of driving licence for drivers.

As with other employment legislation issues, guidelines on unfair dismissal are available from the Department of Employment or HMSO.

Many firms use a standard form for Contract of Employment – see the example below (this firm has also produced a separate book of Staff Notes). However, this is no reason why you cannot issue a Contract in the form of a letter providing that it contains all the required information.

SAMPLE CONTRACT OF EMPLOYMENT

Employer:

Employee: Mr/Ms   Job title:

Your employment began on: 19

Your previous employment does/does not count as continuous *(see staff note 10)*

Your commencing salary is: per year payable weekly/monthly in arrears

Normal working hours: per week

Holiday entitlement: This holiday year   working days

                         Subsequent holiday years   working days
(see staff note 4)

Notice requirements: Employer & Employee

| | Length of service | |
First 3 months	Over 3 months	Over 5 years
One week	Four weeks	One week each completed year

(see staff note 6)

You will not be required to join a Trade Union

For details of sick pay/pension scheme/disciplinary/grievance procedures *see Staff Notes*

Signed for an on behalf of   (Company name):

Manager's signature: Date:

I accept employment in accordance with the conditions laid down in this contract.
I have received a copy of notes for staff.

Employee's signature: Date:

Manager's copy

Employee's copy

Holidays and Sickness

The amount of holiday entitlement is not fixed by law but is a matter for you, the employer, to decide taking into account practice in similar businesses. Once agreed this is included in the Contract of Employment. Remember also that holiday pay is accrued and the contract should indicate how it is calculated to enable employees terminating their employment to know their entitlement.

The Statutory Sick Pay Scheme which came into operation in 1983 requires every employer to pay sick pay to his employees for the first eight weeks of absence due to sickness in any tax year. Details are contained in the appropriate DHSS booklet. The key points to note are that:

- From the fourth day employees must be paid directly a fixed amount of statutory sick pay for each full day's absence.
- The first three days and periods of in excess of eight weeks are excluded from the scheme, although you can make your own agreement on arrangements for payment outside these periods.
- Categories of employees excluded from the SSP scheme include: those over state pension age; those on very short contracts; employees on strike when illness begins; those who have been in receipt of state benefit in the last 57 days; pregnant employees who fall ill after the beginning of the eleventh week before the expected date of confinement; employees who have failed to give satisfactory notice of illness to employers – for those days for which notice has not been provided.

SSP should be on the normal pay day following the start of sickness using the normal payment method. SSP can be topped up to normal pay levels if you wish.

Employees can reduce their contributions to National Insurance and PAYE by the amount of SSP paid out in the related period. Form P11 includes a column for entering SSP reductions.

In addition to the normal DHSS leaflets, there are a variety of publications which describe the Statutory Sick Pay Scheme in detail.

Grievance, Disciplinary and Dismissal Procedures

Human behaviour being what it is – yours or your employees – there will inevitably be occasions when there is disagreement between you. Apart from this, you are obliged to include procedures for handling grievances in the contract of employment. This is merely the method by which an employee can raise any query or complaint about pay or working conditions, and the steps laid down for dealing with the problem.

In the smaller firm this need not be an elaborate process. If your company recognizes a trade union then the procedure is likely to follow the agreed national procedure.

Such procedures should normally identify the various stages which should be followed: e.g. initial complaint to supervisor then, if not settled, to the manager, then director, and so on. Some procedures also specify time limits for each stage, and culminate in the hands of an independent arbiter.

In small organizations it may simply be a matter of allowing employees access to you as the only manager. In dealing with such cases remember your obligations as an employer under contractual law. Hopefully your management style, consideration and effective (two-way) communications system will mean that most potential sources of grievance will be nipped in the bud.

Disciplinary Procedures

The grievance procedure is initiated by the employee often because they are unhappy with something resulting from the behaviour of management. The disciplinary procedure, on the other hand, is initiated by the management because of some aspect of the employee's behaviour. Behaviour, that is, that doesn't conform to the company's rules.

The Advisory Conciliation and Arbitration Service (ACAS) is the best source of assistance in this area. They have published a variety of Codes of Practice including "Disciplinary Procedures in Employment", and will readily provide you with advice on request.

In essence, your disciplinary procedure should include working rules which may be specific to the nature of your business, or more general – covering things like absenteeism, lateness, negligence, unsafe practices, insubordination or theft.

The procedure should also spell out the processes that will be followed in the event of these rules being infringed e.g.:

- oral warnings for minor offences (record them)
- written warnings for repeated offences culminating in a final written warning
- dismissal or suspension
- opportunity for employee to state his or her case
- right of appeal

It is important, too, that employees should be informed their right to be accompanied by their representative. Remember too that except in cases of gross misconduct employees should not be dismissed for a first breach of discipline.

You should obtain a copy of the Department of Employment's booklet on unfair dismissal as well as the ACAS Code of Practice.

The qualifying period for a complaint of unfair dismissal to be accepted by an industrial tribunal is:
- one year (12 months, 52 weeks) for employees whose normal working week is 16 hours or more
- two years where the total number of employees has not exceeded 20 in that two-year period
- five years for those whose normal working week was less than 16 but not less than 8 hours

Redundancy

Employees who work 16 hours a week or more, who are between the age of 18 and normal retirement age and who have worked for you for more than two years are entitled to claim redundancy payments.

There are also special rules where ten or more employees are being made redundant. The Department of Employment will provide details on the Redundancy Payments Scheme including conditions, scale of payments and the procedure for re-claiming a proportion of the payments.

It is important to realize that *a job* is made redundant, not *a person*. You can't declare someone redundant and then recruit another person for the same job.

TRAINING

Having carefully selected your employees you may be tempted to assume that all you need to do now is set them to work. A reasonable assumption perhaps, considering that they may be experienced people who have done this type of work before – whether it be telephone reception or sheetmetal work. Apart from that, you will be conscious of the fact that you are paying them to produce and you haven't time to spend giving lengthy instructions to staff.

Although common, this view is not synonomous with effective business operations.

Training is often confused with education. It is seen as something to do with theoretical concepts which bear little relation to practical realities within the small firm. It is related to colleges, external courses, long periods away from work, and high fees which your company cannot afford!

Further and higher education can contribute, to a considerable extent, to the development and growth of the small firm. Regrettably, however, bad experiences with ultra-theoretical and apparently irrelevant programmes has resulted in an inaccurate general view that:

- education is inappropriate to the needs of small firms
- training is the same as education and is therefore equally inappropriate and unnecessary.

This preconception tends to give a misguided impression of what training is, what it is for, and how it can be carried out. Training, or more appropriately "learning", is about gaining knowledge and developing skills. More to the point perhaps, for you, as the owner of a small business, it is about behaviour – getting your staff to do the things that you want them to do, to the standards that you require, whether it concerns approaching a customer about an outstanding account or assuring the quality of the finished product.

It is important for all potential entrepreneurs to appreciate that these skills can only come from a firm grasp of the philosophy, aims, objectives and standards of the business – gained through the process of training – and are a key factor separating mediocre companies from those that not only survive, but grow.

You may have to use colleges, universities or outside experts in areas where you lack expertise and we will examine this in more detail later; but much of the time you will be able to plan and execute your own training, in-company, on a fairly informal basis.

Induction Training

The need for training starts on Day One. Your new employee, no matter how experienced, is strange to your organization, methods and particular requirements. You couldn't explain everything at the interview, and even if you had attempted to do so, they would only have retained a small proportion of it.

The simplest means of meeting this need is to prepare a checklist of the things *you* want people to know and the things that *they* are likely to want to know during the early stages of employment. Amongst other things, your checklist is likely to include:

- company philosophy, policy, products, services
- organization: who's who; general responsibilities; introduction to immediate superiors and other key members of staff
- customers – the end-users of their products or services
- terms and conditions of employment: method of payment, hours of work, timing of breaks, holidays, sickness procedure, pensions, trade union membership, grievance procedure etc
- safety rules, precautions and procedures, including action in the event of accident or fire and any precautions specific to your product or service
- location of facilities: washroom, kitchen, first aid equipment.

There are many more factors which you will need to consider, but this should provide a general guide to the nature of the points you should cover as part of the induction process.

Of course you don't have to do it all yourself – unless they're your first and only employee – you can delegate appropriate sections to other competent members of staff. Don't try to cover everything on the first day – people can only absorb so much at a time – spread it over a period.

Job Training

All new employees will need some form of job training. This may range from general familiarization for fully qualified and experienced staff to detailed instruction on the operation of unfamiliar equipment or processes.

You have the choice of finding out that training is required by the frequency of mistakes made, or you can approach it systematically by identifying training needs at the beginning. This is a relatively simple process which involves the comparison of the existing knowledge and skills of the employee with that required for the job. If you prepared a job description and personal specification of recruitment, this will make this process even easier.

Having identified what the needs are, list them in terms of:

- what the employee needs to know (knowledge)
- what the employee needs to be able to do (skills).

In essence, you are defining the desired *behaviour* mentioned at the beginning of this section. You can use this list later to check out that your training has achieved what you wanted.

Of course, you will also have to select the most suitable training method.

In-company Training can be carried out by yourself or other members of staff providing that you, or they, have the appropriate expertise. Alternatively you can call in outside specialists to do it for you on a fee-paying basis. In some cases this instruction may be available free or at relatively low cost from the Small Firms Service of the Department of Industry or the Council for Small Industries in Rural Areas (CoSIRA) or, if you're in Scotland: the Scottish Development Agency (SDA). It is also worth checking with the area office of the Manpower Services Commission; the relevant industrial training board or industry training association; or your local enterprise trust. They may not be able to do your training for you, but they can give you sound advice and perhaps identify individuals or organizations that have the ability to provide the type of training that you need.

The actual training method used will depend upon the specific need. In many instances it will be on-the-job instruction. What matters is that is it carried out systematically with employees learning by design rather than haphazardly picking up a mixture of genuine skills and bad habits by watching others doing the job.

Good instruction includes all of the following elements:

- explanation
- demonstration (with the opportunity for clarification)
- practice under supervision
- developing experience, stamina, speed
- checking knowledge, understanding and acquisition of skills.

External Training may be required when neither the expertise, equipment or time is available in the business. Many firms also like to encourage staff to study for qualifications relative to their jobs. Your local college of technology, polytechnic, business school or university will advise you on the range of courses they provide relative to your needs. It's worth making a visit to see the facilities they have and talk to the staff who are teaching the type of course you are interested in.

The quality of certificate and diploma courses is fairly well controlled by education departments, authorities and councils. Short, uncertificated courses are more of a lottery. It isn't just that the quality of lecturing or training staff varies; many courses are necessarily general in nature and designed for a wide range of participants. Inevitably, much of the content of such programmes will not relate specifically to your individual needs. On the other hand, some organizations will design and organize programmes tailored to the particular needs of individual participants.

The answer is to get as much information as you can about the organization, its staff and the course before you commit yourself. As with the selection of accountants and employment agencies, the observations and experience of those who have already experienced the type of course you have in mind can be of value in helping you to reach a decision. Better still, if it is feasible, visit the course organizers and discuss your needs with them. This is the most direct method of assessing whether they are likely to meet your requirements.

Industrial Training Boards and Training Agencies

In 1982, following the Government's review of industrial training, the number of industrial training boards (ITBs) was reduced from around 26 to six. This does not take into account the Agricultural Training Board which continues to operate. Industries covered by the remaining ITBs include: Clothing, Construction, Engineering, Hotel & Catering, Petroleum and Road Transport.

Other industries have introduced voluntary training arrangements as a substitute for ITBs. These agencies are, in most instances, linked to the appropriate trade association.

ITBs and Training Agencies normally levy an annual charge for their services. In return, businesses are awarded grants for specified training; industry-specific training courses are provided; and advice and assistance is provided from specialist training staff.

Detailed information is available from the relevant ITB or training agency. If you have difficulty in locating the appropriate training organization for your particular business contact the Manpower Services Commission area office.

HEALTH AND SAFETY

As an employer you not only have a moral responsibility to care for the health and safety of your employees – you are legally bound to do so. In addition to employers' liability, which is based upon common law – and for which you are required to insure – employers have specific obligations under a variety of Acts of Parliament and related Regulations. Although this may seem to be a matter of common sense you would be well advised to make yourself aware of the responsibilities that health and safety legislation places upon you.

The Health and Safety at Work Act 1974 applies to all persons at work in England, Scotland and Wales. Northern Ireland has its own legislation and there are certain changes to take account of the varying legal systems, but the overall principle and content is similar.

The Health and Safety Commission is the leading body for health and safety matters. The Health and Safety Executive, through its inspectors, is responsible for the operation and enforcement of health and safety legislation. Advice and guidance is available from area offices of the Executive. Some employers have, to their cost, worked on the principle that it is better to avoid the inspectorate until they visit their premises. Unfortunately, this occasion often arises after a costly accident: costly to the employee in terms of his physical wellbeing and livelihood, and costly to the employer in terms of claims for damages, fines and lost production whilst machinery is out of use because of the inspector's prohibition order. Often such regrettable incidents can be avoided by seeking advice at the time that new machinery and equipment is installed. This is also important in terms of the duties of manufacturers and suppliers of equipment under the HASAW Act. They are required to ensure that their product is designed and constructed in such a way as to be safe and without risks to health when properly used. The identification of any inadequacies in equipment supplied to you – as far as safe operation is concerned – at the time of installation, could save you both anguish and expense later on.

Duties to Employees

The duties of employers toward their employees are detailed in Section 2 of the HASAW Act. The principle is encapsulated in the first paragraph, which states:
"It shall be the duty of every employer to ensure, so far as is reasonably practicable, the health, safety and welfare at work of all his employees."
More specifically, employers are required to ensure:

- the provision and maintenance of plant and systems of work which are safe and without risks to health
- safety and absence of risks in the handling, storage and transport of articles and substances
- the provision of the information, instruction, training and supervision necessary to ensure the health and safety of employees
- a safe place of work with the provision and maintenance of means of access and egress
- a safe working environment with adequate facilities and arrangements for the welfare of employees.

This means taking account of every possible hazard to health and safety at work, taking action to avoid risks and providing employees with adequate information and training to ensure that they are aware of the potential hazards and take the necessary precautions.

The most common problems tend to be associated with inadequate guarding, bad lifting techniques, poor ventilation in association with dusts and dangerous fumes, fire hazards associated with sloppy housekeeping and non-existent or unenforced precautions, ignorance of fire-fighting procedures or location and use of equipment, cluttered work spaces. There are, of course, thousands of other possible hazards to health and safety, many of which are covered by special regulations such as that for noise, abrasive wheels, woodworking machinery and lifting equipment. It is in your own interest, as well as that of your employees, to become familiar with those regulations which apply to your business at an early stage.

It is also the duty of every employer – except those with less than five employees – "to prepare, and as often as may be appropriate revise, a written statement of his general policy with respect to health and safety at work of his employees, and the organization and arrangements for the time being in force for carrying out that policy, and to bring the statement, and any revision of it, to the notice of all his employees."

Don't treat this requirement lightly. You are liable for prosecution if you don't produce a statement; if it is inadequate; or if you have not taken sufficient steps to bring it to the attention of your employees. Guidance notes are available from the Health and Safety Commission. In addition, most employers' associations have prepared guidelines for their members.

The written policy statement should cover the general policy and the organization and arrangements for carrying it out.

It should be "a declaration of the employer's intent to seek to provide the safest and healthiest working conditions possible and to enlist the support of his employees towards achieving these ends."

The statement should give the name of the Director, Secretary, Manager or Senior Executive who is responsible for fulfilling the policy, or designate the appointment wherein that responsibility lies.

Where appropriate, other key individuals and their appointments should be named and their responsibilities in relation to health and safety defined. There should also be adequate arrangements to cover the absence of personnel with key safety functions.

Where functional expertise exists to advise line management, e.g. safety adviser, chemist etc, then the relationships and extent of these functions should be clearly defined.

The policy statement should also make it clear that the final level of responsibility is that of each and every individual employee.

Arrangements for training, identification of hazards and related rules and regulations and procedures in the event of fire or injury should also be referred to in the policy statement.

Duties to Persons Other Than Employees

Under the HASAW Act employers also have duties for the protection of other persons, e.g. members of the public, persons visiting your premises, etc. These duties are contained in section 3 of the Act and state that "It shall be the duty of every employer to conduct his undertakings in such a way as to ensure, so far as is reasonably practicable, that persons not in his employment who may be affected thereby are not thereby exposed to risks to their health or safety."

Duties of Employees

The Act also requires employees – which may include members of management – to co-operate with the employer so far as is necessary to enable him to perform his designated duties.

Employees have a duty to take reasonable care for their own health and safety and for that of others who may be affected by his acts or ommissions at work. Section 8 of the Act also prohibits persons from intentionally or recklessly interfering or misusing anything provided in the interests of health, safety or welfare.

Notification of Accidents

The Notification of Accidents and Dangerous Occurrences Regulations 1980 require every employer, irrespective of the type of business with which he is engaged, to notify the relevant enforcing authority of prescribed accidents or dangerous occurrences which have taken place on his premises.

The 'relevant enforcing authority' will depend upon the type of business in which you are engaged. This will be either the District Factory Inspectorate, the Mines and Quarries Inspectorate, the Agriculture, Alkali or Nuclear Inspectorate or, in the case of offices, shops, hotels etc, the local authority health and safety inspectorate.

Notifiable Accidents relates to the 'major injury' or death of any person on an employer's premises. In this event you are required to inform the enforcing authority *immediately*. Not later than seven days after the occurrence you must follow-up this verbal notification with a written report using Form F2508 which is available from Her Majesty's Stationery Office (HMSO).

You must also maintain a written record of the accident including:

- the date of the accident
- the name, sex and occupation of the person
- a description of the injuries sustained
- the place where the accident occurred
- the circumstances which gave rise to the accident

A 'major injury' is: a fracture of the skull, spine, pelvis or of any bone in the arm or leg – other than a bone in the wrist, ankle or foot; amputation of a hand or foot; loss of sight of an eye or any injury which results in hospitalization as an in-patient for more than 24 hours.

Although you need not report accidents which do not result in death or 'major injury' to the enforcing authority you should still record them in the register of accidents. Employees who are absent for three days or more as a result of an injury will claim Industrial Injuries Benefit from the DHSS. This claim will initiate an enquiry to you as the employer, and your response will be communicated to the Health and Safety Executive.

Dangerous Occurrences include a wide range of incidents, whether or not they caused injury but which, taking into account the circumstances, might have been liable to cause major injury to any person, or result in significant damage to plant or premises.

The booklet HS(R)5 "The Notification of Accidents and Dangerous Occurrences", available from HMSO, provides comprehensive guidance on the application of these regulations.

Examples of such occurrences include: the collapse of lifting machinery or equipment; explosion; fires resulting from electrical short-circuits or ignition of materials; release of highly flammable liquids; collapse of scaffolds or buildings under construction or demolition; release of dangerous substances; inhalation of substances resulting in ill-health; similar effects relating to infected material; failure of freight containers while being raised or lowered; bursting of a pipeline or explosion or ignition in a pipeline; overturning or serious damage to road tankers.

The Factories Act 1961 and Offices Shops and Railway Premises Act 1963 and a variety of regulations will apply to you depending upon the nature of your business. You are required to comply with requirements relating to such matters as:

- *Lighting* – which must be sufficient and suitable wherever people work or pass, inside or outside. Windows and skylights must be kept clean.
- *Heating* – rooms must be kept at a 'reasonable temperature'. In factories this means at least 15°C where most of the work is done sitting down and doesn't involve serious physical effort. The temperature can be less if heavy physical work is involved or machinery radiates its own heat. You are also required to have a thermometer in every work room in a place where all employees can see it.

    In general, rooms where people work in shops and offices should be maintained at a temperature of at least 16°C after the first hour at work. There are exceptions, e.g. where goods might deteriorate, site offices, but you must make provision for employees in these situations to warm themselves adequately.
- *Ventilation* – every workroom must have adequate ventilation provided by the circulation of fresh air, and fumes or dust which may be injurious to health should be extracted by an adequate system as near as possible to their source.
- *Seating* – you must provide suitable and sufficient seating for employees who have reasonable opportunities for sitting down without detriment to their work. Seating for employees who do a substantial amount of their work sitting down (e.g.

typists) must be of suitable design, construction and dimensions. You must provide at least one seat for every three employees working in those parts of shops to which the public have access.

- *Space* – factories must have at least 400 cubic feet of space for every worker. The maximum height taken into account for the purposes of this calculation is 14 feet. The maximum number of employees allowed to work in a specific room can also be regulated by the fire authorities as a condition for the award of a fire certificate.

  In shops and offices, every room to which the public is not admitted must have at least 40 square feet of floor space and 400 cubic feet of room space for every worker. The space occupied by furniture and equipment must also be taken into account in this calculation.

- *First Aid* – the Health and Safety (First Aid) Regulations 1981 require you, as an employer, to provide first aid facilities and equipment for all of your employees. This means taking account of employees working away from your premises as well as those permanently located there. The required equipment and facilities are determined by the number of employees, the nature of your business, the size of the premises and proximity to medical services.

  You need to provide at least one first aid box, the contents of which are defined by the authorities in relation to the number of people you employ.

  In situations where hazards are greater, such as factories and warehouses, you should have one person trained in first aid for a workforce of between 50 and 150. In offices and other premises with less potential hazards a qualified first aider is only required if you have more than 150 employees.

  Obviously, all employees should be made aware of the location of the first aid equipment and it should be adequately marked using appropriate signs.

  Detailed information is contained in the booklet HS(R) 11 which is available from HMSO.

- *Accident Book* – if you occupy premises which come within the terms of the Factories Act 1961 or in which 10 or more people are employed you have a duty to maintain an Accident Book. This is also available from HMSO (form BI 510). This relates to the Social Security (Claims and Payments) Regulations 1979 which requires an employee who is injured in the course of his employment to report the matter to his immediate superior without delay, and have the relevant particulars recorded in the Accident Book.

  These regulations also require you as the employer, to investigate the circumstances of every accident reported and, if there are any discrepancies between the facts as recorded and the results of your investigations, these must also be noted in the Accident Book. You must respond to any requests from the DHSS for further particulars and must retain the Accident Book for inspection by the DHSS, if demanded, for a period of 3 years from the last entry in the book.

- *Other factors* – the Acts and Regulations place many other responsibilities on employers depending upon the nature of their business. This includes the displaying of notices and keeping of records in relation to specific regulations and hazards. Safety signs have to be displayed and must comply with certain standards. You may have to make provision for safety representation from among your workforce, allow them time off for training and accede to requests for the formation of a safety committee. You may have to take account of building regulations from the point of view of health and safety. Factories are subject to electricity regulations. There are specific responsibilities in relation to the permissable levels of noise in the workplace. There are regulations concerning storerooms, cloakrooms, lavatory and washing facilities.

Although all of this may appear to amount to a formidable task remember that the authorities concerned have an advisory role and are not only involved in enforcement. Seek their advice and assistance — they can help interpret much of the legalistic prose into everyday practical language.

Fire Precautions

You require a fire certificate if:

- you employ more than 20 people
- you employ more than 10 people anywhere other than the ground floor
- you have a factory in which explosive or highly inflammable materials are stored or used to the extent that they constitute serious additional risks in the event of fire.

If you are in doubt, contact your local fire authority.

Applications for a fire certificate are made on Form FP 1. You will receive a visit from a fire officer who, if satisfied, will approve the award. Alternatively, you will be informed, in writing, of the steps you must take and the time within which you must take them before a certificate can be awarded.

The fire certificate must provide information on:

- the means of escape in the event of fire
- the ways of assuring that means of escape can be safely and effectively used whenever they might be needed
- the type, number and location of fire fighting apparatus on the premises
- the type, number and location of systems provided for providing warning of fire.

You also have a duty to ensure that means of escape are properly maintained and kept free of obstruction; fire fighting and warning equipment is properly maintained; and training on what to do in case of fire is provided for all employees.

PAY AS YOU EARN (PAYE)

Employers are required to deduct income tax from the pay and other emoluments of employees. This not only applies to wages and salaries but also to certain benefits in kind.

General instructions on the operation of PAYE are sent to employers before the start of each tax year. Comprehensive information is contained in explanatory booklets available from any tax office. (Selected examples are listed at the end of this section.) The amount of tax to be deducted will be determined by the employee's tax code which he must provide on commencement of employment (P45). This is applied to the appropriate tax tables which are supplied by the Inland Revenue.

For PAYE purposes "pay" includes salaries, wages, overtime payments, bonuses, fees, commissions and pensions. Holiday pay, payment during sickness or other absence from work and various payments in kind are also classified as "pay" for these purposes. Although there may be a few exceptions, any payment made or benefit provided to an employee can normally be considered as taxable.

Lump sum payments on termination of employment such as "golden handshakes" and severance or redundancy payments of up to £25,000 are exempt from tax. As an employer you are accountable to the Inland Revenue for the PAYE tax on the wages and salaries of your employees. Tax deducted from employees earnings is accounted for monthly – up to the 5th of each month – and must be remitted to the Collector of Taxes within fourteen days of that date. If you fail to meet this requirement it will be you who is considered liable.

The range of pamphlets available from HM Inspector of Taxes is considerable. All are available free of charge from your local tax office. The following selection may be of particular interest to you as a small business owner:

IR 16 (1974) Share Acquisitions by Directors and Employees
IR 18 (1979) Corporation Tax
IR 21 (1980) Income Tax Tables
               (new tables are to be supplied for use after 10 May 1985)
IR 28 (1980) Starting in Business
IR 34 (1981) Income Tax: PAYE
IR 38 (1981) Income Tax: SAYE Share Options
480   (1981) Income Tax: Notes of Expenses, Payments and Benefits for Directors
               and Certain Employees
P7   ⎫ Employer's Guide to PAYE
P7(S)   ⎬ (1982) Supplement
P7(Slip) ⎭ Addenda

NATIONAL INSURANCE CONTRIBUTIONS

The National Insurance Contributions you are required to pay will depend upon the legal form of your business. A sole trader or partner is classified as self-employed and pays contributions in class 2, which is a weekly sum – currently £4.60 per week – and in class 4 based on annual profits.

You can pay your class 2 contributions by direct debit through your bank or National Giro account. Leaflet NI 41 provides specific information on contributions and can be obtained from the local office of the Department of Health & Social Security (DHSS).

It may be possible to arrange for deferment of payment of contributions until your exact liability is known. You should enquire about this at your DHSS office.

A company director pays contributions as an employee and his company pays as an employer. You can therefore end up paying considerably more than if you had chosen to operate as a sole trader or partnership. As a rough guide, you would be better off not trading as a company if you don't expect your profits to exceed £10,000 per annum. But this must also be weighed against National Insurance Benefits which are better for the "employee" director than the "self-employed" sole trader.

Employers must make NI contributions for each employee according to salary level and whether or not they have contracted out of the State Scheme (see Pensions).

Employers who have not contracted out pay a basic 11.45% of salary up to the "upper earnings limit" which is currently £250 per week.

The National Insurance Surcharge which was paid in addition to this basic rate is to be abolished in October 1984.

Employees pay at the rate of 9.0%. Married women and widows who have opted to pay reduced contributions may pay at the reduced rate of 3.85%.

PENSIONS

The subject of pensions is complex but very important – particularly in the longer term. It is too late to realize a year or two before retirement that you have made no provision for future financial support.

In this section we have provided a general summary of the State Pension Scheme and information on schemes for small businesses. In view of the complexity of the subject and the range of options open to you you would be well advised to consult a specialist in this field before committing yourself to any particular scheme.

The State Scheme

The State Pension Scheme was introduced by the Social Security Pensions Act 1975 and was revamped in 1978.

The Pension is paid from the "state pensionable age" which is 65 for men and 60 for women. It is made up from a "base level pension" and an "additional pension". Levels are increased annually, roughly in line with prices, and are announced annually and applied in November.

The base level pension is currently £34.05 per week for a single person or each married person with a full contribution record.

A married couples allowance is also paid where a wife is not entitled to a state pension. This currently stands at £20.45.

The additional pension is based on earnings between lower and upper earnings limits, the levels of which are announced annually; these are £34 and £250 per week at present. In simple terms state pensions, not including the married couple's allowance, are calculated on the basis of these recorded earnings and the number of years in the scheme.

Social security contributions are deducted through the PAYE system. At present the rates are:

Employer – 11.45%
Employee – 9.00%

Although these figures are reduced by 4.1% for employers and 2.15% for employees who have contracted out. This compensates members of occupational pension schemes for taking over the liability for guaranteed minimum pensions.

Contributions are payable on all earnings up to the upper earnings limit. No contributions are payable by you, or by the employee where earnings are below the lower earnings limit.

Employee contributions cease at state retirement age but you must continue to pay the employer's contribution until such employees actually retire.

Contracting Out of The State Scheme

Members of occupational pension schemes are permitted to contract out of almost all of the state additional pension subject to certain minimum criteria:

- a personal pension must not be less than the guaranteed minimum pension, which is the additional pension an employee would have earned had he remained within the full state scheme.
- a widow's pension payable on the employee's death either before or after retirement. This must be at least 1/160th of the employee's final salary for each year of his contracted out service, and must not be less than half his guaranteed minimum pension at the time of his death.
- the guaranteed minimum pension must be revalued every year in line with the general growth in earnings up to state pensionable age. This also applies to previous employees with a right to "frozen" pensions.
- the occupational scheme must be financially sound and evidence of solvency must be actuarially certificated before being permitted to contract out and subsequently at three yearly intervals.

For tax purposes employers contributions to an "exempt approved pension scheme" are allowable as a trading expense. Employee's contributions are accepted as an allowance against income. The recognition of your scheme for "exempt approved" status requires the approval of the Superannuation Funds Office of the Inland Revenue. This will be determined by the scheme's ability to meet certain criteria required under the Finance Act.

Pensions and the Self-Employed

As a self-employed person your National Insurance contributions only qualify you for a basic state pension, and you cannot belong to an approved pension scheme. You can, however, invest in a suitable pension plan (often called a retirement annuity scheme) and if your business is a profitable one, this can prove highly tax-efficient. By selecting the right scheme you can get tax relief at your highest income tax rate, and so get the Inland Revenue to contribute up to three-quarters of your pension. You can also receive the benefit from the pension plan partly as a lump sum free of capital gains tax on the profits made on your contributions; and partly as a pension which will be treated as earned, rather than unearned, income.

You are allowed to contribute up to $17\frac{1}{2}\%$ of net relevant earning to a pensions scheme. This limit is increased to 20% for those born between 1916 and 1933 and marginally more for those born earlier.

Selecting the right scheme is a bit like deciding on an insurance policy. Make sure you get the one that suits your needs rather than the financial ambitions of the agent. If you don't want the frills don't take them – the greater the added extras, the greater the cost. You can go for policy with or without profits or for a unit-linked policy. Over longer periods the latter two are more advantageous. Remember also that unit-linked policies are subject to the fluctuations of the stock market and therefore represent something of a gamble.

As we have already stated, good, preferably independent, professional advice is a must.

Small Self-Administered Schemes

Small self-administered schemes provide considerable tax advantages for small businesses. Unlike insurance-based schemes, they allow the owners of the business control over the scheme's assets and their investment. Only companies, limited or unlimited, may set up an SSA scheme which generally involves fewer than 12 members. Partnerships are excluded.

The rules are explained in the Inland Revenue's Memorandum No. 58 "Small Self-Administered Schemes" which is available from the Superannuation Funds Office (Tel 01-942 8949).

Setting up the scheme is more elaborate and expensive than conventional pension schemes, but this has to be weighed against the undoubted advantages.

Company Pension Schemes

You can set up an occupational pension scheme for your employees. This may be contributory or non-contributory.

The scheme you choose will be determined to a large extent by how much you are willing to pay – or more importantly – how much you can afford. Contributions are usually expressed as a percentage of wages or salaries.

You will also need to consider how your scheme will relate to the state scheme. The Department of Health & Social Security will provide you with guidance on this point.

Make sure you have obtained all of the information you can from the experts and understand your long-term commitments before finally deciding to launch the scheme.

INCENTIVES

As your business develops and the number of staff grow, you may want to consider offering various incentives both as a means of motivating employees to give of their best and to ensure that you remain competitive with the inducements offered by other employers in the area. Examples of common incentives are luncheon vouchers, company cars, profit-sharing schemes, private health insurance, bonus schemes and, of course, a pension scheme.

CHAPTER 8 SUMMARY

- Most businesses need to take on staff, if not initially, when the business grows.
- You need to know what to look for; where, and how, to advertise; how to conduct the interviews and how to assess the applicants you see.
- Once selected, you must be aware of the stringent duties the law imposes on employers and the methods by which you pay PAYE, National Insurance Contributions and pensions, should you decide to offer a pension scheme.
- The staff you select might need to be trained – you can do this yourself or you can send them on an external training course.

Chapter 9
YOUR CUSTOMERS AND THE MARKET PLACE

Optimism is certainly a necessary attribute for the business starter. You have to be able to make positive claims about your business idea right from the outset, in order to keep potential backers, customers and perhaps even your family on the boil.

This is fine while you are "thinking about setting up", but once you decide that you want to commit real resources to the project, you need data not dogma, to succeed. The glib "everyone will want one" will have to be replaced with a well thought-out pre-launch marketing strategy.

Marketing is the name given to the whole area that is concerned with customers, their needs, their view of us and our products, how many of them there are; and what we have to do to make them want our products.

It is the process that takes an idea from the "Wet Bathmat" stage, right through to being a commercially viable business proposition.

In the end every business lives or dies in the market place. A consumer must see more value in what you have to offer than it costs you to put together – or else you are going to lose money. And losing money is *not* what you start up a business to do!

Now obviously making money involves taking risks. The economist views "profit", be it a living wage or having a Rolls in the garage, as the just reward for taking various degrees of risk. The higher the risk the greater the potential reward, in theory.

It would be nice to believe that it was possible to take no risks and still make high profits, but that simply is not possible. What we can and must do, however, is to recognize the nature of the risks associated with our business idea and try to eliminate the worst dangers associated with taking those risks.

Quite simply, we must screen our business idea to see if it can stand up to the rigours of the market place.

"Marketing is the identification of an existing or potential need, and the meeting of that need at a continuing satisfactory profit."

Let's adopt this as our working definition of marketing and read the rest of this chapter keeping your own product or service uppermost in your mind.

UNDERSTANDING CUSTOMERS AND PRODUCTS

Knowing something about your customers and what you plan to sell them seems so elementary that it is hard to believe that any potential business person could start a business without doing so. But it is all too common – and one of the reasons why many new businesses fail.

Here's a story which illustrates the pitfalls:

In 1982 Tim Johnston took voluntary redundancy and decided to start his own business. His redundancy money combined with his savings gave him a total of £15,000, which he put into a vending machine business. He chose vending since he thought that with the demise of the tea lady it must be a growth market.

He surveyed the vending machine manufacturers and selected three machines that were easy to maintain and simple to fill and clean. He bought demonstration models at a discount, and installed them in his newly acquired office cum storeroom. He then looked for suppliers of ingredients, paying particular attention to the flavours since he believed that vended drinks had a poor reputation. Next he arranged with two leasing companies a deal by which they would finance the machines he sold to satisfactory customers.

All this took Tim four months and by the autumn of 1982 he felt certain that he had a good product to offer.

He started to sell. He first called on established, medium-sized local companies. It quickly became clear that they already either had a vending machine or had well-rehearsed reasons for not wanting one. So Tim moved down market and went to see small and new companies – and immediately hit a new problem. The leasing companies he had lined up would only take on clients with a good financial track record. Otherwise they required the directors of the company to provide personal guarantees in case the company defaulted. Now Tim had not only to persuade customers to buy a vending machine but to abandon the shelter of limited liability to do so!

By the end of the first month of his sales campaign, Tim had called on 250 people, seen 28 and given two quotes for machines.

His next tack was to identify likely prospects via the telephone, but the closest he got to an order was from a firm that wanted a vending machine to provide refreshments for night shift workers. The firm didn't care twopence about the quality of the ingredients – their only concern was that the machine could dispense all night on a single fill of drinks.

After six months "in business" Tim closed down. Nearly half his cash was gone and he hadn't got a single order. There was no market for the service he offered.

Satisfying needs

The founder of a successful cosmetics firm, when asked what his business did, replied, "In the factories we make perfume and in the shops we sell dreams."

Businessmen usually define their business in physical terms. Customers, on the other hand, see businesses as satisfying their needs. Compare a Bic with a Parker pen. Basically they are very similar: they both write well; are comfortable to hold; have clips that hold them in place and caps that protect your pockets from ink stains. One costs 10p, the other £3. Customers pay the extra £2.90 for largely intangible benefits such as status or the pleasure the pen will bring as a gift. Bic and Parker are both successful businesses, but the needs they satisfy are poles apart.

Until you have clearly defined the needs of your potential customers, you cannot begin to assemble a product to satisfy them. About the only "need" Tim Johnston identified was that people wanted a good-tasting vended drink. But, in the end, "personal financial security" and "overnight reliability" mattered more.

The American psychologist Maslow says that "all consumers are goal seekers who gratify their needs by purchase and consumption". He classifies consumer needs in a five-stage pyramid: the hierarchy of needs.

Every product or service is bought to satisfy one or more of these needs. So, for example, as people's hunger and thirst needs are satisfied, they move up the hierarchy to satisfy other needs.

Try interesting someone who is starving and cold in "higher" things; or see how much more food you buy if you shop when you are hungry than when you have just consumed a large meal.

Where are your customers on the needs hierarchy, and how can your product or service help them to achieve their goals?

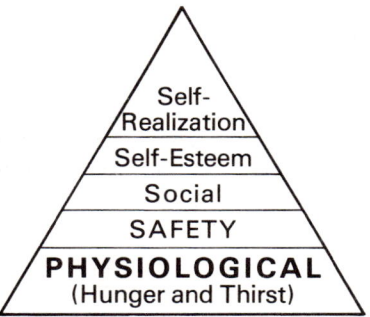

Segmenting the market

Without customers no business can get off the ground, yet alone survive. Some people believe that customers arrive after the firm "opens its doors". This is non-sense. You need to find customers before you even think of launching. If you cannot name with absolute certainty the first twenty people who are going to buy from you, then you are not ready to start your business.

It may not be easy, but then success does not come easily. Just think how much wiser Tim Johnston would have been if he had made this list first.

But naming names is not enough. You have to organize the customers and the potential customers into clusters or groups of "similar" types. For example, a shop or restaurant has regulars and passing trade. The balance between the two is a funda-mental issue that affects everything else the business does.

Also, each of these customer groups is motivated to buy for different reasons and your selling message has to be modified accordingly.

These are some of the ways by which markets can be segmented.

Demographic segmentation groups customers together by such variables as age, sex, education and income. One owner of a corner shop identified two particular groups of customers; schoolchildren, and housewives who had run out of products they would normally buy from a supermarket. For the former the products on offer are sweets, comics, pencils and cheap games. For the latter, small sizes of such items as butter, cereal and washing powder.

Benefit segmentation recognizes that different people get different satisfaction from the same product or service. Most toothpaste manufacturers stress the "benefit" of decay protection, such as the claim "look mum, no cavities". However, others reach a quite different market with their "whiteness" message. White teeth, with the implied attractiveness to the opposite sex, is a more important benefit to some customers.

Geographic segments arise when customer preferences vary by location. For example, the photocopyshop and the motor cycle despatch rider are very much "products" of a city environment.

There are useful rules to help you decide on whether a market segment is worth trying to sell into.

- *Measurability:* can you estimate how many customers are in the segment?
- *Accessibility:* can you communicate with these customers? Just knowing "they are out there somewhere" is not much help.
- *Size:* a segment has to have a "large" number of customers, though exactly what constitutes large will be relative to your business!
- *Open to practial development:* just being a large segment is not enough. The

customer must have money to spend and be able to spend it. Some government departments, for example, are restricted to buying from "approved" suppliers only. So they may be large, but of no interest at all if you cannot sell to them.

Segmentation is an important marketing process, as it helps to bring customers more sharply into focus, and it classifies them into manageable groups. It has wide-ranging implications for other marketing decisions. For example, the same product can be priced differently according to the intensity of customers' needs. The first-class and second-class post is one example, off-peak rail travel another.

Who will buy first?

Customers are not sitting waiting for a new business to open its doors. Word spreads slowly as the message is diffused throughout the various customer groups. Even then it is noticeable that generally it is the more adventurous types that first buy from a new business. Only after these people have given their seal of approval do the "followers" come along.

This adoption process is most noticable with innovative products, such as micro-computers, but the general trend is true for all businesses.

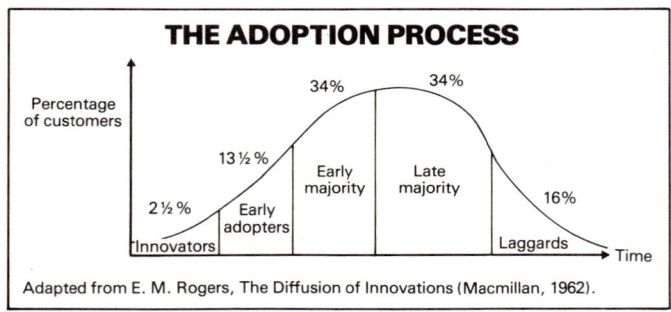

THE ADOPTION PROCESS

Adapted from E. M. Rogers, The Diffusion of Innovations (Macmillan, 1962).

The illustration above shows the process from the 2½% innovators, who make up a new business's first customers, through to the laggards that won't buy from anyone until they have been in business for twenty years.

Until you have sold to the innovators significant sales cannot be achieved. So an important first task is to identify these customers.

Defining the product

Once you know what you are selling and to whom, you can match the features of the product (or service) to the benefits that customers will get when they purchase. *Features* are what a product has, or is, and *benefits* are what that product does for the customer. The example below is part of the Feature/Benefit Analysis for a Renault 5 car.

Feature/Benefit Analysis Chart

Features	Benefits
5 Speed Gear Box	Fuel economy when cruising
Hatch Back	Easy access to luggage space
Fold down back seats	Flexible/expanding luggage space
Rustproofing	Keeps its looks and saves on resprays
Heated rear window	Easy to keep window clear

Remember, the customers pay for the *benefits* and the seller pays for the *features*. So you must communicate both features and benefits if you are to get into business. Do not forget that those benefits must be worth more to your customer than the features cost you to deliver.

Now try this out for your business proposition.

Product life cycles

As well as asking who will buy first, it is important to consider how sales might develop. Any product or service moves through identifiable and to some extent predictable stages from the moment you launch your business. Understanding this "cycle" will help in preparing a sound marketing plan.

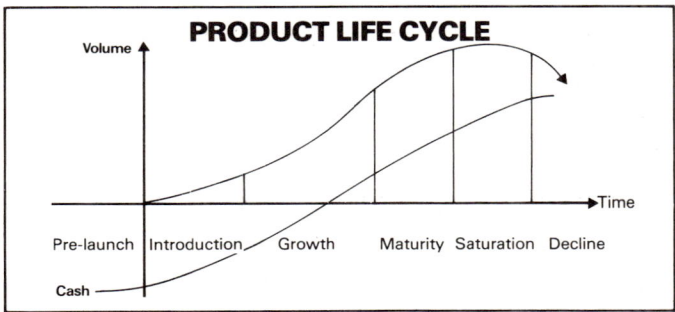

Pre-launch Describes all the work done to bring your business to the opening day.

Introduction In the early days and weeks sales are usually low, no profit is made, and cash is consumed in large quantities.

Growth If all goes well then after several months of trading you should see a steady growth in sales, until you reach an economically viable level. That is when the cash coming in from customers begins to match that going out in wages and to suppliers.

This is also the time when you should be most vigorously promoting your business and encouraging new customers to buy.

Maturity The period when the rate of sales growth begins to slow down. It is a time for consolidation and hopefully profitability. By this stage, which could start to happen during the second or third trading year, your message has reached the bulk of your chosen market.

Saturation This occurs when sales growth stops altogether: new customers are cancelled out by the existing customers being captured by competition. This is a particularly dangerous period for a new business, as the profit level is very often satisfactory at this stage of the cycle. This steady state is a signal that says unless you take new action to improve your product or service, the market will begin to slip away.

Decline The period when sales volume begins to fall. It reveals that your product or service has lost its competitive edge in the market, and a fundamental re-think is called for if you are to survive.

PROTECTING YOUR POSITION

The marketing chain linking you to your customer can, in some instances, be a long one. It can also be vulnerable to interference of the most unwelcome kind. Depending on where your business enters this chain you should look for ways to protect yourself from such threats.

PROTECT YOUR POSITION

Marketing Chain	Protection
Inventor	Patent
↓	
Manufacturer	Licence
↓	
Distributor	Agreement
Customer	Pre-payment
	Credit Insurance

Inventor If your product depends for its uniqueness on some innovative skills, perhaps in the area of technology or design, then you should consider taking out a patent. The subject of patents, copyright and design registration is covered in detail in Chapter 3. However it is worth remembering that however sound your patent, you will need financial resources to defend it. Especially if a big overseas based company is determined to steal your idea.

But successful new product ideas are rare enough, without letting someone else walk away scot free with your one.

NEW PRODUCT IDEAS ARE RISKY

100 Ideas
Business
Screening
Trials
Test
Market
1 Success

For every 100 new product ideas that are thought up only one reaches the market place and is successful.

For every 100 new product ideas that are thought up only one reaches the market place and is successful.

Manufacturer If you plan to make someone else's product, then ensure you have their approval to do so. Companies "licence" the right to make their product, usually in different countries. So, for example, Coca Cola is made and marketed in the UK under licence from Coca Cola Inc. of the USA. A licence is a formal legal document with both rights and responsibilities. One new venture that set out to make a UK version of a very successful American computer game found the owners of the game were happy to licence the product, but only if the rules of the game were rigidly maintained and the quality of written materials was kept to their high standards.

Distributors are very often appointed by manufacturers when they want to get national coverage quickly without too many start-up costs. A small business may become an agent or distributor for several manufacturers to help build up a viable product range, or they may take on someone else's product to add to their own range. Once again it is important to get a formal written agreement, and the Manufacturers' Agents Association (13a West Street, Reigate, Surrey; 07372 43492) has produced a standard version.

Customers are at the end of the marketing chain. If your products or service is sold for cash in a single transaction then usually that point is the end of your main marketing problem. But if, for example, your business is interior design, or some other consultancy, how can you be sure of completing the sale? Your customer could change his mind after you have carried out some work and incurred expenses. Under these circumstances you should look for both a contractual agreement with the task to be done specified clearly. You should also ask for a pre-payment, or stage payments. By the time you have completed your work you should have received all the monies due. If you sell on credit, you can take out insurance to cover yourself against debtors who default.

If you are selling into an export market there are even more risks. The customer's government may decide to freeze foreign exchange, or insist that you take barter goods instead of cash. In most cases small exporters would be prudent to use the Export Credit Guarantee Department to insure that the cash will be forthcoming.

MARKET RESEARCH

The Duke of Wellington defined reconnaissance as the "art of knowing what is on the other side of the hill". Market research is the business equivalent of this military activity.

Market research is the name given to the process of collection, recording, classifying and analysing data on customers, competitors and any other influencers in the buying chain.

Indeed it is the very breadth of this gulf between a new business and its customers that makes this information gathering so vital.

Entrepreneurs very often know a lot about their own product or service, and almost nothing about their customers needs, or likely behaviour. This case study helps to make the point:

Jenny Ross was a late entrepreneur. At 57 it was a toss-up between early retirement, and starting her own business. After ten years as a bookkeeper with a small London accounting practice, the partner she worked most closely with was retiring and this seemed a good opportunity to take stock herself.

Jenny was healthy, energetic and, above all, she enjoyed her work. Her boss suggested that she might like to continue working with some of the practice's smaller clients, and from that base, build up her own bookkeeping business. He told her that new company formations were at a record high and he could see no reason why she could not get a reasonable share of that trade. It meant taking on responsibility for the upkeep of a small office, but she was sure that once "the word got around" business would be brisk.

After about three months, Jenny had no new clients and had lost two of her existing ones. The clients she had lost were not dissatisfied with her work. They had simply changed accountants the "year end" after her old boss had gone. Her outgoings and her income more or less matched up, provided she was prepared to work for 50p per hour. As the custom was not coming to her, Jenny decided to go to it. She placed an advertisement in a paper which advertised small businesses for sale and which she felt was read by the right sort of people.

The results were disappointing to say the least, especially as her advertisement was the only one offering a bookkeeping service! Of the two enquiries she received, one was from a firm miles away on the other side of London; the other wanted a computerized service that he could eventually run for himself. Two repeats of the advertisement brought no better response.

£100 poorer, she went to a Business Advice Clinic in Greenwich Town Hall. Here she was helped to put together a marketing plan designed to get her business successfully "re-launched". Defining her marketplace as two miles in circumference, her customer profile as new firms with less than 20 employees and her product as bookkeeping to trial balance, Jenny set to work with her counsellor's guidance. Using trade directories, she prepared a list of 200 potential customers and sent out a sales leaflet. From this she got four clients, and a further mail shot produced three more.

Jenny Ross is still in business, but she very nearly wasn't. The market research done on her behalf saved her venture.

Why do it?

Jenny Ross survived, so why should anyone want to spend time and money on market research? Well, in this case the sum of money at risk was quite small, so perhaps she did not think it deserved much protection.

If you went out and bought a cheap digital watch you would probably just put it on and forget it. On the other hand if you bought an expensive gold one, with a jewelled movement costing around £1,000, you would not even take it out of the shop until you were satisfied that your insurance policy covered it.

Market research is a form of insurance that a business takes out when it is going to spend relatively large amounts of time or money on a project. Big businesses do it all the time, when they are launching new products, planning on advertising, or simply keeping an eye on the competition.

The amount of research undertaken has to be related to the sums at risk. If your venture calls for a start-up investment of £2,000, spending £5,000 on market research would be a bad investment. However, new and small businesses that do not want to join the catastrophically high first-year failure statistics would be prudent to carry out some elementary market research, whatever level their start-up capital is to be.

The President of the Harvard Business School is reputed to have said, "If you think knowledge is expensive, try ignorance."

What questions can market research answer?

Market research can provide answers to a wide range of questions. For a new business on the threshold of launching out into the marketplace these are the questions that need answering early on.

Where is my market? The starting point in any market plan has to be a definition of the scope of the market you are aiming for. A small general shop may only service the needs of a few dozen streets. A specialist restaurant may have to call on a much larger catchment area to be viable.

You may eventually decide to sell to different markets. For example, a retail business can serve a local area through the shop and a national area by mail order. A small manufacturing business could branch out into exporting.

People all too often flounder in their initial market research by describing their markets too broadly. For example, saying that they are in the motor industry when they really mean they sell second hand cars in Perth; or in health foods, when they are selling wholemeal bread from a village shop.

Whilst it's important to be aware of trends in the wider market this must not obscure the need to focus on the precise area that you have to serve.

How big is my potential market, and is it growing? Until you know something of the characteristics of your potential customers, for example their income bracket or their education level, you cannot begin to calculate how many of them there may be. And until you know how many potential customers there are, you cannot work out your initial sales forecast, and consequently how commercially viable your business is likely to be.

A rough approximation of market size and growth can very often be calculated quickly from published statistics. But sometimes a more sophisticated, or original, method is called for. (We examine methods later on.)

If we were in the home improvements business, for example, we could estimate average expenditure per head using published industry data, and the population of our catchment area from the population statistics. We could then do the following calculations:

Measuring Market Size

Population spent £11.00 per head per annum on Home Improvement products in 1984
Catchment population for my shop is 25,000
So total market potential = £11 × 25,000
$$= £275,000$$

Using the same information for the preceeding year(s) we can measure the growth rate.

Measuring Market Growth

Population spent £10.00 per head per annum on Home Improvement products in 1983
Catchment population for my shop was 24,000
So total market potential in 1983 was £10 × 24,000
$$= £240,000$$

$$\text{Market Growth} = \frac{\text{This Year's Market Potential} - \text{Last Year's Market Potential}}{\text{Last Year's Market Potential}}$$

$$= \frac{275,000 - 240,000}{240,000}$$

$$= 15\%$$

Finally, using the Index of Retail Prices, we can calculate the "real" growth in the market allowing for inflation.

Allowing for Inflation

		%
Unadjusted market growth		15
Retail price rise		6
Real growth in market	=	9

Competition and market share

Once you have calculated the total market potential for your product or service, you will need to look at your competition. Its strengths and weaknesses will play an important part in how you will compete, and what share of the market you can realistically expect.

You need to know everything about them. Their product range, prices, discount structure, delivery arrangements, product specifications, minimum order quantities, terms of trade, their turnover and their profitability.

Use a chart like this to build up a picture of them.

WHO PRESENTLY SUPPLIES YOUR CUSTOMERS

LIST CRITICAL FACTORS FOR SUCCESS

NAME	STRENGTHS	WEAKNESSES

Your competitive strategy will depend as much on recognizing competitors' strengths as on exploiting their weaknesses.

An electrical discount shop, recognizing that it could not compete with a neighbouring giant department store, turned its expertise to advantage. If a customer wanted to discuss the technical merits of, say, one washing machine versus another, they recommended them to go and talk it over with the sales engineers at the department store. But they guaranteed the customer that once he knew what he wanted, they could provide it 30% cheaper.

Returning to our home improvements example in the previous section. If there are already three other shops selling into your market, then it is hard to see, in the short run at any rate, how you could realistically expect to achieve more than a quarter share of the market. In the long run you may outsell them all, but in the short run they will have a body of loyal customers.

Calculating Maximum Initial Market Share

Maximum
Start up Market share

$$= \frac{\text{Total Market Potential}}{\text{Number of competitors} + 1}$$

$$= \frac{£275,000}{4}$$

Your maximum share (25% of market) $= £68,750$

Eventually your competitive strategies may put you ahead. But you would be unwise to pin your financial survival on a sales objective greater than your initial maximum market share.

How can I differentiate my business from the competition?

There has to be something unique either about you or your product that makes you stand out from your competitors. It could be something as obvious as being open later longer, which is where many corner shops score over their bigger competitors. Or it may be a policy, such as the John Lewis Partnership's "Never knowingly over-sold" message, which gives them the edge over other branded goods retailers. Whatever your USP (Unique Selling Proposition) is, communicate it effectively.

How effective is my advertising?

We will be looking at how to advertise later in the chapter, but a legitimate question for market research is how effective is the advertising you decide to do.

The table below shows the advertising results for a small Business Course run in London early in 1984.

At first glance the Sunday paper produced the most enquiries. Although it cost the most, £340, the cost per enquiry was only slightly more than the other media used.

But the objective of this advertising was not simply to create interest. It was intended to sell places on the course. At the end of the day only 10 of the 75 enquiries were converted into orders. An advertising cost of £34 per head. On this basis the Sunday paper was between two and a half and three and a half times more expensive than any other media.

Measuring Advertising Effect

Media used	Enquiries	Cost of advertising £	Cost per enquiry £	Number of customers	Advertising cost per customer £
Sunday paper	75	340	4.50	10	34
Daily paper	55	234	4.25	17	14
Posters	30	125	4.20	10	12
Local weekly paper	10	40	4.00	4	10
Personal recommendation	20	?	?	19	?
TOTALS	190	739	4.35	60	18

This is a classic example of collecting, recording, classifying and analysing market data, to help with business decisions. In other words the purpose of market research.

Other questions which market research for a new business should attempt to answer include:
1. What distribution channels should be used?
2. What price will the market bear?
3. What advertising media do my potential customers see?
4. Are my customers credit worthy?
5. Are customers satisfied with current service levels or quality standards?
6. Is our selling effort adequate?
We discuss these later in this chapter.

How to conduct market research

You must first set *clear objectives*. You want to know as much as possible about the market for your product or service. In research terms this might be defined as: how many people live (or shop) in your catchment area; how many are in the age group you have identified as your target market; what is the sex split (if your product/service is primarily bought by one sex); how large is the market nationwide for the product/service; what is the estimated expenditure per head; what are the trends – up or down; who are the likely competitors and how well do they do. For instance, a publisher who wished to offer a free magazine at Greenwich station might need to discover how many females aged between 18 and 25 travel to work by train each day.

Next, *see if someone else has the answers already*. Market research conjures up images of people with clip-boards accosting you in the street – and you might well have to do that too. But much of the information you need will already be published, so some of your market research activity, at least, can be done in a comfortable chair in a good library. For instance, the official *Census of Population* will supply you with demographic data on size, age and sex of the local populace, and there is a wealth of government and other published statistics to enable you to work out the size and shape of the market nationwide and the expenditure per head of population.

This type of research is called *desk research* and it is well worth doing. We list below some of the most relevant directories and other information sources.

MARKET RESEARCH INFORMATION SOURCES

The A-Z of UK Marketing Data, published by Euromonitor Publications Ltd, provides basic market data for several hundred UK markets from adhesives to zip fasteners, by product area, market size, production, imports, exports the main brands, their market share and a market forecast. A good glimpse at a wide range of markets.

Annual Abstract of Statistics, published by the Central Statistical Office, is the basic source of all UK statistics. Figures are given for each of the preceding 10 years, so trends can be recognized.

ASLIB Directory, Volume I. Information sources in science, technology and commerce, edited by Ellen M. Coldlin, 5th edition, 1982. A valuable reference tool if you need to track down information over a wide range of subjects. This edition has over 3,000 entries from a large number of sources, professional, amateur, big and small. A major factor in including sources was their willingness to make the information available.

BBC Data Enquiry Service, Room 3, The Langham, The British Broadcasting Corporation, Portland Place, London W1A 1AA; 01-927 4338. This is a personal information service drawing on the world-wide resources of the BBC. It is an inexpensive and speedy way of checking facts and drawing on a statistical data bank which covers people, products, countries and events. The service could tell you the price of a pint of milk in 1951 or the current state of the Dutch economy. Ad hoc enquiries can cost as little as £5 or an annual subscription £100.

British Rate and Data, updated monthly. Whatever market you are interested in, it is almost certain to have a specialized paper or journal which will be an important source of market data. BRAD lists all newspapers and periodicals in the UK and Eire which carry advertising, and gives their frequency and circulation volume, price, their executives' names, advertising rates and readership classification.

Business Monitors are the medium through which the government publishes the business statistics it collects from over 20,000 UK firms. They are the primary and very often the only source of detailed information on the sectors they cover. The *Monitors* can help businessmen by indicating trends and tracing the progress of 4,000 individual products, manufactured by firms in 160 industries. *Monitors* can also be used to rate your business performance against that of your industry and measure the efficiency of different parts of your business.

The *Monitors* are published in three main series. The *Production Monitors* are published monthly, quarterly and annually. The quarterly is probably the most useful, with comprehensive yet timely information. The *Service and Distribution Monitors* cover the retail market, the instalment credit business, the motor trade, catering and allied trades and the computer service industry, among others. Finally, there are *Miscellaneous Monitors* covering such topics as shipping, insurance, import/export ratios for industry, acquisitions and mergers of industrial and commercial companies, cinemas and tourism.

The *Annual Census of Production Monitors* cover virtually every sector of industry, and include data on total purchases, total sales, stocks, work in progress, capital expenditure, employment, wages and salaries. They include analyses of costs and output, of establishments by size, of full and part-time employees by sex, and of employment, net capital expenditure and net output by region.

You can use the information – particularly that from the size analysis table – to establish such ratios as gross output per head, net output per head, net to gross output, and wages and salaries to net output. With these as a base, you can compare the performance of your own business with the average for firms of similar size and for that with your particular industry as a whole. For example, you can discover your share of the market, and compare employment figures, increases in sales and so on.

Most of the libraries listed later in this section will have a selection of the *Business Monitor* series. Individual monitors can be bought from HMSO Books, PO Box 569, London SE1 9NH. They are all individually priced.

Guide to Official Statistics is the main guide to all government produced statistics, including ad hoc reports. It is published by HMSO at £18.50. However, a brief, free guide is available from the Press and Information Service, Central Satistical Office, Great George Street, London SW1 3AQ.

Key Note Publications. Publishers of the same name at 28-42 Banner Street, London EC1Y 8QE; 01-253 3006, produce concise briefs on various sectors of the UK economy.

Each Key Note contains a detailed examination of the structure of an industry, its distribution network and its major companies; an in-depth analysis of the market, covering products by volume and value, market shares, foreign trade and an appraisal of trends within the market; a review of recent developments in the industry, highlighting new product development, corporate development and legislation; a financial analysis of named major companies, providing data and ratios over a three-year period together with a corporate appraisal and economic overview; forecasts on the future prospects for the industry, including estimates from Key Note's own database and authoritative trade sources. There is a very useful appendix detailing further sources of information – recent press articles, other reports and journals.

Over 100 market sectors are covered, including such areas as adhesives, after-dinner drinks, bicycles, butchers, commercial leasing, health foods, road haulage, public houses, travel agents and women's magazines. Each Key Note costs £75, falling to £17 for users of their voucher system.

Kelly's Manufacturers & Merchants Directory, published by IPC Business Press, 40 Bowling Green Lane, London EC1R 0NE has an alphabetical list of manufacturers, merchants, wholesalers and firms, together with their trade descriptions, addresses, telephone and telex numbers. In addition, entries are listed by trade classification. A section lists British importers under the goods they import. Exporters are listed by the products they export and the continent and countries in which they sell. The directory covers 90,000 UK firms classified under 10,000 trade, product or service headings.

Kelly's Regional Directory of British Industry is published in eight volumes each October. It provides an exhaustive, town-by-town guide to industry and the products and services offered. This really is most useful if you want to confine your interests to one particular area, perhaps as an aid to a concentrated sales blitz.

Kelly's Post Office London Directory provides business listings by street, so a company's immediate neighbours can be identified. It is useful for finding concentrations of a particular type of business, or for finding gaps in the provision of a particular type of business.

Key British Enterprises, published by Dun and Bradstreet Ltd, 26-32 Clifton Street, London EC2P 2LY; 01-247 4377, contains information on 20,000 UK companies that between them are responsible for 90 per cent of industrial expenditure. KBE is very useful for identifying sales prospects or confirming addresses, monitoring competitors and customers or finding new suppliers. As well as giving the names, addresses, telephone and telex numbers of the main office of each company, it gives branch addresses, products indexed by SIC (Standard Industrial Classification) code, sales turnover (UK and overseas), directors' names and responsibilities, shareholders, capital structure, trade names, and number of employees.

By using the directory you can quickly establish the size of business you are dealing with and what other products or services they offer. It is very often important to know the size of a firm if, for example, your products are confined to certain types of business. A bookkeeping service is unlikely to interest a large company with several hundred employees; they would have their own accounts department. Conversely, a very small company may not need a public relations consultant.

Kompass is published in association with the Confederation of British Industry in two volumes: Volume I is indexed by product or service to help find suppliers, indicating whether they are manufacturers, wholesalers or distributors. It can be very useful indeed on certain occasions to be able to bypass a wholesaler and get to the manufacturer direct. Volume II gives basic company information on the 30,000 suppliers identified from Volume I. It includes the address, telephone and telex numbers, bankers, directors, office hours and the number of employees.

Office of Population, Census and Surveys produce demographic statistics for each county in England and Wales from the 1981 census. These provide data not only on total populations in each area, but also on occupations, economic groups, etc. Similar reports for Scottish and Northern Ireland regions are also available. There is a reference library at OPCS, St Catherine House, 10 Kingsway, London WC2B 6JP; 01-242 0262. More information and answers to general enquiries on these reports are also available from this number on extensions 2009 and 2013.

Overseas Trade Statistics, published by the Department of Industry and Trade, provide a monthly statement of UK imports and exports by volume and value for each product group and individual country. The Bill of Entry Services, operated by HM Customs and Excise, Portcullis House, 17 Victoria Avenue, Southend-on-Sea SS2 6AL (0702 49421 ext. 310), will provide more detailed information at a fee.

Published Data on European Industrial Markets, published by Industrial Aids Ltd, 14 Buckingham Palace Road, London SW1W 0QP; 01-828 5036.

Part I lists over 1,900 market research reports available for purchase at prices from as low as £10 up to several thousand pounds. Although the directory is entitled 'industrial', the interpretation is fairly wide. It covers consumer goods as markets for industrial products, and financial and economic planning studies, where they are considered of possible interest to industry. This could be a relatively inexpensive way of finding out about a distant market place.

Part II is a guide to other sources of information on European industrial markets, including international statistical and individual country sources.

Reports Index, Business Surveys Ltd, PO Box 21, Dorking, Surrey RH5 4EE; 0306 87857. This is an index to reports in every field published and available for sale. Its sources include government publications, HMSO and other market research organizers, educational establishments, EEC, industrial and financial companies. Cost: £94 per annum.

The Retail Directory, published by Newman Books, 48 Poland Street, London W1; 01-439 0335, gives details of all UK department stores and private shops. It lists the names of executives and merchandise buyers as well as addresses and telephone numbers, early closing days etc. It also covers multiple shops, cooperative societies, supermarkets and many other retail outlets. If you plan to sell to shops, this is a useful starting point, with around 1,305 department stores and large shops and 4,821 multiple shop firms and variety stores listed in 1,346 pages. If you are already selling retail, this directory could help you expand your prospects list quickly. The directory also identifies high turnover outlets for main product ranges. There is a useful survey, showing retail activities on each major shopping street in the country. It gives the name and nature of the retail businesses in each street.

A separate volume contains shop surveys for the Greater London area, with 27,830 shops listed by name, street number and trade. The head offices of 1,130 multiples are given, as are 233 surveys showing what sort of shops are in any area. This can be used for giving sales people useful contacts within their territory.

Sell's Directory, Sell's Publications Ltd, Sell's House, 39 East Street, Epsom, Surrey KT17 1BQ, and the Institute of Purchasing Management. It lists 65,000 firms alphabetically, with name, trade, address, telephone number and telex numbers. Using a classified cross-reference system, it covers 25,000 products and services. There is a guide to several thousand trade names, cross-referenced back to each company. The remaining sections include a contractors' section, advertising firms seeking contract work, and a business information section.

If you only know the trade name and want to find out who makes the product, then this directory will help you. You can then use it to find competitive sources of supply of similar products or services.

Finding the information

Now that you have an idea of the considerable mass of data that is available about companies, their products and markets, the next problem that remains is to track it down. Fortunately, many of the directories and publications are kept in reference sections of major libraries up and down the country. If you know exactly what information you want, then your problem is confined to finding a library or information service that has that information.

Specialist libraries

Apart from your local library there are hundreds of specialist libraries concentrated in government departments, major industrial companies, trade organizations, research centres and academic institutes. Two useful publications that will help you find out about these are listed below.

ASLIB Economic and Business Information Group Membership Directory, published by the group and available from the London Business School Library, Sussex Place, Regent's Park, London NW1 4SA; 01-262 5050. This provides a list of over 300 specialist business libraries throughout the country, and gives a very useful guide to their area of specialist interest.

Guide to Government Departments and other Libraries. The 25th edition, published in 1982, is the latest, and is available from the Science Reference Library, 25 Southampton Buildings, Chancery Lane, London WC2A 1AW, price £9. As the title indicates, this book concentrates on libraries in government departments and agencies, and particularly avoids duplicating the ground covered by the ASLIB Directory. The entries are arranged by subject, supplemented by an alphabetical index of the libraries, their locations, phone numbers and opening hours.

Not all the libraries covered in these directories are open to the public for casual visits. However, many will let you use their reference facilities by appointment.

If you are in, or near London you can visit or contact:

The Science Reference Library, Department of the British Library, 25 Southampton Buildings, Chancery Lane, London WC2A 1AW; 01-405 8721, ext 3344 or 3345; patent enquiries ext 3350, telex 266959. This is the national library for modern science and technology, for patents, trade marks and designs. It has the most comprehensive reference section of this type of literature in western Europe. If you have no adequate library close at hand a visit here could save you visits to several libraries. It should also be able to provide you with answers if most other places cannot do so.

The library's resources are formidable. It has 25,000 different journals, with issues back to 1960 on open shelves and the rest quickly available; 85,000 books and pamphlets and over 20 million patents. It has a world-wide collection of journals on trade marks, together with books on law and design. Most of the major UK and European reports are held, as is trade literature and around 1,000 abstracting periodicals.

The services are equally extensive. It is open from Monday to Friday, 09.30 to 21.00, and on Saturday, 10.00 to 13.00. You can visit without prior arrangement or a reader's ticket. Telephone requests for information, including the checking of references, are accepted. Once at the library, staff are available to help you find items and to answer general queries. Scientific staff are also on hand for specialized enquiries. There is even a linguist service to help you inspect material written in a foreign language though for this service you must make an appointment.

The Business Information Service of the Science Reference Library; 01-404 0406. This was set up in January 1981, primarily to support the activities of other business and industrial libraries. However, it will help individual users as much as possible. Staff here can extract reference information quickly, advise on the use of business literature and suggest other organizations to contact. For extensive research you will have to call in person, but they can let you know if a visit would be worthwhile.

Information services

In addition to the many excellent business libraries up and down the country there is an increasing number of organizations that will do the searching for you. The benefits to you are twofold: professionals search out the data, and can alert you to sources that you may not have thought of; they save you time, not just the time you would spend searching. If you are far from a good business reference library you may have a considerable and expensive journey to make. Mostly, these organizations have substantial libraries of their own, but Warwick, for example, will search elsewhere if they cannot find it in their stocks. They claim the second largest statistics collection in the UK, and they have access to several on-line data bases.

Organizations in the field include:

Industrial Aids Ltd, enquiry service at 14 Buckingham Palace Road, London SW1W 0QP; 01-828 5036, telex 918666 CRECON G. This service is geared to supply commercial and technical information, such as who makes what/where/how much. Who is company A's agent in country X? Where are custom manufacturing sources? Details are given of company financial data, affiliations, product literature, consumption patterns, end users, prices, discounts and trading terms, as well as new legislation and standards. The cost is £29 per enquiry, excluding VAT. You can use the service by telephone, telex or letter, and the response is fast.

The Marketing Shop, 18 Kingly Court, Kingly Street, London W1R 5LE; 01-434 2671, telex 262284. This organization provides a wide range of marketing services, but its information service is perhaps the most useful facility for small businesses. It can provide data on practically any topic, either using its own library or outside sources, and will also monitor the media for information on companies, products or markets. The charge is £35 an hour for ad hoc work. The more usual arrangement is for customers to take a block of hours to be used over the year. Block fees start at around £500, which works out at £30 per hour.

Warwick Statistics Service, University of Warwick Library, Coventry CV4 7AL; 0203 418938, telex 31406. Contact: Jennifer Carr or David Mart. The service offers a range of commercial and economic information based on published sources including international statistics, both official and non-official, market research, periodicals, reports, directories, company reports and on-line services. The service can be particularly helpful to a small business with information on market size and share, locating particular types of company and finding out about them, tracing recent articles on a particular product or process, on consumer expenditure data, imports and exports, economic conditions, price trends, advertising expenditure and production and sales figures.

The service will also undertake analysis of the data in question, and provide a written report on their desk research. In general, enquiries are dealt with on the telephone, telex or by post; however, personal visits are welcome. If you telephone beforehand, documents can be assembled for you to look at.

Annual subscribers to the service pay £300 for 25 hours' search time and publication. Occasional users of the service can get information or research assistance on an ad hoc basis at a cost of £20 per hour pro rata, with a minimum charge of £5. All in all, it is very good value.

Their monthly journal, *Warwick Statistics News*, provides a regular source of information on statistical and marketing topics, and costs £25 per annum. The service holds regular one-day seminars on Information Sources for Business Planning and Market Research, costing £30.

FIELD RESEARCH

In some cases the answers to your questions won't exist in published form since no one else will have been interested enough to have researched and published the data – for example, how many people pass a particular shop front each day. There you will need to undertake some *original market research*. This activity, often called field research, means you (or people you employ) have to go out and ask people the questions you want answers to.

Sampling

The first problem you will face is to decide how many people to include in your survey.

Suppose you wanted to find out how many shoppers passed down Kensington High Street every year, and how much they each spent. Clearly you could not stand in the High Street and interview every single person for the whole year. By the time you got the answer it would be too late and the cost too high.

Equally obviously if you asked the first person you saw how much they spent, and then multiplied it by the number of people passing in a day, and then multiplied that by the days in a year, your answer would too inaccurate to be of use.

So somewhere between the whole population and one lies a satisfactory number of people to include in your "sample". Within limits, the larger your sample size the more "accurate" the emerging picture will be. But there are sharp diseconomies. Doubling the sample size, if it is already large, will not improve the accuracy by a significant amount – perhaps a few per cent. But it will double the cost of the survey.

You must also make sure that the sample taken is representative of all the groups of people that you are interested in finding out about. For example men and women; high income and low income; commuters and non-commuters.

The Questionnaire

This is the research technique most commonly used by small and new ventures. Questionnaires can be answered in face-to-face interviews, over the telephone or by post.

Here are some rules to observe when designing a questionnaire:

1. Keep the number of questions to a minimum. People don't have unlimited time and you run the danger of sidetracking the objectives if you ask too many questions.
2. Keep the questions simple. Answers should either be yes/no/don't know, or offer at least four alternatives, e.g. if the question is "How interested are you in going to the theatre?", the respondent should be asked to answer *very, fairly, not very* or *not at all*. This helps you assess what proportion of respondents would almost definitely take advantage of a new product or service and what proportion just might.
3. Make sure the respondent really understands the question – so avoid ambiguity.
4. Avoid opinions, stick to asking for factual answers.
5. Make sure you have a cut-out question to eliminate "unsuitable" respondents. For example, non-decision makers.
6. Make sure you have an identifying question so you can be sure you have an appropriate cross-section of respondents.

Chantal Coady, a 23-year-old design school graduate, brought energy, enthusiasm and impatience in roughly equal proportions to her business start-up. After a spell in the successful chocolate department at Harrods, Chantal felt she knew enough to launch off on her own. She wanted to sell unashamedly luxurious chocolates to a market that expected the best, but could not find it on the doorstep. She believed that London's fashionable King's Road had the right residential customer profile, and there was no source of supply west of Sloane Square. She was less certain of the character and quantity of passing trade, so she devised the questionnaire opposite to confirm or refute her hunch.

Observations

Sometimes it isn't necessary to carry out full-scale surveys. You have probably come across people with counters monitoring the traffic or how many cars have driven over rubber strips in the road. These are "observation research techniques" which are counting the number of people doing something or other. An application for a small business is to count the number of customers, or delivery vans, coming and going to a competitor's premises.

Who can help

There are a large number of specialist market research companies (you can obtain a list from the *Market Research Society,* 15 Belgrave Square, London SW1; 01-235 4709). They will advise you how best to conduct your research, devise tests and questionnaires, and analyse the results.

Professional market research is a sophisticated operation and it isn't cheap: conducting interviews with 100 shoppers, for instance, could cost you £1000.

There are ways to get less expensive help, though. Students on business study courses have to carry out projects as part of their course. Very often this includes a market research task and tutors are keen to ensure that this project resembles real life as closely as possible, so you may be able to get them to undertake some of your

MARKET RESEARCH QUESTIONNAIRE

Date: Location: Time:

1   I am interested in people who buy chocolate – can you tell
     me how often you buy the following:

	Every day	Every week	Once a month	Special occasions
Bars				
Boxes				
Loose chocs				

2   Where do you buy these chocolates?
     Supermarket   ☐
     Sweet shop   ☐
     Woolworths   ☐
     Specialist shop ☐
     Other   ☐

3   When was the last time you were given chocs as a present?
     Some people enjoy receiving chocs as a gift, where would you put
     your self on this scale?

Overjoyed	Very pleased	Pleased	Indifferent	Ungrateful

4   Do you ever buy chocs as a present for anyone?
     The last time you bought chocs for someone, who were they for?
     _____

5   Where did you buy them from?_____

6   How much did you spend?   Up to £1 ☐   Up to £5 ☐   Over £5 ☐

7   Were they wrapped in the shop? (As a gift)

8   Do you have a favourite chocolate bar or box?_____

9   Any preferences for   Dark ☐ Milk ☐ White ☐

10   Do you have a favourite from any particular country?

English	French	German	Belgian	Swiss	Other

11   Some people say that the existing chocolates on the market are
     rather boring, would you agree?

12   If there were a shop which sold a unique range of gifts in
     chocolate, and high quality loose and boxed chocs, how interested
     would you be in buying them?

Extremely	Very	Moderately	Indifferent	Not interested

13   Age group
     Up to 20   ☐
     21 – 25   ☐
     26 – 30   ☐
     31 – 40   ☐
     41 – 50   ☐
     Over 50   ☐

14   Profession _____

15   Income bracket
     Up to £5,000   ☐
     Up to £10,000 ☐
     Up to £15,000 ☐
     Over £15,000   ☐

     Any other comments _____
     _____
     _____
     _____

market reserch for a modest fee. Contact the marketing department of a local college or polytechnic.

Other organizations which offer low-cost help with market research projects are the Institute of Marketing, Moor Hall, Cookham, Maidenhead, Berks SL6 9HQ; 06285-24922 – through their Marketing Advisory Service they can put you in front of an experienced professional marketing person, for a nominal £15 – and the Small Firms Marketing Centre, London Road, Waverley, Bristol BS15 5JH; 0272-677807. Established in 1983 this centre has a small full time staff and a team of part time consultants on tap. Advice on structuring a market research plan is also given by local Small Firms Centres and Enterprise Agencies, listed in Chapter 11.

DISTRIBUTION CHANNELS

Your pint of milk arrives on your doorstep each morning together with your daily paper. Later in the day you may drive out into the country to buy a hand-knit sweater from a country weaver, or a jar of honey direct from the people who made it.

These examples illustrate the two extremes of ways in which a product or service can be "delivered" to a customer.

Most businesses get their products or services to their market via a range of different channels, as these routes are called. Knowing their importance can help you to market your products more effectively.

For example, if you only choose one channel you may be missing out on sales and growth. The daily pint on the doorstep may be ideal for the rural resident – it may even be essential for the elderly and immobile. But it isn't particularly relevant for the itinerant London flatdweller. Flatdwellers consume milk, but they tend to buy it on their way home at the late-night corner shop, just as they buy their papers at the railway station or tube.

Choosing the wrong distribution channels can have disastrous consequences. Freddie Laker's second travel venture was blocked from selling holidays through ABTA (Association of British Travel Agents) members. As this is the key distribution channel for holidays, it proved impossible to build a substantial business without access to it and this was a contributory factor to the collapse of the business.

The chart below gives an idea of some of the routes a product or service takes in getting from the manufacturer to the end consumer. Each stage of the process incurs costs and expects to make a profit margin.

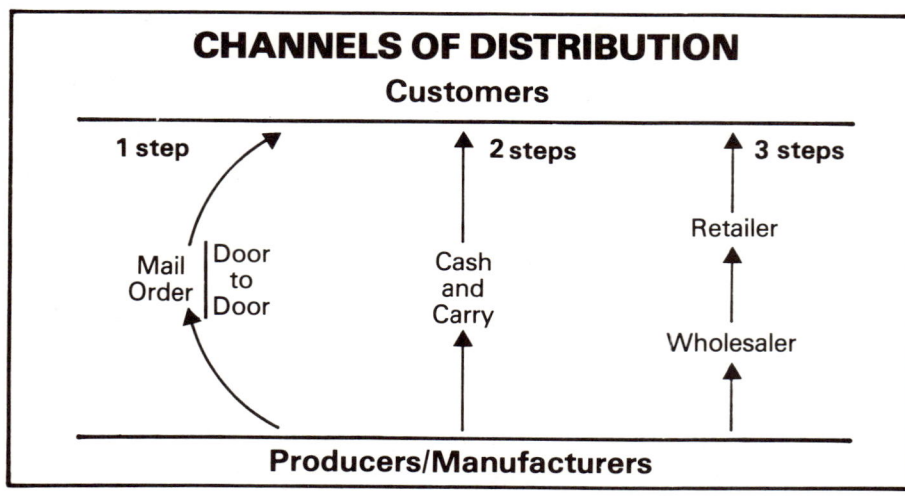

Retail stores This general name covers the great range of outlets from the corner shop to Harrods. Some offer speciality goods such as hi-fi equipment, where the customer expects professional help from the staff. Others, such as Marks & Spencers and Tesco, are mostly self-service, with the customers making up their own minds on choice of product.

Wholesalers The pattern of wholesale distribution has changed out of all recognition over the past two decades. It is still an extremely important channel where physical distribution, stock holding, finance and breaking bulk are still profitable functions.

Cash and carry This slightly confusing route has replaced the traditional wholesaler as a source of supply for smaller retailers. In return for paying cash and picking up the goods yourself, the "wholesaler" shares part of his profit margin with you. The attraction for the wholesaler is improved cash flow and for the retailer a bigger margin and a wide product range. Hypermarkets and discount stores also fit somewhere between the manufacturer and the market place.

Mail order This specialized technique provides a direct channel to the customer, and is an increasingly popular route for new small businesses.

A fruitless search for fashionable, but comfortable, clothes when well into her first pregnancy led Judy Lever to her business idea. Together with her partner Vivian, she launched Blooming Marvellous Ltd four years ago to design, make and market fashionable clothes for the mother-to-be. They could not afford a large stock of products or a wide range. Also the selling season was by definition a short one, and their customers had to be reached quickly. As their potential customers were spread thinly across a wide geographic area it was uneconomic to display their goods in hundreds of shops. They chose mail order as their channel as it gave them the most direct control over their selling effort and put them close to their customers.

Door-to-door selling We've all heard the funny jokes about the foot-in-the-door salesman. This method of distributing has traditionally been used by vacuum cleaner distributors and encyclopaedia companies and is now used by insurance companies, cavity wall insulation firms, double glazing firms and others as well. Many of these businesses use hard-sell techniques which are frequently far from ethical, so door-to-door selling doesn't have a very good name. However, other firms such as Avon Cosmetics have managed to sell successfully by door-to-door without attracting the stigma of unethical selling practices.

Party Plan Selling A variation on door-to-door selling which is on the increase with new party plan ideas arriving from the USA. Agents enrolled by the company invite their friends to a get-together where the products are demonstrated and orders are invited. The agent gets a commission. Party plan has worked very well for Tupperware and other firms who sell this way.

On a more modest scale, we know a man who turned his hobby of making pine bookcases and spice racks into a profitable business by getting his wife to invite neighbours for coffee mornings where his wares were prominently displayed.

Franchising This is a growing method of expanding a business operation – but only for businesses which have been running successfully for some time (we cover franchising in detail in Chapter 2).

Selecting distribution channels

These are the factors you should consider when choosing channels of distribution for your particular business.

1. *Does it meet your customers' needs?* You have to find out how your customers expect their product or service delivered to them and why they need that particular route.
2. *Will the product itself survive?* Fresh vegetables, for example, need to be moved quickly from where they are grown to where they are consumed. Avocado pears

and out of season strawberries are often air-freighted to eager customers who are prepared to pay for the privilege.

3. *Can you sell enough this way?* "Enough" is how much you *want* to sell. Sinclair launched his microvision TV by direct mail because he wanted to *restrict* demand to match his limited capacity to supply.

4. *Is it compatible with your image?* If you are selling a luxury product then door-to-door selling may spoil the impression you are trying to create in the rest of your marketing effort.

5. *How do your competitors distribute?* If they have been around for a while and are obviously successful it is well worth looking at how your competitors distribute and using that knowledge to your advantage.

6. *Will the channel be cost effective?* A small manufacturer may not find it cost effective to sell to retailers west of Bristol, because the direct "drop" size, that is the load per order, is too small to be worthwhile.

7. *Will the mark-up be enough?* If your product cannot bear at least a 100% mark up, then it is unlikely that you will be able to sell it through department stores. Your distribution channel has to be able to make a profit from selling your product too.

8. *Push-Pull.* Moving a product through a distribution channel calls for two sorts of selling activity. *Push* is the name given to selling your product in, for example, to a shop. *Pull* is the effort that you carry out on the shops' behalf to help them sell your product out of that shop. That pull may be caused by your national advertising, a merchandising activity, or the sheer uniqueness of your product. You need to know how much Push and Pull are needed for the channel you are considering. If you are not geared up to help a retailer to sell out your product, and they need that help, then this could be a poor channel.

9. *Physical distribution.* The way in which you have to move your product to your end customer is also an important factor to weigh up, when choosing a channel. As well as such factors as the cost of carriage, you will also have to decide about packaging materials. As a rough rule of thumb, the more stages in the distribution channel the more robust and expensive your packaging will have to be.

PROMOTING THE PRODUCT

Every business has to communicate with its potential customers to persuade them to purchase its products or services. The aim of all promotional activity is to secure as many favourable buying decisions as possible.

The most surprising fact about advertising is not how much money is spent on doing it: in the UK, advertising ranks somewhere between milk and petrol on the national expenditure scale. Rather the problem lies in how much is mis-spent.

Lord Leverhulme said, "Half the money I spend on advertising is wasted. My problem is to find out which half."

Advertising is to some extent an intangible activity, although the bills for it are certainly not. These are the five key questions that you should ask yourself *before* you commit yourself to any promotional expense.

Promotion/advertising check list

What do you want to happen?

How much is that worth?

What message will make it happen?

What media should be used?

How will results be checked?

What are your advertising objectives?

Let's start with the first question, but extend it to give it its full meaning.

What specifically do you want to happen as a result of this promotional activity?

There is no point in informing, educating or pre-selling unless it leads to the opportunity in a significant number of instances for a sale to result. So what does the potential customer have to do to enable you to make these sales? Do you want him to visit your showroom, to phone you, to write to your office, return a card, or send an order in the post? Do you expect him to have an immediate need to which you want him to respond now, or is it that you want him to remember you at some future date when he has a need for whatever it is you are selling?

The more you are able to identify a specific response in terms of orders, visits, phone calls, requests for literature, the better your promotional effort will be tailored to achieve your objective, and the more clearly you will be able to assess the effectiveness of your promotion and its cost versus its yield.

The more you find you are being told that some particular promotional expenditure cannot be identified with a specific objective, but is to "improve your image" or "to keep your name in front of the public", then the more likely it is that particular expenditure is not an effective way of spending your money.

The establishment of specific objectives in the promotional field is sometimes difficult, that is why many people give up rather than try. Assuming that you don't give up and that you establish specifically what you want to happen as a result of spending your promotional money, let's go on to examine how you can go about achieving your objectives.

For a new business the overall promotional task will be to move a core of customers up the "Loyalty Ladder" – that is, from being unaware of your existence to becoming loyal regular customers.

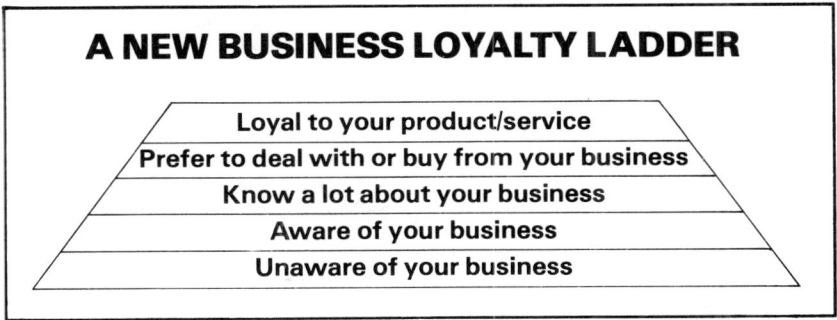

A NEW BUSINESS LOYALTY LADDER

Loyal to your product/service
Prefer to deal with or buy from your business
Know a lot about your business
Aware of your business
Unaware of your business

How much is it worth to achieve your objective?

Once you know what you want a particular promotional activity to achieve it becomes a little easier to set a budget for it. In practice four methods are most commonly used, and they each have their merits, with the exception of the first.

The "What can we afford" approach has its roots in the total misconception of promotional activity, which implies that advertising is an extravagance. When times are good, surplus cash is spent on advertising and when times are bad this budget is the first one to be cut back. In fact all the evidence points to the success of businesses that increase promotional spending during a recession, usually at the expense of their meaner competitors.

The "Percentage of Sales" method very often comes from the experiences of the entrepreneur or his colleagues, or from historical budgets. So if a business spent 10% of sales last year, they will plan to spend 10% next, particularly if things went well. This method at least has some logic and provides a good starting point for preparing the overall budget.

"Let's Match the Competitors" becomes a particularly important criteria when they step up their promotional activity. Usually this will result either in your losing sales or feeling threatened. In either case you will want to retaliate, and increasing your promotion is an obvious choice.

The "Cost/Benefit approach" comes into its own when you have clear and specific promotional goals and an experience base to build on. If you have spare capacity in your factory or want to sell more out of your shop, you can work out what the "benefit" of those extra sales is worth.

Suppose a £1,000 advertisement is expected to generate 100 enquiries for our product. If our experience tells us that on average 10% of enquiries result in orders, and our profit margin is £200 per product, then we can expect an extra £2,000 profit. That "benefit" is much greater than the £1,000 cost of the advertisement, so it seems a worthwhile investment.

In practice, a small business uses all of these last three methods to decide how much to spend on promoting its products.

What message will help achieve the objective?

Let's start again with the marketing concept as defined earlier: "Marketing is the identification of an existing or potential need, and the meeting of that need at a continuing satisfactory profit."

Under a production-oriented company, this becomes "This is what we can make, how do we unload it?" Or, under a selling concept, "This is what we've got, how do we sell it?"

The fact that most advertisers are primarily concerned with helping themselves and *not* their customers becomes glaringly obvious when studying many ads.

The bases of any promotional activity are:
- What to communicate – the message
- How to communicate – the method

To answer the first question a company must look at itself and its products from the customer's standpoint and be able to answer the hypothetical questions "why should I buy your product?" It is better to consider the answer in two stages.
- "Why should I buy your *product*?"

The answer is provided naturally by the analysis of factors which affect choice. So the analysis of buying motives or satisfactions is an essential foundation of promotional strategy.
- "Why should I buy *your* product?"

The only logically satisfactory answer is: "because it is different". The difference can arise in two ways.

We – the sellers – are different

Establish your particular niche.

It – the product – is different

Each product should have a unique selling point, based on fact.

Your promotional message must be built around these factors and must consist of facts about the company and facts about the product.

The stress here is on the word "fact" and whilst there may be many types of facts surrounding you and your products, your customers are only interested in two. The factors which influence their buying decision, and the ways in which your business and its products stand out from the competition.

These *facts* must be translated into benefits. Another look at the ascending scale of human needs will help you to understand why people buy.

Ascending scale of human needs
Freedom from pain
Freedom from hunger
Freedom from discomfort
Continuance of the species
Security/dislike of change
Company
Affection/love
Satisfaction of curiosity
Ego gratification
Intellectual stimulation
Aesthetic satisfaction
Spiritual needs/immortality

There is an assumption sometimes that everyone buys for obvious logical reasons only, when we all know of innumerable examples showing this is not so.

Does a woman only buy a new dress when the old one is worn out?

Does the boss have a desk that's bigger than his subordinates because he has more papers to put on it?

It's often easy to understand in selling to domestic consumers what fundamental human motivations influence their buying needs and, therefore, what benefits your product or service must offer if it is to fulfil that need.

In the case of professional buyers who are buying for others to consume/use, or to resell to others, the identification of buying motives may be more difficult. The bigger the buying decision or the closer the use of the item purchased is to him, the stronger will be the influence of personal emotions/motivations – the more minor the decision or remote the use, the stronger will be the influence of dispassionate, logical purchasing decisions.

Therefore, to identify the message you want to communicate, you must first establish what are the needs your product can satisfy, what benefits can you offer that will meet those needs, and how are you going to communicate your message.

Your message should be put together to satisfy these four steps:

Attention
Interest
Desire
Action

Having decided on the objective and identified the message, how do you choose the most effective method of delivering your message?

What media should you use?

Not all methods of communication have an equal impact. We are much more likely to be favourably influenced if a trusted and respected friend recommends a product or service to us, than by a door to door salesman. Like every aspect of business there is a logic to help you find which avenue of communication to use. That logic is based on an "ascending scale of power of influence".

We show the scale overleaf together with the practical advantages and disadvantages of each method.

Ascending Scale of Power of Influence

Method	Advantages	Disadvantages
1. Personal, recommendation/advice of individual whose opinion is trusted and known to be unbiased	Most effective means of influence/communication	Difficult to relate to specific potential customer. Alright for general spread of customer loyalty, slow to communicate specific message.
2. Personal recommendation by individual whose judgement has not been validated, but who is unbiased by personal gain	Second most effective means of influence/communication. Can use group opinion leaders	Slow process to educate and convert them. Difficult to assess effectiveness.
3. Personal recommendation by individual who appears to be knowledgeable and honest, but who stands to gain by his recommendations	More control since "salesman" can be trained	Limited number of communicators available to use compared to size of target audience.
4. Direct approach by 'phone	Immediate. Opportunity to gain responses. Easy to assess effectiveness	Identification of potential purchases can be difficult. Staff need careful training.
5. Direct and individualized approach by mail	Relatively cheap and immediate methods of assessing effectiveness easily incorporated	Takes time to create good mailing list.
6. Unbiased comment in "general media"	Inexpensive. Immediate. Large audience	Not totally under one's own control. No way of building in assessment of effectiveness.
7. Participation in promotional activity, such as an exhibition	Immediate. Can generate other free publicity. Medium audience. Way of identifying potential customers	Needs considerable organization and flair.
8. Biased recommendation in the general media.		

Much of the conventional activity of promotion and advertising is concentrated at the bottom end of the ascending scale of influence. A review of the various media open to a small business, and the advantages and disadvantages of each, are listed below.

Media	Advantages	Disadvantages
Television (and cinema)	(a) Conviction. (b) Combines movement and spoken word in the home. (c) Can demonstrate product. (d) Creative flexibility: realism or entertainment, animation. (e) Media flexibility: can concentrate on one area or cover majority of country. (f) Production flexibility: advertisement can be changed at short notice (a few weeks). (g) Trade reaction usually very favourable.	(a) High absolute cost (although cost per viewer can be low) – (b) Advertisements are ephemeral (viewer cannot refer back).

Media	Advantages	Disadvantages
Local radio	(a) Media flexibility – can cover one area or a number of areas. (b) Production flexibility – ads can be changed at short notice. (c) Some stations, e.g. Capital Radio, have special small business packages providing up to ten spots for as little as £3000.	(a) No national coverage (b) Listeners cannot refer back. (c) High absolute cost at peak times (although cost per listener can be low for the right audience).
National press	(a) Low cost per 1000 readers with large coverage. (b) Permanence: reader can return to advertisement. (c) Authority: advertisements borrow some of the reader's loyalty to paper. (d) Size: large advertisements are conspicuous in relatively thin papers. (e) Copy: intricate statements can be printed for study at leisure. (f) Favourable impression on traders.	(a) Readership subject to many influences, e.g. position in paper, impact of dramatic news. (b) Production quality not very high. (c) Impact difficult to achieve except in big spaces. (d) Media flexibility almost non-existent.
Local newspapers	(a) Permanence: reader can return to the advertisement. (b) Authority: advertisement borrows some of the readers loyalty to the paper. (c) Size: large advertisements are conspicuous in relatively thin papers. (d) Copy: intricate statements can be printed for study at leisure. (e) Media flexibility: can cover any group of population from small town to major city and environs. (f) Local promotion: can tie in with dealer's efforts. (g) Authority: local papers very real and friendly to readers.	(a) High cost per 1000 readers. (b) Printing quality sometimes very low. (c) Make-up: frequently very crowded and complicated with high number of local advertisements.
National magazines	(a) Low cost per 1000 readers with large coverage (b) Permanence: reader can return to the advertisement (c) Authority: advertisement borrows some of the reader's loyalty to the paper. (d) Size: large advertisements are conspicuous in relatively thin papers. (e) Copy: intricate statements are printed for study at leisure. (f) Favourable impression on traders and in addition: Colour though expensive can be very useful.	(a) Readership subject to many influences e.g. position in paper, impact of dramatic news. (b) Impact difficult to achieve except in big spaces. (c) Media flexibility almost non-existent and limited variety of publications. Mostly for women.

Media	Advantages	Disadvantages
Specialized magazines (*Practical Householder* etc.)	(a) Permanence: reader can return to the advertisement. (b) Authority: advertisements borrow some of the reader's loyalty to the paper. (c) Copy: intricate statements can be printed for study at leisure. (d) Favourable impression on traders. Preconditioned readers interested in particular subject. Colour printing. Relatively low cost.	(a) Very competitive climate, adjacent to directly competitive advertising. (b) Thick magazines crowded with advertising.
Posters	(a) Media flexibility: can be posted in any numbers down to one, in almost every populated area. (b) Colour and impact can be considerable with large posters. (c) "Readership" (on lines of a quick glance) very high.	(a) Information about actual readership and effect is imprecise. (b) Creative limitations considerable, very short message required for quick impact. (c) Trade reaction not specially favourable.
Leaflets	(a) Low cost. (b) Simple to put into operation. (c) Can be done quickly. (d) Can be concentrated into any geographic area. (e) Can be mailed or distributed by hand. (f) Easy to monitor results.	(a) No permanence. (b) Low status. (c) Low response.

How will the results be checked?

This is very much down to you. A glance back to advertising analysis in the market research section of this chapter will show how one organization tackled the problem.

As a general guide you should record the information in the table below, for each promotional activity.

Monitoring Results

Promotion: _____ Date: _____

Media: _____ Responsibility: _____

Costs: _____

Objective (quantify)	Results (quantify)	Variance (objects-results)	Consequences (profit or loss)

At the end of the day the consequences of promotional expenditure will result in a profit or loss to the business, as will every other business decision. The only way you can learn from your mistakes, which you will undoubtedly make, is to recognise them in the first place.

PUBLIC RELATIONS

"Public relations is about presenting yourself, your business and your products/ services in a favourable light to your various 'publics' – suppliers, creditors, bankers, the general public, and of course your customers ... at little or no cost."

The sting in the tail of that description is why it is so vital for small businesses to get favourable media comment. But it is also important because it is a more influential method of communication than general advertising.

If you cannot wait for the press to beat a path to your door, then you will have to go to theirs. The starting point, as with all promotion, is to decide what you want to achieve. Once you have done that, prepare a short press release, using the style of language of the type of media you are aiming for.

Put down some important facts and give the "story" some human interest. Send it (or phone it) not to the editor but to the particular section of the paper or journal you want to get into. It may be the business editor or features editor for example. Better still, get the person's name. Don't be disappointed if your first "press release" doesn't get instant national coverage. Keep up the pressure, and once the ball gets rolling it can move very fast indeed. Chantal Coady's Rococo had nearly thirty important stories published in media ranging from *Vogue* and the *Sunday Times* to the London *Standard* and local radio. All for the price of a few dozen stamps.

SELLING TECHNIQUES

Salesmanship is the domain of the secondhand car dealer, in popular folklore. The reality is rather different. While a vivid imagination and an outgoing personality are not a hindrance to a salesperson, they are not a prerequisite either.

Every entrepreneur is heavily involved in selling, whether the customers come to them, as they hopefully would if the business is retail, or if they have to go out to the

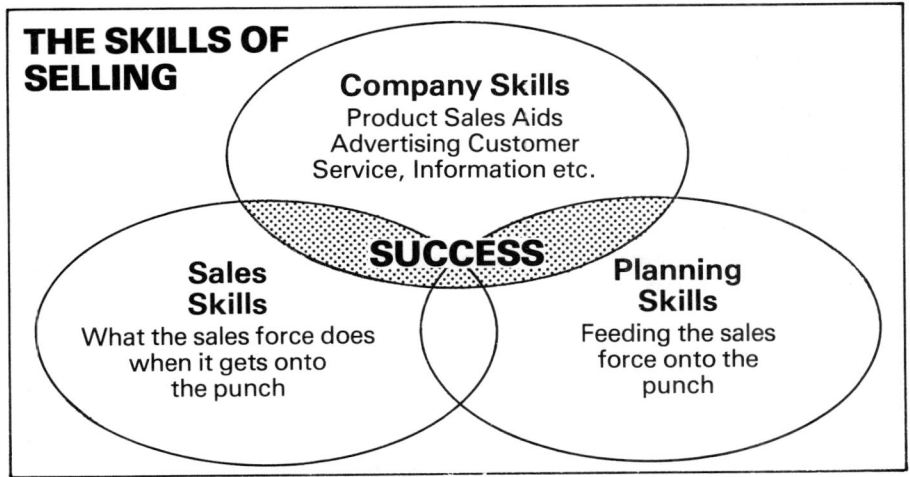

THE SKILLS OF SELLING

Company Skills
Product Sales Aids
Advertising Customer
Service, Information etc.

SUCCESS

Sales Skills
What the sales force does
when it gets onto
the punch

Planning Skills
Feeding the sales
force onto the
punch

customers. The old adage "90% perspiration and 10% inspiration" can aptly be applied to selling. Good organization and an understanding of the selling process is the key to developing selling skills.

To be successful in selling you need skills in these three areas. All these skills have to be brought to bear at the same time to achieve results.

Product knowledge

The founder (or prospective founder) of a business has considerable advantages over the professional salesperson. They have an unrivalled knowledge of what products are on offer and what they can do for the customer. They can also decide on advertising levels and the way information, such as leaflets, are prepared and presented.

Customers place great importance on dealing with someone knowledgeable and authoritative, and this is a strength the small business owner has and the big company salesperson very often does not.

Planning skills

Businesses that have salespeople have them because they believe that spending time with customers is an important, if not the most important, marketing function.

Not all businesses share this belief – for example, in mail order no physical contact is made before the product is sold. But for the vast majority of enterprises a major task is to get as much "selling time", as this face-to-face contact is known, as possible.

Unfortunately events usually conspire to make time slip away, with the field salesperson suffering the most. The field salesperson has to travel to his customer and frequently has to wait to be seen, or to call back at a more convenient time.

Sales force working day analysis

40% travelling	3 hours
30% waiting/meals/tea etc.	2 hr. 30 mins.
30% contact time	2 hr. 30 mins.
	8 hour day

But effective contact time = 15% = 1 hour 15 mins.

The table above is a reliable estimate on how a salesperson spent his time in a major national salesforce.

On average 70% of the working day was spent out of contact with customers. Barely two hours was spent in face-to-face selling and about half of that was wasted or ineffective.

With this fact in mind, time and territory planning is a vital problem for anyone who has to go out to get customers.

Sales skills

Every sale goes through a number of stages and by understanding them the chances of success can be improved.

Find out what the customer wants. If someone goes into a car showroom and the salesman enthusiastically tries to sell them a Porsche he will probably fail. The opening questions must probe the customers to find out their needs. Do you want a new car or a secondhand one? Are you looking for a family saloon and how much have you got to spend? The questions may not be as blunt as that, but these are the facts you have to know before you can move on to the next stage.

Match your product to their needs, and show how they will get the value they want by buying from you. Using your product and business knowledge you should now begin to steer the "prospect" towards a specific product.

Build up a body of agreement with the customer by posing questions which call for a "yes" answer.

This car is in your price range? YES

You did say you wanted four doors? YES

If you cannot get this body of agreement then you may have to go back to the previous stage and find another product.

But don't be put off by a few "No" answers, these may be signs that the "sale" is progressing well.

Overcoming objections. Objections are not a bad sign, on the contrary they are a sure sign of interest. But before trying to overcome them you should see if they are valid objections or false objections.

Objections

Customer	Salesperson
I would rather have it in blue	I can get it in blue for you next week
I really want to take it with me	I will phone our other branch and have it sent over within the hour
I'm not sure if I can really afford it anyway	

In this example the colour is not a real objection but perhaps the price is.

Close the sale. You would be surprised how many people either do not recognize a "buying signal" when they see one or keep on "selling" long after the customer is ready to buy. At this stage in the sale you should be firming up on the order by closing the sale and these techniques can help you.

The assumptive close

Salesperson	Customer
We will deliver and plumb the washing machine in on Thursday	Good

The special situation close

Salesperson	Customer
This is the last one we have and no more will be coming in this month	I'd better take it now

The Churchill close, so called because he is reputed to have used this technique when persuading the Americans to join the last war, calls for a summary of questions along these lines.

The Churchill close

Salesperson	Customer
You like the colour?	Yes
The size is just right?	Yes
You want to wear it tonight?	Yes
	———
	3 × Yes

But it's a little more than you planned to spend.
Well, that makes 3 "yes's" to one "no".

A final closing technique often overlooked is to simply ask for the order. You may get a lot of refusals, but you will also get some orders that would never have arrived by any other route.

Telephone Selling

The telephone can be a powerful selling tool, and it can save all that travelling time too. It is usually no substitute for face-to-face selling, but for some products or services there is no other economic way to sell. Imagine trying to sell "small ad" space in a newspaper without the telephone!

Selling on the telephone follows all the general principles already covered and the techniques apply too. But it calls for super organization and the following extra factors have to be borne in mind.

Smile when you use the phone. The person you are speaking to cannot see you and they rely completely on the tone of your voice. A friendly reassuring tone is the best selling voice and a smile helps that to come across.

Speak distinctly. A good telephone voice is a real asset. In most face-to-face discussions people can lip read or follow mannerisms, which help clarify ambiguous points. Not so on the telephone.

Have all the relevant material to hand. Keeping people waiting on the phone breaks the flow of the sale. Be organized, have all information, questions, answers to likely queries, delivery dates, discounts etc prepared in advance.

Keep it short. As well as being expensive, long calls are counterproductive. A telephone call is often an intrusion on a more immediate task. If you have ever had to get out of the bath to take a wrong number call in a freezing hallway you will understand the problem. So be brief, businesslike and to the point.

HOW TO CALCULATE YOUR SALES/PRICE EQUATION

One of the big chicken-and-egg questions in marketing is: what should your selling price be?

At first glance the problem looks simple enough. You just add up all your costs and charge a bit more. The more you charge above your costs, provided the customers keep on buying, the more profit you make. A look over your shoulder at what the competition are charging gives you another clue.

But as soon as you begin to do the sums, the problem gets a little more complicated. For a start, not all costs have the same characteristics. Some, for instance, don't change, however much you sell. If you're running a shop, the rent and rates are relatively constant figures, quite independent of the volume of sales. On the other hand, the cost of the products sold from the shop is completely dependent on volume. The more you sell, the more it "costs" to buy stock.

You can't really add up these two types of costs until you've made an assumption about volume – in other words, how much you plan to sell.

Let's take an elementary example: a shop that sells only one product and has only two relatively fixed costs, rent and rates.

Rent and rates for shop	£2,500
Cost of 1,000 units of volume of product	£1,000
Total costs	£3,500

So until you decide to buy, and hopefully sell, 1,000 units of the product, you cannot total the costs. Knowing the volume, you can then work out a cost per unit of product (total costs ÷ number of units or £3,500 ÷ 1,000) of £3.50.

Now, provided you sell out at a price above £3.50 you will always be profitable. But what happens if you don't sell all of the 1,000 units? Say you fix a selling price of £4.50. If you sell all 1,000 units, you would make a profit of £1,000. But if you only sell 500 units, your total revenue drops to £2,250 and you actually *lose* £1,250.

This very simple example (which ignores the fact that the product may or may not be perishable and might be able to be stored for sale later) shows that all these decisions are intertwined. Costs, sales volume, selling price and profits are all linked – a decision taken in any one of these areas has an impact on the other areas.

Breaking even

So how do you keep all these different factors in focus at the same time? The answer lies in the sales volume/price equation. Understanding how it works can pay dividends.

The chart below gives a picture of how volume/price/costs and profits relate to one another. The figures are all hypothetical and only there to show how the equation works in practice:

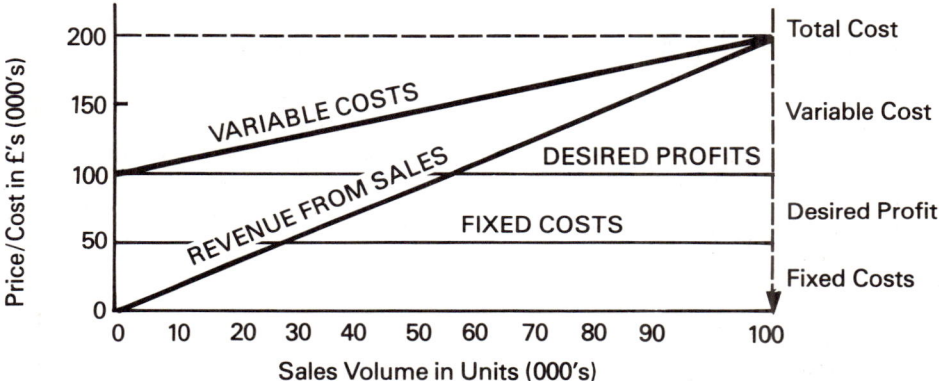

The vertical axis shows the value of sales and costs in £s thousands and the horizontal shows units of sales volume in thousands. In this case, the volume is 100,000 units.

The first horizontal line is the fixed costs, those that don't change as volume increases. The chart uses an example giving fixed costs of £50,000.

The next horizontal line shows the profit objective, in this case also £50,000.

The angled line running from the top of the profit line represents the variable costs. These are costs such as raw materials, which vary directly with output. Every extra unit produced needs £1 of extra variable costs.

Profitable pricing

Only one element is needed to complete the picture, the sales line. If we connect the bottom left-hand corner of the chart (the 0,0 co-ordinate) with the top right we can see how much sales revenue is needed to cover fixed costs, variable costs and to make a satisfactory profit. In this case you have to sell 100,000 units for £200,000 to reach your desired profit (let's call it the "Break Even Profit Point"). This means a selling price per unit of £2.00.

You don't have to draw the chart every time. The sales/price equation, deduced from the chart, looks like this:

$$\text{Break Even Profit Point} = \frac{\text{Fixed Costs} + \text{Profit Objectives}}{\text{Selling price} - \text{Unit Variable Costs}}$$

The great strength of this equation is that each element can be changed in turn on an experimental basis to arrive at a satisfactory and achievable result.

For instance, suppose you decide that it is highly unlikely that you will sell all 100,000 units but that 80,000 is achievable. Now what would your selling price have to be to make the *same* profit?

Using the sales/price equation you can calculate the sum:

$$\text{BEPP} = \frac{\text{Fixed Costs} + \text{Profit Objectives}}{\text{Selling Price} - \text{Unit Variable Costs}}$$

$$80,000 = \frac{50,000 + 50,000}{£x - 1}$$

$$£x - 1 = \frac{100,000}{80,000} = 1.25$$

$$£x = 1.25 + 1 = £2.25 = \text{new selling price}$$

If the market will bear £2.25 all is well; if it won't then the ball is back in your court. You have to find ways of decreasing the fixed or variable costs rather than just accepting a lower profit as inevitable.

The equation works equally well for a more complex operation. In a multi-product company, you simply allocate a proportion of fixed costs to each product or product group. In the case of our shop, the product group might be sweets or cigarettes. Say the fixed cost rent of the shop is £4 per sq. ft. Then if the product (or product group) takes 200 sq. ft. on shelf space, its share of those fixed costs is £800.

Setting your selling price for the first time

The greatest danger in setting a price for the first time is to pitch it too low. Raising a price is always more difficult than lowering one. There are great temptations to undercut the competition at the outset. Usually this argument is rooted in the mistaken belief that you do not have their overheads. But you will not have their buying power or experience either, which surprisingly enough counts for more.

Every product or service has its own demand curve. This can help you to predict how a change in price will effect your sales volume.

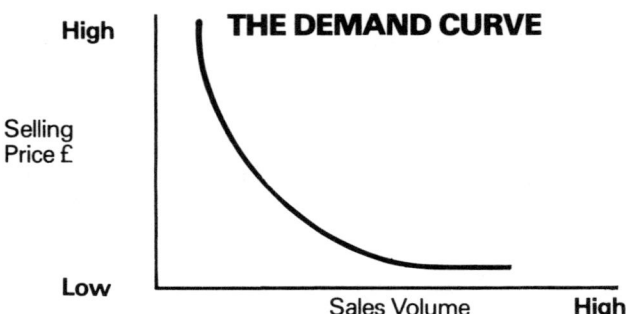

The sensitivity of demand to price changes is called "price elasticity". If demand increases more than proportionately when a product's price is reduced, then the demand is elastic. If it does not, it is inelastic.

Sales of Rolls Royces are not likely to be improved significantly by lowering prices. In fact, the snob appeal may be diminished, so this is an inelastic demand curve. You have to quickly get a "feel" for how your sales volume is affected by price changes.

CHAPTER 9 SUMMARY

- Understanding the needs of your customers and how to communicate them is fundamental to the success of your business: no customers, no business.
- It's important to define the different segmentations of your particular market and to promote accordingly: not all customers, for instance, get the same benefits from buying a product. Someone who buys a watch as a gift gets the pleasure of "giving"; someone who buys a watch for himself gets a timepiece.
- You need to decide who your potential first-buyers will be and to define accurately the *benefits* of your product or service.
- Products don't last forever, though, so you need to understand product life-cycles and how to protect your position.
- Market research is a crucial activity in determing whether a product or service is needed – how should you carry it out? What questions can it answer? There are various sources of market research information which can help you carry out basic research from your desk. But there are also market research techniques which aren't too difficult to carry out yourself or, if you can afford it, with the help of professionals.
- You must identify, understand and select the right distribution channels for your product or service. They range from door-to-door selling, selling through retail outlets to franchising your idea.
- You must also promote your product. What is the best message to project? Which of the many media channels will be the best bet for your particular business? You need to learn the skills and methodology of selling and know how to calculate the right price for your product or service.

Chapter 10
MAKING YOUR BUSINESS GROW

Big companies are only small companies that succeed. Once your business is launched and running, your thoughts will turn to how to make it grow. Expansion poses new problems for the entrepreneur, and, to some extent, each step along the road is similar to starting up all over again.

Expansion must be properly planned to be worthwhile. If you set clear objectives, and learn to plan from the outset your business will be prepared for growth. If you don't, not only will the need for an overall plan become more apparent but adopting one at a late stage may be extremely difficult.

Planning is useless without the ability to monitor and control progress against the plan, which emphasizes the importance of keeping regular accounts and setting up a system of budgetary control, otherwise you might go to the wall through overtrading (we pointed out the pitfalls in Chapter 7).

Expansion will almost certainly require changes within the business structure and its working methods. You, the owner, will need to be flexible enough to adopt new ideas if they make sense for the business, and be prepared to delegate (often difficult for people who have successfully run their business single-handed) since inevitably, you will have to employ more staff.

You may also – even if you haven't done so already – need to raise money from a financier, and this may involve parting with shares in your business (see Chapter 4 for an explanation of equity finance).

PLANNING FOR GROWTH

For a new or small business, looking more than a year or two ahead in any detail is really just crystal-ball gazing. Too many things are changing and new factors are coming into play. So it is more sensible to prepare a short-term plan for the next one and two years, and update and extend it regularly.

Concentrate your planning initially on the area of business you are currently involved with or one closely linked to it – diversifying into new areas is more risky and the present successful business might fail as a result.

Here's how Chantal Coady set her objectives: Chantal started her shop Rococo in 1982 to sell "unashamedly" luxurious chocolates and sweets in Chelsea's Kings Road – an area that could afford and would appreciate them. After 12 months trading she began to look for ways to overcome the cyclical nature of the business. Chocolate sales peak over Christmas and Easter and there is a deep trough in the summer – the unusually long, hot summer of '82 nearly scuppered her business.

Cash resources for new stocks and for advertising were very limited, but she had one asset – a relatively unused and large basement. Chantal's plan for the next 12 months was to find some way of improving cash flow in the lean summer months which would be compatible with her business philosophy, and which meant utilizing the basement area. She allocated a certain proportion of her meagre cash resource to achieving that goal. We'll come back to Chantal's plans in a minute.

Once objectives have been set and resources defined, here are some growth strategies you can adopt.

DO WHAT YOU DO NOW – BUT BETTER

Sell more effectively: examine your selling methods and selling literature and improve on them. Allocate more time to selling. Many people running young enterprises find they get so bogged down in detail that they neglect this vital side of the business.

Here's how Joe and Ted resolved their problem. Shortly after launching their mail order business, Joe and Ted found they were transformed from Chairman and Managing Director into a couple of mail boys. After a day collecting, packing and running down to the Post Office there was no time or energy left for anything else; never mind extending their customer base. So they farmed out their business to a specialist mailing house which took over everything from processing customers' cheques to despatching the goods. Weekly sales figures, customer lists and data on the effectiveness of each advertisement placed being provided by the mailing house's computer. Ted and Joe now concentrate their energies on getting their products right and selling them properly – and the business goes from strength to strength.

If more small business managers were prepared to subcontract aspects of their activities which they know they aren't expert in, or haven't the time to do there would probably be fewer business failures. Writing advertisements and press releases, hiring personnel and preparing regular accounts are examples of work which can be put out – and this is frequently more cost-effective than employing someone to do it or doing it yourself.

Find more customers. You probably have only a small share of the market so there is plenty of potential. You might decide to increase you advertising within your defined catchment area or to extend your market by offering your product through the mail.

You can rent mailing lists from specialist list brokers (contact the British List Brokers Association, King House, 1 Westbourne Grove, London W2; 01-221 1500) or compile your own by using trade directories to flush out possible customers.

Here's more of Chantal Coady's expansion plan:

The catchment area for Chantal's Rococo chocolates was very small – a mile or so around the shop, plus passing trade. Her tins of chocolates had a long shelf life and a distinctive image which made them an ideal "catalogue" product. She bought a list of wealthy people from a specialist mailing house, and sold her product effectively to them by post.

Reduce costs. Any steps you can take to lower the amount of working capital or fixed assets employed in the business – so long as it doesn't harm your sales – will obviously improve your profitability. Had Chantal Coady been able to sell off her underused basement she could have doubled her profit margin thus:

Profit now	=	£10,000pa	= 10%
Overheads (shop and basement)	=	£100,000 (shop and basement at £50,000 each)	
Profit after sale of basement	=	£10,000	= 20%
Overheads (shop only)	=	£50,000	

Carrying out a cost analysis of the activities you take for granted can often throw up the fact that they have no value. The table below convinced one small shopkeeper that opening most evenings was a waste of time, at least for his business:

Activity	Cost	Benefit	Net Value
Open after 6 pm	Overtime £50 pw	Increased sales of £100 at 40% mark up	£10 loss (i.e. £40-£50)
Open Saturday	Overtime £50 pw	Increased sales of £250 at 40% mark up	£50 profit (i.e. £100-£50)

SELL NEW PRODUCTS TO EXISTING CUSTOMERS

Find other products/services that you can sell to existing customers. These should be things they want, which you have the skills to supply and which will make you a profit.

Let's return to Chantal Coady. Analysing how she could bump up summer trade, she identified ice-cream as a "summer" product but with year-round sales. She needed an ice-cream which was compatible with her upmarket image so she searched around for the best. She was lucky enough to be put in touch with a skilled specialist ice-cream maker who was himself looking for new retail outlets to increase his sales. He was prepared to invest in his own refrigeration plant and to house it in Chantal's basement, also to provide counter staff to sell his products. In return Chantal would take a royalty on sales. This was the ideal growth route for Chantal – it conserved her cash, utilized her basement, brought in extra profit to the business and, most importantly, maintained a steady flow of customers to the shop throughout the year.

NEW MARKETS FOR EXISTING PRODUCTS

Look around for other market segments (see Chapter 9) who may be interested in your product but who, for one reason or another, you are not currently trying to sell to.

As we saw above, Chantal Coady decided to sell by mail order to widen her customer base. She had also identified the local business community as potential buyers – particularly restaurants which offered or would be prepared to offer after-dinner chocolates to clients. She hadn't initially made any approaches to this segment of the market since they (a) required a delivery service and (b) expected credit terms, neither of which she was in a position to afford during the first year of operation. But this will be her new target market during 1985.

You might also consider selling your product or service in another geographical area by opening a branch office.

Franchising is another method of expanding a business. (We explain how franchising works in Chapter 2.) Launching your business as a franchise isn't cheap, but it is extremely cost-effective since your franchisees are, in effect, taking most of the risks. If you decide to explore franchising, keep these rules in mind:

- Talk to your lawyer, accountant and bank manager before doing anything. The contract between you and your franchisee is a crucial document and must be well thought out.
- Make sure your business concept is well-documented. Your franchise package must cover every area – e.g. product knowledge; selling skills; marketing; book-keeping and accounting.
- Start with a small-scale pilot franchise, learn from that experience and don't try to grow too fast.
- Select only franchisees who appear to have the necessary experience to succeed. Just because they can afford the franchise fee doesn't make them good business people.
- Set up a sound system to monitor the franchisees' performance as your future income will depend on their success.

Putting a marketable and viable franchise proposal together can take several months and the costs start in the five-figure bracket. Contact the British Franchise Association for more information.

Here's how Roger Coate franchised his business:

Roger's business, APC Alarms Ltd, operates in the domestic security field – a growth market if ever there was one. This year he decided the only way to rapidly exploit a new security system was to franchise it "If we just used our own capital and ploughed back profits it could take us 10 years to reach the position that franchising will get us to in three," he says.

In effect, APC shares the capital burden with its franchisees, using their fees to meet some of the costs of growth. The APC franchise package includes a comprehensive accounting system, and as this is where novices are most likely to go wrong, it is a very big plus for franchisees. The marketing element of the package includes a custom-made video starring Gordon Jackson.

The complete package will cost franchisees £11,500 and they will need a further £8,000 or so to finance stock and working capital. The franchisee also pays a royalty on sales of 8%.

Franchising's great strength for Roger is that it improves cash flow. Most of the selling expenses are where they belong, at the point of sale with the franchisee.

Exporting is another method to expand sales of existing products into new markets. It poses the same problems as selling to the home market and additional complications in the areas of distribution, communications and paperwork.

Fortunately, there is plenty of help available to new exporters from a wide number of different organizations. We give the addresses of the more important bodies at the end of this chapter.

First, you need to establish whether an export market exists for your product or service and, if so, where it is. Starting points: *The Overseas Trade Statistics for the UK* published monthly by the HMSO. This lists all UK imports and exports, by category, by amount, by value and by country of origin and destination. More information on overseas markets can be found in the Department of Trade's Statistics and Market Intelligence Library and from the British Overseas Trade Board who offer advice, and sometimes even financial assistance to the UK exporter. When it comes to preparing the necessary documents, SITPRO (the Simplification of International Trade Procedures Board) can offer invaluable help.

If you decide you can't afford the time and energy to set up your own export operation, there are two other ways into overseas markets which you can adopt without leaving your desk. There is a *Directory of Export Buyers* which lists people who negotiate export orders on behalf of overseas firms. The directory shows which countries they buy from, which products they are interested in and the foreign firms they buy for.

Alternatively you can use an export house (contact their association listed at the end of this chapter). Export houses undertake a whole range of activities from simply acting as your agent to, in effect, becoming your export manager and even financing your export trade.

NEW MARKETS FOR NEW PRODUCTS

Diversifying your activities is virtually the same as starting all over again and just as risky. The only useful resources you can bring to bear on this type of growth are your entrepreneurial talent – and cash.

Firms diversify for a variety of reasons: to avoid risk, say, or to compensate for declining markets and seasonal trade or to grab an opportunity for expansion.

Adrian Clarke, for instance, decided to contract his family-run 100-year-old department store and embark on a new venture because he could syphon profits from his existing enterprise into a gamble that could pay dividends in the long-run.

Adrian's 100,000 square foot Berwick department store was really too large to be profitably occupied especially since retailing trends had moved away from department stores to shopping precincts and discount houses. So in 1981 Adrian contracted the store to 50,000 square feet, which allowed him to concentrate on the profitable side of the business, sold off the remaining 50,000 and invested the money in a computer software house. Although he realized that the computer industry was a risky business, he knew that it was highly profitable for those who succeeded. With the stable platform of the department store and its high cash-flow behind him, he decided that it was therefore worth the risk. Two years later the software house is showing a much greater return on investment than the department store.

Diversification is probably the last of the ideas for growth we've mentioned that you should consider. Look at the others first and see what ideas they give you.

MAKING A CHOICE

Ask yourself these questions before pursuing any growth plans:
- It is consistent with my philosophy of the business and its market?
- Will it really help me achieve my goals?
- Can I afford it?
- Will the rest of my business survive if this plan goes wrong?
  Unless you can answer "yes" to all these questions, don't do it.

GROW OR BECOME EXTINCT

If your sales are growing steadily each year and you are showing profit, why take the risk of adopting a chancy new expansion plan? Because it's possible that your market might be slipping away without you being aware of it. When analysing your sales figures have you accounted for inflation?

Here's an unadjusted table of sales figures.

Year	Sales	Growth	% growth year on year
1	£100,000	–	–
2	£130,000	£30,000	30
3	£145,000	£15,000	11.5

Looks good doesn't it? But in periods of inflation pounds don't have the same value year-on-year. To adjust the figures to allow for inflation you need to consult the Retail Price Index.

Let's assume that the indices figures for years 1, 2 and 3 were 104, 120, 135 respectively. We use the latest figure as the basis for comparison.

This is the sum to convert pounds in year 1 and year 2 to current pounds.

$$\text{Current pounds} = \frac{\text{Index for current year}}{\text{Index for historic year}} \times \text{historic pound}$$

For year 1 sales now become $135/104 \times £100,000 = £129,808$
For year 2 sales now become $135/120 \times £130,000 = £146,250$
For year 3 sales now become $135/135 \times £145,000 = £145,000$

Here's the *real* sales growth over the past three years:

Year	Adjusted sales	Adjusted growth	% change
1	£129,808	–	–
2	£146,250	£16,442	12.7
3	£145,000	–£1,250	–0.9

Not so rosy is it? Sales are in fact declining rather than growing.

Another reason why you can't afford to ignore planning for the future is because products have a natural life cycle that turns full circle (we explained product life cycles in Chapter 9). You mustn't be lulled into a false sense of security by believing that natural growth can go on for ever. The final stage in the cycle is "decline" and unless your product is constantly re-launched for new customers that is bound to happen. Even books written by authors long dead are repackaged with new covers and re-sold – George Orwell's *Nineteen Eighty-Four* has probably sold more copies this year than any year since it was published.

The moral is never sit back and relax once your business is going – constantly review, revise, revamp and, most important of all, lay down plans for the future.

USEFUL ORGANIZATIONS

British Direct Marketing Association, 1 New Oxford Street, London WC1 1NQ (01-242 2254) can supply you with details of Direct Mail Houses who prepare and produce lists of prospective customers.

The Marketing Advisory Service, The Institute of Marketing, Moor Hall, Cookham, Maidenhead, Berks SL6 9HQ (06285-24922) can put you in contact with an experienced marketing advisor at a relatively low cost.

The Institute of Sales Promotion, Panstar House, 13-15 Swakeleys Road, Ickenham, Middlesex UB1D 8DS (08956-74281/2)

British Franchise Association, (see Chapter 2) can advise you on how to offer your business as a franchise.

Local Chambers of Commerce can help with advice on opportunities within the locality.

Enterprise Agencies, listed in the final chapter, can also advise on plans for expansion.

For Exporting

H.M. Customs & Excise, King's Beam House, Mark Lane, London EC3R 1HE (01-626 1515)

Statistics and Market Intelligence Library, 1 Victoria Street, London SW1H 0ET (01-215 5444/5)

British Overseas Trade Board (BOTB) 1 Victoria Street, London SW1H 0ET (01-215 7877)

British Export Houses Association, 69 Cannon Street, London EC4 (01-248 4444)

The Directory of Export Buyers in the UK, Trade Research Publications, 6 Beech Hill Court, Berkhamstead, Herts (04427-3951)

Simplification of International Trade Procedures Board (SITPRO), 11/12 Waterloo Place, London SW1Y 4AY (01-930 0532)

The Small Firms Exporters Scheme, Exports Credit Guarantee Department, Aldermanbury House, Aldermanbury, London EC2P 2EL (01-606 6699)

CHAPTER 10 SUMMARY

- Planning for growth is essential for every business as "natural" growth begins to slow down and competitors erode your share of the market.
- Entrepreneurs need to establish a product/market strategy and clear and quantified objectives. The four ways to expand your business are: (1) Doing what you do now but better. (2) Selling new products to existing customers. (3) Finding new markets for existing products. (4) Finding new markets for new products.
- Whichever method you choose it should be affordable, consistent with your business philosophy, and should not put your existing operation at risk.

Chapter 11
WHERE TO GO FOR HELP

Last year over 500,000 people who were starting up, or running a small business used the services of a business advisory organization. Most were simple telephone enquiries but others involved face-to-face counselling sessions – perhaps to help raise money or to cope with an in-depth tax problem. There are now over 300 organizations concerned with providing help, advice and resources (including finance) for small businesses and those starting them. For the most part, these services are provided free or at a very low cost. In order to give a better understanding of their nature and purpose it will help to look at them as divided into three categories: general business advisory agencies, business associations, and other useful organizations.

BUSINESS ADVISORY AGENCIES

Although all the agencies and advisory services have their roots in the local community, the direct initiative for starting them often came from a central body. Five such bodies are in the forefront of these initiatives:

Small Firms Service

This service, which is provided by the Department of Trade and Industry, is an information and counselling service to help owners and managers of small businesses with their plans and problems. It is also an advisory service to those thinking of starting their own business. The service operates through a nationwide network of twelve Small Firms Centres backed up by over 80 Area Counselling Offices.

The Service can help with almost any type of business enquiry and will provide information on such topics as raising finance, government grants, sources of supply, industrial training, exporting, planning, industrial relations, new technology and marketing. It can also put you in touch with the right people in government departments, local authorities, chambers of commerce, the professions or any other body that can help in solving your problems. As well as answering enquiries over the telephone the Small Firms Centre can arrange for a meeting with a Small Firms Business Counsellor who is himself an experienced businessman and who can offer impartial and confidential advice and guidance. Such meetings can either be at local area counselling office or at the client's own premises. However, the decisions you make on the basis of advice given are your responsibility and yours alone.

The information service is free. For counselling, the first three sessions are free; if further counselling is required a modest charge of about £20.00 is made for the fourth and subsequent sessions. To contact your regional Small Firms Centre dial 100 and ask the operator for Freefone 2444, or you can telephone direct or walk in and talk to them.

The Small Firms Service doesn't operate as such throughout the length and breadth of the UK. A similar service is offered by the following bodies in Scotland, Wales, Northern Ireland and for rural areas of England.

Scotland

The Scottish Development Agency, Small Business Division, Rosebury House, Haymarket Terrace, Edinburgh EH12 5EZ (031-337-9595). Contact: Peter Carmichael, Director.

They provide a free confidential information and advice centre, and a national counselling service available on Freefone 2444. The SDA publishes a comprehensive range of booklets and can advise on finance, government aid, marketing, market research, exporting, diversification, training, industrial relations, and of course high technology.

The agency is also the largest provider of industrial space in Scotland – factories, workshops and industral estates. Sizes range from a couple of hundred square feet, to many thousands. The SDA can make finance available for certain small industrial and service enterprises, and has a strong interest in the craft field.

The Highlands and Islands Development Board, Bridge House, 27 Bank Street, Inverness, IV1 1QR (0463-234171) offers a wide range of help, including grants, to businesses who plan to locate in the Highlands and Islands area.

Wales

The Welsh Development Agency, Head Office, Treforest Industrial Estate, Pontypridd, Mid-Glamorgan CF37 5UT (044-385-2666). Contact: A. A. Williams, Deputy Controller, SBU.

The SBU is the focal point for business advice in Wales and comprises some 60 full and part-time staff who provide assistance to more than 3,500 potential and existing businesses annually. The SBU is able to provide general and specific advice on all areas of business, e.g. general management, government legislation, technical advice, business counselling.

Specifically, the SBU has expert advisers on marketing, accountancy, engineering, production management, woodworking, pottery, wrought iron work. Additionally the SBU is responsible for administering the Counselling Service in Wales on behalf of the Department of Industry. This service utilizes the expertise of retired and semi-retired successful businessmen who make their practical experience available to existing businesses and people hoping to start up in business.

Northern Ireland

The Local Enterprise Develpment Unit (LEDU), Lamont House, Purdy's Lane, Newtownbreda, Belfast BT8 4TB (0232-691031). Contact: George Mackey, Chief Executive.

This Small Business Agency can help manufacturing, craft or service businesses which employ up to 50 people. Their Product Ideas Licensing Library can help you to find a start-up area, or their Research and Development Grant Scheme can help you to bring your own product to market. They maintain a register of private and public property and can provide technical advice on a wide range of matters.

Their Business Centre in Linenhall Street has been specially designed to hold trade shows, and is available for small businessmen to mount their own exhibitions. They operate a counselling service and have Local Area Officers keen to assist.

Council for Small Industries in Rural Areas (CoSIRA)

141 Castle Street, Salisbury, Wiltshire, SP1 3TP (0722-336255). This is an agency of the Development Commission and its objective is to revitalize country areas in England by helping small rural firms to become more prosperous. CoSIRA is government financed but the staff in each rural county are backed up by a voluntary committee of local people. Their range of advice includes:

Business Management Advice Accountancy, book-keeping, profit planning, cash flow forecasting, costing, applications for loans and overdraft facilities.

Marketing, market research, product planning, pricing and distribution, advertising and sales, export, exhibitions. Production management, planning and control of production, buying and stock control, staff recruitment, employment legislation, statutory sick pay, supervisor training, use of microcomputers.

Technical Advice Building and estimating, structural engineering, joinery, building conversions, thatching, dry stone walling. Mechanical engineering, electrical engineering, industrial safety, welding techniques, CNC machine tools, low-cost automation, jig and tool design, workshop layout, fibreglass lamination, thermoplastics, clay products technology and pottery, abrasive wheels, vehicle electrics.

Furniture making, antique furniture restoration, upholstery, woodworking machinery, spraying and finishing. Sawmill management, timber technology, saw doctoring. Farriery, forgework, saddlery and leather work. Engineering projects and prototypes.

CoSIRA's own workshops can undertake the design and production of jigs, press tools and special-purpose machinery for small firms. They will also develop prototypes. This service is particularly valuable to non-engineering businesses.

Finance CoSIRA has its own limited loan fund which can be used in appropriate cases to finance part of the cost of a project, up to a maximum of £75,000. Repayment may be between two and twenty years according to the type of loan.

Grants In priority areas only, grants are available towards the cost.

Action Resource Centre (ARC)

Henrietta House, 9 Henrietta Place, London W1M 9AG (01-629-3826). Contact: Cecilia Allen. This was set up in 1973 by a group of businessmen to research and demonstrate how business skills could best be used for the community. Since 1976 ARC has concentrated on helping to create employment opportunities, using people seconded from industry and business to work on selected projects. Each ARC project is chosen with specific local needs and conditions in mind. For example, in the London Borough of Islington they run a Small Business Counselling Service; in Dundee, they assisted Goodwill Enterprises Ltd which takes in old furniture, refurbishes it and sells it to the public, thus creating work; in Nottingham ARC has introduced a financial advisory service (CAS Unit) for community organizations in the area. With financial and other support from several hundred major companies, and with 100 professional business advisers seconded from those companies working on projects up and down the country, their local impact is significant.

BSC (Industry) Ltd

NLA Tower, 12 Addiscombe Road, Croydon CR9 3JH (01-686 0366). Contact: John Northcott. This company, a subsidiary of British Steel Corporation, aims to help businesses in 18 locations in Scotland, England and Wales, with the objective of helping to put back sound jobs in those areas where the British Steel Corporation has discontinued or substantially reduced its activities.

In each of the 18 areas BSC Industry is associated with a local Business Opportunity Team, usually an Enterprise Agency but sometimes some other local organization which exists to support businesses in the area. BSC Industry itself will provide financial assistance, where such assistance is necessary for a project to proceed: the assistance usually takes the form of an unsecured loan at below commercial rates of interest.

BSC Industry has also provided small industrial workshops in a number of its areas. These units range in size from a few hundred to a few thousand square feet, and are made available on a 3-month rolling licence agreement with a minimum of formalities.

The 18 areas where BSC Industry help is available are: Derwentside, Hartlepool, West Cumbria, Teesside, South Humberside, Rotherham, Sheffield, Corby and Dudley in England; Lanarkshire, Cambuslang and Garnock Valley in Scotland; Deeside, Llanelli, Blaenau Gwent, West Glamorgan, South Glamorgan and South Gwent in Wales. Phone the Croydon office for contact points.

Co-operative Development Agency

Broadmead House, 21 Panton Street, London SW1Y 4DR (01-839 2988). The agency was established by Parliament in 1978 with all-party support, to promote the concept of cooperatives. It gives advice on the mechanics and philosophy of cooperatives to people starting a new business or wanting to convert an existing business that might otherwise be sold or closed down. There is also a network of local co-operative development agencies – phone the number above for details.

Local Enterprise Agencies

Local Enterprise Agencies or Trusts have been formed in about two hundred places up and down the UK. Some have been in existence for a decade, but the great majority were formed in the last two or three years. They have in common the objectives of encouraging new and small businesses to start up in a particular area, and of helping businesses in their area to survive and prosper.

These agencies are usually run by a small staff (The largest has 21 people and the average is 3) who can call on the wealth of expertise within the organizations sponsoring the agency. Sponsors include local government, chambers of commerce, colleges, industrial and commercial companies, banks and other concerns.

England

ACCRINGTON,
> Hyndburn Enterprise Trust, c/o GEC, Blackburn Road, Clayton-le-Moors, Accrington, Lancashire BB5 5JW (0254-33241)
> Contact: H. Patterson.

ALDERSHOT,
> Blackwater Valley Enterprise Trust Ltd, The Old Town Hall, Grosvenor Road, Aldershot, Hants. Tel: 0252-319272.
> Contacts: Walter Oakey (Director), G. Vaux.

ALTON,
> East Hampshire Enterprise Agency Ltd, c/o Bass Brewery (Alton) Ltd, Manor Park, Alton, Hants GU34 2PS. Tel: 0420-87577.
> Contact: Robert Dutton.

ASHFORD,
> Enterprise Ashford Ltd, 28 North Street, Ashford, Kent TN24 8JR. Tel: 0233-30307.
> Contact: A. J. Duncan.

ASHTON-UNDER-LYNE,
> Tameside Venture Trust, c/o Council Offices, Wellington Road, Ashton-Under-Lyne, Greater Manchester OL6 6DL. Tel: 061-344-3407.
> Contact: Mrs Millman.

BARNSLEY,
> Barnsley Enterprise Centre, Pontefract Road, Barnsley S71 1AJ. Tel: 0226-298091.
> Contact: R. A. Brown, Business Development Officer.

Employment Promotion & Development Unit, South Yorkshire County Council, County Hall, Barnsley S70 2TN, South Yorkshire. Tel: 0226-86141.
Contact: R. L. Briant, Employment Promotion & Development Officer.
BARNSTAPLE,
North Devon Enterprise Group, Bridge Chambers, Barnstaple, N. Devon EX31 1HE. Tel: 0271-76365.
Contact: Mr J. Goodenough, Organizer.
BARROW-IN-FURNESS,
Furness Business Initiative Ltd, 111 Duke Street, Barrow-In-Furness, Cumbria LA14 1XA. Tel: 0229-22132
Contacts: P. Marsden, Mrs G. A. Clouter.
BASINGSTOKE,
Basingstoke & Andover Enterprise Centre, 9 New Street, Basingstoke, RG21 1DF. Tel: 0256-54041.
Contacts: Bernard Affleck, Director, D. Pilkington, Secretary.
BATH,
Mendip & Wansdyke Local Enterprise Group, Ammerdown, Radstock, Bath BA3 5SW. Tel: 0761-35321.
Contact: Mr P. Whiting.
BIRMINGHAM,
Birmingham Venture, Chamber of Commerce House, PO Box 360, 75 Harborne Road, Edgbaston, Birmingham B15 3DH. Tel: 021-454-6171.
Contact: Mr D. Bullivant, Manager.
Small Business Centre, University of Aston, 200 Aston Brook Street, Birmingham B6 4SY. Tel: 021-359-4647.
Contact: D. Jones.
BLACKBURN,
Blackburn & District Enterprise Trust, c/o Blackburn & District Chamber of Industry & Commerce, 14 Richmond Terrace, Blackburn BB1 7BH. Tel: 0254-664747.
Contact: J. A. McKinstry.
BODMIN,
Mid Cornwall Industrial Group, c/o Co-operative Retail Services Ltd, 2 Fore Street, Bodmin, Cornwall. Tel: 0208-77512.
Contact: Mrs J. Thomson.
BOLTON,
Bolton Business Venture Ltd, 46 Lower Bridgeman Street, Bolton BL2 1DG. Tel: 0204-391400.
Contact: R. McMullan, Director.
BRAINTREE,
Braintree Encourages Enterprise (BEES), Enterprise Office, Town Hall Centre, Market Square, Braintree, Essex CM7 6YG. Tel: 0376-43140.
Contact: Stuart Beckwith, Adviser.
BRIDGWATER,
Small Industries Group Somerset, 68 Friarn Street, Bridgwater, Somerset TA6 3LJ. Tel: 0278-424456.
Contact: Fred Wedlake.
BRIGG,
SOHBAC (South Humber Business Advice Centre Limited), 7 Market Place, Brigg, South Humberside DN20 8HA. Tel: 0652-57637/8.
Contacts: Roger Thackery, Derek Marshall.
BRISTOL,
Aid to Bristol Enterprises (ABE), 16 Clifton Park, Bristol BS8 3BY. Tel: 0272-741518.
Contacts: Mike Mears, Colin Jones, Pat Cook.

New Work Trust Company Limited, Avondale Workshops, Woodland Way, Kingswood, Bristol BS15 1QH. Tel: 0272-603871/575577.
Contacts: Ms P. Underwood, Ms R. Wagstaffe, Mr M. Pope.

BURTON-ON-TRENT,
Burton Enterprise Agency, The Grain Warehouse, Derby Street, Burton-on-Trent. Tel: 0283-37151/2.
Contacts: Peter Harris, Ms C. Heathcote.

BURY,
Bury Enterprise Centre, 12 Tithebarn Street, Bury, Lancs. BL9 0JR. Tel: 061-797-5864.
Contact: D. Gough.

CAMBORNE,
West Cornwall Enterprise Trust Limited, Wesley Street, Camborne, Cornwall TR14 8DR. Tel: 0209-714914.
Contacts: Philip S. Staton, Mrs G. Beeching.

CARLISLE,
Business Initiatives Carlisle, Tower Buildings, Scotch Street, Carlisle CA3 8RB. Tel: 0228-34120.
Contact: A. W. Dickinson.

CHATHAM,
Medway Enterprise Agency, Railway Street, Chatham, Kent, ME4 4RR. Tel: 0634-400301.
Contact: Guy Sibley, Director.

CHESTER,
Employment Promotion Group, Cheshire County Council, Commerce House, Hunter Street, Chester CH1 1SN. Tel: 0244-603155.
Contacts: Mr M. Cordwell, Mrs F. Southorn, Mr I. Lawrence.

CHESTERFIELD,
Chesterfield Business Advice Centre, 34 Beetwell Street, Chesterfield, Derbyshire S40 1SH. Tel: 0246-208743.
Contact: Robert Taylor, Manager.

CLEVELYS,
Wyre Business Agency Ltd, Colchester House, Burnhall Industrial Estate, Fleetwood Road, Fleetwood FY7 8JS. Lancs. Tel: 0253-864014.
Contact: Michael Burton, Director.

COLCHESTER,
Colchester Business Enterprise Agency, Gate House, High Street, Colchester, Essex. Tel: 0206-48833.
Contact: Director, Mr Tom Ford.

CONSETT,
Derwentside Industrial Development Agency, Derwentside Industrial Centre, Berry Edge Road, Consett, Co. Durham DH8 5EU. Tel: 0207-509124.
Contact: L. Haveron.

CORBY,
Corby Business Advisory Bureau, Douglas House, 37 Queen's Square, Corby, Northants NN17 1PL. Tel: 0536-62571.
Contacts: L. C. Howard, Mrs M. Hunter.

COVENTRY,
Coventry Business Centre Limited, Ground Floor, Spire House, New Union Street, Coventry CV1 2PW. Tel: 0203-552781.
Contact: Mrs C. A. Jarvis.

CRANFIELD,
Interwork Business Development Centre, Cranfield, Bedford MK43 0AL. Tel: 0234-752767.
Contacts: Prof. B. Wilson, Paul Stait, Gilbert Jenkins, Eileen Williams.

CROYDON,
  Croydon Business Venture Limited, 26 Barclay Road, Croydon, Surrey CR0 1JN.
  Tel: 01-681-8339.
  Contact: Mrs N. Chessum.
DARLINGTON,
  Darlington & S W Durham Business Venture, Imperial Centre, Grange Road,
  Darlington, Co. Durham DL1 5NQ. Tel: 0325-480891.
  Contacts: Cyril Beere, Keith Ormrod.
DERBY,
  Derby & Derbyshire Business Venture, Saxon House, Heritage Gate, Friary
  Street, Derby DE1 1NL. Tel: 0332-360345.
  Contacts: M C Powell, Executive Director. Lynn Green, Secretary/P.A.
DUDLEY,
  Dudley Business Venture, Falcon House, The Minories, Dudley DY2 8PG, West
  Midlands. Tel: 0384-231283.
  Contacts: Mr John Standish, Mr David Needham.
DURHAM,
  Enterprise North, Durham University Business School, Mill Hill Lane, Durham
  DH1 3LD. Tel: 0385-4191.
  Contacts: Derek Craven, Margaret Robertson.
FLEETWOOOD,
  Lancashire Enterprises Ltd, 6 Fish Trades Building, Fleetwood, Lancs FY7 6PP.
  Tel: 0772-735821.
  Contact: Mr Banford.
GLOUCESTER,
  Gloucestershire Enterprise Agency, 90 Westgate Street, Gloucester GL1 2NZ.
  Tel: 0452-501411.
  Contacts: Jack Tester, Director, Brian Hurley.
GRAVESEND,
  Gravesham Industry Enterprise Agency, 8 Parrock Street, Gravesend, Kent DA12
  1ET. Tel: 0474-27118.
  Contacts: Paul Beard, Mrs H. Gray.
  Gravesham Industry Ltd, Gravesham Borough Council, Civic Centre, Windmill
  Street, Gravesend, Kent DA12 1AU. Tel: 0474-64422 ext. 274/5.
  Contact: Mr R. Dewar.
GREAT YARMOUTH,
  Great Yarmouth Business Advisory Service, 165a King Street, Great Yarmouth,
  Norfolk NR30 2PA. Tel: 0493-58157.
  Contacts: John Norton, Roy Northcott.
GRIMSBY,
  Great Grimsby Small Firms Advisory Bureau, Devonshire House, Grimsby. Tel:
  0472-59161.
  Contacts: John Robertson, Mel Pretious.
HALIFAX,
  Cadlerdale Small Business Advice Centre, 4 Clare Road, Halifax. Tel:
  0422-69487.
  Contact: Ron Chandler, Director.
  Cadlerdale Information Service for Business & Industry (CALDIS), Library
  Centre, Percival Whitely College of F. E., Francis Street, Halifax W. Yorkshire
  HX1 3UZ. Tel: 0422-58221.
  Contact: D. Manley.
HARLOW,
  Harlow Enterprise Agency, 19 The Rows, The High, Harlow, Essex. Tel:
  0279-38077.
  Contact: Dennis Williams.

HARROW,
  Enterprise Agency, Brush House, Rosslyn Crescent, Harrow, Middlesex HA1
  2SE. Tel: 01-427-6188.
  Contact: Richard Robinson, Executive Director.
HARTLEPOOL,
  Hartlepool Enterprise Agency Ltd, 5th Floor, Titan House, York Road, Hartle-
  pool, Cleveland TS26 9HL. Tel: 0429-221216.
  Contact: Alan Humble, Director, Geoff Coates.
  Hartlepool New Development Services, Old Municipal Buildings, Upper Church
  Street, Hartlepool, Cleveland. Tel: 0429-66522 ext. 374.
  Contacts: Mrs B. Morley, C. C. Doram, R. Preece.
HASTINGS,
  Hastings Business Ventures, 6 Havelock Road, Hastings, East Sussex TN34 1BP.
  Tel: 0424-433333.
  Contact: Victoria John.
HEBDEN BRIDGE,
  Pennine Heritage Ltd, The Birchliffe Centre, Hebden Bridge, W. Yorkshire HX7
  8DG. Tel: 0422-845100.
  Contact: Bill Breakell, General Manager.
HONITON,
  East Devon Small Industries Group, 115 Border Road, Heath Park, Honiton,
  Devon EX14 8BT. Tel: 0404-41806.
  Contact: A. D. Johnson, Development Officer.
HULL,
  Business Advice Centre, 24 Anlaby Road, Hull, HU1 2PA. Tel: 0482-27266.
  Contact: A. G. Spice.
IPSWICH,
  Enterprise Trust (IPSENTA), 30a Lower Brooke Street, Ispwich, Suffolk. Tel:
  0473-59832.
  Contact: Director, David Rolfe.
LANCASTER,
  Business for Lancaster, St. Leonards House (Room B32), St. Leonards Gate,
  Lancaster LA1 1NN. Tel: 0524-66222.
  Contacts: Peter Stiles, Mrs A. Morris.
  Enterprise Lancaster, Town Hall, Lancaster LA1 1PH. Tel: 0524-65272.
  Contact: R. H. Kelsall.
LEEDS,
  LCVS Enterprises Ltd, 31-35 Aire Street, Leeds LS1 4HT. Tel: 0532-435897.
  Contact: W. Shutt.
  Leeds Business Venture, 4th Floor, Merrion House, The Merrion Centre, Leeds
  LS2 8LY. Tel: 0532-446474 and 457583.
  Contact: Mike Riley.
LEICESTER,
  Leicestershire Business Advice Centre, 30 New Walk, Leicester LE1 6TF. Tel:
  0533-554464.
  Contact: Mrs Jane Burgess, PA to Director.
  Leicestershire Small Firms Centre, 8 St. Martins, Leicester LE1 5DD. Tel:
  0533-29684.
  Contact: Mr C. M. Britt, Director, Mrs J. A. Dewhurst, Consultancy Admini-
  strator.
LETCHWORTH,
  Letchworth Garden City Business Centre, Works Road, Letchworth Garden City,
  Hertfordshire SG6 1LB. Tel: 04626 78272.
  Contact: Colin Fricker.

LIVERPOOL,
   Business in Liverpool Ltd, The Innovation Centre, 131 Mount Pleasant, Liverpool L3 5TF. Tel: 051-709-1231.
   Contact: L. T. Williams, Director.
LONDON,
   Business Advice & Consultancy Service (London Borough of Newham), Town Hall, Barking Road, East Ham, London E6 2RP. Tel: 01-552-5324.
   Contact: Tom Brandon (Ind. Co-ord. Officer).
   Camden Enterprise, 57 Pratt Street, Camden Town, London NW1 0DP. Tel: 01-402-2128.
   Contact: Laurie Ewins, Manager.
   The Fashion Centre, 46 Great Eastern Street, London EC2A 3LE. Tel: 01-729-0962.
   Contacts: David Jones, Director, Ann Priest.
   Hackney Business Promotions Centre, 16 Great Eastern Street, London EC2A 3EP. Tel: 01-739-9606.
   Contact: Mr A. G. Wood for Business Advice, Mr D. Griffin for property.
   Hammersmith & Fulham Business Rescources Ltd, c/o Ind. Development Unit, PO Box 501, Hammersmith Town Hall, King Street, London W6 9JU. Tel: 01-741-7248.
   Contact: Michael Smith, Executive Director.
   Kensington & Chelsea Resources Centre, 9 Thorpe Close, London W10 5XL. Tel: 01-969-9455.
   Contact: M. Lewthwaite.
   Lambeth Industrial Entreprises, 62 Tritton Road, London SE21 8DE. Tel: 01-670-4411.
   Contact: John Morris.
   Lambeth Business Advisory Service, Directorate of Town Planning and Economic Dev., Courtenay Hse., 9-15 New Park Road, London SW2 4DU. Tel: 01-674-9844.
   Contact: Richard Boulter.
   London Enterprise Agency, (LENTA), London Chamber of Commerce & Industry, 69 Cannon Street, London EC4N 5AB. Tel: 01-236-2676, or 01-248-4444.
   Contact: Brian Wright, Director.
   Park Royal Enterprise Trust, Waxlow Road, London NW10 7NU. Tel: 01-961-2717.
   Contact: R. L. T. Jones, Chairman.
   Spitalfields Small Business Association Ltd, 170 Brick Lane, London E1. Tel: 01-247-1892.
   Contact: Kay Jordan, Co-ordinator.
   Tower Hamlets Centre for Small Businesses Ltd, 99 Leman Street, London E1 8EY. Tel: 01-481-0512.
   Contact: B. Kennon.
   Wandsworth Business Resource Service, (LENTA) 140 Battersea Park Road, London SW11 4NB. Tel: 01-720-7053 and 720-7097.
   Contact: Clare Nesbit, Manager.
LOUGHTON,
   Forest Enterprise Agency Trust (FEAT), c/o Central Library, Traps Hill, Loughton, Essex IG10 1SZ. Tel: 01-508-7435.
   Contact: Peter Scarlett.
LOWESTOFT,
   Lowestoft Enterprise Trust, 1 All Saints Road, Pakefield, Lowestoft, Suffolk NR33 0LJ. Tel: 0502-63286.
   Contact: Chris Barnes, Manager.

LUTON,
Bedfordshire & Chiltern Enterprise Agency, (BECENTA) Enterprise House, 7 Gordon Street, Luton LU1 2QP. Tel: 0582-452288.
Contact: D. J. Upcott, E. R. Pearce.

MACCLESFIELD,
Macclesfield Business Venture, c/o Josolyn & Co. Silk House, Park Green, Macclesfield, Cheshire. Tel: 0625-615113.
Contacts: John Rosthorn, Anita Crawshaw.

MAIDSTONE,
Maidstone Enterprise Agency Ltd, 25a Pudding Lane, Maidstone, Kent ME14 1PA. Tel: 0622-675547.
Contact: John Lee, Director.

MALDON,
Colchester & Maldon Business Enterprise Agency, Maldon District Council, Market Hill, Maldon, Essex CM9 7QN. Tel: 0621-54477.
Contact: Anna Cronin.

MANCHESTER,
Greater Manchester Enterprise, Gt. Man. Economic Development Agency, Bernard House, Piccadilly Gardens, Manchester M1 4DD. Tel: 061-236-4412.
Contact: M. E. E. Morton.
Manchester Business Venture, c/o Tootal Group PLC, 56 Oxford Street, Manchester M60 1HJ. Tel: 061-228-1144.
Contact: Brian Bawden, Director.
North West Industrial Development Association, Brazennose House, Brazennose Street, Manchester M2 5AZ. Tel: 061-834-6778.
Contact: John Timperley, Information Officer.

MIDDLESBROUGH,
Cleveland Enterprise Agency, 52 Corporation Road, Middlesbrough, Cleveland TS1 2RN. Tel: 0642-222836.
Contacts: George Brown, Director, Ken Anderson, John Hufton, Alan Pounder, Alan Sykes, Marilyn Twidale.
New Enterprise Centre, Silver Street, St. Hildas, Middlesbrough TS2 1NF. Tel: 0642-224839.
Contact: Mr J. E. Corbett, Manager.

MILTON KEYNES,
Milton Keynes Business Venture, Sentry House, 500 Avebury Boulevard, Central Milton Keynes MK9 2LA. Tel: 0908 660044.
Contacts: John Carpenter & Doug Strachan.

MITCHAM,
Merton Enterprise Agency, Vestry Hall Annex, London Road, Mitcham, Surrey CR4 3UD. Tel: 01-640-5182.
Contact: Richard Pook, Manager.

MORPETH,
Northumberland Business Centre, Southgate, Morpeth, Northumberland NE61 2EH. Tel: 0670-514343.
Contact: John Hamilton, Manager.

NEWCASTLE-UPON-TYNE,
Project North-East, 5 Saville Place, Newcastle-Upon-Tyne NE1 8DQ. Tel: 0632-617856.
Contacts: David Grayson, David Irwin.
Tyne & Wear Enterprise Trust Ltd, (ENTRUST) SWS House, Stoddart Street, Newcastle-Upon-Tyne NE2 1AN. Tel: 0632-619122.
Contacts: Director, John Eversley, Tim Atterton.

NEWPORT,
  Isle of Wight Enterprise Agency, 6/7 Town Lane, Newport, Isle of Wight PO30
  1NR. Tel: 0983-529120.
  Contact: Christopher Young, Director.
NORTHAMPTON,
  Northamptonshire Enterprise Agency Limited, 67 The Avenue, Cliftonville,
  Northampton NN1 5BT. Tel: 0604-37401.
  Contact: David Mann, Managing Director.
NORWICH,
  Vale Royal Small Firms Ltd, (Business back-up), Mid Cheshire Business Centre,
  Winnington Avenue, Winnington, Northwich, Cheshire CW8 4EE. Tel:
  0606-77711.
  Contact: John Bone, General Manager.
  Norwich Enterprise Agency Trust (NEAT) Norwich Chamber of Commerce &
  Ind., 112 Barrack Street, Norwich NR3 1TX. Tel: 0603-613023.
  Contact: Director.
NOTTINGHAM,
  Nottinghamshire Business Venture c/o John Players, Nottingham NG7 5PY. Tel:
  0602-787711.
  Contact: Gordon Mackenzie, Director.
  Nottingham Community Project, Baker Gate House, Belward Street, Nottingham
  NG1 1JZ. Tel: 0602-581933.
  Contact: P. Teague.
  Nottinghamshire County Council, Economic Development Unit, County Hall,
  West Bridgford, Nottingham NG2 7QP. Tel: 0602-023823.
  Contacts: L. D. Harker, G. B. Anderton.
  East Midlands Initiatives, Lyndhurst House, Malvern Road, Mapperley, Notting-
  ham NG3 5GZ. Tel: 0602-626089.
  Contact: Brian Hopewell, Director.
  Hyson Green Workshops Limited, Lindsey Street, Radford Road, Nottingham.
  Tel: 0602-708779.
  Contact: Brian Stanley, Manager.
OLDHAM,
  Business in Oldham, Orme Mill, Greenacres Road, Waterhead, Oldham OL4
  3JA. Tel: 061-665-1255.
  Contact: Roy Newton, Manager.
OXFORD,
  Oxford, Enterprise Trust, c/o Taylor & Co., 125 London Road, Headington,
  Oxford. Tel: 0865-63092.
  Contact: J. C. W. Burrough.
PENRITH,
  East Fellside & Alston Moor Project, c/o Eden District Council, Mansion House,
  Penrith, Cumbria CA11 7YG. Tel: 0768-64671.
PETERBOROUGH,
  Peterborough Enterprise Programme, Broadway Court, Broadway, Peterborough
  PE1 1RP. Tel: 0733-310159.
  Contact: John Duckworth, Director.
PLYMOUTH,
  South Hams Small Industries, The Croft, Brixton, Plymouth, Devon. Tel:
  0752-880210.
  Contact: Alan Lovering.
PORTSMOUTH,
  Portsmouth Area Enterprise, First Floor Offices, 27 Guildhall Walk, Portsmouth
  PO1 2RY. Tel: 0705-833321.
  Contact: Bill Summer, Jim Pryer, Alex Addison.

READING,
Berkshire Enterprise Agency, The Old Shire Hall, The Forbury, Reading, Berks RG1 3EJ. Tel: 0734-585715.
Contact: R. D. Hale.

ROCHDALE,
Metropolitan Enterprise Trust Rochdale Area, c/o TBA Industrial Products Ltd, PO Box 40, Rochdale OL12 7EQ. Tel: 0706-356250.
Contact: Mr Islwyn M. Jones.

ROSSENDALE,
Rossendale Enterprise Trust, 29 Kay Street, Rawtenstall, Rossendale, Lancashire BB4 7LS. Tel: 0706-229838.
Contact: Mr Bruce Harris.

ROTHERHAM,
Rotherham Enterprise Agency Ltd, Guardian Centre, Rotherham, South Yorks S65 1DD. Tel: 0709-2121.
Contacts: George Linney, Geoffrey Morris.

RUNCORN,
Business Link Limited, 62 Church Street, Runcorn, Cheshire WA7 1LD. Tel: 09285-63037 and 73549.
Contact: B. W. Burton, General Manager, A. G. Griffiths, J. Forrester.

SAFFRON WALDEN,
Small Business Advisory Service, 18 St. John's Close, Saffron Walden, Essex CB11 4R. Tel: 0799-27853.
Contact: John Martin.

ST. AUSTELL,
Restormel Local Enterprise Trust Ltd, Low Penarwyn, St. Blazey, Par, Nr St. Austell, Cornwall PL24 2D. Tel: 072-681-3079.
Contact: A. G. Tourell, Honorary Director.

ST. HELENS,
Community of St. Helens Trust Limited, PO Box 36, St Helens, Merseyside. Tel: 0744-692570.
Contacts: Mr D. Boult, Dr R. Halford, G. White.

SCUNTHORPE,
Industrial Development Enterprise Agency, Civic Centre, Ashby Road, Scunthorpe, South Humberside DN16 1AB. Tel: 0724-869494.
Contacts: Mr R. I. Robertson, Mr I. Hutchison, Mrs J. C. Knox.

SHEFFIELD,
Sheffield Business Venture, 317 Glossop Road, Sheffield S10 2HP. Tel: 0742-7551721.
Contact: Brian Perkins, Director, John Dickson, Adviser.

SHREWSBURY,
Shropshire Employment Promotion Association, Shirehall, Abbey Foregate, Shrewsbury, Shropshire SY2 6ND. Tel: 0743-222379.
Contacts: Stuart Morris, Ron Shone, Ruth Mochrie.

SITTINGBOURNE,
SWIM/SWAP, Swale Workshop Action Project, Newington Enterprise Centre, Wardwell Lane, Newington, Sittingbourne, Kent ME9 7BS. Tel: 0795-843802.
Contact: W. A. Penney.

SOUTHAMPTON,
Southampton Enterprise Agency, Solent Business Centre, Millbrook Road West, Southampton SO1 0HW. Tel: 0703-788088.
Contact: John Townesend, Director.

SOUTHPORT,
Southport Enterprise, 54 West Street, Southport, Lancashire. Tel: 0704-44173.
Contact: B. E. Cresswell, Secretary.

STAFFORD,
   Staffordshire Development Association, Staff Business Advisory Centre, 3 Martin Street, Stafford ST16 2LH. Tel: 0785-3121 ext 7370.
   Contacts: Mr A. F. Davidson, Mr M. S. Cox, Mr P. Wilson.
STEVENAGE,
   Stevenage Initiative, Business and Technology Centre, Bessemer Drive, Stevenage, Herts SG1 2DX. Tel: 0438-315733.
   Contacts: R. M. Hamill, F. E. Tippler.
STOCKPORT,
   High Peak Business Centre Limited, Shudehill House, Hayfield, via Stockport SK12 5EP. Tel: 0663-42701.
   Contact: Edwin A. Whiting.
STOKE-ON-TRENT,
   Business Initiative, North Staffs & District, Gordon Chambers, 36 Cheapside, Hanley, Stoke-on-Trent ST1 1HE. Tel: 0782-279013.
   Contact: David Gage, Carol Probyn.
SUNDERLAND,
   New Enterprise Advisory Service, Citizens Advice Bureau, 48 John Street, Sunderland, Tyne & Wear SR1 1QH. Tel: 0783-44027.
   Contact: Ivor Saville.
SWINDON,
   Swindon Enterprise Trust Limited, 1 Commercial Road, Swindon, Wilts, SN1 5NE. Tel: 0793-487793.
   Contact: R. H. D. Hardy.
TELFORD,
   Industrial Development Unit, Telford Industrial Centre, Stafford Park 4, Telford, Shropshire TF3 3BA. Tel: 0952-610329.
   Contact: A. E. Johnson, D. Chiva.
   Shropshire Enterprise Trust, Nat West Bank Chambers, The Green, Church Street, Wellington, Telford, Shropshire TF1 1DN. Tel: 0952-56624.
   Contacts: Mr R. B. Williams, Mr R. C. Jebb.
WAKEFIELD,
   Kirklees & Wakefield Venture Trust, Walker House, 12 Rishworth Street, Wakefield WF1 3BY. Tel: 0924-381343 and 0484-31352.
   Contact: L. Mullins, Director.
WALSALL,
   Walsall Small Firm Advice Unit, Jerome Chambers, Bridge Street, Walsall WS1 1EX. Tel: 0922-646614.
   Contact: Jeff Hughes.
WARRINGTON,
   Warrington Business Promotion Bureau, Barbauld House, Barbauld Street, Warrington WA1 2QY. Tel: 0925-33309.
   Contact: Brian Rick.
WARWICK,
   Warwickshire Enterprise Agency, Northgate South, Northgate Street, Warwick CV34 4JH. Tel: 0926-495685.
   Contact: C. D. Edwards, Director, Mrs C. M. Heath.
WASHINGTON,
   Tyne & Wear Small Business Club, Usworth Hall, Stephenson District 12, Washington NE37 3HS Tyne & Wear. Tel: 09141-75555.
   Contacts: Mrs G. M. Wright, General Manager, Mr B. L. Wilson, Chairman.
WATFORD,
   Watford Enterprise Agency, 7 Clarendon Road, Watford, Herts. Tel: 0923-47373.
   Contact: K. W. Hards.

WEMBLEY,
Brent Business Venture Limited, 12 Park Lane (off High Road), Wembley, Middlesex HA9 7RP. Tel: 01-903-7300/7329.
Contact: A. C. Nicholls.

WEST MIDLANDS,
Sandwell Enterprise, 22 Lombard Street, West Bromwich, West Midlands B70 8RT. Tel: 021-569-2231.

WIGAN,
Wigan New Enterprise Ltd, 11 Bridgeman Terrace, Wigan WN1 1SZ. Tel: 0492-496591.

WIRRAL,
ENTEP Trust Limited, 118 Whitby Road, Ellesmere Port, South Wirral L65 6TF. Tel: 051-356-3555.
Contact: C. D. Leatherbarrow.
In Business Ltd, Small Business Centre, Claughton Road, Birkenhead L41 6ES, Wirral Merseyside. Tel: 051-647-7574.
Contact: Paul Farrow.

WISBECH,
Fens Business Enterprise Trust, 2 York Row, Wisbech, Cambridgeshire PE13 1EB. Tel: 0945-587084.
Contact: Ron Wheeler, Director.

WOLVERHAMPTON,
Wolverhampton Enterprise Ltd, Business Advice Centre, Lich Chambers, 44 Queen's Square, Lich Gate, Wolverhampton, WV1 1TS. Tel: 0902-713737.
Contact: Mr R. P. Thompson, Director.
Wolverhampton's Small Business Consortium, Marston Road, Wolverhampton WV2 4LU. Tel: 0902-714582.
Contact: John B. Thomas, Manager.

WORCESTER,
Business Promotion Centre, Hereford & Worcester County Council, Taylors Lane, Worcester WR1 1PN. Tel: 0905-21312.
Contact: John Chidlow.

WORKINGTON,
Moss Bay Enterprise Trust (MOBET), Mobet Trading Estate, Workington, Cumbria CA14 3YB. Tel: 0900-65656.
Contact: T. Winterbottom, Manager.

YORK,
Vale of York Small Business Assoc., Lower Friargate, York YO1 1SL. Tel: 0904-641401.
Contact: Gil Elliott, Director.

Scotland

AIRDRIE,
Monklands Enterprise Trust, Unit 2, 17 Upper Mill Street, Mill Street Industrial Estate, Airdrie ML6 6JJ. Tel: 023-64-69255.
Contact: Mr W. M. Martin.

AYR,
Ayr Local Enterprise Resources Trust, (ALERT), ALERT Office, 88 Green Street, Ayr. Tel: 0292-264181.
Contact: Mr Hugh Frew.

BATHGATE,
Bathgate Area Support for Enterprise (BASE), 19 North Bridge Street, Bathgate. Tel: 0506-634024.
Contact: Mr M. J. Fass, Director.

DUNDEE,
  Dundee Industrial Association, Blackness Trading Precinct, West Hendersons Wynd, Dundee DD1 5BY. Tel: 0382-26001/2.
  Contact: Mr Ron Bear, Mrs G. Doyle.
EDINBURGH,
  Edinburgh Venture Enterprise Trust (EVENT), Hanover Buildings, Rose Street, Edinburgh EH2 2YQ. Tel: 031-226-5783.
  Contacts: Mr J. MacMillan (Chairman), N. K. Campbell (PR & Research), J. F. Jacobs (Asst. Director).
  Leith Enterprise Trust (LET), 25 Maritime Street, Leith, Edinburgh EH6 5PW. Tel: 031-553-5566.
  Contact: Mr J. Prettyman.
FALKIRK,
  Falkirk Enterprise Action Trust (FEAT), Suite A Haypark, Marchmont Avenue, Polmont, Stirlingshire FK2 0NZ. Tel: 0324-716808.
  Contact: Mr J. M. Jackson, Director.
GLASGOW,
  McPhail Street Properties Limited, Greenhead Bridgeton Factors, 23 McPhail Street, Glasgow G40 1EL. Tel: 041-556-2433.
  Contacts: Mr W. Hibberd, Mrs B. G. Ogston.
  Strathclyde Regional Council Industrial Development Unit, Strathclyde House 4, 3 India Street, Glasgow G2 4PF. Tel: 041-227-3866.
  Contact: Garrath Le Sueur, Industrial Development Manager.
  Glasgow Opportunities Enterprise Agency (GO), 7 West George Street, Glasgow. Tel: 041-221-0955.
  Contact: Mr George Paterson, Director, Jim Andrew, Tony Deeley, John Whitehead.
GLENROTHES,
  Glenrothes Enterprise Trust (GET), North House, North Street, Glenrothes, Fife KY7 5NA. Tel: 0592-757903.
  Contact: Mr Brian Turnbull, Director.
INVERNESS,
  Highland Craftpoint, Beauly, Inverness IV4 7EH. Tel: 0463-782578.
  Contact: Donald McFall, Head of Development Services.
KILMARNOCK,
  Kilmarnock Venture, Clydesdale Bank, 30 The Foregate, Kilmarnock. Tel: 0563-44602.
  Contacts: Mr Willie McPhail, Director, A. Ferguson, Tech Proj. Manager, G. Rutherford, Project Manager, Liz Graham, Secretary.
MOTHERWELL,
  Lanarkshire Industrial Field Executive (LIFE), 1-11 High Road, Motherwell ML1 2HU. Tel: 0698-66622.
  Contacts: Terry Currie, Ian Long, David Hawkes.
  Motherwell Enterprise Trust (MET), 54 Brandon Parade, Motherwell ML1 1UJ. Tel: 0698-69333.
  Contacts: Andrew Christie, Mrs C. Abraham.
PAISLEY,
  Local Enterprise Advisory Project, Westfield Annex, Paisley College, Paisley. Tel: 041-887-1241 ext 286.
  Contact: John Pearce, Duncan McTavish.
SALTCOATS,
  Ardrossan-Saltcoats-Stevenson Enterprise Trust (ASSET), 21 Green Street, Saltcoats, Ayrshire. Tel: 0294-602515.
  Contacts: Douglas Martyn, Director, G. Weir, Project Officer, W. S. McArthur, Enterprise Fund.

STIRLING,
  Ind. Dev. Dept., Central Regional Council, Viewforth, Stirling FK8 2ET. Tel: 0786-3111 ext 216.
  Contact: Industrial Development Manager.

Wales

CARDIFF,
  Cardiff & Vale Enterprise, 5 Mount Stuart Square, Cardiff CF1 6EE. Tel: 0222-494411.
  Contact: A Atkinson, Managing Executive.
  Mid Glamorgan County Council, Industrial Dev. & Promotional Unit, Greyfriars Road, Cardiff CF1 3LG. Tel: 0222-28033 ext 143.
  Contact: Mr D. Griffin, Industrial Development Officer.

DEESIDE,
  Deeside Enterprise Trust Ltd, Park House, Deeside Industrial Park, Deeside, Clwyd CH5 2NZ. Tel: 0244-815262.
  Contact: Peter Summers, Director, Norman Stuart, Felicity Agar.

HAVERFORDWEST,
  Pembrokeshire Business Initiative, Lombard Chambers, 14 High Street, Haverfordwest, Dyfed SA61 2LS. Tel: 0437-67655/6.
  Contact: P. L. M. Davies OBE, Managing Director, J. E. Lloyd.

LLANDRINDOD WELLS,
  Powys Self Help, Old Town Hall, Temple Street, Llandrindod Wells, Powys. Tel: 0597-4576.
  Contacts: Mrs S. Bailey, Roger Palmer.

LLANELLI,
  Llanelli Enterprise Company, 100 Trostre Road, Llanelli, Dyfed. Tel: 055-42-2122.
  Contacts: Mr A. W. G. Giles, D. C. Williams, Mrs J. M. Mactavish.

MERTHYR TYDFIL,
  Merthyr Agency for the Development of Enterprise Ltd, The Enterprise Centre, Merthyr Ind. Park, Pentreback, Mid Glamorgan CF48 4DR. Tel: 0443-692233.
  Contact: Mr J. Pride, Director.

NEATH,
  The Neath Partnership, 7 Water Street, Neath, West Glamorgan SA11 3EP. Tel: 0639-54111.
  Contact: J. A. Filmer-Bennett (Chairman), E. A. J. Carr (Business Development Director), Ellen Pierce (Tourism Development Manager).

NEWCASTLE EMLYN,
  Antur Teifi Limited, Swyddfair Graig, Castell Newydd Emlyn, Dyfed SA33 9BK.
  Contact: Wynfford James, Development Officer.

NEWPORT,
  Newport Enterprise Agency, Enterprise Way, off Bolt Street, Newport, Gwent NPT 2AQ. Tel: 0633-54041.
  Contact: John Crowley, General Manager.

NEWTOWN,
  Development Board for Rural Wales, Business Advisory Service, Ladywell House, Newtown, Powys SY16 1JB. Tel: 0686-26956/27168/27518.
  Contact: Mr Jackson.

PONTYPRIDD,
  Industrial Resource Centre, Treforest Industrial Estate, Pontypridd, Mid Glamorgan CF37 5YL. Tel: 0443-85-4133/4/5/6.
  Contacts: Mr Peter Davies, Mr Ray Howorth.

SWANSEA,
  Swansea Centre for Trade and Industry, Singleton Street, Swansea SA1 3QH. Tel:
  0792-476666.
  Contact: J. R. W. Evans, Director, D. R. Nutt, Business Services Manager, M. E.
  Burns, Assistant Director.
  West Glamorgan Enterprise Trust, 12a St. Mary's Square, Swansea, West
  Glamorgan SA1 3LP. Tel: 0792-475345.
  Contact: George Atkins, Director.

Northern Ireland

BANGOR,
  North Down Economic Development, Town Hall, The Castle, Bangor BT20
  4BT. Tel: 0247-54371.
  Contact: Mr T. Boal.
BELFAST,
  Belfast Development Agency, 2nd Floor, Canada House, 22 North Street, Belfast
  BT1 1LA. Tel: 0232-249655.
  Contact: Mr T. G. Crawford.
CARRICKFERGUS,
  Enterprise Carrickfergus, c/o Courtaulds Industry Centre, 75 Belfast Road,
  Carrickfergus, Co. Antrim BT38 8PH. Tel: 09603-68005.
  Contact: P. J. Conway, Chairman.
ENNISKILLEN,
  Fermanagh Enterprise Organization, Project House, Regal Pass, Enniskillen, Co.
  Fermanagh.
  Contact: Mr G. Burns.
LISBURN,
  Economic Development Organization, Town Hall, Castle Street, Lisburn BT27
  4ST. Tel: 084-62-2259.
  Contact: H. Anderson.
LONDONDERRY,
  Enterprise House, Little James Street, Londonderry. Tel: 0504-264015.
  Contact: Con McAlister.
  North West Ulster Enterprise Development Agency, 1/3 Clarendon Street,
  Londonderry BT48 7EP. Tel: 0504-265817.
  Contact: Dr V. Furness, Director.
NEWRY,
  Newry & Mourne Co-operative Ltd, 71 Hill Street, Newry BT34 1DG. Tel:
  0693-67011.
  Contact: Mr F. Dolaghan.
STRABANE,
  Strabane Industrial Development Co. Ltd, c/o 3/4 Abercorn Square, Strabane, N.
  Ireland. Tel: 0504-882505.
  Contact: D. McLaughlin.

BUSINESS ASSOCIATIONS

Alliance of Small Firms & Self-employed People Ltd, 42 Vine Road, East Molesey,
  Surrey KT8 9LF. (01-979-2293). Represents the interests of its members at
  national and local level. It has a Members Enquiry Service which can give advice
  and information on a wide range of tax, legal and employment matters. It also
  has a legal expenses insurance scheme.

Association of Independent Businesses, Trowbray House, 108 Weston Street, London SE1 3QB. (01-403-4066). Maintains close links with Whitehall and Westminster in its efforts to remove discrimination against independent business, in existing and proposed legislation.

Association of British Chambers of Commerce, Sovereign House, 212a Shaftesbury Avenue, London WC2H 8EW. (01-240-5831/6). A co-ordinating body for Chambers of Commerce.

Black Business Development Unit, Polytechnic of the South Bank, Manor House, 58 Clapham Common Northside, London SW4 9RZ. (01-223-8977/8). Helps promote business opportunities for ethnic minorities.

Chambers of Industry and Commerce, Sovereign House, 212a Shaftesbury Avenue, London WC2H 8EW. (01-240-5831/6). Apart from playing an important role in providing information and help for existing businesses, chambers of commerce have been a major force in the launching of many of the most prominent and effective Enterprise Agencies. They are a very important source of information, advice and help for new and small businesses.

Confederation of British Industry (CBI), Centre Point, 103 New Oxford Street, London WC1A 1DU. Their Smaller Firms Council carries out research and publishes papers concerning the needs of smaller firms.

Federation of Medium and Small Employers, Enterprise House, Pack and Prime Lane, Henley-on-Thames, Oxon RG9 1YU. (04912-6161).

The Forum of Private Business Ltd, Ruskin Chambers, Drury Lane, Knutsford, Cheshire WA16 6HA. (0565-4467). They research and run a referendum periodically throughout the year, keeping members informed and asking their views on a number of topical business issues.

The Institute of Directors, 116 Pall Mall, London SW1Y 5ED. (01-839-1233). The Institute represents the interests both of the directors of large companies and owner directors of smaller ones.

The National Federation of Self-Employed and Small Businesses Ltd, 32 St. Annes Road, West Lytham St. Annes, Lancashire FY8 1NY. (0253-720911). Press and Parliamentary Office: 140 Lower Marsh, Westminster Bridge, London SE1 7AE. (01-928-9272). A campaigning pressure group in business to promote and protect the interests of the self-employed, and owners and directors of small businesses.

Scottish Enterprise Foundation, University of Stirling, Stirling FK9 4LA (0786-3171). Founded in 1982 to encourage enterprise programmes and research in the small business field.

The Small Business Bureau, 32 Smith Square, London SW1P 3HH. (01-222-9000). Publishes a monthly newspaper called *Small Business* and runs an advisory service for its members.

Small Business Research Trust, 3 Dean Trench Street, Westminster, London SW1P 3HB. (01-222-4684/5). Contact: Bert Nicholson. The trust intends to become an independent research organization for small businesses in the UK. Formed in 1983 with a wide base of industrial, institutional and professional support.

Small Firms Information Service, of the British Institute of Management, Parker Street, London WC2B 5PT. (01-405-3456). The BIM runs a small firms information service to help with the management problems the smaller firm might encounter, and a sign-posting service to other sources of assistance in the area of general business information.

The Union of Independent Companies, Alan Randall, 71 Fleet Street, London EC4. (01-583-9305). A non-political organization formed in 1977 by a number of small independent industrialists, its aim is to help create an environment which will stimulate the independent sector of the economy and generally to further the interests of the small independent company, in both the manufacturing and service sectors.

OTHER USEFUL ORGANIZATIONS

Names and addresses of relevant organizations are given in each chapter. Here are some others you might find useful.

The Advertising Association, Abford House, 15 Wilton Road, London SW1V 1NJ. (01-828-2772).

Banking Information Service, 10 Lombard Street, London EC3V 9AR. (01-626-8486).

British Consultants Bureau, Westminster Palace Gardens, 1-7 Artillery Row, London SW1P 1RJ. (01-222-3651).

British Venture Capital Association, Leith House, 47-57 Gresham Street, London EC2V 7EH. (01-606-8513). Acts as a clearing house for people wishing to make contact with a member venture capital company.

The Building Centre, 26 Store Street, London WC1E 7BT. (01-637-1022). This has the most extensive library and information service on the whole building field, including building regulations and sources of professional advice. Their free information service (01-637-8361) will provide answers to almost any building problem.

The Chief Registrar of Friendly Societies, 15-17 Great Marlborough Street, London W1V 2AX. (01-437-9992).

Communication Advertising and Marketing Education (CAM) Foundation, Abford House, 3rd Floor, 15 Wilton Road, London SW1V 1NJ. (01-828-7506). This is the authoritative body on what and where to study in the marketing field.

Corporation of Mortgage, Finance & Life Assurance Brokers Ltd, PO Box 101, Guildford, Surrey GU1 2HZ. (0483-35786/39126).

The Design Council, 28 Haymarket, London SW1 4DG. (01-839-8000).

Direct Selling Association, 44 Russell Square, London WC1P 4JP. (01-580 8433).

Discount Market Association, 39 Cornhill, London EC3V 3NU. (01-623-1020).

The Equipment Leasing Association, 18 Upper Grosvenor Street, London W1X 6PB. (01-491-2783).

IMAGE Marketing Services, 359 The Strand, London WC2. (01-836-7086). Contact Andrew Ferguson. They run a scheme called Sharex to help small firms take part in exhibitions.

Industrial Market Research Association, 11 Bird Street, Lichfield, Staffs WS13 6PW. (05432-23448).

The Industrial Society, Peter Runge House, 3 Carlton House Terrace, London SW1Y 5DG. (01-839-4300).

Institute of Chartered Accountants in England & Wales, PO Box 433, Chartered Accountants Hill, Moorgate Place, London EC2P 2BJ. (01-628-7060). The society provides a free booklet, You Need a Chartered Accountant.

Institute of Chartered Accountants of Scotland, 27 Queen Street, Edinburgh EH2 1LA. (031-225-5673).

Institute of Cost and Management Accountants, 63 Portland Place, London W1N 4AB. (01-580-6542).

Institute of Credit Management, Easton House, Easton on the Hill, Stamford, Lincolnshire PE9 3NH. (0780-56777). The professional body for people interested in credit management. Produces a quarterly journal, *Credit Management*.

Institute of Management Consultants, 23-24 Cromwell Place, London SW7 2LG. (01-584-72856).

Institute of Personnel Management, IPM House, 35 Camp Road, Wimbledon SW19 4UW. (01-946-9100).

Institute of Public Relations, Gate House, St. John Square, London EC1M 4DH. (01-253-5151).

The Law Society, 113 Chancery Lane, London WC2. (01-242-1222).

Local authorities. Each has a Planning Department, which can give information and opinions on planning applications and other matters relating to your premises; a Building Control Department, covering building regulations; an Environmental Health Department, covering health and safety at work; and an Industrial Liaison Department, giving general advice to encourage industrial development.

Local Councils can very often provide small sums of start up finance, or money for market research. Contact your local council's Industrial Development Officer.

The London Society of Chartered Accountants, 38 Finsbury Square, London EC2A 1PX. (01-628-2467).

The Mail Order Traders Association of Great Britain, 25 Castle Street, Liverpool L2 4TD. (051-227-4181).

Management Buy-out Association, The Chairman, 71 Padleys Lane, Burton Joyce, Notts. NG14 5BW. (060-231-2499). Founded in 1982 by George Bloomfield, to offer impartial advice to managers contemplating "buy-outs".

National Association of Pension Funds, Sunley House, Bedford Park, Croydon CR0 0XF. (01-681-2017). Some pension funds are prepared to invest in promising small businesses. The Secretary of this association could put you in touch with such a fund.

The Post Office, provides an introductory offer for first time users of their Direct Mail, Business Reply, Freepost and Overseas direct mail shot services. As a small business you would be prudent to think of using Direct Mail and with the Post Office paying for the first 1200 of your letters, you can save money too. Contact: Kay Manley, Post Office Director Mail Section, Room 604, 22-25 Finsbury Square, London EC2B 2QQ.

PRESTEL CITISERVICE, Page 5991, provides a weekly update of important changes in the pattern of government finance for new projects. (Service provided by Peat, Marwick & Mitchell & Co.)

Public Relations Consultants Association, 37 Cadogan Street, Sloane Square, London SW3 2PR. (01-581-3951).

Regional Newspaper Advertising Bureau Ltd, Grosvenor House, 141 Drury Lane, London WC2B 5TD. (01-836-8251). Contact: Peter Edwards. Single point of entry to book advertising in any of 1,000 local newspapers. They offer a computerized database service that can provide all relevant facts and figures about these local papers and the areas in which they operate

Small Firms Marketing Centre, London Road, Warmley, Bristol BS15 5JH. (0272-677807). The centre has a small full-time staff and a team of part-time specialist consultants on tap. It was established in 1983 to provide practical help to small and young enterprises at a modest cost.

The Society of Company & Commercial Accountants, 11 Portland Road, Edgbaston, Birmingham B16 9HW. (021-454-8791/2).

Trade Associations, to be found through *Directory of British Associations* published by CBD Research Limited, Beckenham, Kent. Most business fields have a trade association, such as the Brewers Society, the Federation of Fish Friers or the Booksellers Association. They are a useful source of help and advice to potential new entrants to their trade. This directory lists all such associations.

Chapter 12

FIVE START-UP OPPORTUNITIES ANALYSED

In this chapter we take a closer look at five popular start-up ideas: a small hotel; a private day nursery; a health food shop; a clipping/grooming service for dogs; a driving school.

We offer some guidelines on the amount of money needed to get the business underway, the skills needed by the entrepreneur himself and indicate the possible rewards – and the risks – together with inside tips from those who have done it.

These analyses are adapted from articles which appeared in the *Business Ideas Letter* and we thank the publishers, Stonehart Publications Ltd, for permission to reproduce them.

A SMALL HOTEL

Start-up money: varies depending on value of the business – but quite a lot.
Skills/qualifications needed: ability to manage on four to six hours sleep a night, good head for figures, previous experience useful but not essential.
Time involved: full-time, and then some.
Potential rewards: a business-subsidised life-style plus a net profit of, perhaps, 25% of revenue.
Likely snags: choosing the wrong location, finding honest staff, a 7am to 1am working day.

Estate agents who specialize in hotel sales say there is a growing trend for people to chuck in the rat race, sell up and invest everything in a small inn or guest house deep in the country. As often as not, it's a place where they previously enjoyed a holiday, usually Devon, Cornwall or Somerset.

Far be it for us to pour cold water on people's dreams, but what with the recession, the growth of holiday self-catering and an occupancy rate in many West Country hotels dropping to below 50% even in high season, small resort hotels are no longer such a good bet, especially if you're a beginner. Neither are those small country hotels that rely entirely on charm or the quality of the food to bring in the paying customers. It's more than likely that a change of management will result in a change of chef and, whoosh, you've lost your clientele. No, for anyone who is determined to make money in the hotel game the best type of hotel to choose is one with 18-20 bedrooms on the fringes of London or in a provincial town, which attracts a mixture of businessmen and tourists and which doesn't rely too heavily on its bar and restaurant trade. We'll come back to that in a moment. First, it's important to establish what special qualities, if any, you need for success. Who's most likely to make it as a hotelier? The answer we got from one expert was "ex-Inland Revenue employees", which perhaps isn't as crazy as it sounds. They have stickability and a head for figures, which are two of the qualities you need, plus a special understanding of how to make the most of the tax advantages, which are one of the perks of the hotel business.

Fully half the people who go into small hotels have no previous experience, as that's not an essential. Those who succeed have something much rarer, the capacity to work an 18-hour day, seven days a week, and still come up smiling. You're never really off duty when running a hotel. And if you've gone into it as a way of meeting people, wait till you meet some of the people you'll have to meet! One hotelier we know built up his business from scratch while running a garage at the same time. According to him, "you need a lot of self-discipline to make it a success, which is hard at the beginning if you've been used to a nice, organized nine-to-five job."

The Hotel & Catering Industry Training Board runs a course on buying a hotel (for address see below). It finds that 95% of the applicants come from other fields, ranging from law to the civil service, and all have a more or less equal chance of success. Of course, it helps to have some idea of the workings of the trade. At the very least, it would pay to visit a variety of hotels in the category we're talking about and work out exactly why they're making a success or not. Attention to detail is usually the give-away: clean cutlery and china, no delays in answering the telephone, a big and well-organized car park.

A small establishment of only 10 bedrooms can often be a viable proposition if it has a flourishing restaurant and bar trade, but for beginners looking for a family-run hotel the optimum size is 18-20 bedrooms. Reasons?

- It will be manageable with a minimum of staff (good people are hard to find and even more difficult to keep).
- Room revenue is the biggest profit-maker in a hotel. Bar and restaurant takings, the other two main sources of income, incur much higher costs.
- If you've little or no experience of catering, it makes sense not to go for a hotel that relies too heavily on its food and drink operation.

So you want to look for a hotel with a reasonable number of rooms, and you want to look for one that has a maximum occupancy all week long, year round. By maximum, we mean an average of 65% – no hotel is full all the time. To achieve that, you must choose a hotel in the right location, which more than anything else is what it's all about. Conrad Hilton is supposed to have said (it's a truism in the property business as well) that the three most important considerations in buying a hotel are "location, location and location". Get that right and you shouldn't go too far wrong.

You not only have to consider the area of the country but also the exact location within that area. Ideally, you want a place that attracts business customers from Monday to Thursday and tourists over the weekend. Certain inner-fringe areas of London such as Bayswater, Paddington or even Kensington are worth considering, in spite of the high prices – London is thick with visiting businessmen, especially to exhibition centres like Earls Court and Olympia, and it draws 80% of all tourists to the UK.

That being said, you should also examine the London suburbs and dormitory towns, especially those which are attracting businesses moving out of central London.

Provincial towns are another strong possibility for setting up small hotels. Miles Quest, author of the definitive book *How to Buy your own Hotel*, reckons them to be the best bet of all. "Unlike London and one or two major cities, there has been no dramatic increase in the number of hotels in many provincial cities although rooms and other extensions have been added to existing hotels, competition is not so keen. Many provincial hotels have built up a steady trade with commercial and business traffic or could build it up in the future."

What can you expect to pay?

As a rough guide, something between £70,000 and £175,000 for the sort of hotel we're talking about, depending on such factors as area, turnover, tenure and so on. To get a better idea of what's on offer, take a look through the "Hotels, Guest and Apartment Houses" section in *Dalton's Weekly*.

How much can you borrow? From clearing banks, up to 50% of the purchase price, repayable over 7-10 years on freehold properties, and 5 years on leasehold. The size of the loan will depend on profitability; the banks don't seem to worry over much if you have no previous experience in the hotel trade.

If you're looking for more money or a longer repayment period, try one of the venture capital lenders such as the Industrial & Commercial Finance Corporation (see Chapter 4).

Don't overlook the help you can get from estate agents. There are a number of good ones who specialize in hotels and guest houses, and they can not only provide suitable properties for you but also assess your needs and abilities and help you find finance, too. For the latter service, they'll charge a fee of 2%-3% of the amount borrowed (or "facility arranged", to use the jargon). Here are a handful of useful agents to contact:

- Robert Barry & Co., Cotteswold House, Cirencester, Glos and 11 Charlotte Street, Edinburgh 2.
- Brodie Marshall & Co., 36 Ebury Street, London SW1W 0LW.
- Lawson & Herman, 8 Abingdon Road, London W8 6AF.
- Oliver, Kitchen & Flynn, 30 Albion Place, Leeds 1.

Key points to watch out for

What you pay for a hotel is, of course, very much affected by the state of the building and the standard of contents and fittings. It is essential to check the fire precautions. Even though the hotel may already have a fire certificate, the authorities often make a point of reinspecting a building when it changes hands, and suggesting various improvements. You may also have to update existing equipment (improving emergency lights, installing smoke detectors, and the like), so it's wise to consult the local Fire Prevention Officer before making your final decision.

Talk, too, to the local planning authority about planning consent for expansion. If the business proves successful you don't want to be hampered by lack of space. Better still, choose a hotel that already has outline planning for an extension.

With alterations or improvements generally, you should be able to programme them so that at least part of the hotel stays open and you can use the income to defray building costs. It wouldn't make sense to close the hotel down unless you were completely refurbishing it, but what are you going to live on in the meantime?

If the hotel only has a "breakfast room", you should consider whether you want to expand the catering facilities or whether offering bed-and-breakfast is enough. In London, because of intense competition from outside restaurants, it's a waste of time offering restaurant facilities in a hotel of less than 100 rooms. In a provincial town, however, where the competition is much less fierce, a restaurant with a limited menu of high-quality standard dishes (steaks and grills) could work well, and increase the pulling power of the hotel.

Here are some other points to watch for when looking at hotels:

- *Is the car park big enough?* Nearly everybody who uses your hotel, or the restaurant, will come by car. So an adequate car park is vital. Don't be lulled by an apparent sufficiency of street parking – what happens if the local authority suddenly decides to restrict it? And don't think you can rely on nearby commercial car parks, which are almost bound to be closed just when your guests want to use them.
- *Is the boiler too old?* A hotel without hot water is like a bank without money, and likely to stay in business about as long. So if the boiler is more than 25 years old, get an expert to look at it.
- *Is the building listed?* If it is, you'll end up living in the planning authority's pocket. You won't be able to anything, not even knock down an internal wall, without their permission. And an extension could well be prohibited.

● *What about insurance?* Your bank will expect you to take out insurance on the building from the day contracts are exchanged. That's simply to cover their investment in case the place burns down. In addition, you will have to insure the contents of the building and, under the provisions of the Occupiers Liability Act, the safety of your customers.

You may also want to take out a profit protection policy to provide you with some sort of income in case the hotel goes up in smoke.

Before exchanging contracts your solicitor will need to apply on your behalf for a liquor licence, or for the transfer of the existing licence to your name. If the licensing justices don't like anything about your character or background, they can object to the application and you may not get the licence. If you don't, and if the contract to buy the hotel is conditional on you getting the licence, which it should be, then the deal collapses. So get your application in early enough. There are five main types of licence in England, and no less than seven in Scotland.

What about stock?

Before exchange of contracts you will also have to agree on the inventory which the vendor will have drawn up. You have to check that all items included in the sale are as listed and haven't been cunningly replaced with second-rate substitutes. If the hotel is leasehold, there will be two inventories – one listing the fixtures bought from the freeholder, the other listing the fittings bought from the leaseholder. Make sure, incidentally, that the contents you buy are actually the contents you get; overnight swops have been known to take place, with the Royal Doulton becoming Royal Woolworth.

On takeover day itself, the valuer and stock-takers will value all saleable liquor on the premises at wholesale cost prices (assuming the hotel had a liquor licence in the first place), together with all the food stocks. When the value of the stock has been agreed, you and the vendor will have to reach a settlement and the purchase of the stock will be completed immediately after the stocktaking. The settlement will include not only the purchase of wet and dry stocks but any necessary adjustments in the general and water rates.

Income and outgoings

Most hotels derive their income equally from three main sources – one third from room revenue, one third from liquor sales and one third from food. This gives you three legs to stand on, and the business won't fall over if one of the legs is temporarily shorter than the others. Room revenue, as we've said, is much more profitable than food and drink sales.

With both of those, you have to aim for a gross profit of 55%–65% to make them worthwhile. Taking the business as a whole, you want to achieve a net profit of at least 12%–16%, which can be ploughed back for expansion.

With a small hotel you will be doing a lot of the work yourself, though you will need to hire certain staff, even if only part-time. Cleaning staff are comparatively easy to find and it is best to hire your linen unless the hotel is small enough (12 bedrooms or less) to allow it to be washed on the premises. If you decide that you're going to provide anything more than breakfasts you will need a chef and perhaps serving staff. A chef who's worth his salt can be a great help in achieving the right level of gross profit on food – he'll know exactly how to get the most out of each item.

Up to 35% of your operating expenses can be on staff because this is a service industry – a more likely level, though, is 20%–25%. The accompanying panel shows a simple profit and loss account for a 16-bedroom hotel – it is for guidance only; no two hotels will produce the same set of figures, even in an identical location.

Actual profit and loss account after first year of operation

	%	£	£
Sales:			
Rooms	23.7	37,860	
Food	38.4	61,418	
Liquor/tobacco	35.7	57,140	
Other	2.2	3,589	
TOTAL SALES			160,007
Less: Cost of Sales			
Food	37.4	23,002	
Liquor/tobacco	47.4	27,105	50,107
GROSS PROFIT	68.7		109,900
Less: Wages	27.8		44,556
NET MARGIN	40.8		65,344
Less: OPERATING EXPENSES			
Electricity		1,634	
Oil		2,297	
Gas		867	
Insurance		605	
Rentals		1,115	
Laundry		4,538	
Advertising, etc		495	
Music and entertainment		1,851	
Postage		350	
Print and stationery		733	
Rates		2,618	
Telephone		842	
Cleaning materials		794	
Flowers/decorations etc		1,922	
Miscellaneous		1,440	
TOTAL	13.8	22,101	22,101
OPERATING PROFIT	27		43,243
Less: Maintenance and depreciation			3,123
NET PROFIT	25.1		40,220

From: *How to Buy Your Own Hotel* by Miles Quest (Brodie Marshall, 1979).

What food and drink to provide

A bar, as we've seen, can be a valuable source of revenue, though sales costs are comparatively high. It's vital to keep a close eye on bar staff, though, because this is one area where pilfering can be rife. The remedy is to have a stocktaking once a month. The value of your wet stock could well be over £5,000, so it's worth protecting. Bar snacks are a good idea because they bring in extra revenue and encourage people to drink more. Cigarettes aren't big revenue producers but they are a necessary part of the service.

Breakfast must be the crowning glory of your service, whether or not you decide to serve other meals. It is the one thing that all travellers look forward to, especially those from abroad, and you mustn't disappoint them. After all, Kipling said: "You can dine well in England – provided you eat three breakfasts a day."

The English Tourist Board's Development Guide on *Starting a Small Guest House* is very sensible on the subject of breakfasts:

"Breakfast should consist of fruit juice, breakfast cereal or porridge, followed by the usual cooked breakfast of eggs, bacon, sausage, etc., and tea or coffee plus rolls or toast. Remember that some of your visitors may be staying more than one night or have had the same breakfast in a dozen other guest houses. Offering a choice of main course, be it only a boiled egg instead of a fried breakfast, can suffice, but you could be more imaginative by offering kippers or smoked haddock. Breakfast is the last impression people have of your establishment so it helps for it to be as good as possible so that visitors may be tempted to return."

Here is an ETB example for costing a breakfast (1982 prices) to give a 50%-60% profit.

1 glass fruit juice	
or	
½ grapefruit	
or	
1 bowl cereal plus milk & sugar	10p
1 egg	7p
2 rashers bacon	20p
1 sausage	10p
1 tomato	8p
2 slices toast	5p
2 cups coffee or tea	8p
Milk, sugar, butter, marmalade/honey	10p
	78p

Suggested selling price: £1.50-£2.00.

Now the question of providing an evening meal. The considerable extra cost in terms of food and, possibly, staff, plus overheads such as heating and repairing and replacing equipment, make it a question that needs careful examining. Broadly speaking, an evening meal is unnecessary if the hotel is in London – there are too many alternative eating places and you'd be hard put, anyway, to compete with them in price.

If the hotel is in provincial town or an outlying suburb, then the argument for providing an evening meal is much stronger. You should aim to provide the highest possible quality that is compatible with the price and the market – in other words, you offer the best mixed grill in town, and at the best price. Keep the menu limited and keep it conservative, concentrating on old favourites such as steak and kidney pie, roasts and grills. A small menu is best because it makes it easier for the kitchen and cuts down mistakes in serving.

You'll have to cost your dishes accurately, ensuring that the major items give you a gross profit of between 60-70%. If the prices that your customers are willing to pay won't allow that, you'll have to find a cheaper supplier – most hotels use local cash-and-carry wholesalers – or, as a last resort, serve small portions. The best way to get your costing right every time is to stick to standard recipes so that the ingredients don't vary too much.

Hotels are a very vulnerable business. For one thing, they have very high fixed costs which have to be met even if there isn't a single guest. For another, they offer a commodity which, unlike shoes or cosmetics, can't be sold tomorrow if it didn't sell today. This means you have to work extra hard at marketing and publicity in order to keep the beds filled.

Apart from all the normal procedures, such as getting yourself listed by the local authority, contacting local travel agencies and advertising in the local papers, there are various marketing consortia that individual hoteliers can join. By pooling membership fees, each hotel in the consortia gets considerably greater marketing and sales clout than they could possibly afford on their own.

In addition, the consortia offer advisory services to individual members. You have to be vetted before you're allowed to join.

Two of the best known consortia are:

Best Western Hotels, 26 Kew Road, Richmond, Surrey TW9 2NA 01-940 7566. There is a once-only joining fee of £750 and an annual subscription of £2,663 for hotels with up to 10 bedrooms (£88.25 extra per room for hotels with between 11-200 rooms).

Inter-Hotel, 29 Harrington Gardens, London SW7 4JT.

Further Action

Two organizations that can provide a great deal of help and advice are: *The British Tourist Authority*, 64 St. James Street, London SW1A 1NF (01-499 9325) and *The English Tourist Board*, 4 Grosvenor Gardens, London SW1W 0DH (01-730 3400). The ETB publishes a series of Development Guides which cost £1.50 each, post free. *The Hotel and Catering Industries Training Board* is at Ramsey House, Central Square, Wembley, Middlesex HA9 7AD (01-902 8865).

How to Buy Your Own Hotel by Miles Quest is available by mail from Brodie Marshall Hotels, 36 Ebury Street, London SW1W 0LW (01-730 9974) at £10, which includes postage and packing.

A PRIVATE DAY NURSERY

Skills/qualifications needed: experience with under-5's is essential, property/ construction and commercial skills desirable.
Start-up money: from around £10,000 if you're leasing old premises with not too much conversion work needed, up to around £30,000 for new portable buildings.
Time involved: full time plus.
Potential turnover: £16,000 to £30,000 p.a. depending on location, much more if staffing ratios were brought more into line with nursery classes in infants' schools.
Likely snags: bureaucratic interference, some invasion of home life, especially if you run a transport service.

There can't be many businesses around at the moment with four customers on the waiting list for every one they can serve. This is the happy position of many of Britain's private day nurseries, and it's an area which seems set for spectacular growth in the years ahead.

There is, however, one important qualification to be made. One of the major checks on growth is the irrelevant and pettifogging nature of some of the official regulations. Our favourite example decrees that you issue each child with its own freshly laundered hand towel every day, to be hung on pegs spaced six to nine inches apart. The idea is to cut out the risk of cross-infection.

Picture the scene: 24 little monsters milling around, paws in and out of each other's food and in each other's mouths. They seethe en masse into the washroom, grab the first towel they see, drop it on the floor, hang it back wherever they can until the nursery nurse can sort out the towels. One to a peg. All that time and energy going into the laundry for no good reason at all.

Rules like these are made by people who never seem to question their logic or the cost of observing them. Unfortunately, the people running day nurseries will attack the rules only in private, since their licence to trade depends on outward compliance with them, and nobody wants to "rock the boat".

Day nurseries of all sorts are licensed, regulated and inspected by the Social Services Departments of the local authorities.

Thanks to the stringent regulations, and the generous nature of building specifications in the public sector, it can cost a local authority well over £100,000 to build on their own account a small day nursery for some 30 infants. As a direct result, many local authorities have no nursery provision of their own at all, and they rely heavily on private concerns to accept needy children referred through Social Services.

Even in the best provided areas, like the London boroughs, the number of children at risk is so great that all the available places in the local authority day nurseries are filled by specially referred children, and the ordinary working mum has very little chance of finding a nursery place for her child.

In a market like this, you really can't go wrong as long as you run a good nursery. In the small towns day nurseries report waiting lists of up to 100 children; in the cities desperate parents offer to pay twice and three times the going rate to have their child jump the queue.

The Department of Health doesn't issue separate figures for the private and public sectors of nursery care, but the total figures for all types (England and Wales, 1980) are as follows:

Under 5's attending full-time 266,000
          attending part-time 197,000

The number of children in each group, however, is as follows: under one year old: 639,000; one year: 614,000; two years: 566,700; three years: 556,300; four years: 583,700; five years: 611,600.

The biggest growth recently has been in the numbers of very young children now attending nurseries because mother has to work as father's job looks precarious. Playgroups only offer the occasional play session, so the alternatives for the working mum are a childminder, a nanny or a day nursery. It's generally reckoned that about half the mothers of children in this age group would prefer to go out to work if facilities existed for good day care. Clearly the 463,000 places available would only have met the needs of one in three children.

Let it get around that you're going to open a nursery if you can find good premises cheaply and you'll probably find you get to hear about every possible building even before it's advertised. In small regional towns it's still possible to sign up large buildings in a central position for as little as £250 down and £10 a week in rent. (Calculate your rates bill at the same time, however. One such low-rent property we found pays over £800 a year in rates).

One of the most common and cheapest choices is the large Victorian house rented on a medium-term lease. Before you start hunting you'll need to take advice from the County Fire Officer on what to look for and what to avoid in terms of layout, as it could cost you a fortune to convert an unsuitable building. Generally speaking the authorities prefer to keep the children on the ground floor, with other accommodation (kitchen, office, washrooms, rest room etc.) on the first floor. You must also get approval for the position of staircases, exits and fire doors.

Other snags with old buildings are the lack of safe parking space and the high cost of insulation and heating. Many nursery owners who installed secondhand night storage heaters in the mid-70s now bitterly regret it. They're paying up to £1500 a year to keep premises at the regulation 65°F. Gas central heating is much cheaper to run, but more expensive at the outset.

For the more intrepid property fanciers it's undoubtedly cheaper to get something purpose-built – if you can stand the upheavals. One husband and wife team, Chris and Wendy Wardman, benefited each other's business very neatly. He runs a building and demolition business and she runs two day nurseries, so all her construction and conversion work was handled in the family. Chris Wardman was in regular contact with the Estates Department of his County Council which disposes of local authority surplus equipment through a tendering system. Interested parties just make a bid for the items that interest them. In 1979 the Wardmans bought two secondhand portable buildings, one double and one single unit, for just £2,500. Their insured value today is £15,000.

Buying secondhand may be a bargain, but there are a few catches. You have the considerable expense and inconvenience of dismantling and moving the buildings yourself, and you have to make good the torn up tarmacadam and the damage done to lawns etc, in getting the crane and low-loader on to the school or hospital grounds. The Wardmans had actually spent £15,000 by the time they opened the finished nursery. This included the building and fitting out of a "junction section", housing the kitchen, washrooms and all the mains drainage and plumbing, and a new roof for the entire "L" shaped building. It makes for thought-provoking comparison, however, with the copy book approach of the local authority architect who spends £100,000 of rate-payers money to achieve the same end.

Whether you convert an old building, build a new one or use a portable unit, you will need to install special fixtures and fittings. The biggest single shock will be the cost of the child-size loos and wash-basins – half the size but twice the price of standard fittings. The regulations also oblige you to have three basins in the kitchen – one for washing up, one for washing hands and one for preparing vegetables.

One final note for the budget: don't forget to check what you need outside – you must have a securely fenced play area and a standing area for prams.

Here are a few hints on what equipment you need in the nursery, including tips on making the money go further:

- *Flooring:* non-slip, easily mopped floor tiles are your best bet. Exhibition contractors might be able to get them for you at cost price.
- *Kitchen equipment:* you can pick up most items as bankrupt or secondhand stock, but buy ovens, freezers etc new and with full maintenance cover.
- *Food:* get a cash-and-carry card and learn how to make a little money go a long way. You get reimbursed for a third of a pint of milk per child per day and, using this in puddings etc you should be able to provide lunch and tea for 24 children and lunch for four members of staff on £40 per week.
- *Nursery furniture:* suppliers of school tables and chairs tend to charge an absolute bomb (again because of local authority regulations). Try and get a local carpenter to make you up large, low tables with tubular legs and Formica tops, seating about ten children. Chairs must be robust and durable, and you can find sturdy little chairs among Third World imports for as little as £1.50 each.
- *Medical/health items:* an appeal to local GPs can produce a remarkable quantity of thermometers and first aid materials, since they receive so many free gifts from the drug companies. Ask parents to provide nappies each day for babies and toddlers and a clean hand towel for the older ones.
- *Play equipment:* most of this can be made or bought secondhand from private homes, playgroups closing down, jumble sales etc. Look for bargains in toys, indoor climbing frames, Wendy houses, blackboards, baby walkers, play pens. Good secondhand colour tellies repossessed from defaulting clients can be bought cheap through TV rental firms.
- *Miscellaneous:* cots, fireguards, stair gates, harnesses, changing mats, sterilizing units – all this kind of gear can be got secondhand. For fire extinguishers try demolition contractors. A day nursery for 24 children can easily get through £300 worth of paper in a year. Check whether anyone knows a charitable printer for free supplies.

To get financial backing for a day nursery you will need to present a budget to your bank, so your first task is to work out costings and how much you will be able to charge.

Current rates vary quite widely, from £15 in small towns for a full 8am to 6pm week, to over £30 in cities where the day tends to be longer due to mother's journey time to and from work. Many nurseries run a minibus to pick up the children from home and take them back.

This is popular with parents, saves staff time, but is likely to fill your evenings with telephone messages about how so and so is ill and can't come. Half days are generally charged at more than half rate, e.g. £2 for half day, £3.50 for a full day.

On the costs side, the single most problematic area is the cost of converting or constructing premises. Long delays are commonplace and time costs a great deal of money. If you can attract a professional into helping you force the pace on all the approvals, arrival of materials, honouring of contracts etc. It will take a great load off your mind and save money. One nursery erecting new premises on a site leased from the local authority made it a condition of the lease that they would not be liable to pay rent until the building was ready for business.

Heating is a particular expense in a day nursery. Here modern buildings (including current portable structures) can be 100% cheaper to heat than rambling old buildings.

Staffing is another major expense. Though rates of pay are very low, between £1 and £1.50 an hour at the lower-priced end of the range, the regulations require you to have one member of staff on duty for every six children you are licensed to care for.

This is another source of friction between private and public sectors. The Education Authorities will cheerfully put a class of 24 four-year-olds in the charge of one nursery teacher, but those self-same children would have to have four supervising adults in a day nursery controlled by Social Services Regulations. If you want to take the children for a run in the park or to a nearby beach for the afternoon, you're supposed to increase this to one adult per two children. All the rule achieves is an enforced no-outings policy.

The established trend in the USA and in other European countries is toward more and more freedom for the mothers of young children, and therefore towards better provision of day care. In Britain frustration at the shortage of nursery places is mounting. As and when we start getting fuller employment, changes will have to be made to an antiquated, pedantic and largely irrelevant set of regulations. This in turn will encourage large nurseries (a sole trader is restricted in the number of children he's licensed to care for, *regardless* of how many staff he employs) and more individual establishments throughout the country.

A day in the life of a day nursery proprietor is pretty demanding in itself without the "lightning inspection visit" that usually ends up as a waste of time. He or she is responsible for a huge amount of paperwork: register of attendance, weekly menus including special diets, shopping lists for cash-and-carry, record keeping on Social Services referrals, medical record keeping, general bookkeeping, wages etc.

Any of this work is liable to interruption at any time if he or she is needed to change a nappy, show a new parent round, mend a gate, instruct a member of staff, phone the health visitor about head lice, Social Services about bruises or take a child to the doctor. "You need patience at the best of times," explained one owner, "but to put up with some of the more inexperienced people who come round you need to be a bloody saint. They'll make you hunt through the children's bags until all the towels are hanging on those damned hooks, or they'll turn up on the day the cook's got 'flu and your producing a lunch for umpteen children and all they can say is 'you shouldn't be doing this, you know!'

Fortunately, people who work with children tend to be very resourceful, with a rich fund of humour and patience to draw on, and it's just as well they are. Running a day nursery is demanding work, but it's rewarding both financially and personally.

Further Information

The British Association for Early Childhood Education, (Montgomery Hall, Kennington Oval, London SE11 5SW; 01-582 8744) issues a useful set of publications.

A HEALTH FOOD SHOP

Start-up money: £10,000 plus.
Skills/qualifications: a belief in, and some knowledge of, natural foods; tact and patience.
Time involved: full-time.
Potential rewards: a steady income.
Likely snags: choosing the wrong area.

Health food shops are a good deal more popular than their late-Sixties image of grains, beans, herbs and hippies might suggest. They now sell a far wider range of products, catering not just for the alternative stomach but for a whole naturally healthy lifestyle and are aiming at the mass market. Some chains like Holland and Barratt, have already brought health foods to the high streets very successfully.

A wider awareness of the damage processed foods can cause – the growing list of substances found to be carcinogenic, for instance, and the linking of heart disease to unhealthy eating habits – has led to much greater public interest in natural foods. As well as guarding against later ill-health, a change in diet can actually solve immediate problems – for instance, hyperactive children have been tamed virtually overnight by removing foods with certain additives from their diet.

Although health food shops are mushrooming at a rapid rate, saturation point is still reckoned to be a long way off. The density of health food shops to population in the UK is still only a third of that in other European countries – West Germany and Sweden, for instance.

What you'll need

To run a health food shop you'll need robust health yourself, money, a good site, a head for business and some knowledge of nutrition and natural foods.

It is estimated that suburban shopping centres and towns with a population density of around 20,000 will support a health food store. Ideally, you want a site where there is heavy pedestrian traffic. A prime site amongst large supermarkets, though, is not necessarily the best in ratio of rent to sales volume terms. And many sites located at the beginning, end or just off the high street have proved to be success-ful.

A recommended size of store is one with between 300 and 500 square feet of sell-ing space, but a smaller store in a better location, even if it costs as much in rent, can have a much higher sales potential.

If you take over existing premises, remember you will probably have to pay a premium as well as rent. A very rough guide to the amount of rent for a 500 sq. ft. shop is £5,000 per annum.

The cost of equipping the shop will depend very much on the state of the premises. Here is a guide (again, very approximate) to the sort of costs involved for a 500 sq ft health food store assuming no structural building work, and a shop front in good condition:

Perspex fascia – projecting sign	350
Wood-edged or laminated shelving units/cash desk	4,000
Floor covering carpet or vinyl	700
Dairy cabinet	650
Cash register/scales	500
Shopping baskets, price guns and tickets etc.	250
Standard display material	100
Provision general decoration, electrics	250
Initial stock to fill store	5,000
Sundry items	200
Total	£12,000

An analysis of health food shops carried out in 1982 suggested that average weekly sales were in the region of £2,000 per week, and operational costs (excluding wages) equalled 12% of sales.

You need to develop systems for ordering and controlling stock. You must monitor the speed at which products sell and weed out slow movers. Also, make regular checks for products that have passed their shelf life. This is extremely important since selling deteriorating products will deal your blossoming reputation a heavy blow. Be particularly vigilant in the summer months. Also, check new stock for shelf life and don't accept products with only a few days to go. Products should also be spot-checked for weight, and any weighing you do yourself from bulk purchase should be done with care. Many products, especially dried fruit, lose a little weight drying out while on the shelf, so allow for this.

As a food shop you will be visited by Weights and Measures Inspectors and Public Health Inspectors. Your scales should always be correct and all foods packaged for protection. The shop must, of course, be spotlessly clean and the storeroom should also be clean, dry and cool.

Products must be labelled according to regulations with details of ingredients, country of origin, weight and price. Some products, flour and sugar for instance, can no longer be sold in imperial measures. You can be fined for inadequate labelling or selling underweight.

The main difference between running a health food store and any other food shop is the need to know about nutrition, health and natural foods. Nobody asks the shop assistant in a supermarket what to buy for migraines but such questions and many more serious ones (questions about digestion, the menopause, even cancer) occur daily in a health food shop. The advice aspect can be time-consuming but it is a vital part of building your reputation, and feeling you are helping others is rewarding in itself.

You don't have to have any qualifications in this country to give dietary advice (unlike the US) but it's only sound and helpful advice that starts the word of mouth recommendations which increases your trade. If the thought of advising cancer sufferers alarms you, take heart – you can't do much harm by recommending a healthy, balanced diet. Be careful, though, not to make exaggerated claims for the curative properties of foods and supplements – you can be had up under the Trade Descriptions Act, even for verbal claims.

It's useful to contact doctors in your area and let them know what you stock so that they can refer patients with special dietary needs to you.

There is a certain mystique surrounding natural foods. You can take a three-month course at the Kushi Institute in London which covers all the principles and practice of macro-biotics along with the "Shiatsu message, Order of the Universe, and Nutrition and Spiritual Development". For the more practical-minded, there are correspondence courses run by the National Association of Health Stores, dealing with all aspects of running a health food store and details of the products and their benefits. There are also plenty of books on the subject.

One good one is: *Let's Get Well* by Adelle Davis.

You'll need to know something about vegetarian cookery, too, as customers may not know how to use certain foodstuffs.

What to sell

The pills, potions and elixirs sold in health shops are the biggest money-spinners of all. They are highly priced, take up little shelf space and sell well. However, many health foods shops are dead against these supplements, believing that just changing peoples' eating habits is the key to healthy living.

You will need to balance the profit motive against your own philosophy. Telling someone to change their lifestyle to calm their nerves isn't easy, but suggesting natural sources of vitamins (unrefined cereal grains or molasses instead of B6) should help you retain your customer's confidence and custom although you may lose out financially. Remember, you want to build a reputation for long-term success.

Decide what to stock early on since it affects other decisions, such as the fittings and layout of the shop. Visit other health foods stores and note down names and addresses of suppliers for goods you like.

Here are some guidelines on stock:

- keep it simple. If people want to choose between 10 brands they'll go to the supermarket. Find, say, one brand of muesli which you like at a good price and stick with it.
- don't try to compete directly. If you're next to an excellent bookshop there is probably no point selling books. Similarly, don't stock foods which supermarkets sell cheaper – some honeys, for instance.
- try to get customers to come in frequently by selling items which people regularly need – bread, vegetables, eggs – as well as the grains and beans which might only be bought periodically.
- stock items for impulse buying – cosmetics, books, confectionery etc.

The traditional stock of a health food shop is grains, beans, dried fruit, nuts and muesli but consider the following too. *Wholemeal bread* is extremely popular, although a low profit item. Cakes and scones sell well, and at higher profit. Contract out to a local baker after sampling and comparing a few bakeries first. Purists regard *dairy products* as unhealthy and don't sell them but many customers expect them (you will, though, need to invest in a refrigerated cabinet). *Eggs* are fast sellers – "free range" or "fresh farm eggs". *Organically grown vegetables* pull in the crowds.

Vitamins, minerals and natural remedies are very profitable. They have a mark-up of 33%-50% and people will often spend around £25 on a month's supply

Cosmetics and skin care products are popular and as profitable as the supplements. There are many ranges made without animal or synthetic ingredients from flowers and herbs, cucumber, honey etc. Keep some at the end of the customer "traffic flow" for impulse buying.

Books on such subjects as macrobiotics, vegetarian cookery, natural healing and homeopathy. Stick to a small range of practical books too.

Items of *cookware* which aren't readily available elsewhere can attract attention – clay ovens, copper pans and woks for instance.

Takeaway food is an extremely popular area. Ideas include grain and vegetable pasties, falafels (made with chickpeas), hiziki rolls (whole grains, cooked vegetables and sea vegetables in a pastry case), carob brownies and other things. Consider offering a sandwich service at lunchtime using wholemeal bread, houmous and a variety of salads as a way of attracting people to the shop. But you may need to get clearance from the local authority to provide a takeaway service.

Planning the shop

Health foods stores are still new enough as a concept to need careful planning to allay any psychological resistance on the part of customers about coming through the door. The window displays should be fairly unobtrusive so that there is a good view of the interior. It's best to avoid the "shop for cranks" look with sacks of grain all over the floor and "Save the Whale" posters on the wall. But, equally avoid, the cold clinical look of a supermarket. The way you plan the shop should match the products and the philosophy behind them – a more natural way of life. Warm colours, wooden shelving (often cheaper than metal shelving anyhow) and carpeted floors are all welcoming features.

You must decide at the beginning how much self serving you want customers to do. If you buy grains and beans in bulk, you can avoid the tedious process of weighing, packaging and labelling by displaying them in large wooden bins and allowing customers to weigh the amounts they require. However, unless you have plenty of space, this can cause chaos!

Since the stock itself is a major part of your decor be imaginative with it. Keep the arrangement simple and logical, but move it around and change the window display regularly – a different look catches the eye of the passer-by.

Further information

The National Association of Health Stores (Queens Road, Nottingham NG2 3AS; 0602 866615). They advise would-be health store owners on all aspects of opening, fitting and stocking a shop and run training courses which lead to a Certificate or Diploma in Health Food Retailing. There is a buying group for members.

Realfare (Healthways House, 45 Station Approach, West Byfleet, Surrey KT14 6NE. Byfleet 41133). Realfare is the trade development arm of Booker Health Foods, a sister company of Brewhurst, the Holland and Barrett retailing chain, and Newman and Turner, the main book distributor for the health food trade. Realfare sell five useful booklets entitled "So you want to own a health food store" which contain information on the business aspects of running a store, shopfitting, merchandising and the products. They also offer a consultancy service on site analysis and shop fitting which is available to anyone. They do, though, offer a membership scheme which offers full consultancy, weekly deliveries of all supplies from Brewhurst and various promotional opportunities.

A CLIPPING AND GROOMING SERVICE FOR DOGS

Start-up money: under £2,000.
Skills/qualifications needed: a love of dogs, patience, strength, a training course lasting about a month.
Time involved: full-time.
Potential rewards: no fortune, but a reasonable living.
Likely snags: your customers sometimes bite.
Risk factor: low.

Man's best friend is his dog. Not to put too fine a point on it, in many British households the loyal and faithful Labrador ranks marginally higher in the affections of the hapless owner than the nagging spouse or rampaging kids. If your love for the dog extends beyond the family pooch to envelop all canine creatures from the diminutive chihuahua to the Great Dane, then you may be interested in setting up a dog grooming service.

During the Swinging Sixties the miniskirt came into fashion and so did the poodle. With it came the chic poodle parlour, Dutch cuts, lion cuts, pink bows and tartan tailored dog coats. More than a clipping service, the poodle parlour provided a whole new image for Candy, Lulu and Mimi – and for their owners. The 1960s represented the heyday of the poodle. Since that time many have closed. The poodle is now ranked only eleventh in the popularity polls. Top dog today is the Yorkshire Terrier.

However, all dogs need grooming and, as many dog owners will know, good clipping and grooming services are few and far between. Appointments often have to be made several weeks in advance. Country areas seem to be particularly badly provided for; dogs are often transported many miles to be trimmed. With over five million dogs in the country there is an obvious demand for this service and with a few weeks' training, capital of under £2,000 (but more if you need premises) and the right attitude towards your canine customers you could be in business filling the gap.

What sort of qualities do you need? Apart from an obvious love for and affinity with *canis familiaris* you will need firmness, patience, a strong back and a dogged determination to succeed. Training courses are available but costs vary, so shop around before committing yourself. "The Poodle Parlour" in Iver, Bucks runs a training course for trainee groomers which lasts for between two and eight weeks. The cost is £150. They teach you all aspects of dog grooming.

To find a training course in your area read the advertisements in the two major dog magazines, *Dog World* and *Our Dogs*. Rather than investing large sums of money on training courses, you could try and persuade an experienced groomer to instruct you free of charge in exchange for helping out in the kennels, pet shop or salon while you're learning. Go to the dog shows and familiarise yourself with the different breeds. Get catalogues from suppliers of dog-grooming equipment. Two of the largest are Allbrooks Ltd, Witton House, Lower Road, Chorleywood, Rickmansworth, Herts WD3 5L2 (Chorleywood 4204) and Brookwick Ward & Co. Ltd., 8 Shepherd's Bush Road, London W6 7PQ (01-743 1847). An invaluable book for all dog groomers is *The All Breed Dog Grooming Guide* by Sam Kohl and Catherine Goldstein available from John Gifford Ltd., 119 Charing Cross Road, London WC2 (£5.95 plus p & p). It's a comprehensive guide to clipping over 120 breeds from Afghans to Yorkies. Remember though that the most important quality needed is knowing how to handle a dog. As one groomer told us: "If you can't do that you might as well trim hedges rather than dogs."

How To Start

It's not necessary to have a smart salon. If you want to avoid expensive overheads set up the business in your own home. But be well organized or you will find your house overrun with dirty and disruptive dogs. Confine your operation to one room or better still convert the garage or garden shed.

Certain plumbing and rewiring work may be required. You will need a large sink or bath at waist height in which to wash the dogs, and a hand-held shower. After bathing, it is essential that dogs are well dried. Large industrial dryers are available (Allbrooks sell the Standard Tornado for £129.95 and the Major Tornado De-Luxe for £210.25). Two driers, perhaps a hand-held machine and a floor model, should be adequate to start with.

It's generally a good idea to give your clients a rest after their dousing (you too might appreciate a breather if Fido is an energetic bather), so invest in a couple of dog-sized cabinets. Allbrooks sell a 30x20 carrying cage for £58.65 (inc VAT), the largest from Brookwicks is 26x18 and costs £39.35 (exc. VAT). With a large flexible hose fitted to your hairdrier and directed through the bars of the cabinet door you can keep the dog warm and hasten the drying process while attending to your next customer. You'll need a bench or table on which to groom your dogs. Allbooks manufacture the ultimate in grooming tables – hydraulically operated height adjustment, double socket electric power point, complete holding frame with back bar and accessories – the Groomaster costs £356.21 (inc. VAT). However, if you are prepared to make do with something a little less ambitious Brookwicks offer a basic grooming table for £46.50 (exc. VAT) or get your local handyman to build you a sturdy wooden bench for less. Provide a rubber mat to prevent your dogs slipping. For the novice a grooming stand is a useful piece of equipment; complete with adjustable chain and harness, it enables you to work with both hands free.

Make sure you have an adequate number of well-positioned plugs for both the driers and electric clippers. Of the latter you will need at least two sets, more if you can afford them. Oster clippers are among the best and cost £99.89. You will also need a variety of blades, prices range from £15-£20, to perform the different cuts and for clipping the different parts of the animal's body.

Stock up with a range of scissors, including thinning scissors, blunt scissors for clipping delicate ears and nail clippers. Buy good quality and keep them well sharpened and they should last for years. A selection of combs and brushes will also be needed. A large choice is available from the big suppliers.

Invest in good quality dog shampoos and conditioners. Simpson's of Ely in Cambridgeshire are one of the major manufacturers. The choice is almost as large as that available to us humans. Don't try and cut costs by washing dogs in Fairy Liquid. You risk inflicting rashes and other complaints on sensitive skins and it's not worth it. Shampoos are available in economical gallon containers.

Large towels will be needed but don't buy the best. Try buying towelling by the metre from the local market – it's cheaper. Keep a supply of collars and leads for those dogs who arrive with choke chains or even string around their necks. You will also want ample supplies of cotton wool, as well as flea spray, surgical spirit, tweezers and a pair of surgical gloves.

Tips on grooming

If a dog is regularly clipped the grooming process should be more or less routine. Ideally, poodles should be clipped every six weeks and most other breeds three times a year. After general brushing to remove tangles (roughing out), ears should be cleaned, claws clipped and teeth brushed. Some groomers won't touch teeth, preferring to leave this sometimes dangerous operation to the vet. Note any infections the dog may have and inform the owner. Your concern should be with the general well-being and good health of the animal and not just with turning out a pretty and sweet-smelling creature. Roughing out is followed by bathing, drying, then clipping according to the guidelines laid down for each breed. An experienced groomer should be able to "process" a dog in under an hour.

Dogs, like all animals, are subject to parasites – ticks, fleas, lice and mites are just some of the uninvited visitors your customers may bring with them. Most of these pests can be removed by using an insecticidal shampoo at bath time. Old dogs, like old people, tend to develop warts. Avoid nicking these with clippers or scissors – they tend to bleed profusely. Try and ensure that your customers have been "walkies" before they arrive. It will reduce messy accidents while they are with you. Keep a medicine chest to hand. Talk to your local vet and get him to advise you on emergency aids. A dog may become ill while in your care – perhaps suffer a heart attack or have a fit.

Be prepared. Whisky or brandy is a useful stimulant and even if the dog fails to respond, a medicinal nip will probably do wonders for you in an emergency.

Animals can be unpredictable, particularly in strange surroundings away from their owners, and while many will positively enjoy your attentions, some will actively resist them.

For some dogs the only solution is sedation but this is not to be encouraged. Not only is it not good for the animal but if the dog can't stand up it is extremely difficult to clip its legs and belly. Muzzles can be useful; sometimes the presence of the owner may be enough to reassure a nervous pet.

One groomer we spoke to with over 20 years experience with all breeds of dogs tried to separate two fighting Kerry Blues while they were in her charge. She was severely bitten and bruised and ended up in hospital with 12 stitches in both hands, bandaged ribs, not to mention tetanus jabs and antibiotics. Her injuries curtailed her work for two months. It is therefore vital to have adequate insurance cover for both yourself, your dogs and your home.

What to charge

We telephoned some dog groomers to see what they charged for an Irish Terrier, an Old English Sheepdog and a Springer Spaniel. Prices ranged from £5.50-£10.50 for the terrier, £15-25 for the sheepdog, £6.50-£14.50 for the spaniel. Gauge your charges according to the difficulty of the cut required, the time it takes, the condition of the dog when it is delivered to you and the size of the animal. Charge extra if you have problems controlling the animal or have to scissor cut or hand strip, but don't overcharge.

When you first start your business advertise in the local papers or have some hand bills printed and drop them through letterboxes. Once established, you will find the best form of advertising is personal recommendation. Send out reminders to ensure repeat business and for customers who bring their pets to you regularly offer a discount.

If you have limited facilities at home a mobile service might be the answer. Many old people are unable to get out and about and would be glad of a visiting groomer. All you need is a small van in which to transport your hairdrier and other equipment. The advantage of a mobile service is that your water and electricity costs are eliminated as well as the wear and tear on your home.

A DRIVING SCHOOL

Start-up money: around £4,000.
Skills/qualifications: clean driving licence, ADI examinations, calm disposition.
Time involved: 40-hour week if you don't under-charge.
Potential turnover: £15,000-£20,000 on your own, more when you employ other staff.

This is a popular start-up opportunity since it's easy to run the business from home which means you can minimise the costs of setting up.

There are currently some 27,000 approved driving instructors and about 2,500 trainee driving instructors. The figures do, however, disguise a fairly high casualty rate. Last year some 199 instructors failed to renew their licences and while some were retiring, others were switching careers to find an easier way of making a living.

Qualifications

There is no way you can contemplate becoming a driving instructor unless you have held a *clean* ordinary driving licence for at least the last four years. You have then to pass the Approved Driving Instructors examinations set by the Department of Transport. These consist of a written test of theoretical knowledge of driving matters, a driving test in which the candidate is required to drive to a much higher standard than the ordinary L-Test and a practical test of ability to give instruction. Legislation being introduced in 1984 requires would-be instructors to pass the written and driving test part of the qualifying exam before receiving a licence to instruct as a trainee instructor. You then both take and give tuition under supervision of an approved driving instructor before going for the exam which tests your ability to instruct.

Training for the Approved Driving Instructor exams is widely advertised in trade magazines such as *Driving* (see further information). The cost is upwards of £400.

You could go to a large driving school where you still usually get a fairly standardized course, sitting in the back of the car and watching the tutor for a good part of the time. Or, if you prefer a more personalized approach, you could ask the Motor Schools Association (see below) for a list of their approved tutor instructors in your area. David Hambly, an instructor we talked to, for instance, likes to give people a two-hour assessment drive (cost £25) so that both he and the trainee can decide whether or not the person is likely to make the grade as an instructor. If so, the would-be instructor then signs on for a three-week course at a fixed cost of around £380. The course includes preparation for both the written and driving tests.

Once you've passed the first two parts of the exam you are paid trainee wages while gaining the experience needed to take the final part.

Many people who intend to go on their own find that, once qualified, it makes sense to put in some time working for a local driving school, both to gain experience and build up capital and contacts before splitting off to set up their own school. This way you can be earning regular income from the start.

So that's what you need in the way of *official* qualifications, but have you a suitable temperament? Here's a classic scenario for failure: an engineer who's a good driver gets £5,000 redundancy pay, passes his exams and starts a driving school. All his working life has been spent with machinery rather than with people.

Suddenly he's dealing with nervous housewives, punk teenagers, foreigners who are a bit slow to understand his instructions, brash young executives – the whole range of Joe Public, all at less than their best in the nerve-stretching experience of learning how to drive. Some of us find it hard enough to be nice to the people we like all the time. A driving instructor has to put dozens of perfect strangers at ease for many hours a week. He has to tune into their individual reasons for wanting to learn, and pitch his level of instruction to their level of understanding, their ability and their varied emotional states.

If you've worked in any service business, says David Hambly, you've got the right kind of experience. It doesn't matter whether you work in a shop, a hotel or an airline, so long as you've really developed the art of being nice to people and looking after them in the course of your work. People who've worked in splendid isolation for years find the change very stressful, they get irritable with the customers and pack up after 18 months or so, through lack of repeat business and recommendation.

What You Need

The £4,000 plus start-up money suggested at the beginning of the article is based on: £450 for training and test fees; £100 for fitting dual controls to your car; £100 for promotion; around £200 increase in your insurance premium; £200-£400 for ancillaries such as a telephone answering machine, L-plates and "livery" for the car plus, say, £3,000 subsistence money for your first three months of trading.

Although you can fit dual controls to your own car for around £100, you must be sure of both its reliability and its suitability for learner drivers. Don't forget, though, that you will need to change the arrangements with your insurers to give you comprehensive cover as a driving instructor.

However, you might decide it's preferable to acquire another car for your business. And one of the biggest surprises is that you can acquire a dual-control vehicle quite cheaply – you can lease one for between £26-£50 per week. When selecting a car, efficient fuel consumption is a main criteria – you're likely to clock up 50,000 miles a year. Adjustable seats, all-round visibility, ease of handling, insurance rating and frequency of servicing should also be important considerations.

Driving magazine reports that the top ten cars amongst driving schools (in order of popularity) are:

Datsun Sunny, Ford Escort, Ford Fiesta, Austin Metro, Austin Mini, Datsun Cherry, Mazda 323, Toyota Corolla, Toyota Starlet, Vauxhall Chevette, Vauxhall Astra and the Volkswagen Polo.

Once you've got the car, you need to give it a "livery". There are no specific requirements as yet except for L-plates and the fact that you must display your driving instructors licence in the vehicle. However, your "image" isn't something to be neglected if you want to project a professional approach. Official looking plates, roof-mounted and other signs, can be bought from Driving Schools Suppliers Ltd, 227 Aston Lane, Penny Bar, Birmingham B20 3H4 (021-356 7467). They can also supply stationery, audio-visual aids and other necessities, as well as organizing a dual-control system in your existing car.

What else do you need? A telephone answering machine is a must. First it gives a 24-hour response to people who suddenly decide to take the plunge (if they get no answer, they'll just try further down the list until they do). It also prevents people from saying "Well I did ring to cancel the lesson but you were out."

Although experience suggests that some 70% of bookings come from recommendations, it's worth both ensuring you have an entry in the Yellow Pages and that your entry in the ordinary telephone directory is set in bold type. This costs a few pounds extra but it means your name stands out and makes it quicker for people to identify you.

Customers

Once they bite, you must treat them with care. They are all different and will need different amounts of instruction as well as different approaches. As a rule of thumb, the calculation to apply, is that people need (roughly) 1½ lessons for every year of their life (that's for people between 17-70).

It's sensible to send them a letter confirming their contract and setting out your terms. As an example David Hambly's letter is shown overleaf.

If, like David, you are also in the business of training would-be instructors you can offer customers a reduced rate if they are prepared to be "guinea-pigs" and allow a trainee-instructor to guide them.

Costs

The Association of Professional Driving Instructors calculate that the proper current standard rate for driving tuition at the time of writing should be £11.00 an hour. In practice you find people advertising tuition as low as £5.45 an hour and working 50-60 hours a week to make the business pay. You need to set your prices with care.

David Hambly has just raised his fees to £8.50 an hour and is the market leader in his local area; when he puts up his prices the other schools follow suit. As a family man he refuses to work Sundays and limits Saturday lessons to mornings only.

He has a strong daytime trade and gives his last lesson at 7pm each day.

Here's a breakdown of his driving school finances.

INCOME		
40 hours a week at £8.50 an hour, 48 weeks a year (not registered for VAT)		£16,320
EXPENDITURE		
Petrol, oil		£3,000
Servicing at £100 per 10,000 miles		£500
Insurance		£200
Advertising, telephone, accountants fees		£1,200
	TOTAL	£4,900
GROSS PROFIT PRE TAX		£11,420

Obviously, if you are prepared to work more than 40 hours per week you stand to make a larger profit.

One way to increase custom is to offer pupils a commision if they introduce a new pupil to your driving school David Hambly offers £10 once the new pupil has completed ten hours tuition.

You can also offer extra "post-test" services such as teaching the techniques of motorway driving.

Another potentially profitable area is tutoring company executives for the ROSPA Advanced Motorists Test. Big companies are increasingly asking their

Ref:
Date:

Dear

Thank you very much for contacting us with regard to a
course of driving instruction. We aim to give a friendly
service to all our pupils, and feel very privileged to
count you amongst our pupils. Enclosed is a copy of our
rules, like any company we have to have a few, and we
are always open to suggestions about them.

The price of the lessons at the present time is £8.50
per hour. As the price of petrol and servicing goes up
from time to time, we try to absorb the cost as long as
possible before passing on the prices increases to
yourself.

We confirm that your first lesson is on: _____
at _____.

If you need to ring us and we are out, we have a
telehone answering machine, all you need to do is to
leave your name and telephone number and we will ring
you back.

Looking forward to meeting you at the above time,

Yours faithfully,

David A Hambly

executives to take the advanced test since this enables the companies to obtain a reduction on their fleet-hire insurance.

There has been a considerable amount of concern recently about driving tuition – low standards of teaching, too easy to qualify, cut-price driving schools which don't provide value for money and economise on mileage to save petrol costs at the pupils' expense, second-rate instructors who frequently work excessive hours (80 hours a week is not unknown) which is not in the interest of any road user.

Various initiatives are now being taken to remedy the situation. Legislation under Part V of the Road Traffic Act will raise qualifying standards since trainee instructors won't be granted a licence until they have passed the first two parts of the ADI exams. The Department of Transport are also likely to be scrutinizing driving schools more carefully in future since they now maintain records showing which driving school is responsible for which pupil taking the test. Instructors whose pupils consistently fail on various aspects of test requirements will probably be checked on.

Also, some individual driving instructors, anxious to give their business a good name, have banded together to form the *Association of Professional Driving Instructors* (see below for address). This totally independent body will require its members to have passed the Advanced Driving Test and to conform to a Code of Practice.

If running a driving school appeals to you, there is one thing you really must not do – drink and drive. A conviction would put you out of business for at least four years.

Further information

The Driving Instructors Handbook by John Miller and Nigel Stacey (Kogan Page).
The Driving Instructors Association, Lion Green Road, Coulsdon, Surrey CR3 2NL (01-660 3333). The DIA publishes the bi-monthly magazine *Driving*, and offers various pension, insurance and vehicle leasing schemes to members. They also have regional groups around the country.
The Motor Schools Association, 12 Tilton Street, London SW6 7LR (01-385 3589) can provide names of approved tutor instructors for the ADI exams.
The Association of Professional Driving Instructors, Russettings, 16 Long Avenue, Clevedon, Avon (0272 871825). This new trade association is campaigning for higher professional standards. It also offers various benefits like a test date exchange scheme between member instructors and instructor exchange in emergencies.

INDEX

Note: Individual organizations and publications have been omitted from the index. For further information please refer to the relevant subject area.

ADVERTISERS' INDEX